THE UNIVERSITY OF
WINCHESTER

THEATRIC REVOLUTION

Theatric Revolution

Drama, Censorship and Romantic Period Subcultures 1773–1832

DAVID WORRALL

OXFORD

UNIVERSITY PRESS

OXFORD

UNIVERSITY PRESS

Great Clarendon Street, Oxford OX2 6DP

Oxford University Press is a department of the University of Oxford.
It furthers the University's objective of excellence in research, scholarship,
and education by publishing worldwide in

Oxford New York

Auckland Cape Town Dar es Salaam Hong Kong Karachi
Kuala Lumpur Madrid Melbourne Mexico City Nairobi
New Delhi Shanghai Taipei Toronto

With offices in

Argentina Austria Brazil Chile Czech Republic France Greece
Guatemala Hungary Italy Japan Poland Portugal Singapore
South Korea Switzerland Thailand Turkey Ukraine Vietnam

Oxford is a registered trademark of Oxford University Press
in the UK and in certain other countries

Published in the United States
by Oxford University Press Inc., New York

© David Worrall, 2006

The moral rights of the author have been asserted
Database right Oxford University Press (maker)

First published 2006

British Library Cataloguing in Publication Data
Data available

Library of Congress Cataloging in Publication Data
Data available

Typeset by Laserwords Private Limited, Chennai, India
Printed in Great Britain
on acid-free paper by
Biddles Ltd, King's Lynn, Norfolk

ISBN 0-19-927675-7   978-0-19-927675-2

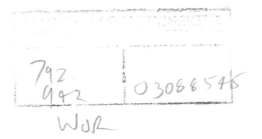

Preface

THEATRIC REVOLUTION has not been an easy book to write. Researching it was rather like walking through glue, trying to recover hundreds
of lives connected through a common involvement in the heavily
regulated Georgian theatre. This sort of historical research has a
habit of humbling the best efforts of scholars so I will leave others to
point out where my history has gone awry.

I came to Georgian drama from the belated realization that
London's radical presses were sited in the same vicinity as its Royal
theatres. I was in my element once I had satisfied myself that it was
more or less possible in 1819 (with only a little historical licence) to
have gone to Wych Street (a thoroughfare long since swept away,
now beneath the road between the present-day former BBC premises
at Bush House and the Aldwych Theatre), to have bought a copy of
the radical activist Robert Shorter's journal, the *Theological Comet;
or, Free-Thinking Englishman* at no. 49, had a beer at the White
Lion tavern in the same street—perhaps sitting in on the Cato
Street conspirators plotting Spencean revolution in the pub's back
room, unwittingly observed by a Home Office spy—and then to
have walked across the street to see William Thomas Moncrieff's
extraordinary burletta of 1817 (still going strong), *Giovanni in
London; or, The Libertine Reclaimed*, at the tin-roofed Olympic
Theatre. Once I realized this, an entire new world of London
theatrical subcultures opened up.

To have arrived at this point, I am most of all grateful to the Arts
and Humanities Research Board who gave me my sole experience
of sabbatical leave, allowing me to escape my twenty-sixth year of
consecutive full-time teaching. The British Academy awarded me
funds to visit the Larpent collection at the Huntington Library,
California and, a couple of years later, a two-month Huntington
Fellowship allowed me to return there. Along with two glorious weeks

at the Lewis Walpole Library, Farmington, right at the end, these were life-savers. The staff of the British Library Rare Books Room have provided an uninterruptedly friendly and excellent service over many years. I have also worked comfortably at Westminster City Archives, the British Museum Department of Prints and Drawings, the V&A Museum, Tate Britain Archives, the London Library, the Public Record Office, the Houghton Library of Harvard University, the Folger Shakespeare Library, Washington, DC, and the Beinecke Library of Yale University.

My thanks to Sophie Goldsworthy and Elizabeth Prochaska for overseeing this project and also to their choice set of constructively engaged readers. Over several years, various scholars have listened to me ramble about this project with patience beyond my deserving. Unknown even to themselves, particular colleagues helped me at crucial moments. These include Tim Burke, Steve Clark (who also read a late draft), Jeff Cox, Phil Cox, Kevin Gilmartin, Bridget Keegan, Saree Makdisi, Jane Moody, and Anne Janowitz. Brian Ridgers, Christine Riding, and Michael Gamer also proved lively sources of support and information. The Enlightenment and Romanticism Reading Group at Senate House has continued to be the most stimulating and challenging seminar I have ever encountered. My past and present research students Keri Davies, Will Easton, Sibylle Erle, and Minne Tanaka have also listened to me beyond the call of duty.

My new colleagues at Nottingham Trent University are uniformly wonderful and inspiring in their good sense and energy. I am immensely proud to be associated with them and, at long last, to be in such a supportive institution. Mei-Ying Sung has given me throughout her gentle and sustaining love.

Contents

viii   *Contents*

Introduction

THEATRIC REVOLUTION will trace the political and popular culture of
Georgian period drama, with particular emphasis on its Government
regulation and the social context of the artisan radicalism to which
it was conjoined. Although theatre's relationship with contemporary
popular culture will be a primary concern of the book, the dominant
characteristic of writing for the stage at this time was the practice
of censorship. Before proceeding to outline the structure of *Theatric
Revolution* and some of its methodologies, this regulatory factor
needs to be emphasized because it was the determining feature of all
contemporary theatrical expression. Writing for the stage constantly
negotiated at least one of three types of regulation: direct control via
the Lord Chamberlain's Examiner of Plays; indirect control via local
magistrates; and, finally, the more subtle and social politicking of the
Royal theatres.[1]

At the height of the Romantic period, a historical moment placing
a high value on natural rights and the liberty of expression, drama for
the stage was the *only* literary form to be subjected to statutory Government censorship. Imagine the flood of books, learned articles, and
Ph.D. dissertations had contemporary novels or poetry encountered
these restrictions. And yet the Lord Chamberlain's Examiner of Plays
expunged, excised, and refused dramatic texts on a weekly basis. In
other words, in the age of Blake, Byron, the Shelleys, Keats, and

---

[1] Watson Nicholson, *The Struggle for a Free Stage in London* (London: Archibald
Constable, 1906) still remains a useful work in this field.

Wordsworth, during a period notable for the way in which its poetry and novels reflected with exceeding complexity the period's considerable political controversies resulting from the French Revolution, a long and divisive war, an unprecedented industrial revolution coupled to sporadic social unrest, stage drama was the only literary form continuously under Government regulation.

The methodology of much of this book is an attempt to describe a social anthropology of Georgian theatricality in the form of its recovery and reconstruction as a mode of everyday contemporary behaviour. Theatricality was a mode of public being, a representation of the self which was not confined to dramas performed in the playhouses. Indeed, although it is not specifically an argument of *Theatric Revolution*, the censorship and monopolistic economics of Georgian stage drama was probably so fundamentally constrictive of dramatic performativity that a dispersal or dissemination of theatricality into general public culture or behaviour is not an unexpected, or unreasonable, response to officially regulated drama in the theatre. However, Georgian theatricality was probably not, as Betsy Bolton has implied, principally a mode of access to political debate via a specifically 'theatrical analogy' of public discourse.[2] Bolton may be correct as to theatricality's usefulness to women but this effect is a secondary, rather than a primary, function of the role of the dramatic in everyday life. Something of this was picked up over forty years ago in E. P. Thompson's memorable insight that 'the vice of the English Jacobins . . . was self-dramatization'.[3] Certainly the link between political radicalism and a propensity for theatricality will be a persistent undercurrent in this book. Thompson's exploration of significant layers of working-class subculture is also paralleled here. One of the principal arguments of *Theatric Revolution* is that theatrical subcultures, similar to the political subcultures discovered by Thompson in working-class movements, were constitutive of the

[2] Betsy Bolton, *Women, Nationalism, and the Romantic Stage: Theatre and Politics in Britain, 1780–1800* (Cambridge: Cambridge University Press, 2001), 11–21.

[3] E. P. Thompson, *The Making of the English Working Class* (1963; Harmondsworth: Penguin, 1980), 173.

general culture and that, by virtue of their visibility in public space, their extraordinarily rich records portray a series of often discrete emergent microcultural groups.

Theatric Revolution is intended to be precisely located within Georgian contemporary culture. Wherever possible, explanation and interpretation will be drawn directly from the evidence base of the history it seeks to recover. Its working methodology will be to elaborate a reconstructive anthropology of Georgian drama. However, in order that major components of its terminology can be clearly understood and defined, there here follows an explanation of significant words or phrases, together with an attempt to document the period's print culture and its specific relationship to the period's growing fascination with theatre. It is particularly important to describe the significance and complexity of the contemporary print culture because London's playhouses, like those located in the provinces, were surrounded by presses often characterized by radical political leanings and an eye for the age's increasing theatricality. Links between theatre, the visual arts (including prints), and the popular press provide much of the basis for understanding Georgian behaviour.

With the exception of the term 'subcultures', most of the key terms employed in this study are historically grounded. Subcultures refers to socially marginal groups whose members communicate with each other by speech or writing structured in relationships augmented through connections of friendship or kinship. The beliefs and behaviour of many of these Georgian groups are sufficiently ideologically marked as to be traceable with some degree of historical certainty. That such subcultures existed during the period is nowhere better demonstrated than in the account of the occasional poet and ex-London Corresponding Society member—turned Government spy—William Hamilton Reid, whose *Rise and Dissolution of the Infidel Societies in this Metropolis: including the origin of modern deism and atheism ... from the publication of Paine's Age of Reason till the present period* (1800) was based on his direct surveillance of London's republican, deistical and rationalist gatherings. The links between subcultures and theatricality are explicit even in this relatively obscure case. Typically for the theatrical tastes of the age, William Hamilton Reid had also tried his hand at playwriting, composing a lost satire on political 'Secret Societies' entitled *The Democrat Cured; or, The Upholsterer of Dantzick*, a drama he had worked up from a German translation of a Danish original and then further adapted explicitly in the style of Arthur Murphy's Drury Lane farce *The Upholsterer, or What News?* (1758).[4] Like another ex-London Corresponding Society spy and dramatist, James Powell (the subject of Chapter 8), Hamilton Reid was familiar with London's political subcultures, and had an interest in writing plays, adjacent concerns. A feature of these subcultures is that they were sufficiently tenacious to be able to adapt themselves into configurations which had the ability to evade repressive political conditions and to diversify into alternative discursive repertoires.[5] The transmission of specific ideologies through these subcultures can be documented through the records of their surveillance and their determinable presence within an increased print culture often closely related to contemporary London theatre.[6]

The medium of connection within and between these subcultures was sociability, another key term in *Theatric Revolution*'s lexicon although one which the Georgians would have understood more straightforwardly as 'conviviality'.[7] Someone like the obscure republican Spitalfields typefounder and pressman Robert Hawes

---

[4] William Hamilton Reid, *The Rise and Dissolution of the Infidel Societies in this Metropolis* (1800), 99–100; Iain McCalman, 'The Infidel as Prophet: William Reid and Blakean Radicalism', in Steve Clark and David Worrall (eds.), *Historicizing Blake* (Basingstoke: Macmillan, 1994), 24–42.

[5] David Worrall, 'Robert Hawes and the Millenium Press: A Political Microculture of Late-Eighteenth-Century Spitalfields', in Tim Fulford (ed.), *Romanticism and Millenarianism* (Basingstoke: Palgrave, 2002), 167–82.

[6] David Worrall, 'Artisan Melodrama and the Plebeian Public Sphere: The Political Culture of Drury Lane and its Environs, 1797–1830', *Studies in Romanticism*, 39 (2000), 213–27; David Worrall, 'Kinship, Generation and Community: The Transmission of Political Ideology in Radical Plebeian Print Culture', *Studies in Romanticism*, 43 (2004), 283–95.

[7] For a variety of recent perspectives, see the essays collected in Gillian Russell and Clara Tuite (eds.), *Romantic Sociability: Social Networks and Literary Culture in Britain, 1770–1840* (Cambridge: Cambridge University Press, 2002).

(whose work is referred to in Chapter 5) could print a list of *Constitutional Toasts, Good Wishes, &c. An humble Offering To the Friends of Liberty* (*c.*1789) seamlessly celebrating such things as 'No Oppression', 'Natural Rights', 'No Window Tax' alongside injunctions to 'Mirth & Good Humour' and 'Convivial Decorum'. Hawes's *Constitutional Toasts* were intended for the sometimes politicized, often philanthropic, convivial assemblies which were a recurrent feature of Georgian life, often with clear links to theatre. James Cawdell, a comic actor popular on the northern England circuits in the 1770s and 1780s, performed for the philanthropic Liberty Club, Manchester, claiming that he 'Wrote [a song] during the Evening's conviviality ... [which was] sung after the undermentioned Members had sung the following airs ...'[8] Such sociability or conviviality was not only freely associated with communal political expressions, as in the Hawes and Cawdell examples, these gatherings also served to reinforce popular attitudes to topical events. The theatrical pressman John Duncombe exploited the comic actor John Liston's role in John Poole's hit comedy *Paul Pry* (1824), when he published *John Duncombe's [Fifth] Edition. Liston's Drolleries; A Choice Collection of Tit Bits, Laughable Scraps, Comic Songs, Tales and Recitations* (*c.*1825). Appended to *Liston's Drolleries* was the anonymous 'The Parson's Clerk. A Celebrated Comic Song, sung at most Convivial Assemblies'. 'The Parson's Clerk' was a satire on the disgraced dissenting preacher Alexander Fletcher of Albion Chapel, Moorfields, and his jilted lover, Eliza Dick. It was a minor scandal of 1824 whose sexually transgressive and anticlerical opportunities were swiftly exploited by radical pressmen ('Near Moorfields is a House of Prayer, | Which every Chapel goer knows, | Pious folk they do go there, | To—sport their Sunday clothes'). Although 'The Parson's Clerk' was consciously puffed up by Duncombe as 'sung at most Convivial Assemblies', there can be little doubt that such anticlerical communal singing actually took place. In this close community of

---

[8] James Cawdell, *The Miscellaneous Poems of J. Cawdell, Comedian: ... to which is annexed An Answer to a late libellous Compilation called The Stockton Jubilee* (Sunderland, 1785), 96.

London's radical print culture in the early 1820s, Duncombe's career
was increasingly taking him into theatrical imprints and away from
the days back in 1819 when he could be indicted at King's Bench
for selling anti-Prince Regent squibs, appearing in the same session
as Mary Jane Carlile (Richard's sister), Robert Shorter (the editor of
the radical journal *the Theological Comet; or, Free-Thinking Englishman*) and the coloured slave's son and orator, Robert Wedderburn.[9]
This community of speech, song, and the printed word often acted
cohesively: the pressman John Fairburn's comment on the event was
the opportunistically titled *Dick Versus Fletcher, For A Breach Of
Promise Of Marriage!!!* (1824) while the radically inclined press of
Sherwood [Neeley] and Jones (the first piraters of Southey's drama
Wat Tyler in 1817), brought out the more sober *Trial of the Rev.
Alexander Fletcher, minister of Albion-Chapel, Moorfields, before the
United Associate Synod* (1824). Such an exponential expansion of
print comment on topical events parallels widely dispersed practices
of sociability. This now obscure case was sufficient to bring together
an impressive range of the capital's pressmen and for Duncombe to
think it fit to append 'The Parson's Clerk' to his *Liston's Drolleries*
aimed at the theatrical market. This vigorous popular press, often
centred around radical presses actively engaged with theatrical titles,
supplemented rather than replaced the Georgian free-and-easies or
'song-and-supper' clubs discussed below. These fugitive interper-
sonal activities existed in complex layers of assembly and association
but almost inevitably with explicit links to contemporary theatre.

Contemporary cultural expressions of sociability could be formal or
informal. At its most formal level was the organization of assemblies
with specific beliefs or categories of restrictive entry. The Freemasonry
of de Loutherbourg's circle, discussed in Chapter 4, would be an
example of this type of sociability, one which existed on the fringes of
London theatre as early as the 1770s. However, de Loutherbourg was
far from unique. After arriving in England in 1765, another well connected Freemason working in London's entertainment industry, the

9 PRO K[ing's] B[ench] 10/63 pt. 1.

violinist and conductor François-Hippolyte Barthélemon, by 1776 had graduated from the difficult conditions of directing the music at Marylebone Gardens pleasure grounds to leading the orchestra at the Haymarket King's Theatre opera house. François-Hippolyte, together with his composer wife, Maria Barthélemon, actively supported the Freemason's Charity School for Female Children, an institution standing within sight of the Royal Circus (later the Surrey Theatre), and the couple also organized concerts for distressed Spitalfields weavers.[10] Such philanthropy typifies the deeply embedded nature of Freemasonry within contemporary practices of both sociability and sensibility. Nevertheless, the charitable and creative efforts of François-Hippolyte and Maria Barthélemon stand as a stark contrast to the repressive behaviour of John and Anna Margaretta Larpent (the Examiner of Plays and his wife) described in Chapter 3, whose labours were dedicated to curtailing Georgian theatrical expression. The formalized societies favoured by the Barthélemons, despite their restrictive practices, provide good examples of sociability taking place on a scale where its influence encompassed thousands of persons, either as performers, as audiences, or simply as the recipients of charitable activity. At the other end of the spectrum to these formal organizations were more informal, often plebeian, practices of sociability.

That particular practices of plebeian behaviour were not only widely dispersed into contemporary culture, but also capable of being understood and denoted in the theatre, is clearly evidenced in the Adelphi's play, *The Fancy's Opera* (c.1823), where the taproom of a tavern is described in the stage directions as '*fitted up for a Free & Easy*'. A 'free and easy' was the singing, drinking—yet

[10] François-Hippolyte Barthélemon, *Selections from the Oratorio of Jefte in Masfa, Composed at Florence in the Year 1776 ... [with] Memoir of the Late F. H. Barthélemon, Esq.* (1827), 5–6; Maria Barthélemon, *The Weavers Prayer Composed and Sung by Mrs. Barthelemon at the Concert For the Benefit of the Distress'd Weavers London: Printed for the Authoress ...* (c.1780), see also H. W. Pedicord, 'White Gloves at Five: Fraternal Patronage of London Theatres in the Eighteenth Century', *Philological Quarterly*, 45 (1966), 277–8; H. W. Pedicord, 'Masonic Theatre Pieces in London 1730–1780', *Theatre Survey*, 25 (1984), 154–7.

superficially formalized—convivial entertainment convened by the clientele attending working class taverns. They were the earlier, more vernacular, versions of the 'song-and-supper' clubs founded in London in the late 1820s in the vicinity of the Strand, and described in Chapter 7. In *The Fancy's Opera*, the drinkers nominate a president and vice-president for the evening (punned as 'Mr Vice'), and the Adelphi's anonymous author even tried to reconstruct Cockney speech patterns with one Heavyswell declaring that 'though I'm not in werry good woice to night, Mr Vice, but however I'll do my best, I never likes to disturb Harmony and conviviality'. The taking of turns, the volunteering of song and drink, the maintenance of civil speech, were all aspects of Georgian sociability ('Why Gemmen, as I likes to mix up a little sentiment with my Conviviality, I'll give you if you please [the song] "Luck in a Bag, and shake it out whenever you want it"').[11] The Harmony of a free-and-easy, that part of the tavern evening formally given over to mutual entertainment, exemplifies contemporary plebeian sociability. These were highly provisional venues which continued to develop throughout the first half of the nineteenth century.

Crucially, in the Strand almost directly across the road from the Adelphi Theatre, by 1819 a tavern called the Coal-Hole had become part of a fugitive series of Georgian private theatres, a louche category of playhouse strongly associated with disorder and financial irregularity.[12] A decade later, the Coal-Hole appears to have reverted back to its tavern origins, becoming one of the best-known of the 'song-and-supper' clubs described in Chapter 7. Although the Coal Hole ceased being a private theatre, its 'song-and-supper' incarnation attracted not only the celebrated actor Edmund Kean, but also Charles Sloman, the later star of the Victorian music hall (music hall being the true descendant of these clubs). As well as Sloman, then at the very beginning of his career, the Coal Hole regularly featured (perhaps conferring on

---

[11] Larpent 2333, Huntington Library and Art Gallery, San Marino, California.
[12] Listed in *The Critics Budget, or, a Peep into the Amateur Green Room* (1819), cited in Harry R. Beaudry, *The English Theatre and John Keats*, Salzburg Studies in English Literature (Salzburg: University of Salzburg, 1973), 22–3.

them some valuable measure of self-esteem) obscurer singers such as the ageing Joe Wells, whose renditions were chiefly remembered at the end of the century for their 'coarseness and vulgarity'.[13] Like the playwright Theodore Edward Hook, author of the anti-Methodist (heavily censored), *Killing No Murder* (1809), Charles Sloman used the venue to exercise his theatrical skills in improvising verses or songs for the Coal Hole drinkers although, by that time, he was already starring at playhouses such as the Royal Coburg Theatre, where he performed acts such as the complex three-part solo 'Comic Medley' written by William Thomas Moncrieff, a performance proving sufficiently famous for Sloman's role to seize the frontispiece (captioned, 'Mr Sloman, as Dressed in Character for his Three part Medley') of the printed edition of the Coburg's *Crockery's Misfortunes; or, Transmogrifications* (1821). This transition of the Coal Hole from tavern to private theatre and onwards into an incarnation as a 'song-and-supper' club of the later 1820s, tells us much about the complex vitality of late Georgian London sociability and its connections with the personnel and intricate textualities of contemporary theatre.

The plebeian tavern free-and-easies, and their theatrical successors the 'song-and-supper' clubs, illustrate both the dissolution of public and private space within the environs of the London theatres and yet also the maintenance of distinctions between people who had agreed upon a kind of consensual orderliness validating the continuity of their gatherings. The changing awareness of boundaries between public and private space is an assumption about much of the contemporary culture examined in *Theatric Revolution*. Contentious arguments over public and private space were symbolized in the strict monopoly over the spoken word which Covent Garden and Drury Lane enforced (effectively a privatization of dramatic speech) and which the challengers to their hegemony insisted was a natural right. Transposed like this, as a metaphor mirroring the politics of national life, the boundary between public and private in the playhouses was

---

[13] Charles Stuart and A. J. Parks, *Variety Stage: A History of the Music Halls from the Earliest Period to the Present Time* (London: Fisher, Unwin, 1895), 23.

a surrogate of the debate between nomination and representation in English political structures. If only the Royal theatres were allowed to speak, what happened to the voices excluded from the Royal patent? Were the Royal theatres, like the unreformed Houses of Parliament, the privileged and notionally nominated agents of the English national drama, or were they merely components within a wider unrecognized franchise of emergent playhouses and their audiences?

The Royal theatres' monopoly over spoken drama was a constraint on the freedom of public theatrical space which was continually under challenge. Many parallel expressive registers to this protest can be found in the conflicts between public and private space encountered in other areas of contemporary London life in the vicinities of the playhouses. These aspects of metropolitan street sub-culture inevitably erupted as challenges to highly regulated Georgian drama. The complexity and paradoxes of contemporary metropolitan viewing of elite visual arts and their relationship to the playhouses is registered in the close physical proximity of the two Royal theatres and the Royal Academy's exhibition hall at Somerset House. David H. Solkin's collection of essays *Art on the Line: The Royal Academy Exhibitions at Somerset House* (2001) has argued that the Royal Academy gallery at Somerset House provided a kind of democratized public and private viewing space during its 'carnivalesque' annual shows.[14] According to Solkin's interpretation, the Royal Academy exhibitions represent a kind of inclusive Georgian liberalism. However, for any hypothetical contemporary visitor walking from the Royal Academy to the Theatres Royal, Covent Garden, or Drury Lane (only a few hundred yards away), the actual experience would have been one of profound visual disruption, a restriction of visual liberty. As Marc Baer has shown in *Theatre and Disorder in Late Georgian London*, audience disquiet at visual inclusiveness within the Covent Garden playhouse prompted the 1809 'Old Price' (or

---

[14] David H. Solkin, '"This Great Mart of Genius": The Royal Academy Exhibitions at Somerset House, 1780–1836', in David H. Solkin (ed.), *Art on the Line: The Royal Academy Exhibitions at Somerset House, 1780–1836* (New Haven and London: Paul Mellon Center for Studies in British Art and the Courtauld Institute Gallery, 2001), 8.

OP) riots. In addition, new publications arising to satisfy the public's appetite for theatrical comment, such as the *British Stage, and Literary Cabinet*, often carried lengthy reviews of Royal Academy shows but these commentaries only served to embody the contrasts between the two types of Royal venue since, by definition, the readers of the *British Stage* were also potential visitors to the Royal Academy exhibitions. The Royal Academy shows themselves increasingly reflected the age's growing interest in drama. The Academician George Henry Harlow's grand oil painting *The Court of the Trial of Queen Katherine* (Sudeley Castle Trustees, 1817) illustrated a scene from Shakespeare's *Henry VIII*—depicting Sarah Siddons's definitive role as Katherine—but the 1817 show also included numerous other minor art forms on theatrical subjects such as 'laborious' copies derived from prints of the French tragedian François-Joseph Talma (1763–1826), or a 'very neatly executed Medallion of [Edmund] Kean'.[15] While the floor of the Academy's exhibition room, with its inwardly angled walls above the 'line', may have fixed the spectator into some kind of nominal public act of spectating pictures hung above the line (or else of privately interiorizing the paintings hung below it), the nearby Royal playhouses maintained, in their physical interiors, material spaces which were not only bisected by different horizontal floor levels but also intersected by vertical partition walls. All classes were present but not all classes were equally visible.

However, the 1809 OP rioting was only the most vocal set of occurrences in numerous undercurrents of social unrest already latent within the London population. Disorderliness, even when viewing the visual arts, was a commonplace for anyone walking the capital's streets. On London's thoroughfares, public activities of spectating into print shop windows had none of the relative decorum and privacy of viewing oils at the Royal Academy. Old Bailey court records show that criminals consistently targeted viewers crowding in front of the capital's print shops, ensuring that spectating was

---

[15] *The British Stage, and Literary Cabinet*, June 1817, 134–6.

often challenged by public disorder.[16] By the early 1800s, the owners of a number of these print shops were intimately connected not only with radical politics but also with theatrical imprints.

The environs of London print shops, such as those belonging to Thomas Tegg and John Fairburn, with their potentially violent mix of viewers and criminal activity, are important in facilitating precise locations of a popular print culture which had material links to disruptions of the type occurring at Covent Garden. The politicization of the print culture serving the capital's contemporary theatrical market was highly contingent. While some pressmen like John Duncombe moved out of radical politics and into selling cheap editions of plays, theatrical songs, and thespian anecdote, other plebeian printmen moved in the opposite direction. Remarkably, T. J. Wooler, now best-known in his later incarnation as editor of the radical journal the *Black Dwarf* (from 1817), had been the first editor of the weekly periodical, *The Stage* (1814–15).[17] The format of Wooler's satirical pamphlet *Political Lecture on Heads. By the Black Dwarf* (1820), self-consciously imitated George Alexander Stevens' *Lectures on Heads* (1765), one of the most durable comic hits of the eighteenth-century dramatic repertoire. Amongst aspiring plebeian pressmen, theatrical publications presented a growing market closely connected with their more overtly political activities. Thomas Tegg had been an early entrant into publicizing the debate about private boxes at Covent Garden.

---

[16] James Gillray's well-known caricature of a crowded pavement of viewers peering into (his dealer) Mrs. Humphrey's shop, *Very Slippy Weather* (10 February 1808), is a misleadingly genteel version of the criminality associated with such gatherings. There were instances of both servants and (presumably physically well built) publicans being assaulted and robbed in their vicinity, sometimes by solitary thieves, at other times by gangs which, on one occasion, included 'Lascars' (ethnic sailors employed by the East India Company). See Joseph Hedford, 16 September 1801 in *Proceedings of the Old Bailey*: T18010916-22; John Booker, 10 May 1815, ibid. T18150510-59; John Jones, 21 April 1819, ibid. T18190421-57; John Brown, John Franks, 23 October 1822, ibid. T18221023-51 (the print shops in Sweeting's Alley are identifiable as belonging to Samuel Knights and J. Heskett); James Dovey, Roger Adams, 17 February 1825, ibid. T18250217-35.

[17] Beaudry, *The English Theatre and John Keats*, 206, 216.

Tegg's edition of Thomas Gilliland's *Elbow Room, a Pamphlet* (1804), subtitled 'remarks on the shameful increase of the private boxes of Covent Garden', anticipated by some five years the issues of exclusion and visibility that marked the outbreak of rioting in 1809.[18] Gilliland argued that annual subscriptions to reserve 'private Boxes' established an unacceptable form of property ownership which infringed contemporary notions of natural rights: 'theatrical property is different from every other species of right . . . the Managers cannot take the same liberty with a Theatre, that a merchant or a common dealer can with his own articles of commerce and private property'.[19] As early as 1804, *Elbow Room* presciently described the grievances underlying the public disorder of 1809: 'the Manager of a Theatre cannot shut his audience from the convenient parts of the house without a dreadful breach of public right, the legal letter of their patents, and a gross insult to the nation'.[20] Gilliland's acuity in noting this 'breach of public right' was exactly concerned with resisting Covent Garden's shifting demarcation between public and private space. Tegg's role in acting as a publisher of *Elbow Room* clearly suited his growing involvement with caricature prints and general theatrical publications. Similarly, the pressman John Fairburn's career in print publishing and theatrical pamphlets (such as *The Life of Wm. Henry West Betty, The Celebrated and Wonderful Young Roscius* (1804)), would lead him to become the champion of the rioters' perspective and to combine these two callings in his commentary on the disturbances, *Remarks on the Cause of the Dispute Between the Public and Managers of the Theatre Royal, Covent Garden . . . illustrated with a large Caricature Frontispiece of the House that Jack built* (1809). Again, the pamphlet's author (if it is not Fairburn himself), noted that the new boxes (quickly nicknamed 'pigeon-holes') destroyed the

---

[18] Thomas Gilliland, *Elbow Room, A Pamphlet: containing remarks on the shameful increase of the private boxes of Covent Garden, with a variety of original observations relating to the management of that theatre. Also a comparative view of the two houses, shewing the puerility of a great man's prophecy, who was to have turned Drury Lane Theatre into a 'splendid desert', &c. &c.* (1804).

[19] Ibid. 15.   [20] Ibid. 16.

connection between the public areas of the playhouse and those parts
of the audience hidden away in private boxes which had no shared
'sense of seeing and hearing ... what passes on the Stage'.[21]

The September 1809 Old Price riots were precisely about Covent Garden's introduction of physical partitions separating theatre
audiences from each other in an asymmetry of public and private
space. As Fairburn's pamphleteer wrote, the private rooms leading
off from the boxes were decidedly not public spaces ('In the interior
of these "sanctum sanctorums", our profane feet have not found
admission'). The playhouse's new configuration had created 'what is
vulgarly called private [rooms], and to each is an approach through a
private anti-chamber, furnished with every accommodation for convenience, luxury, and indulgence'.[22] If it is true that the viewing gaze
was democratized at the Royal Academy, the occupation of Royal
playhouse space was increasingly restricted by private boxes and inner
lobbies. Of course, this is a complex picture of sometimes seemingly
paradoxical cultural attitudes. Thomas Gilliland, the defender of
the natural rights of public space in *Elbow Room* (1804), that same
year wrote in another work on theatre, *A Dramatic Synopsis*, that
the burletta playhouses provided entertainment fit only for 'Holiday
Folks', 'Dumb Shew [for] the tasteless amusements of the giddy and
thoughtless', a popular demand he thought already well served by
Astley's Amphitheatre and Sadler's Wells.[23]

The glimpses offered here of the disruptive, occasionally multi-
ethnic, pickpocket-ridden 'mobs' on the pavement outside London's
print shops, and the sheer variety of the politicized theatrical prints
and imprints these premises supported, is only a partial indicator
of the enormous social changes then occurring. This was a society

[21] *Remarks on the Cause of the Dispute Between the Public and Managers of the Theatre Royal, Covent Garden, With a Circumstantial Account of the Week's Performances and the Uproar ... illustrated with a large Caricature Frontispiece of the House that Jack built* (1809), 9.

[22] Ibid. 9–10.

[23] Thomas Gilliland, *A Dramatic Synopsis, Containing an Essay on the Political and Moral Use of a Theatre; Involving Remarks on the Dramatic Writers of the Present Day, and Strictures on the Performers of the Two Theatres* (1804), 51.

whose print culture had become enormously generative yet whose Parliamentary representation remained unreformed even as its theatrical entertainments were left severely circumscribed. It was not an exclusively London phenomenon. Conditions in provincial England were very similar to the metropolitan picture, with ample evidence of thriving print cultures attached to local theatres. In Manchester, by then a rapidly growing industrial town, the invasion uncertainties of 1803 had spawned a journal, the *Townsman . . . Addressed to the Inhabitants of Manchester on Theatricals* (1803), whose profits were donated to the 'Patriotic Fund'. The *Townsman* reviewed Manchester performances of plays such as Matthew Lewis's *The Castle Spectre* (1798) and James Boaden's *The Maid of Bristol* (1803), the latter presumably performed complete with George Colman the Younger's loyalist Epilogue, 'Address to the Patriotism of the British People'. However, this Mancunian enthusiasm became misplaced after the *Townsman* was renamed as the more explicitly theatrical *The Thespian Review; an Examination of the Merits and Demerits of the Performers on the Manchester Stage, Pro & Con* (1806). The Manchester *Thespian Review* described an extraordinary local theatrical spectacular entertainment, obviously intended to dignify a national tragedy, which had misfired on stage. A painted mechanical 'Panorama' of Nelson's funeral, constructed from 'pasteboard, canvas, and [wooden] ribs of deal', was presented by the local theatre but 'tumbled down' in front of both the audience and the *Thespian*'s reviewer. This disaster required that, on the second next night, Nelson's panorama was supplemented by a farce.[24] Nelson's ill-fated Manchester pasteboard funeral spectacle demonstrates that expressions of provincial political activism, in this case loyalist in character, were closely linked to local theatricality.

The energy and interest with which local theatricals were pursued can be judged by the Manchester *Thespian Review* engendering two further pamphlets, *The Theatrical Inquisitor; or, An Enquiry*

---

[24] *The Thespian Review; an Examination of the Merits and Demerits of the Performers on the Manchester Stage, Pro & Con*, 7 (1806), 55–6.

into What Two worthy Managers have promised, and what performed (Manchester, 1804), and *A Little Amusement for the Gentlemen of Monmouth-street, Rosemary-Lane, and the Neighbourhood; Vulgarly Called Cannon-st. and M'Donald's-lane [sic]. With Observations on Clerical, Military, Mercantile, & Theatrical Characters* (Manchester, 1804).[25] Even in the backwater of Boston, Lincolnshire, an annual *Impartial Critique, or, A Peep into the Boston Theatre, During the Season of 1813 [1814]; Being, a Comprehensive View of The Corps Dramatique* (Boston, 1813, 1814) generated enough local feeling for the Boston *Adviser* to warn that it was compiled by 'two well-known slaves to Bacchus ... [who] used to frequent the Red Lion tap-room, to beg a *gill* from any industrious tradesman, or to spunge' from local drinkers.[26] What is unmistakable, particularly in the Manchester example, is not only the ability of the theatre and the theatrical print culture to reflect local squabbles over personality and literary aspiration and thereby to lend a variety of civic cohesion, but also to respond to significant national events such as Napoleon's threat of invasion and the death of Nelson.

Within this populist context, even play texts themselves had become commodities sufficiently prized to draw the attention of criminals. Although this new print culture ensured plays were printed in ever greater numbers and with wider circulations, the texts still remained scarce enough to be valuable. Plays were sold under increasingly sophisticated conditions of commercial activity under complex patterns of distribution. Thomas Dolby's play series, *Dolby's British Theatre*, was published in fifty-nine volumes between 1823 and 1825. A major feature of Dolby's edition was that it did not limit itself to the Royal theatre repertoires but gathered its material from all the London playhouses. It is scarcely an exaggeration to say that Dolby's edition has been vital in preserving much of the canon of Georgian drama, and it was certainly crucial in disseminating contemporary

[25] *The Townsman ... Addressed to the Inhabitants of Manchester on Theatricals. The Profits Given to the Patriotic Fund*, 1, 7, and 13 (1803–4); *Thespian Review*, 7 (1806).
[26] *The Adviser* (Boston), 29, Tuesday, 27 April 1813, 226–7.

play texts ranging from standard repertoire pieces such as Isaac Bickerstaffe's *Love in a Village* (1763), to John Howard Payne's very recent *Charles the Second, or, The Merry Monarch* (1824). From his principal outlet on the Strand, Thomas Dolby seems to have entered into a commercial relationship with a relative, Samuel Dolby, who kept a pair of interconnecting tobacconist and bookseller shops in Wardour Street which he worked with his wife, Charlotte. On 1 May 1824 a 17-year-old man, William Ramsden Robinson, was convicted of stealing twenty volumes of *Dolby's British Theatre* from Samuel Dolby's shop. Robinson had listed them on a scrap of paper as 'Dolby's acting plays', perhaps confusing Charlotte Dolby by also calling ('in rather a raised tone') for the latest issue of A. F. Crell and W. M. Wallace's new periodical, *The Family Oracle of Health, Economy, Medicine and Good Living* (1824–8).[27] At the time, Thomas Dolby was still busy with political publications, some of which he jointly sold from the Wardour Street premises, including works written by radical luminaries such as *Memoirs of Henry Hunt, esq.: Written by himself, in His Majesty's jail at Ilchester* (1820) and Major John Cartwright's *A letter to Mr. Lambton: A petition to the Commons, maintaining that ninety-seven lords appear to usurp two hundred seats in the Commons House, in violation of our laws and liberties* (1820). This snapshot of the books available in Dolby's shops, which would have included periodicals on domestic economy, multiple-volume play editions, and interventionist radical imprints (some of which clearly figured in Robinson's criminal planning), helps denote the highly intricate theatrical print culture which forms the basis for the reconstructive anthropology presented in *Theatric Revolution*.

Gillian Russell's *The Theatres of War: Performance, Politics, and Society 1793–1815* (1995) was perhaps the first study to rediscover considerable quantities of these extraordinary manifestations of theatricality in her recovery of distinctive military subcultures located in Georgian army camps and in the ships of the Royal Navy. Now

---

[27] William Ramsden Robinson, 15 July 1824, *Proceedings of the Old Bailey*; T18240715-101.

that Jane Moody's excellent study *Illegitimate: Theatre in London,
1770–1840* (2000) has narrated the parameters of Georgian and
early Victorian dramaturgy, it seems appropriate to attempt a recovery of the extraordinary mentalities and subcultures, both political
and spiritual, which founded the expansion of London's theatre-
going audience. The reclamation of female actors and dramatists by
Catherine Burroughs and Judith Pascoe has done much to initiate
our sense of the potential of the complex vitality of the contemporary
theatrical scene, as well as its role as a mediating cultural influence,
but the purpose of my book is both to analyse the legal forces
affecting drama and to discuss the politics and sociability of how
these powers were negotiated.[28] *Theatric Revolution* offers a study of
the theatrical subcultures which emerged during the long adversarial
battles fought out between the theatres and the Government's role
in enforcing regulation, monopoly, and censorship.[29]

  Censorship as a formative feature of Georgian drama has tended
to be occluded from the otherwise growing field of scholarship in
this area. Typifying recent academic practice has been a special
2003 issue of the *European Romantic Review* devoted to 'Romantic
Drama: Origins, Permutations, and Legacies' but which displaces
the problem of censorship—the daily experience of the national
Royal theatres as well as the theatres in Westminster—to just one
reference and two footnotes.[30] The contributors seem unworried
either by censorship or that spoken tragedy and comedy was the
perquisite of just two London theatres, and burletta the *requisite* of
the rest of the capital's houses.[31] Burletta was the hybrid form of

---

[28] Judith Pascoe, *Romantic Theatricality: Gender, Poetry, and Spectatorship* (Ithaca,
NY: Cornell University Press, 1997), Catherine Burroughs, *Women in British Romantic
Theatre: Drama, Performance, and Society, 1790–1840* (Cambridge: Cambridge Univer-
sity Press, 2000).

[29] The 'monopoly' might more precisely be called a 'duopoly' but the role of the
summer players and the provincial patent houses complicates the nomenclature without
removing the fact of a monopolistic national drama.

[30] *European Romantic Review*, 14 (2003), 30 n. 1; 46 n. 4; 120.

[31] Phyllis T. Dircks states the position correctly ('In the forced absence of spoken
drama, the minor theatres cultivated burletta') but does not follow through the political

recitative musical and spoken declamation or song which the non-patent theatres had evolved as a means of circumventing the ban on five-act spoken drama. This single rule helps define the reason why so much dramatic writing of the Georgian period has come to be so poorly valued by later literary historians.

Incredible though it may seem in the era of the Shakespeare Jubilee of 1769, the Boydell Shakespeare Gallery which opened in 1789, and the emergence of the Bard as a central figure in the national pantheon, the only dramatic genre in London permissible outside the Royal theatres was burletta. Above all, it is burletta which has barred Georgian drama's entry into the literary canon, yet Romantic period writing for the stage was formed on these twin templates of censorship and burletta. This happened not by choice but because of the continued legal intervention of the Examiner of Plays and the hegemonic role of the Royal theatres.

The absence of this historical circumstance from scholarly analysis exemplifies the process whereby problems are collectively relegated to the status of non-problems, has been well established from Ludwik Fleck's *Genesis and Development of a Scientific Fact* (1935) to Thomas S. Kuhn's *The Structure of Scientific Revolutions* (1962).[32] One can only speculate to what extent ground-breaking critical works on the Romantic period's attitudes to drama, such as Jonathan Bate's *Shakespearian Constitutions: Politics, Theatre, Criticism 1730–1830* (1989), would need to be modified when set beside a full realization that the period's dominant issue concerning the staging of Shakespeare was not quibbling about Nahum Tate's happy-ending

implications of the circumstance, particularly with reference to the post-1800 period, *The Eighteenth-Century English Burletta* (Victoria, BC: English Literary Studies, 1999), 14. As will be discussed below, even the Examiner of Plays had problems defining burletta. In this study, all productions outside of the Royal theatres will be assumed to have been burlettas (which was what they had to be). In practice, my study will further define some productions as pantomime or harlequinade since these adopted standard conventions of characterization.

[32] Ludwik Fleck, *Genesis and Development of a Scientific Fact*, ed. Thaddeus J. Trenn and Robert K. Merton, trans. Fred Bradley and Thaddeus J. Trenn (Basel: Benno Schwebe, 1935; Chicago: University of Chicago Press, 1979); Thomas S. Kuhn, *The Structure of Scientific Revolutions* (Chicago: University of Chicago Press, 1962).

King Lear, but the profound cultural effects of the Covent Garden and Drury Lane monopolies and the enforced prohibition of all performance of spoken drama outside of the royal playhouses or the strictly private theatres. Outside of literary studies, the influential modern historian John Brewer, in his account of Georgian drama in *The Pleasures of the Imagination: English Culture in the Eighteenth Century* (1997), also underestimates both the intrusiveness of direct censorship and the longevity of theatrical regulation. Remarking that, 'By the first decade of the nineteenth century he [the Lord Chamberlain] was using his discretionary powers to license new theatres, like the Olympic and the Adelphi on the Strand', Brewer fails to mention that they were licensed only for burletta while, similarly, his conclusion that 'Over the next twenty years [from the 1810s] the patentees' monopoly became a dead letter', seems to miss something of the political dynamic of this confrontation during the era of an unreformed Parliament.[33] As late as 1809, an attempt to establish a series of comic operas at premises in Argyll Street previously used as a concert hall was denied licensing by the Lord Chamberlain almost certainly on the grounds that allowing Italian *opera buffa* there might introduce a precedent for the performance of vernacular burletta.[34] Elsewhere, Brewer has oversimplified how 'Juggling, music, dancing, opera, pantomime, entr'act, tragedy, and comedy were all lumped together on the London stage.' This would be a wonderful example of the freewheeling 'absence of discrimination between cultural forms' which Brewer wishes to describe but, actually, the list of genres could only be found present in its entirety in London at Covent Garden and Drury Lane, and then only after interception by the censor.[35]

---

[33] John Brewer, *The Pleasures of the Imagination: English Culture in the Eighteenth Century* (London: HarperCollins, 1997), 388–9.

[34] Henry Francis Greville, *Mr. Greville's Statement Of Mr. Naldi's Case* (1811), 10, 14–15.

[35] John Brewer, '"The most polite age and the most vicious": attitudes towards culture as a commodity, 1660–1800', in Ann Bermingham and John Brewer (eds.), *The Consumption of Culture 1600–1800: Image, Object, Text* (London: Routledge, 1995), 341–61, 348.

This sense of a whole set of issues concerning Georgian drama being of only passing concern to modern scholarship has become commonplace. Typically, a recent work such as William Jewett's *Fatal Autonomy: Romantic Drama and the Rhetoric of Agency* (1997), a study of the dramatic writings of Southey, Wordsworth, Byron, Coleridge, and Shelley, quickly dismisses drama's entire contemporary social environment as beyond the scope of the book, simply by declaring that 'Others are better equipped to write that work than I' (p. 4). Again, there seems only a residual amount of usefulness in examining Romantic period spoken tragedy, by far the minority mode of contemporary dramatic expression in the playhouses, without at least referring to the role of the Examiner of Plays or the monopoly (actually *duopoly*) position of Covent Garden and Drury Lane.[36] That such disregard continues unabated is even more remarkable amongst critics who contribute to the recovery of women dramatists. Despite Betsy Bolton's *Women, Nationalism, and the Romantic Stage: Theatre and Politics in Britain, 1780–1800* (2001) being concerned with 'the English state as a stage: a place of genre-governed performance' in which Bolton reconstructs 'the performative politics shaping the public woman and her role in England's national romance', she has just three half-sentences on monopoly and licensing and none at all on burletta or the cartel over spoken drama.[37] The polemical issue at stake is that, increasingly after 1800, the majority of women actors on the London stage negotiated not only a censored theatre but one which, inevitably, would produce them as singers of burletta. It is also easy to forget in Judith Pascoe's discussion of the actress Sarah Siddons—typified in Sir Joshua Reynolds's portrayal of her as *The Tragic Muse* (1798, Henry

---

[36] To further refine this already complex idea of a monopoly or duopoly, it should be stated that the dramatist Samuel Foote was granted a licence to perform spoken dramas at the Haymarket, but only during the summer season from 15 May to 15 September, P[ublic] R[ecord] O[ffice], Kew, Chancery and Supreme Court of Judicature: Patent Rolls 66/3706.

[37] Betsy Bolton, *Women, Nationalism, and the Romantic Stage: Theatre and Politics in Britain, 1780–1800* (Cambridge: Cambridge University Press, 2001), 13, 146, 148, 232.

E. Huntington Library and Art Gallery)—that Siddons's career reached its zenith in a censored duopolistic theatre. On the other hand, the constrained limits of Jeffrey N. Cox and Michael Gamer's introduction to the *Broadview Anthology of Romantic Drama* (2003) provides a recent welcome indication of the relevant materialities of theatre, including censorship, which represented the infrastructure for contemporary drama.

Much of *Theatric Revolution* will be engaged with tracing the legacy, and strategies for evasion, of these regulatory bodies and of the monopolies originally formed in the largely pre-constitutional era of Charles II, and still unreformed in the Romantic period.[38] The growth of burletta was inevitably exponential in the Georgian period because the monopoly over five-act spoken drama remained with the Royal theatres. With the two royal patent monopoly theatres stranded in the West End, the upward growth of a London working-class theatre-going population situated to the south and east of the metropolis became the occasion for a constitutive change in the culture of drama.

One of the ways this cultural change found expression was through different attitudes to actors' labour and to the audiences which evolved in the playhouses. This is clearly the concern of the actress Elizabeth Macauley, whose pamphlet *Theatric Revolution; or, Plain Truth Addressed To Common Sense* (1819) was a response to her rough treatment at the hands of the patent theatres. The model of its prescient intervention into the theatre debate of the late 1810s also provided the title of this book, one of whose aims is to recover the lost lives of these Georgian theatre workers. In place of her own hardships, Macauley hoped acting would become a communitarian activity as part of a collectivized movement of dramatic workers rather than as simply a series of isolated hirings, firings, and vituperative reviews. A review of her pamphlet appearing in a journal, the *British Stage, and Literary Cabinet,* reflects something of her

---

[38] For the evolution of the patentees, see Robert D. Hume, *Henry Fielding and the London Theatre, 1728–1737* (Oxford: Clarendon Press, 1988), 2–14.

predicament in dismissing her in vicious terms, 'We hope to hear no more of Miss Macauley, for she writes and reasons worse than she acts.'[39] However, *Theatric Revolution; or, Plain Truth Addressed To Common Sense* conveys a sense of both the economic and the ideological loss in the contemporary position of theatre employees:

It is that we are enemies to each other. Instead of linking ourselves in one unanimous body; aiding and assisting each other; the wise instructing the ignorant, and the strong protecting the weak; we are guided by selfish views alone each striving to be himself a sun, and disdaining the petty stars around him. (p. 13)

Idealized though her struggle may have been (even if her subtitle, *Plain Truth Addressed To Common Sense*, shows its grounding in late eighteenth-century radical dissent), Elizabeth Macauley's objective for her colleagues was that 'Actors should be the philosophers of the age' (p. 14). Such a claim is every bit as uncompromising as P. B. Shelley's argument in *A Philosophical View of Reform* written the same year (and repeated in *A Defence of Poetry*) that poets and philosophers are the unacknowledged legislators of the world. Not least, Macauley's own agenda would make little sense of her own situation if her plan, right from its origin, did not already include a leading role for female actor-philosophers. Sadly, five years later she still felt obliged to publish a pamphlet entitled *Facts Against Falsehood! Being A Brief Statement Of Miss Macauley's Engagements At The Winter Theatres; The Subterfuges By Which She Has Been Driven From The Regular Exercise Of Her Profession, And Withheld From At Least Two Thirds Of The Public Of This Metropolis. Also Her Letters Of Appeal To The Present Managers* (1824).

If Elizabeth Macauley articulated, however briefly, an ideological role for drama and its practitioners, Charles Mathews, her immediate contemporary, is another useful representative to consider in order to understand how a new relationship between actor and audience came

---

[39] *British Stage, and Literary Cabinet*, 30 (June 1819), 169–70.

into being.[40] Mathews's experience of theatrical grandees was similar to Macauley's. His highly successful series of one-man shows were themselves the cause of disputes between different agents who felt they had been cheated of a share in his profits.[41] Although Mathews had trailed and prototype-tested parts of his *At Home* entertainment over more than ten years, its later incarnations such as the hit *Earth, Air, And Water*, as pirated by ex-radical pressman John Duncombe, is one of the first identifiable manifestations of that popular rapport with an audience contrived through a mixture of arch innuendo, the debunking of authority, and outrageous comic claims which emerges as a surprisingly Rabelaisian eruption into the Regency. Duncombe pictured Mathews in the crudely coloured and etched frontispiece to his edition of *The Theatrical Album; or, Comedian at Home ... Sketches from Mr. Mathews's Entertainment of Earth, Air, And Water* in the role of Major Longbow ('The Modern Munchausen'). Longbow's tall tales and outrageous physical confidence are still funny today: 'there's muscle hard as iron—feel me all over—hit me with a sledge hammer; can't hurt me, 'Pon my life its true what will you lay it's a lie—.' The invitation to 'feel me all over', the mock assertion to the audience (''Pon my life its true'), as well as the repeated catchphrase wager 'what will you lay it's a lie[?]' all denote, even when here clipped into a frontispiece caption, a new kind of proximity to the audience and the disappearance of cultural deference between Mathews and the English Opera House audience.[42]

In their very different ways, both Macauley and Mathews are representative of the individual agency of performers who migrated from being merely the servants of their craft to being its innovators. With a number of performance precedents for topical commentary

---

[40] For an excellent survey of Mathews's career and comic innovation, see Jane Moody, *Illegitimate Theatre in London, 1770–1840* (Cambridge: Cambridge University Press, 2000), 191–7.

[41] S. J. Arnold, *Forgotten Facts in the Memoirs of Charles Mathews, Comedian, recalled in a letter to Mrs. Mathews, his biographer* (1839).

[42] Charles Mathews, *Second Edition/Duncombe's Edition. The Theatrical Album; or, Comedian at Home ... Sketches from Mr. Mathews's Entertainment of Earth, Air, And Water* (1821), frontispiece.

and satire already established by Samuel Foote in the mid-eighteenth century, when his mimicry of prominent Methodists such as George Whitefield skirted on the edge of the licensing laws, the early nineteenth century was ready for a new type of ideological commitment in its drama.[43] In Macauley's case there is a sense that drama's collectivity enables the social function of an ideology. In the case of Mathews, the disappearance of boundaries of deference between actor and audience signals a new and deeply theatricalized population. In both their cases, the central cultural function of elite literature has been largely abandoned.

In following the implications of these admittedly rather divergent examples drawn from Elizabeth Macauley, the pamphleteering actress, and Charles Mathews, the pirated stand-up comic, my book *Theatric Revolution* will adopt a methodological format which is intended to be both historically and empirically robust. Generally, this book will not sustain its argument by reference to parallels in contemporary elite culture but, rather, will closely examine several types of contemporary theatrical microculture. *Theatric Revolution* takes it as axiomatic that these microcultures are constitutive not only of the drama of this period but also of the more general contemporary popular culture. Close reference to contemporary documentation in the form of unpublished manuscripts, Public Record Office papers, journals, chapbooks, sheet music, prints, correspondence, spy reports, playbills, etc., much of it either never printed or else unreprinted in modern times, aims to make it distinctive in current scholarship on Romantic period drama. However, this empirical base is not without its difficulties.

While researching *Theatric Revolution*, I encountered a number of unnerving problems relating to the reliability of the corpus of modern scholarship on Georgian drama, problems which I never

---

[43] Matthew J. Kinservik, 'The Censorship of Samuel Foote's *The Minor* (1760): Stage Controversy in the Mid-Eighteenth Century', *Studies in the Literary Imagination*, 32: 2 (1999), 89–104; Matthew J. Kinservik, *Disciplining Satire: The Censorship of Satiric Comedy on the Eighteenth-Century London Stage* (Lewisburg, Pa.: Bucknell University Press, 2002).

quite surmounted. Some of this was of a factual nature; other issues concerned practices of interpretation. It will be for others to point out my own shortcomings but there were a number of unsettling empirical flaws in the secondary scholarship which, ultimately, proved significant enough to warn me off incorporating some recent criticism. One type of problem is that characterized by William Jewett's *Fatal Autonomy* (1997) or else by the special issue of the *European Romantic Review*. These concern questions of absence rather than of a confusion in the evidence base. The continued omission of certain types of historical source, where this appears to have been principally brought about by scholars wilfully foreshortening or narrowing the range of material they consider to be relevant, stands in danger of becoming compounded into a self-legitimizing collectivity, a blindness within the scholarly community. However, there are also other, more straightforward, empirical obstacles.

For example, Marc Baer's frequently cited *Theatre and Disorder in Late Georgian London* (1992), an influential study of the cultural context of the 1809 Old Price Riots at Covent Garden, has caused particular concern. Baer's examination of Home Office and King's Bench papers in the Public Records Office has been unverifiable by the present writer. The notation Baer uses in *Theatre and Disorder* is to refer to sources such as Home Office '42/67–99; 43/17; 48/14; 49/6' and to cite them in this format, without further specificity (p. 93 n. 16). The problem for anyone wishing to replicate Baer's findings is that the documents referred to are numbered in the PRO as consecutive files (e.g. HO 42/67, HO 42/68, HO 42/69 and so on), but each separate file usually contains about 400 pages, typically manuscript letters of correspondence, usually some two or three pages in length, occasionally interspersed with pamphlets, newspapers, or similar printed material. In other words, Baer's notes, as exemplified in the single set of sources referred to above, allude to some 15,000 pages of information. Relocating individual documents without further specifity as to date, addressee, addresser, etc. has proved impossible. In particular, it has not been possible to re-locate the apparently crucial affidavits

of the Covent Garden prompter, Joseph Glassington, which Baer
cites as being deposited at King's Bench 1/35/2 (pp. 30 n. 46; 116
n. 5). In another area, as indicated in *Theatric Revolution*'s Chapter
7, Baer's neglect of a number of discharged inductees at the OP
riots, including the wayward playwright son of the architect Sir John
Soane, somewhat compromises his conclusions as to the audience
composition. Other pitfalls awaiting unwary modern historians of
Georgian drama are exemplified in George Taylor's failure in *The
French Revolution and the London Stage, 1789–1805* (2000) to
notice that censorship by the Examiner of Plays, John Larpent, was
thwarted by the simple expedient of the co-authors, Robert Merry
and Charles Bonnor, sending the censor only the dialogue of *The
Picture of Paris taken in July 1790*. Sending Larpent the text is all
Merry and Bonnor were required to do but the printed version
of the piece makes it clear that the silent pantomime part was a
much more violent representation of the Revolution than Larpent
could have imagined when he licensed it.[44] With commendable
diligence, Taylor worked from the manuscript submitted to Larpent
but without apparently realizing that, in this particular instance, the
printed copy provided a fuller—and more provocative—guide to
the production. Such instabilities of contemporary drama texts have
alarming consequences for the modern critic. In a similar fashion,
David Mayer III's excellent *Harlequin in his Element: The English
Pantomime, 1806–1836* (1969), the only full-scale scholarly study
of pantomime, overlooks the significance of 'product-placement' on
the Georgian stage, as typified in the eponymous *Harlequin in his
Element* (1807), perhaps because Mayer did not have access to a
variant contemporary printed edition, such as that of Scales, which
included scenic descriptions.

Although changes in the scholarship of consumerism may have
made parts of Mayer's ground-breaking book outmoded, scholarly
elision sometimes amounts to a paradigm difficult to surmount

---

[44] George Taylor, *The French Revolution and the London Stage, 1789–1805* (Cambridge: Cambridge University Press, 2000), 61–2.

because of what I have earlier indicated as continued omission. Such a case is Julia Swindells's *Glorious Causes: The Grand Theatre of Political Change, 1789 to 1833* (2001). Despite Swindells's choice of dates, and her obvious interest in censorship, *Glorious Causes* never makes a single reference to John Larpent, the Examiner of Plays from 1778 until his death in 1824. In other words, the political role of censor for the greater part of the historical period covered by Swindells's book is ignored. What is the credibility of a discussion concerning drama and 'political change' in a study purporting to cover the period beginning 1789 if it fails to particularize about Larpent's occupation of the Examiner role for the thirty-five years from that date until his death? Swindells discusses Larpent's successor from 1824, George Colman the Younger, but even here fails to comment on Colman's increasingly ideologically motivated role as Examiner, as publicized by himself in the unnoticed *Observations On The Notice Of A Motion To Rescind Certain Powers Of His Majesty's Lord Chamberlain* (1829) written in 1825, barely a year after his appointment.

Such failures or omissions, when individually considered, may not amount to much. However, when these problems cover issues such as the independent verifiability of the historical archive, considerations of the double materiality of contemporary play texts sometimes simultaneously existing as Lord Chamberlain manuscripts and printed editions, plus the cursory significance attached to Larpent's role as Examiner during significant years of European political upheaval beginning in 1789, it may perhaps be understandable that the present writer, on balance, has chosen largely to rely on the interpretation of first-hand documents rather than on the insights of modern criticism. It appears that the pitfalls, if not elephant-traps, inherent in researching Georgian period drama have yet to be much alleviated by an accurate and enthusiastic modern scholarship.

Chapter 1 will set out some of the regulatory intricacies of Georgian drama, indicating the basic constraints on the theatres and the context of its reception. Chapter 2 then focuses on the Royal theatres' suppression of one particular playhouse in 1787, the Royalty Theatre, Tower Hamlets, in London's East End. By chronicling the

Royalty's attempts to evade closure, much can be uncovered about how that theatre integrated into its local environment. With so much of this book necessarily referring to the role of the Lord Chamberlain's Examiner of Plays, Chapter 3 will examine the day-to-day censorship practices of John and Anna Margaretta Larpent (that is, the Examiner and his wife) in the early 1790s as they encountered a wave of dramas touching on the French Revolution.

Chapters 4 and 5 both present examinations of the context of regulation and control of the playhouses and their writers. They have in common their attempt to recover the microhistories of personnel working for London's theatres. Of these, perhaps Chapter 4 is the most ambitious because it indicates the presence of a spiritualized set of microcultures primarily focused on the scene painter Philip de Loutherbourg. It attempts to recover the evidence of several levels of sociability connected through networks of skill and alternative spirituality in the London playhouses of the 1770s. The chapter begins with the manifestations of Freemasonry on stage at Drury Lane before moving to connections between firework-making, print-selling, alchemy, and alternative medical regimens centred on personnel linked to the London pleasure ground Marylebone Gardens. Chapter 5 examines the recurrence of a specific marginal political discourse temporalized in the distressed Spitalfields area of London, a discourse concerning the price and abundance of food, and its sudden re-emergence in a drama written for Covent Garden in 1800 during a period of civil unrest surrounding grain forestalling and food price rioting. The censoring and withdrawal of this play, T. J. Dibdin's *Two Farmers*, is an indicator not only of the continuous role of censorship throughout this period (and the subsequent loss to the canon of a fascinating dramatic text) but also of how contemporary drama potentially figured topical events revealing of ideological fractures between radical and loyalist perspectives.

British culture during the period surveyed in *Theatrical Revolution* was thoroughly theatricalized. The strategy of Chapters 6 and 7 is to present a synchronic analysis of the social and political role of drama during the Romantic period. They elaborate an historical anthropology of theatricality and its adjacent subcultures aiming to present a crucial selection of evidence denoting contemporary theatricality, in this case broken down hierarchically into class and economic components, from elite to vagrant. This synchronic approach aims to retain descriptive accessibility without the limitations of the survey of theatre and leisure in J. H. Plumb's contribution to the otherwise influential *The Birth of a Consumer Society: The Commercialization of Eighteenth-Century England* (1982).[45] Both chapters set out the core of the empirical evidence for *Theatric Revolution*'s argument that theatrical culture and theatricalized subcultures permeate the period and are best understood as a kind of historical anthropology, a set of social behaviours and patterns determined by complex relationships of class, economics, and ideology. Although such a survey can never escape being representative, it will lean towards an attempt to be exhaustive in its treatment of theatrical microcultures. Chapter 6 is largely concerned with the implications of Queen Caroline's visit to the Royal Coburg Theatre in 1821 while Chapter 7 comprises a lengthy examination of the general sociability of the theatrical in Georgian society. The special claim of Chapter 7 is that it uncovers, sometimes for the first time, the microhistories of drama's personnel (including such forgotten figures as the 'tumbler' James Pack who graduated to Drury Lane from agricultural fairgrounds), as well as its institutions, including the scarce records of the late Georgian London 'private theatres' which operated on the fringes of legality. Although these microhistories and microcultures of theatre operated often quite discretely from one another, *Theatric Revolution* claims that, cumulatively, they were constitutive of contemporary popular culture.

The constitutive role of these subcultures is one of *Theatric Revolution*'s foremost assertions. For example, to return to Covent Garden's *Harlequin in his Element* (1807) and the

---

[45] J. H. Plumb, 'Commercialization and Society', in Neil McKendrick, John Brewer, and J. H. Plumb (eds.), *The Birth of a Consumer Society: The Commercialization of Eighteenth-Century England* (London: Europa Publications, 1982), 265–334.

'product-placement' of branded goods aimed at the Georgian consumer discussed in Chapter 7, such features found in the relatively fugitive theatrical form of the harlequinade or pantomime betray the presence of a complex set of economic and social relations centred on the manufacture and retail of consumer goods. Their presence implies the existence of a highly developed culture of luxury consumption at a time when, paradoxically, the nation was fully engaged in a European-wide war. While the harlequinades have largely escaped consideration for inclusion in the literary canon, they were clearly at the forefront of the relationship between theatres and their audiences. Coade's artificial stone products for garden ornamentation and building embellishment, together with Hancock & Shepherd's glassware for domestic lighting, were exhibited onstage in front of a Covent Garden audience which could number up to 3,000 people nightly. Whatever the exigencies of the continuing bloodshed of the Napoleonic War, these manufacturers were clearly sensing the presence of an audience whose literary appetite was for genres now considered marginal yet whose spending power was already in the luxury class. A little over ten years later, the Royal Coburg Theatre would seek to satisfy these twin tastes of a popular London culture which was comfortable with its consumption of luxury goods and happy to have its aspirations incorporated into its theatrical display. This culminated in what Jane Moody has described as 'visual magnificence of the minor theatres', with the Coburg by 1822 featuring an astonishing sixty-three-piece glass curtain in front of the stage where the packed audiences could spectate their own reflections before the performance began.[46]

Chapter 8 further traces radical and loyalist aspects of contemporary drama by contrasting two microhistories, that of the extraordinary context of James Powell, the Government-paid spy and playwright author of the abolitionist Drury Lane Christmas entertainment, *Harlequin Negro*, and that of a group of hard-core metropolitan Spencean revolutionaries who wrote a closet drama,

---

[46] Moody, *Illegitimate Theatre in London*, 151–4, plate 10.

Plots and Placemen, to promote their cause and satirize Government during the 1817 suspension of Habeas Corpus.

The final two chapters of the book, 9 and 10, return to precise geographic locations by indicating that, by the late 1810s and 1820s, both provincial English and working-class areas of London, sustained by a growing plebeian print culture, had developed a complex and sophisticated theatricality capable of responding to specific events in the life of the nation. Although much of *Theatric Revolution* is concerned with the culture of theatricality in London, Chapter 9 indicates that, by the late 1810s, provincial dramatics—or, at least, dramatic writing—had become a surprisingly agile and responsive vehicle for popular expression, in this case focused on a notorious murder. Perhaps unexpectedly, this chapter shows that the London theatres responded to the initiatives of a provincial press. Finally, Chapter 10 examines a five-act 'People's tragedy', *Swing, or, Who are the Incendiaries?* (1831), written by the blasphemous priest Robert 'the Devil' Taylor and performed at the veteran, much-imprisoned, pressman Richard Carlile's Rotunda in Blackfriars Road at the height of the 'Captain Swing' agricultural unrest of 1831. The ascetic and rationalist Carlile's exploitation of drama's popularity amongst working-class audiences is a good indicator for how plays written beyond the reach of the Royal theatres served to further local political activism. As an intriguing facet of this story, a Government spy attended and noted every performance of *Swing*.

The chapters which constitute *Theatric Revolution* aim to discuss both a representative range of drama, to give some consideration to the variety of playhouse venues available and, not least, to portray some of the unexpected mentalities and ideologies involved concerning people whose working lives touched upon Georgian theatre. However, because British drama had emerged and developed over a considerable period, and was subject to a complicated array of legal and official sanctions and privileges, it is first necessary to give a preliminary outline of these pressures. The mode of presentation in Chapter 1 will be to outline a few of the principal issues in order that they can be more swiftly returned to in subsequent chapters.

1

Customs and Practices: The Regulation of the Theatres

THE basic structure of British drama during this period was largely determined by the effects of two political and legal realities. The first was the role of the two London Royal theatres in Covent Garden and Drury Lane. Employing patents or monopolistic authorities originating from the Restoration, the two patent theatres were the only playhouses within London's Westminster allowed to produce drama of the type most readily recognizable to modern readers as the five-act spoken drama familiar to us from Shakespeare's plays. The second determinant was the office of the monarch's Lord Chamberlain who employed an Examiner of Plays to vet and censor not only the appropriateness of the texts of dramatic entertainments but who also helped, effectively, to safeguard the privileges of the patent houses. Theoretically, the Lord Chamberlain's remit did not extend beyond Westminster except for the provincial Royal theatres such as those in Edinburgh, Norwich, or York. In Ireland the Lord Chamberlain's role was subsumed under the authority of a Lord-Lieutenant.[1] The fate of much of London theatreland lay in negotiating, on a day-to-day basis, the extraordinary cartel on spoken drama operated by Covent Garden and Drury Lane, on the one hand and, on the other, the regulation of texts by the Examiner of Plays.

---

[1] The basic conditions are given in L. W. Conolly, *The Censorship of English Drama, 1737–1824* (San Marino, Calif.: Huntington Library, 1976); John Russell Stephens, *The Censorship of English Drama 1824–1901* (Cambridge: Cambridge University Press, 1980).

In practice, there were many variations, contradictions, and bizarre paradoxes to the summary given above. Despite the apparent restriction of the Lord Chamberlain's jurisdiction to Westminster, this effectively meant that virtually the whole of 'London' as it then existed came under his control. The reach of the Lord Chamberlain was further compounded by the support extended to the patent theatres. The playwright Isaac Jackman, writing a defence of the Royalty Theatre, Tower Hamlets, in 1787, objected that the London Royal theatres 'desire a MONOPOLY OF THE WHOLE METROPOLIS, extending from Knightsbridge to Blackwall . . . and expect the legislature to countenance it'.[2] In other words, the actual reach of the influence of the Royal theatres went far beyond their official boundaries. Although tightrope walking and tumbling performances were excluded in practice (but not in theory), the submission of new work to the Examiner comprehensively included all types of texts, that is any entertainment performable on a stage containing text, including new prologues, epilogues, songs and lectures. In addition to receiving a salary, the Examiner also took a fee of 2 guineas per piece submitted. The charge was the same for a three-act burletta as for one new song or prologue added to a previously licensed work. Another perquisite of the office was that, at least for the King's Theatre opera house, Haymarket, Examiner Larpent (and even some of his officials) had free entry for themselves '& Friend'. These tickets were so heavily used that an official 'Perpetual Ticket' in solid silver had to be authorized and engraved by the Lord Chamberlain's office.[3] Free tickets to the opera for you and your spouse were just one of the many corruptions which increasingly provoked those involved in London's theatre industry who were themselves denied political franchise and the means to have their cause represented in Parliament.

These complicated rules of jurisdiction, silver tickets, fees, and salary are good indicators of the Byzantine structure of custom and

---

[2] Isaac Jackman, *Royal and Royalty Theatres. Letter to Phillips Glover, Esq of Wispington, In Lincolnshire; in a Dedication to the Burletta of Hero and Leander, now performing, with the most distinguished applause, at the Royalty Theatre, in Goodman's Fields* (1787), 42.

[3] PRO L[ord] C[hamberlain] 5/205. fos. 312–14.

practice, legal enforceability—and plain muddle—that is best seen in its cumulative form in the Parliamentary *Report from the Select Committee on Dramatic Literature* published in 1832, the committee having been chaired by Edward Lytton Bulwer.[4] The dating of the inquiry is itself indicative of how, in the era leading up to the Reform Bill of 1832, the Government wished to come to some sort of consolidation or accommodation of its position with respect to theatre. This body, on which sat the playwrights Shiel and Jephson, was almost certainly convened just to get the tiresome patent theatres off the back of the Government. Censorship was an issue which no doubt Government did not feel averse to continuing, but protecting the capital investment of the patentees from the competition of the minor theatres cannot have been very much on their agenda. As Tracy C. Davis notes throughout her excellent account in *The Economics of the British Stage 1800–1914* (2000), by the beginning of the nineteenth century there existed a complex economic network of monopolistic assertions and counter-claims to a theatrical free trade.[5] The objections made by writers such as Isaac Jackman—who had noted that the Royal theatres 'expect the legislature to countenance' their monopoly—was beginning to make the protectionist case wear thin by the late 1820s if the state's case for censorship was always to be enfeebled and muddled by its yoking to the claims of the patentees. Within this legal and political framework operated the types of dramatic writing to be discussed in this book.

Only staged drama was subject to censorship or control by the magistracy. Of course, in wider spheres of general literary culture, writers did occasionally fall foul of the law and politics. For example, the journalists Leigh and John Hunt were gaoled in 1812 for an issue of *The Examiner* attacking the Prince Regent, while the blasphemous pressman Richard Carlile was imprisoned in 1819 for publishing

[4] *Report from the Select Committee on Dramatic Literature: With The Minutes of Evidence . . . 2 August 1832*, Parliamentary Papers (1831–2), vol. vii.

[5] See the important chapter 'Monopoly and Free Trade; Fair and Unfair Competition', in Tracy C. Davis, *The Economics of the British Stage 1800–1914* (Cambridge: Cambridge University Press, 2000), 17–41.

Paine's *Rights of Man*, Part III. Earlier, the poet and artist William Blake had been indicted in 1802 for speaking seditious words. However, none of these authors wrote works which required them first to be submitted to a censor. Yet dramatists and others concerned with the theatre felt acutely the long-term effects of Governmental control. Writing in a flourish of wounded frustration at the extensive cuts required for his Irish insurrectionary tragedy *Alasco* (1824), the future ennobled President of the Royal Academy, Martin Archer Shee, protested that 'The dramatic writer is put out of the pale of the constitution . . . blotted out of theatrical existence in a flourish of red ink.' Nearly twenty years later in 1840 another commentator complained that 'The body of dramatists are still subject to the wills of two individuals.'[6] These routine acts of censorship, running daily all the way through the period covered in this book, definitively establish the primary level of interference by Government in the production of dramatic writing.

Printed drama intended solely for reading ('closet drama', as it is sometimes called) probably reached some level of development and attention precisely because it escaped authoritarian sanction. Staged drama had to fend for itself and negotiate official regulation. As Catherine Burroughs has fascinatingly shown, these rather coarse distinctions may truncate a sense of the rich inclusiveness of general theatrical writing but my concerns are not particularly close to those of literary history.[7] While it is useful to remember of such closet dramas that, as well as providing useful modes of access for experiments in social conduct (perhaps particularly for women), their existence as a sub-genre is due to the specific displacement of literary, spoken, drama from the stage. In an environment where new writers had to surmount the obstacles of the monopolies of the

---

[6] Martin Archer Shee, *Alasco: A Tragedy, in Five Acts . . . Excluded from the Stage by the Authority of the Lord Chamberlain* (Sherwood, Jones & Co., 1824), p. xxiii; Edward Mayhew, *Stage Effect: or, The Principles which Command Dramatic Success in the Theatre* (1840), 27.

[7] Catherine B. Burroughs, *Closet Stages: Joanna Baillie and the Theatre Theory of British Romantic Writers* (Philadelphia: University of Pennsylvania Press, 1997).

patentees (which restricted the available venues for new writing), the censorship vagaries of the Examiner of Plays, not to mention the inevitable inertia of established playhouse repertoires, it is little wonder that 'closet drama' became an attractive and, indeed, wholly understandable option. It has been argued that such an unperformed 'mental theatre' was enabling for literary culture, allowing the safer haven of 'cautionary fables rather than ... theatrical fiascos', but whether that is so or not, it seems sensible to recognize that closet drama was a rational response to the judicial scrutiny of the theatre.[8] Indeed, Chapter 5 will discuss an ultra-radical closet drama, strongly associated with London's armed revolutionaries and which, quite obviously, would have had no chance of performance by any contemporary theatre which valued its patent or magistrates' licence. Nevertheless, throughout the period, it was possible and entirely legal, to *print* censored plays, complete with the Examiner of Plays' cuts restored, but performance on stage at the Royal Patent theatres and within Westminster first had to undergo either the scrutiny of the Lord Chamberlain's office or, outside of his jurisdiction, to suffer a more generalized licensing of theatres by local magistrates. Under such conditions, the writing of closet drama was an entirely reasonable means of avoiding both the Examiner's interference on expression or the remoteness of the Royal theatres selection process.

What controls were exercised over drama intended for representation in the theatre? The answer is not straightforward either in theory or in practice. Indeed, much of this book will be concerned with frequently returning to the actuality of the issues encountered on a day-to-day basis by writers and playhouse managers as they sought to negotiate the ill-defined customs, practices, and legalities which were considered to be relevant. The theory was relatively straightforward. By the end of the eighteenth century, all new plays, prologues, epilogues, songs, interludes, recitals, indeed anything containing new text that was due for representation in one of the Royal Patent

[8] Alan Richardson, *A Mental Theatre: Poetic Drama and Consciousness in the Romantic Age* (University Park and London: Pennsylvania State University Press, 1988) 17.

theatres and/or within a 20-mile radius of the City of Westminster
had to be submitted (prior to performance) and a licence obtained
from the Lord Chamberlain's Examiner of Plays (who also took a
fee).[9] When asked to give a legal opinion at the end of the 1800s,
a consultant Middlesex magistrate, acting on behalf of the patent
theatres Covent Garden and Drury Lane, found a precedent in
Lord Kenyon's judgment that, '"Tumbling and Fencing"' excepted
('because no copies of these amusements can be sent to the Lord
Chamberlain, for his appropriation, previous to the Acting'), the
remit comprehensively covered all 'Tragedies, Comedies, Operas,
Farces Masques, Burlettas Pantomimes, Grand Ballets, Ballets of
Action Descriptive of Particular Stories, Prologues, Epilogues, Melo
Dramas, and Songs Between the Acts of Plays and Farces.'[10]

This censorship also included newly discovered Shakespeare plays.
When the forger William Henry Ireland's *Vortigern. A Tragedy in
Five Acts* (1796) was scheduled for performance at Drury Lane—on
the understanding that it was possibly an undiscovered work by
William Shakespeare—it too had to be censored (with a passage
referring to Vortigern's incest being struck out).[11] Clearly, censoring
Shakespeare created few aesthetic or moral problems for the Examiner
of Plays.

While the above describes the basic regulatory environment
governing drama for the stage, the wider legislative framework controlling theatrical representation became ever more oppressive. In the
early aftermath of John Larpent's appointment as Examiner in 1778,
the relationship of the Lord Chamberlain's office to theatres beyond
Westminster was extremely confused. Charles Dibdin, who opened
his Royal Circus equestrian venue in 1782 beyond Westminster on
the Surrey side of the Thames, soon fell foul of the Lord Chamberlain

[9] John Russell Stephens, *The Censorship of English Drama 1824–1901* (Cambridge:
Cambridge University Press, 1980), ch. 1: 'Licensing and the Law'.

[10] *The number of little Theatres already opened ... having greatly injured the Theatres
Royal* ... (*c*.1810), 9.

[11] Larpent 1110, *Vortigern. A Tragedy in five Acts, Theatre Royal Drury Lane. February
4ᵗʰ 1796*, Huntington Library, Calif.

as responsibility passed to and fro between the Chamberlain's office and the local magistracy. Significantly, in October 1782 Dibdin's chief riding master, Charles Hughes, was put into the Bridewell on the Lord Chamberlain's authority.[12] Indeed, Dibdin's *Royal Circus Epitomized* (1784), although principally written to complain about his financial partners, provides an extraordinarily complex set of incidental documentary evidence as to the confused regulatory division between the Lord Chamberlain's office and the Surrey magistrates. But in any case, by 1797 the humourless Royal theatres were still seeking the prosecution of one Jobson, a Bartholomew Fair puppet-showman, for allowing his puppets to speak.[13]

Rumblings and grumblings about the power of the Royal theatres' patents and the role of the Lord Chamberlain continued for more than two generations. *The Report Of The Lord Chancellor ... On The Investigation of the Subject Of The Different Theatrical Petitions* (1831), which was intended to answer the latest bout of anti-patent theatre protest, concluded 'that the power [of granting patents] is vested by law in the King, beyond the reach of doubt or question'.[14] This was the context in which much theatrical writing existed, bounded as it was by a fairly comprehensive set of legal controls and requirements. In theory, the financial penalties for infringement were draconian.

Theoretically, fines for performing without the licence of the Lord Chamberlain were £50 *per* performer *per* performance *per* indictment. This exponential tariff of penalty was fully understood by the owners of the Royal theatres. One of the attempts by the patentees to scare the Royalty Theatre when it had opportunistically opened itself under the alleged authority of the Lord-Lieutenant Governor of the Tower, was backed by the pamphleteer's legal

[12] Charles Dibdin, *Royal Circus Epitomized* (1784), 19.
[13] Thomas Frost, *The Old Showmen, And the Old London Fairs* (London: Tinsley Brothers, 1874), 208.
[14] *The Report Of The Lord Chancellor And The Other Judges To His Majesty On The Investigation Of The Subject Of The Different Theatrical Petitions Was As Follows* [19 Feb. 1831].

counsel issuing a stern warning. In the blunt *A Very Plain State of the Case, or The Royalty Theatre Versus the Theatres Royal* (1787), the author threatened that all the Royalty's personnel, 'from the Manager and *honest* Charles Bannister [the comedian] down to Leoni's [a singer] little Pupil', were all liable to become the subject of 'a separate information', a discrete offence personal to each employee which could be 'lodged at any time within six months from the day on which each offence was committed'.[15] Charles Dibdin's principal Royal Circus horseman, Charles Hughes, for example, was committed to Bridewell as the result of 'a new information'.[16] The effects of these liabilities were of much concern to the Royalty's supporters. The playwright Isaac Jackman noted that the legislation dictated that the theatre's liability was that 'every person offending, shall for every such offence forfeit the sum of 50*l*'.[17] As a final piece of intimidation, because the magistrates were 'obliged to take the informations from whoever shall come forward', it was made clear that 'the numberless needy wretches about the metropolis, to whom a few pounds is so much an object, will [not] suffer so inviting an opportunity ... to pass unembraced'. In other words, London's East End beggars would be subtly induced to make complaints to magistrates.[18] This exponential tariff of fines, when multiplied by an unquantifiable number of beggars' indictments, would have been completely ruinous if regularly initiated. However, recollecting these real and supposed conditions as they applied in 1832, the editor and antiquarian John Payne Collier, in discussing the penalties, noted that the patent theatres seldom enforced their rights to fine in the courts preferring, as he put it, for 'the Lord Chamberlain to take upon himself the odium of closing profitable minor theatres by his own

[15] Michael Leoni was a German Jewish opera singer who died in Jamaica, where he had fled to escape his creditors: R. Humphreys, *The Memoirs Of J. Decastro, Comedian ... Accompanied By An Analysis Of The Life Of The Late Philip Astley, Esq. ... Also An Accompanying History Of The Royal Circus, Now The Surrey Theatre* (1824), 9–10 n.

[16] Charles Dibdin, *Royal Circus Epitomized*, 19.

[17] Jackman, *Royal and Royalty Theatres*, 9.

[18] *A Very Plain State of the Case, or The Royalty Theatre Versus the Theatres Royal.* (1787), 50–3.

authority', which he never seems to have done.[19] Nevertheless, the patentees ensured a climate of coercion, and confrontation coloured all theatrical ventures coming under their purview. As they clearly realized, much of their power lay in their intimidatory posture of truculent benevolence, the patronizing but unreliable *noblesse oblige* of a complacent ruling class.

The Royal Patent theatres guarded their rights more by this kind of bluster and manoeuvring than by actual direct intervention. In short, the Government office of the Lord Chamberlain's Examiner was the principal vehicle for safeguarding their privileges. This was done via the straightforward exclusion from the minor theatres of serious or five-act spoken drama, forms which Larpent could readily enough identify, even if the exact configuration of the permissible form of 'burletta' was more difficult to establish. However, when the Olympic Theatre in Wych Street opened in October 1815 within a hundred yards or so of both the Royal theatres, Drury Lane and Covent Garden began to complain, especially as another theatre, the Sans Pareil (later the Adelphi), had opened in the Strand. Essentially, the argument was about the diminishment of takings occasioned by the new theatres, that is, an argument about the loss of capital rather than the erosion of literary value. Although Robert William Elliston of the Olympic immediately sensed a threat, it was not until 1816–18 that the Royal Patent holders began to try a different tack. Still addressing themselves ostensibly to the Lord Chamberlain, they managed to move the locus of their complaint to the Home Office.

This was a significant development in Government strategy. As early as 1795 London's emerging spymaster, Sir Richard Ford (the future controller of the playwright-spy, James Powell; see below Chapter 8), whose reports were returned to the Duke of Portland at the Home Office, had intervened into the political regulation of theatres when he had tried to put pressure on the New Circus Theatre (the popular name for Astley's Amphitheatre post-conflagration

---

[19] John Payne Collier, *An Old Man's Diary, Forty Years Ago; For The First Six Months Of 1832* (London: Thomas Richards 1871) 81–2.

rebuild) to change the contents of its playbills. In the politically
sensitive year of 1795, amidst civil unrest and poor harvests, the
authorities appear to have become nervous at some of the New
Circus's productions. Ford (or his assistant, John King) had sent a
memorandum to the Bow Street magistrates (on whose bench Ford
later sat), directing them to 'represent to ... [Astley] ... *not in a
public manner*' (my emphasis) that 'allusions in his [play]Bills ... may
be the means of the Magistrates refusing a renewal of his licence'.[20]
If such ambitions of Government control were already present in
the mid-1790s, even if implemented discreetly, the moving of the
complaint in 1818 from the purview of the Lord Chamberlain to
that of the Home Office appears to signal the readiness of that
department of state to play a role in the regulation of the stage, in
this instance by putting pressure on magistrates. While such a move
may have been done with some wariness by the Home Office in
1818, it was a decisive official shift. Although apparently shortlived,
the Government must have been aware that, indirectly at least, the
Home Office's involvement gave the Royal theatres potential access
to the system of spying and informer activity which the department
of the Home Office had employed over the last twenty years, with a
belligerence glimpsed in dealings with Astley's New Circus.

At first the target of the Royal theatres was to reduce, as Elliston
described it, 'the term of the seasonal license of the Olympic
Theatre, in each year, [by] nearly one half; that is, to the period from
Michaelmas to Easter'.[21] Elliston's own position was unenviable
because he was, simultaneously, 'not merely the proprietor of the
little Theatre called "the Olympic"; but [also] the holder of one
Theatre Royal of magnitude [Birmingham]; and of other regular
Theatres of respectability and consideration' (p. 37). In other words,

[20] R. R. Nelson, *The Home Office, 1782–1801* (Durham, NC: Duke University Press, 1969), 115–16; 18 April 1795, HO 43/6. I have not been able to identify the production which gave offence.

[21] Robert William Elliston, *Copy Of A Memorial Presented To The Lord Chamberlain, By The Committee Of Management Of The Theatre-Royal Drury-Lane, Against The Olympic And Sans Pareil Theatres; With Copies Of Two Letters, In Reply To The Contents Of Such Memorial, Addressed To The Lord Chamberlain* (1818), p. iv.

Elliston had to operate, as part of his day-to-day management activity, as an owner working both within and without the patent licensing system.[22] The London Royal Patent holders jointly presented their own arguments to the Home Office and Elliston was forced into the position of handwriting a lengthy response which he later published, together with the patent-holders' arguments, as a *Copy Of A Memorial Presented To The Lord Chamberlain, By The Committee … Of The Theatre-Royal Drury-Lane, Against The Olympic And Sans Pareil Theatres; With Copies Of Two Letters, In Reply To The Contents Of Such Memorial, Addressed To The Lord Chamberlain* (1818).

Elliston's main line of attack was to ridicule the Royal Patent holders' allusion to their theatres as the principal seats of the 'National Drama'. Although neither the busy 'multi-plex' manager Elliston nor the capital shareholders of the Royal theatres were in a position to give much in the way of a considered, philosophically informed, set of arguments about what constituted the 'National' dramatic heritage of Shakespeare, Jonson, or Otway, the debate was being forced along by the risk to both capital interests and livelihoods in resolving a formulation of the exact relationship between theatre and literature. Furthermore, such a contestation also served to raise questions about the role of monopolistic interests in post-Napoleonic War Britain. Fortunately, the pomposity of such opinions provided Elliston with many quotable passages which he was pleased to re-address back in his own defence, arguing that 'the corruption of "the national drama", and not its "support", has been one of the manifest consequences of these measures [of monopoly]' (p. 36). Addressing the Lord Chamberlain as 'The Guardian Of The National Drama' (p. 7), the lessees of Drury Lane and Covent Garden claimed that, through the diversion of audiences away from them to the Olympic and Sans Pareil theatres, 'the two Patent Theatres are deprived of their Chance Of Profit; And The Means Of Supporting The Dignity

---

[22] In 1819 Elliston became a lessee of Drury Lane and, under the terms of his new agreement, had to sell up the Olympic: Edward Wedlake Brayley, *Historical and Descriptive Accounts of the Theatres of London* (1826), 88.

Of The National Drama' (p. 5). Elliston's reply, essentially, was that the Royal theatres were already themselves encroaching on the looser entertainments to which the minor theatres were limited by 'engrossing the whole store of stage exhibition, from the deepest pathos of tragedy to the highest flights of tight rope dancing, from the amblings of the poet to the amblings of the riding-house', or, as he put it, from Congreve to Puss-in-Boots (p. 25). As far as he was concerned, the current state of affairs was the protector 'not of "the national drama", but of the mongrel system which has been engrafted upon it' (p. 36). Such defences must have been extremely time-consuming to compose, especially for a man as busy as Elliston. These references are to the pagination of the printed *Copy Of A Memorial Presented To The Lord Chamberlain* (1818) Elliston published but, first of all, he had to send a labouriously produced handwritten submission to the Home Office (no doubt dictated and copied out by a hapless theatre scribe) while he fought off the attack by the patentees.

Caught between the two opposing sides, the Home Office was forced into attempting to establish some kind of evidential basis for the charges by sending informers to the theatres. One witness went to see *The Sportsman and Shepherd! or, Where's My Wig* at the Sans Pareil, Strand, while another saw Moncrieff's hit *Giovanni in London* (1817) at the Olympic, Wych Street. Inconclusively, the *Giovanni in London* informer reported only that it was 'performed in a kind of Doggrel [*sic*] the whole of the performances were well received by a respectable and crowded Audience'.[23] The attempt, perhaps instigated at Cabinet level in dialogue with the Lord Chamberlain, to incorporate the Home Office into decision-making about the ultimate relationship between the patent theatres' monopoly and the enforcing power of the Lord Chamberlain, probably signals a degree of frustration by central Government. The episode is a highly significant event within the workings of Government's dealings with the theatre. It shows that the bureaucracy adapted itself

[23] PRO H[ome] O[ffice] 119/4, 2, 18 March 1818.

to recognizing the political and legal dimensions of the legacy of seventeenth-century theatrical patents but also that they attempted to find some way of working which was more suited to the changed conditions of post-war Britain.

The legality of the Royal Patents indirectly conferred power of censorship onto the Government office of Lord Chamberlain, particularly by way of restrictions of genre; but unfortunately what also came into the package of the Lord Chamberlain's responsibilities were the capital sensitivities of the lessees and their tiresome urgings about the consequences for 'the national drama': 'unless your Lordship exerts your power to suppress these two minor theatres, which have thus so scandalously abused their licenses' (p. 6). The seventeenth-century legislation, as it stood, also gave some projection of London-based Government control into provincial England and Scotland since the regional patent theatres were included in the Lord Chamberlain's jurisdiction. Of course, what was revealed in the ramshackle nature of the authorities' practical day-to-day control of their jealously guarded rights of licence was that the provincial Theatre Royal owners often did not understand their subjugation to the Lord Chamberlain's control. The incoming of a new Examiner revealed the shaky theoretical base which underpinned the Lord Chamberlain's powers and the real (or more likely feigned) misunderstanding of his role as provincial playhouse managers probed Colman's resolution.

When George Colman the Younger took over in 1824 as Examiner after the death of John Larpent, the ex-playwright faced a rapid learning curve. No doubt testing the water soon after his first appointment, the executors of the Royal theatres in Hull and York, then in the hands of creditors, attempted to perform seven plays which they claimed had been 'only performed at the Minor Theatres of the Metropolis, not under the jurisdiction of the Lord Chamberlain'. Colman replied that, if it were the case that previous performances had occurred at 'Astley's, the Surrey, the Coburg, & some other Minor Theatres', then they were specifically 'without the License requisite for the York & Hull Theatres', since the proposed theatres for performance were both Royal theatres.[24] This attempt to wrong-foot the new Examiner was not the only incidence of chancing with the Lord Chamberlain.

Close on the heels of this exchange about two Yorkshire theatres, two weeks later came a piece from the Olympic Theatre, Wych Street, which was 'under the very noses' of Drury Lane and Covent Garden, which claimed its genre as a 'Burletta' but which was a term Colman thought he needed more clearly defined if he was to do his business.[25] The Olympic Theatre was only a few yards from the Theatre Royal Drury Lane but, as a 'minor' non-patent theatre, it still fell under the control of the Lord Chamberlain because it was in Westminster. Five-act spoken drama remained the perquisite of Covent Garden and Drury Lane alone: elsewhere, burletta was the only legitimate generic form.

Meanwhile, a baffled Colman, who had been a successful and highly experienced playwright for over thirty years, tried to decide what a burletta was. Colman wrote to Lord Montrose, the Lord Chamberlain: 'Surely a Burletta must be interspersed throughout with songs at least, whatever may be the other characteristics of a Burletta[?]'[26] The moment is very revealing because Montrose scarcely betrayed any thoroughly thought through literary or philosophical grounds for maintaining burletta's position as the one dramatic form not likely to infringe the Royal Patents. 'I think I may fairly say, that it is easy sometimes to say what is not a Burletta, tho' it may be difficult to define what a Burletta is' was Montrose's rather unhelpful reply. The Lord Chamberlain went on to indicate that a burletta was 'where the songs make a natural part of the Piece (& *not forced into an acting piece*, to qualify it as a Burletta)'. If this was muddled (a burletta, according to the Lord Chamberlain, is only where song is a 'natural' and not a 'forced' element of the

---

[24] B[ritish] L[ibrary] Add. MS 42865. fos. 431, 432; 4th, 8 March 1824.

[25] The phrase is one used at the time, see *Account of the Proceedings Before His Majesty's Most Hon. Privy Council Upon the Petition For A Third Theatre in the Metropolis* (1810), 54.

[26] BL Add. MS 42865, 22 March 1824.

text), Montrose was even less sure about 'whether a Burletta must not [always] be in verse, & the whole sung, not *said*'. Montrose expressed it this way round because the minor theatres were only protected from prosecution by the litigious Royal theatres if they exclusively performed burletta ('which makes the question dangerous, for These Theatres, as the Great Theatres may prosecute, under the Licence granted to the Minor Theatres'). In other words, under Montrose's understanding of the patents, burletta would have to be strictly interpreted as something approaching the modern definition of opera, a piece whose texts are wholly set to music, including the notional musicality of recitatives. With the power over public performance of drama so deeply embedded in the Lord Chamberlain's official role, it is amazing that he concluded his letter to Colman by advising him to maintain a discreet distance from the issue of generic definition ('Perhaps you had better say you do not think yourself called upon to give the definition of a Burletta, & therefore cannot presume to take that definition on yourself').[27] There is not much point assuming that Georgian drama was plunged into the aesthetic quagmire of burletta out of choice: burletta was the only legitimate form outside of the Royal theatres. To attempt to use speech was to invite certain prosecution. However, the reverse was not true. While burletta could be freely used by the Royal theatres, the plays of Shakespeare—or any other type of spoken drama—was forbidden to the non-patent houses.

This combination of an absolute lack of principle coupled to a complete intention of implementing authority is a defining characteristic of the Government regime controlling the representation of theatrical writing during this period. If anything, Colman's written inquiries to Montrose show a certain level of commendable bureaucratic procedure: if he did not know the answer himself, at least he was prepared to ask Montrose. In other words, Colman was astute enough not to let the buck rest with him: he made certain it was passed to the Duke. As will be shown in Chapter 3, Colman's

[27] Ibid.

predecessor, John Larpent, was much less organized or prepared to be even notionally accountable.

A principal aim of *Theatric Revolution* is to show how drama evaded or negotiated these types of Government censorship. This censorship was manifested not only as an immediate Government control over play texts through the Lord Chamberlain's office, but also as the more widely dispersed coercive effect of the monopolistic Royal Patent lessees on the increasing number of London 'minor' theatres. However, far from it becoming a *cause célèbre* of radical sensitivities to injustice (as was to happen to some extent in the late 1820s), one of the paradoxes of political radicalism's relationship with theatrical censorship was that it was not always bothered about it. During the Covent Garden 1809 OP riots, for example, the 1790s Jacobin Henry Redhead Yorke in the *Political Review* (16 September 1809) fulminated against 'that unfeeling Jewess [the singer], Angelica Catalini' (alleged to have been hired at £4,000 per year), declaring, 'I am for a rebellion; and, let me tell King John [Kemble, manager], that if he will not give us the English spirit of Garrick, we will give him and his Frenchified crew, the spirit of Marat', yet Yorke wrote not a single word about censorship.[28] It is noticeable that, over the long term, the literary history of this period has been less frequent in noting the statutory censorship of drama than it has in charting the rise of the radically-inclined Romantic period lyric poets.

The bifurcation of the paths between drama and the advancement of canonical literary status for poetry is perhaps most starkly seen in the shortlived periodical the *Newgate Monthly Magazine*. The *Newgate Monthly* was published by an array of Richard Carlile's shopmen, some of whom were still in prison subsequent to their convictions for publishing Carlile's *Republican*. The political fervour and moral rectitude of these men (and some women) is not in doubt but the problems of stage censorship were only of passing interest. In one of the first issues of the *Newgate Monthly Magazine*, Thomas R. Perry (one of the imprisoned shopmen) wrote a short piece

---

[28] *Covent Garden Journal* (1810), 377–85.

entitled 'The Stage versus The Pulpit', which objected to Methodist harassment of theatre companies, particularly in the provinces, arguing that the office of Examiner of Plays was 'a disgrace to this age and nation'.[29] Under Carlile's leadership, the *Newgate Monthly Magazine* was happy to be politically and socially progressive enough to publish a letter from 'A Female Materialist and Republican', and it was personally supportive enough for the imprisoned contributor W. Haley to reflect in his piece, 'Life in Newgate', that he 'saw the Coronation, and I have seen many other grand fooleries . . . But the interior of a Theatre presents to me a delightful spectacle' without actually using the magazine to polemicize against stage censorship.[30] However, the *Newgate Monthly Magazine* would subsequently go on to neglect the politics of drama and is now best known in literary history for its ardent championing of the poetry of P. B. Shelley. It is unlikely that this was a deliberate shift in emphasis—the Government repression, including periods in gaol, disrupted the editorship of the journal—but, given the profile of the theatre as a political issue, the fact that it was supplanted by Shelley's poetry in the pages of the magazine is nonetheless remarkable.

During the course of its two or so years of publication, the journal published a series of essays (as well as one 'Sonnet to Shelley') aimed at explaining and widening Shelley's reputation.[31] It is possible to conjecture that the pseudonymous author of these essays ('C') was either the shadowy pressman George Cannon, or the shoemaker poet Robert Charles Fair. The point of interest to the profile and reputation of Georgian period drama is that these writers for the *Newgate Monthly Magazine* were amongst the first to identify the importance of Shelley's politics and to place these politics within a radical tradition dating back to 1790s Jacobinism ('The Mab of Shelley bears a strong resemblance to the Genius of Volney'); and that they did this within an understanding that his poetry was both

[29] *The Newgate Monthly Magazine, or Calendar of Men, Things and Opinions*, October (1824), 78–82.
[30] Ibid. (1824–5), 224–30.
[31] Ibid. 275, 415–22, 460, 476, 478–9, 517–27.

subversive of oligarchy and supportive of working-class culture. As one article on Shelley put it, 'There is yet, no poet's works which contain bolder strains of poetry and stronger attacks upon the absurd systems, whose supporters have so long preyed upon the industrious plebeians.'[32] The bifurcation of the literary road which, later in the nineteenth century, saw Shelley raised to iconic status amongst working-class radicals begins here.

Drama dropped out of the roll-call of honour at the expense of poetry. While the politics of drama were clearly recognized, they found no ideological champion in the *Newgate Monthly Magazine*. The singularity of this position is perhaps at its most evident in the *Newgate*'s willingness to confront in its pages one of drama's most persistent opponents, the Society for the Suppression of Vice.[33] At the very least, the contradiction of this position implies that much of the strength of early nineteenth-century radicalism, particularly under Carlile, was overwhelmingly devoted to tackling the stranglehold of the established Church. This unfortunate direction in literary history became even more paradoxical when, in the early 1830s, Richard Carlile opened up his own theatrical space at the Rotunda, Blackfriars Road, the subject of Chapter 10 of *Theatric Revolution*. Although poetry was an important vehicle of expression for many aspirant artisans, Carlile had eventually to concede the attractions of drawing nightly audiences to his polemics. However, in the long-term development of literary criticism's sense of its own history, Shelley's gain was artisan drama's loss.

One of the literary implications of the development of the burlettas was, indeed, a perceived decline in the absolute literary quality of drama which, arguably, the literary taste of the *Newgate Monthly* mirrors. The complexities and questionable evidence of this decline is a subject implicit in the argument of this book but the classic position, as influentially put by Allardyce Nicoll, also alleges a net

---

[32] *The Newgate Monthly Magazine, or Calendar of Men, Things and Opinions*, (1824), 476.
[33] 'Proceedings of the Vice Society', ibid. 547–52.

detrimental effect on the perceived social value of dramatic writing, an argument which cannot be sustained.[34] Coupled to this perceived decline in literary value was, inevitably, an apparent loss in drama's role as a moral force in the arts.

Drama always had a difficult time being understood as morally beneficial but a general awareness of its social purpose had survived much of the eighteenth century surprisingly intact. Even in provincial Lincolnshire, where the coaching town of Stamford's limited theatre season was timed to coincide with the local horse-racing calendar, a pit ticket dating from the late 1790s was printed showing four clasped hands and the words 'Liberty/Truth/Justice/Friendship', an emblem denoting the shared civic ideals of both the town and its theatregoers.[35] However, these ephemeral examples from the period's generally burgeoning print culture also reflect the age's polarized views about the stage. In 1799 the Religious Tract Society published a one-penny anti-stage pamphlet, *Theatrical Amusements; Or, A Dialogue Between Mr. Clement and Mr. Mortimer, In Which The Present State of the Stage is Fully Considered . . . No. 542*, in a format embellished by a woodcut vignette picturing a theatre entrance lugubriously captioned 'Mortimer reading the Inscription on the wall | The Way To The Pit☞'. Symptomatic of the ideological fractures surrounding the physical sites of contemporary drama, with only a little imaginative licence it is possible to envisage some hypothetical Stamford theatregoer at the end of the 1790s arriving at the playhouse bearing a 'Liberty/Truth/Justice/Friendship' entrance ticket only to be lobbied by moral activists at the door to buy (or accept gratis) a copy of the Religious Tract Society's *Theatrical Amusements*.[36] The steady condemnation of drama by the patrician ruling class was a constant factor which ran in parallel with drama's

---

[34] The classic modern verdict of literary decline is Allardyce Nicoll, *A History of English Drama, 1660–1900* (1930; Cambridge: Cambridge University Press, 1960), v. 58–78, 'The Reasons of Decline'.

[35] Playbills, Stamford Town Hall, Lincolnshire.

[36] For Religious Tract Society's leafleting of the Adelphi Theatre's W. T. Moncrieff *Tom and Jerry* in 1822 and Robert Taylor and Richard Carlile's *Swing* at the Rotunda in 1831, see Chs 7 and 10 below.

gradual development away from its control by theatrical monopolies and interventions by the Lord Chamberlain and the magistrates. It is not surprising, therefore, that some commentators, such as the playwright Elizabeth Inchbald in an 1807 piece about novelists, were led to comment unfavourably on this changing relationship in which the stage drama was less confidently supportive of the patrician outlook and its moral roles. Nevertheless, Inchbald recognized clearly enough the political implications of dramatic censorship, that while the novelist 'lives in a land of liberty . . . the Dramatic Writer exists but under a despotic government'. However, although Inchbald noted 'the subjection in which an author of plays is held by the Lord Chamberlain's office', she argued that the dramatist 'is the very slave of the audience'.[37] In concluding that dramatists dared not 'expose upon the stage, certain faults, almost inseparable from the indigent' or 'expose in a theatre, the consummate vanity of a certain rank of paupers, who boast of that wretched state as a sacred honour, although it be the result of indolence or criminality' (p. 17), she had reckoned without huge changes in popular theatrical culture. While this may have been true of attitudes in the early 1800s period when Inchbald was writing, by the early 1820s—in a social transformation at least partly brought about by the emerging burletta houses—conditions had changed. The Adelphi's 1821 hit play *Tom and Jerry* could positively flaunt its crowd-pulling 'gammoning' St Giles' beggars, African Sall, Dusty Bob, Little Jemmy, and Billy Waters.

One of the earlier turning points of drama's movement away from modes of cultural deference and towards a recognition of its alterity as a mainly plebeian public sphere can be identified in the moment of Drury Lane's production of William Henry Ireland's Shakespeare forgery, *Vortigern* (1796). While it was, strictly speaking, a symbolic moment rather than signifying any structural change in the material conditions of theatre writing, Ireland's *Vortigern* usefully marks the latest moment when writers still felt the need to compromise their writing by attempting to replicate a mode of literary expression

---

[37] Elizabeth Inchbald, *The Artist*, 13 June 1807, 9–19, 16.

which was solely the preserve of two London theatres and the provincial patentees. After Ireland's debacle, playwrights began to explore the rather different forms of literary expressivity allowable in the burlettas of the non-Royal theatres. As the number of non-patent theatres increased, particularly in London, the attractiveness of kowtowing to the obscure selection processes of the Royal theatres became less and less attractive. The uncertain reception of spoken five-act plays continued to cause problems about which younger writers must certainly have been aware.

As late as 1824, the fate of Martin Archer Shee's five-act tragedy of *Alasco* (1824), a work intended for Covent Garden, provided a disconcerting warning to aspirant writers wishing to pursue spoken drama. What was so daunting about the episode of *Alasco* was that Shee was already comfortably socially placed as a highly successful portraitist, a profession whose calling particularly demands that painters be both decorous in their affairs and acceptable to the higher echelons of society. By 1824, Shee's sitters had already included royalty ([the future] *King William IV*, *c.*1800, National Portrait Gallery), politicians (*John Freeman-Mitford, 1st Baron Redesdale*, speaker of the House of Commons, *c.*1802, National Portrait Gallery) as well as many eminent lawyers, high-ranking soldiers, and divines. Six years after writing *Alasco*, Shee achieved the recognition of his peers by being elected President of the Royal Academy in 1830. However, these social networks did not spare his Polish tragedy the drastic cutting demanded by the new Examiner of Plays, George Colman the Younger. As he refused to submit to the substantial cuts required, *Alasco* was withdrawn, but Shee was quickly able to publish *Alasco* as a play text, along with his own lengthy remonstrating preface complete with Colman's deletions indicated. The publishers were the radical firm of Sherwood, Jones & Co., whose house had pirated the Poet Laureate Robert Southey's 1794 drama, *Wat Tyler*, back in 1817.[38] It is quite probable that Shee's social status was instrumental in rapidly securing *Alasco* a production at the New York Theatre,

[38] Shee, *Alasco*.

New York, in December of 1824 (where its American reprint was puffed as *Alasco ... Excluded from the English Stage*).[39] However, the problems of the dramatist did not end there. In addition to having *Alasco*'s Covent Garden production thwarted, Shee also had to face the socially unpredictable effects of adverse press comment, a situation potentially damaging to a portraitist whose practice of his profession depended on commissions from affluent potential sitters and their families.

An anonymous reviewer in *Blackwood's Magazine* wrote a review of the printed edition headed, 'Pike Prose, and Poetry', where the writer made a sustained series of references to *Alasco*'s parallels with the Irish situation, despite the play's overtly Polish setting. The reviewer was contemptuous of its 'foul stream of Whiggery', of 'Mr Shee's Covent-Garden Whiteboyism' (the latter being the *Blackwood's* reviewer's knowledgeable reference to a contemporary Irish rebel group), while it also fulminated against the play's stage directions of '"*Daybreak*—The Entrance of a cavern—a *peasant* armed with a PIKE", the instrument of the rebels in Ireland. Had the scene been meant for Poland, in which it was laid, the author would have given his Whiteboy a lance.'[40] Neither was it the case that Colman's interdiction of *Alasco* remained a purely bureaucratic affair. Colman had also written privately to Sir William Knighton, a physician and close confidant of George IV, remarking with reference to *Alasco* that such 'plays ... built upon conspiracies, and attempts to revolutionise a state, stand upon ticklish ground; and the proposed performance of such plays is to be contemplated with more jealousy when they pourtray the disaffected as gallant heroes and hapless lovers'.[41] Clearly, for someone of the standing

[39] Martin Archer Shee, *Alasco: A Tragedy, in Five Acts ... Excluded from the English Stage by the Authority of the Lord Chamberlain, Performed, for the first time, at the New-York Theatre, on Thursday evening, Dec. 16, 1824* (New York, 1824).

[40] *Blackwood's Magazine*, 15 (1824), 593–7.

[41] Quoted in Richard Brinsley Peake, *Memoirs of the Colman Family, including Correspondence with the most distinguished personages of their time*, 2 vols. (1841), ii. 400–1.

of Shee, with the potential to become President of the King's Royal Academy of Art, such well connected correspondence could be seriously damaging.

As well as encountering this barrage of hostility from *Blackwood's Magazine*, and the guilt-by-association suggested in Colman's correspondence with the eminent courtier, Shee had also to suffer further artistic dismemberment when *Alasco* was produced by the Surrey Theatre in April 1824. Of course, the Surrey Theatre's eagerly opportunistic billing of 'Last Week Before Easter! | New & Suppressed Tragedy of Alasco!' (Shee's name was omitted from the playbill) exposes the limitations of Colman's authority as Examiner of Plays, a role which stopped at Waterloo Bridge and did not run to the south side of the Thames. The Surrey management had evidently read Sherwood, Jones & Co's edition as well as 'the very pithy and clear delineation given by the highly talented Author in the Preface of this Publication', but, as the playbill explained, they undertook to perform only 'a selection' of 'the above celebrated Tragedy compressed and arranged as a Melo-Drama'.[42] That the Surrey's *Alasco* was a 'selection' 'compressed and arranged', as well as being generically redefined from tragedy into 'Melo-Drama', is a clear indication that, at the least, the playhouse both shortened the play and very probably imported music to be played between the scenes. For Shee, it was a highly equivocal outcome: if he ever thought of proceeding with a censored version at Covent Garden, then it too would have been cut so as to comply with Colman's strictures. However, the Surrey's 'compressed' version was also an abridgement although, tantalizingly, it is possible to imagine that the management provocatively chose to perform the very parts about which Colman had made most objection (and which had been highlighted in Shee's printed text). Whatever happened, performance in either playhouse would have been a bastardization of Shee's original plan. Even if Colman ran out of jurisdiction at the Surrey Theatre, the hegemony of the Covent Garden and Drury Lane patentees over

---

[42] BL Playbills, Surrey Theatre, 1822–8. Monday, 5 April 1824.

speech on the stage ensured that the Surrey *Alasco* was not to be performed as the straightforward spoken drama Shee had intended. Indeed, it is very probable that the Surrey's designation of *Alasco* as being 'arranged as a Melo-Drama' meant that Shee's text was wholly set to music, a stipulated licensing requirement for the Surrey. While Shee might have felt some satisfaction at having finally found an outlet for his tragedy, its 'compressed' nature and probable musical setting could hardly have matched his original intentions of writing a five-act play with complex, if covert, allusions to Irish nationalism.

The fall-out of the *Alasco* episode of 1824 shows that, long after *Vortigern's* 1796 performance, if dramatic writers were either forced into pretending to be Shakespeare (as in William Henry Ireland's case) or else had to watch helplessly as a tragedy such as Shee's allegorizing a serious contemporary issue was censored, abridged, and hounded in the literary press, then the burlettas of the minor theatres potentially offered welcome freedoms. Ultimately, the most telling aspect of what happened to *Alasco* was that it was the Surrey Theatre which had attempted something approaching a rescue, and it was the unregulated New York playhouse which had finally achieved its production. Back in London, the attractions of unimpeachable burletta on the south side of the Thames, together with the proximity of south London's greater audience catchments, continued to make the prospect of writing spoken dramas for Covent Garden or Drury Lane an extremely poor risk.

Revealingly, it was an almost certainly pirated comic sketch of Charles Mathews, whose *At Home* monologues similarly traversed an indistinct area of regulation, which most clearly summarized the situation of stage drama obtaining in the mid-1820s when a musical piece called 'Memoranda in Confusion' was printed as *Duncombe's Edition ... Mr. Mathews' Memorandum-Book, of Peculiarities, Character, and Manners, Collected by him in his various Trips* (1825). The existence of Mathews's piece demonstrates that the *Alasco* episode was one whose implications were widely understood to be not merely the misfortunes of one unlucky dramatist. In 'Memoranda in Confusion' (sung to the refrain 'Four-and-twenty

Actors all of a row'), Mathews satirized how 'Coleman [*sic*] who wrote the *Heir at Law* [1798] and *Broad Grins* [1802] now sets up to correct all our sins.' In this song Mathews comically bemoaned the loss of 'Mr. Shee that the Deputy Licenser would not let us see'.[43] Mathews's sketch, reaching large audiences on the comedian's tours as well as via Duncombe's cheap printed edition, would have ensured that the issue both reflected, and furthered, the circulation of the circumstances of the *Alasco* incident far into contemporary popular culture.

Even by virtue of their location, theatres like the Royal Coburg (now Old Vic) in the Cut, on the Surrey side of the Thames, were much closer to their audience hinterlands. Simple economic factors of travel within the metropolis did much to dictate the demographics of attendance. Horace Foote's *Companion to the Theatres* (1829) gave the hackney carriage fare for someone travelling from Blackfriars Road to Astley's Amphitheatre as one shilling and sixpence as opposed to three shillings to reach Drury Lane.[44] As its building proposals put out to potential backers outlined, although the Coburg was to be built in 1817 on cheap swampy ground, it was 'situated on the site of Seven Roads, one of which proves to be the nearest way to Westminster for all the Population of the East end of the Town'.[45] Not only could south London audiences more easily see theatrical performances at the Coburg, after the opening of Waterloo Bridge in 1817 the traditional audiences of Covent Garden and Drury Lane audiences could just as easily come to them.

There were also other more politicized movements at work which tended to radicalize the social role of drama. At its simplest, the struggle against the Royal Patent theatres, culminating in a Parliamentary *Report from the Select Committee on Dramatic Literature* (1832), became a proxy or surrogate for the struggle for Parliamentary

---

[43] Mathews, *Second Edition/Duncombe's Edition*, 4–6.
[44] Horace Foote, *A Companion to the Theatres; and Manual of The British Drama* (1829), 148.
[45] BL, Miscellaneous Institutions: Theatres, *Royal Coburg Theatre. In order to form a just opinion* ... (1817).

reform.[46] The political dimension of reform of the Royal Patent theatres was widely understood as a mature cultural metaphor for the more general political Parliamentary reform of the electoral franchise. The reformist discourse of the one was simply mapped onto the reformist discourse of the other. The equation between a monopolistic, unreformed theatre and an unreformed, narrow franchise for Parliament was a ubiquitous political observation and one which increases quite visibly the nearer the 1832 Reform Bill is approached.

The richness of popular understanding of the issues involved in this equation, and of their deep social dispersal, is made evident in the material vocabularies and expressive repertoires deployed by contemporaries. During the Old Price (OP) riots at Covent Garden in September 1809 theatregoers could 'contemplate the various banners that were flying in different parts of the house' carrying various slogans which seamlessly equated political and theatrical reform. These banners were made up and smuggled into the theatre by the audience in order to ensure the newspapers reported the arguments of the rioters as well as noticing the general level of fracas. On the third night of the uproar, amongst the banners displayed over the balconies of the theatre were ones reading 'No private Rooms—Opposition, persevere and you must succeed—No snug Anti-rooms [*sic*] ... No privileged Orders in the third circle ... No monopoly—No private accommodations before the curtain.'[47] The rioters' grievances were not only about raised prices, but also about the visibility of the 'privileged Orders' and the 'monopoly' of the Royal theatres in successfully limiting theatrical competition. Noticeably, one of the banners displayed that night, 'Opposition, persevere and

[46] Only Covent Garden, Drury Lane, and the Haymarket held the Royal Patent, although the Italian opera house in the Haymarket held a royal licence specific to opera. The Lyceum or English Opera House sometimes titled themselves in playbills as a Royal theatre but this arises from the theatre being a temporary home when Covent Garden burned down; see Brayley, *Historical and Descriptive Accounts of the Theatres of London*, 42.

[47] John Bull [John Fairburn], *Remarks on the Cause of the Dispute Between the Public and Managers of the Theatre Royal, Covent Garden, With a Circumstantial Account of the Week's Performances and the Uproar ... illustrated with a large Caricature Frontispiece of the House that Jack built* (1809), 19.

you must succeed', was a self-reflexive maxim conveying meaning about a more generalized political struggle as well as the immediate OP objective of reduced prices and greater public visibility in Covent Garden Theatre.

Indeed, unrest at price rises following Covent Garden's reopening after a devasting fire mobilized other equally far-reaching concerns including explicit criticism of upper class immorality. The radical pressman John Fairburn implied that the newly restructured interior of Covent Garden would facilitate the sexual debaucheries of the upper classes. During the rebuild, the theatre's interior had been reconfigured so that the gentry would

approach through a private anti-chamber, furnished with every accom-modation for convenience, luxury, and indulgence; there the weary, whose delicate frames are exhausted by the fatigue of viewing the performance from a chair, may, in the security of their extreme privacy, hide them 'from the day's garish eyes', and repose in soft indolence between the Acts, or during the performance, on a couch, with which indispensable convenience these delicious boudoirs are respectively furnished.[48]

Beyond the levelling, equalizing moral gaze of the pit, the gentry would be hidden but up to their tricks, or as Fairburn's *Remarks on the Cause of the Dispute* put it, 'No snug hiding places' (p. 15). On the fourth night of the OP riots, as if to emphasize the alignment of theatrical and political concerns which ran in tandem with this moral criticism, one of the placards simply read, 'No theatrical taxation' (p. 25). In other words, the riotous OP crowds distinctly recognized that Government regulation of the theatre, whether through the exercise of the patentees' privileges or the Lord Chamberlain's censorship role, were all part of an economy in which politics, morality, and capital colluded as a cartel over dramatic representation.

This mapping of the discourse of political reform onto the debate was thoroughly understood on all sides. In an exchange during the taking of evidence for the *Report . . . on Dramatic Literature*, George

---

[48] Ibid. 10.

Colman the Younger, the then Examiner, was asked if he would 'strike . . . out' 'the word reform' from any play he read:

970. In the exercise of your censorship at the present moment, if the word reform should occur, you would strike it out?

[COLMAN.] — No; I should say, 'I think you had better omit it; I advise you to do so for your own sakes, or you will cause a hubbub.'

The potential to cause 'a hubbub' was a fear which glances back towards the notoriety of episodes such as the OP riots when the former London Corresponding Society member Francis Place played a prominent role in organizing the more measured civil protest aspects of the public's encounter with the Covent Garden management.[49] Overt theatricalization and role-playing at the OP riots by many members of the audience will be discussed later but the behaviour of the riot supporters also included a complete breakdown in customs of deference. Arriving unawares on the first night of the riots, the Duke of York stepped from his carriage to be greeted by 'exclamations of "Dukey", "My Darling", &c.'[50] With Parliamentary reform very much on the national agenda in the early 1830s, Colman must have feared the audience seizing on the word 'reform' and hijacking the performance. Predictably enough, as if anticipating such a collapse, in 1832 the owners of the Royal theatres Drury Lane and Covent Garden had complained that any de-regulation would be comparable to that attempted in freeing-up theatre building in France during 'the height of the revolutionary mania'.[51]

Activism in support of theatrical reform was widespread. Eugene Macarthy, in *A Letter To The King, On The Question Now At Issue Between The 'Major', And 'Minor' Theatres* (1832), attacked the

[49] See Marc Baer, *Theatre and Disorder in Late Georgian London* (Oxford: Clarendon Press, 1992), 94, for Place's first involvement. Place was born opposite the south side of Drury Lane Theatre and later married the Covent Garden actress Louisa Simeon Chatterley: *The Autobiography of Francis Place, 1771–1854*, ed. Mary Thale (Cambridge: Cambridge University Press, 1972), pp. ix, 23, 258.

[50] *Covent Garden Journal* (1810), 148–9.

[51] *The Humble Petition of the Proprietors of the Theatres Royal Drury Lane and Covent Garden* (1832), 2.

'arrogant and despotic edicts of a Theatrical Oligarchy' of patentees while the anonymous author of *Major And Minor Theatres. A Concise View Of The Question* (1832) adopted the contemporary reformist discourse more directly: 'It has been one of the pleas of the corruptionists (of the Boroughmongers of the Playhouses), that the public do not wish for a regular Drama—that they do not wish for a reform.'[52] In adopting an activist stance by organizing a petition, the author of *Major And Minor Theatres* not only summoned 'ye shades of the O.P. rioters', as part of a twenty-two-year collective memory of agitation, but the Home Office's surveillance system also took an interest in the pamphlet where it was directly filed alongside copies of the *Poor Man's Guardian* newspaper and William Benbow's *Grand National Holiday, and Congress of the Productive Classes* (1832), a work important to labour historians in first outlining the concept of a general strike.[53] Thomas James Thackeray's pamphlet *On Theatrical Emancipation, And the Rights of Dramatic Authors* (1832) made the association between corruption, privilege, and monopoly, versus the rights of unenfranchised labour, even more explicit when he wrote about 'the anomaly of *two institutions* arming themselves with unjust laws, and, at the expense of the well-being of more than two thousand of their fellow-labourers, endeavouring to establish ever more firmly all the abuses of *privilege* and the selfishness of *monopoly*'.[54] Thackeray's comments on the numbers employed in theatrical work identify a not insignificant component of London's place as a centre for the manufacture and provision of luxury goods and services. Perhaps less easy to establish as evidence, but no less important, were the allegations of sexual misconduct made against patentees. Although it was beyond Larpent's jurisdiction because of

---

[52] Eugene Macarthy, *A Letter To The King, On The Question Now At Issue Between The 'Major', And 'Minor' Theatres* (1832) 10; anon., *Major And Minor Theatres. A Concise View Of The Question, As Regards, The Public, The Patentees, And The Profession With Remarks On The Decline Of The Drama, And The Means Of Its Restoration To Which Is Added The Petition Now Lying For Signature* (1832), 13.

[53] *Major And Minor Theatres*, 13. A copy of the pamphlet is in PRO HO 64/17.

[54] Thomas James Thackeray, *On Theatrical Emancipation, And the Rights of Dramatic Authors* (1832), 3.

geography, the Dublin Theatre Royal's patent holder, Richard Daly, paid starvation wages to his male actors and, as the memoir of the comedian Jacob Decastro put it, 'the women he kept by the same means, in a state of compliance with his desires'.[55] These issues of theatrical privileges and cartels, and their wider resonance in national political discourse, had been thoroughly understood for over fifty years. The revealingly titled pamphlet *Theatrical Monopoly; Being an Address to the Public on the Present Alarming Coalition of the Managers of the Winter Theatres* (1779) urged the playwright George Colman (the future Examiner's father) to try to obtain a patent specifically to establish a new theatre capable of breaking the hold of the current Royal theatres.[56]

To counter this monopoly, there were the usual time-honoured options available to the public. As Gillian Russell and Marc Baer have pointed out, much of the cultural politics of the 1809 Covent Garden 'Old Price' or OP riots is intelligible in terms of E. P. Thompson's analysis of the moral economy of Georgian crowd behaviour.[57] At the height of the OP riots, a letter to *The Times* all but identified the riots as symptomatic of the moral economy of the crowd, 'Covent Garden Theatre possessing a monopoly, its proprietors have thought proper to raise the price of the article in which they deal. The public who is the buyer, thinks this an unfair price, and shows its disapprobation by modes from time immemorial used for the purpose.'[58] This identification of corrupt practices provoking the riots through the agency of an artisan or plebeian audience is a clear example of the exercise of a moral economy amongst contemporary theatre audiences. As the writer concluded in commenting on the lack

[55] Humphreys, *The Memoirs Of J. Decastro*, 52.

[56] *Theatrical Monopoly; Being an Address to the Public on the Present Alarming Coalition of the Managers of the Winter Theatres* (1779), p. viii.

[57] Gillian Russell, 'Playing at Revolution: The Politics of the O.P. Riots of 1809', *Theatre Notebook*, 44:1 (1990), 16–25; Baer, *Theatre and Disorder in Late Georgian London*, 9, 23, 26.

[58] The classic accounts of this phenomenon are E. P. Thompson, 'The Moral Economy of the English Crowd in the Eighteenth Century' and 'The Moral Economy Reviewed', in *Customs in Common* (Harmondsworth: Penguin, 1993), 185–258, 259–351.

of fair competition, 'at the present, the public have no choice. They must buy from the house possessing the monopoly or not at all.'[59] As part of the public sensitivity towards the political dimensions of theatrical monopoly, there was a swift radicalization of those not prepared to remain as mere bystanders.

The perceived abuse of privilege also extended to the high-handed way in which much new writing was excluded from the patent theatres. One of the more extraordinary (if not entirely uncommon) manifestations of the plain inefficiency of Drury Lane was when one author found that his translation of a French drama, submitted for consideration in 1803, was left unacknowledged but put into production in 1805.[60] The adaptor, James Powell, was himself unusual in that he was also a long-term government spy and informer. In fairness to Drury Lane, although the language is closely similar in part, it is evident that the manager, R. W. Elliston, had extensively revised and shortened Powell's original translation of *The Venetian Outlaw*.[61] Portentously, in 1812 the first advocate and excerpter of Shelley's *Queen Mab*, the Smithfield radical shoemaker Robert Charles Fair suffered the rejection of his (first recorded) poetic effort, an address for the reopening of Drury Lane Theatre, when he lost out to Lord Byron.[62] Certainly, there was a ready enough interest

[59] Quoted, *Covent Garden Journal* (1810), 543–4.

[60] James Powell, *The Venetian Outlaw, His Country's Friend. A Drama, in Three Acts, Now Performing at the Theatre Royal, Drury-Lane, with unbounded Applause … Altered from the French of A. Pixiricourt* (1805), pp. iii–iv; Larpent 1449, application made 22 April 1805 by Richard William Elliston, Huntington Library, Calif.

[61] R. W. Elliston, *The Venetian Outlaw, A Drama in Three Acts, As Performed at the Theatre Royal, Drury Lane* (1805). Elliston noted that he had received his translation from 'Mr Bingley, jun'. who had seen it performed at the Duke of Brunswick's theatre (p. 58). Elliston included in his edition an affidavit distinguishing his own translation from that of Powell (p. 60).

[62] BL Add. MS 27899, fo. 10, 'Drury Lane Theatre Rejected Addresses, 1812'. Drury Lane had organized a poetry competition to choose a reopening address. There was great controversy surrounding Byron's successful 'Address, Spoken at the Opening of Drury-Lane Theatre … October 10, 1812' which does not appear to have been entered. When read alongside Byron's riposte to the ensuing fuss, 'Parenthetical Address, by Dr. Plagiary', what emerges is a smugly patrician viewpoint which greatly contrasts to the (less poetically vivid) more ideologically open piece by Fair. For the context, see Michael

among radical pressmen to print plays rejected by the two theatres, thus creating opportunities of obliquely attacking such high-profile examples of the corrupt, unreformed monopolies paralleled in the nation's general political structure. Robert Charles Fair's fellow Spencean, the Whitefriars pressman Thomas Davison (who was also John Murray's main printer of Byron's works during the 1810s) published J.W.S.'s *The Innocent Usurper, A Musical Drama, founded upon the Demofoonte of Metastasio. As offered to the Managers of Covent Garden Theatre, June, 1819* (1821), shortly before he himself went to gaol for printing Richard Carlile's *Republican*. This proximity between London's radical press and theatrical writing is a consistent feature of metropolitan political culture and it worked in quite intricate ways. As well as publishing many other plays, the London Corresponding Society (LCS) pressman Henry Delahay Symonds innocently furthered the career of a dangerous informer when he published James Powell's *The Narcotic and Private Theatricals. Two Dramatic Pieces by James Powell of the Custom House* (1793). Powell's infiltration as Secretary of the second incarnation of the LCS led in 1798 to his escape to Hamburg, where he was involved in spying on United Irishmen and possibly associating with William Wordsworth.[63] Similarly, after his play was turned down the dramatic writer F. A Wilson turned to the anti-Royalist pressman Effingham Wilson to publish his *Epistolary Remonstrance to Thomas Morton Esq, Dramatic Writer And Professed Critic and Reader to Captain Polhill and His Majesty's Servants of Drury Lane Theatre* (1832). Hard on the heels of the 'Rejected Addresses' fiasco at Drury Lane, several spurned plays were published together as being representative of *The New British Theatre; a Selection of original drama, not yet acted; some of which have been offered for representation but not accepted* (1814). In keeping with the political reform-by-proxy agenda described above,

---

Simpson, 'Re-Opening after the Old Price Riots: War and Peace at Drury Lane', *Texas Studies in Literature and Language*, 41 (1999), 378–402.

[63] See Kenneth Johnston, *The Hidden Wordsworth* (London: Norton, 1998), 457, 896 n. 71.

the New British Theatre's Advertisement stated that the volume was intended to 'promote the Reformation Of The Stage' while its editorial matter referred to 'the want of competition' created by the Royal theatres, noting that 'We may frequent what tavern we please, reside where we choose, read what we will; but in our amusements we must be slaves to the patentees of Drury Lane and Covent Garden' (p. vii). Although the plays in *The New British Theatre* are of variable quality, such publications served to keep alive other aspects of collective literary memory. Introducing Sophia Lady Burrell's *Theodora*, the volume's editor compared her favourably to Madame de Staël, a 'philosophess, celebrated more on account of her political connexions than her merits deserve', adding that de Staël's talents were 'far below the almost forgotten Mary Wollstonecraft, both in dignity of thought and eloquence of elucidation'.[64]

Neither was this debate about the power of the patents exclusively a feature of different parts of Grub Street or between rival theatre managers. New and innovative forms of stage entertainment inevitably challenged the customs and legalities of both the theatre managers and the Lord Chamberlain's powers. The one-man hit show *At Home*, by the comic impressionist and social caricaturist Charles Mathews, concluded its first forty-night run at the English Opera House, Strand, in 1818 with the actor giving an extraordinary farewell speech to the audience attacking the Royal theatres. It was a remarkable decision on Mathews's part, perhaps prompted in part by his own feelings at having been slighted by the patent houses; perhaps also it was a response born out of a sense of being forced to narrowly skirt around the laws requiring the submission of texts to the Lord Chamberlain for prior approval. When asked by the 1832 Parliamentary *Select Committee on Dramatic Literature*, 'Are Mathews' entertainments licensed?' Colman's reply was an unequivocal, 'Yes, certainly', but the reality was somewhat different.[65] It

---

[64] *The New British Theatre; a Selection of original drama, not yet acted; some of which have been offered for representation but not accepted* (1814), 337.

[65] *Report from the Select Committee on Dramatic Literature: With The Minutes of Evidence. . . 2 August 1832, Parliamentary Papers* (1831–2) vol. vii, Question 900, p. 63.

looks very probable that Mathews managed to skirt around Larpent's interference while he was in office up to 1824, but Colman's assertion for the post-1824 period is likely to have been over-optimistic as to the actual effectiveness of the Lord Chamberlain's control.

Located firmly within Westminster, the English Opera House fell under the jurisdiction of the Lord Chamberlain. However, although texts were soon pirated into printed editions cobbled together from sketches heard at Mathews's *At Home* and other entertainments, a great deal relied on Mathews' ad-lib impromptu insertion; something he was hardly in a position to be able to first notify to Larpent. Not least, Mathews was also loath to risk the pirating of his 'Monopolylogues' directly from Larpent's office. In 1832 John Payne Collier was at a theatrical dinner where he heard Mathews recollect this worry and also that, in any case, he had 'only forwarded for approval the merest sketch of the performance, without ... the songs'. The sketches 'had never yet been in black and white' because 'he trusted entirely to his memory and to the promptings of the moment'.[66] In other words, for much of the time, Mathews was able to escape regulation purely on account of his inventing new material, or making modifications of past material, at every performance. On the last night of *At Home* in 1818, Mathews stood before the audience to say that although he understood 'that my performances are within the strict letter of the law', he would also 'resist strenuously and firmly any measures that may be pursued to support an injurious monopoly to my injury'. The particular 'measures' Mathews mentions almost certainly refers to covert machinations by the Royal Theatres, disgruntled at their own inability to anticipate the unexpectedly successful run of the *At Home* shows, to invoke their considerable influence and privileges in removing this competition. It was certainly an odd way to end a show performed by a mimic ventriloquist comedian, advising the audience in measured terms that he was 'contending in the cause of the

---

[66] John Payne Collier, *An Old Man's Diary, Forty Years Ago; For The First Six Months Of 1832* (London: Thomas Richards, 1871), i. 40.

public, who have no right to be curtailed of their lawful amusements, or to be told by Patentees, "If you won't come and laugh with us, we will take care you shall not go and laugh elsewhere"'. Not surprisingly, Mathews finished the performance by saying he hoped to 'make you laugh again and again' and that he would, next time, 'choose a merrier subject than Patent Theatres and Monopolies'.[67] Nevertheless, the episode is a revealing indicator for how precarious Mathews felt his position to be in that *At Home* was both evading the requirement to submit texts to the Lord Chamberlain's office for their approval but also infringing the perquisite of the patentees and their monopoly over stage speech.

Although Mathews was beloved of the artisan class who bought the Duncombes' crude piratings of his performances, he swiftly moved on to a hard-working but comfortable gentility.[68] Nevertheless, his *At Home* was symptomatic of the written and spoken expression of a plebeian public sphere which articulated, not least through the sort of expanding and radicalized print culture typified in the Duncombes' pirating of Mathews' performances, the development of a new type of drama whose roots were based in that class of artisans who found their way into the minor theatres. The one-man show, brought to its earliest success with Mathews, was soon being developed by its supporting plebeian print culture in a racy combination of nationalism, domesticity, song, and humour. One such example is the so-called Peter Plagiary's compilation aptly titled *The Song Smith and Story Stitcher* (1818), published near the Strand theatreland and alternating songs with stories and anecdote 'grotesque, lively, and humorous; intermingling, by way of a salad ... a few of our national airs, and home-spun lays'. Plagiary's *Song Smith* was a perfectly performable, presumably domestic, series of anecdotes, manipulating national, professional, and sexual stereotypes but also prepared to be risqué in its story of 'an after-dinner wedlock *teté a teté*

---

[67] Anne Mathews, *Memoirs of Charles Mathews, Comedian* (1838), ii. 472.

[68] Moving to Highgate, he was sought out by S. T. Coleridge; Anne Mathews, *Memoirs of Charles Mathews*, iii. 188–98.

2

The Suppression of the Royalty Theatre in the East End of London

THE history of the Royalty Theatre in Tower Hamlets provides a good case history of how late eighteenth-century drama faced a double attack from the authorities.[1] Although the Royalty's fugitive status has rendered a full history of the playhouse incomplete, enough remains for a remarkable narrative to be recovered of its resistance and adaptation. For those theatres falling within the jurisdiction of the Lord Chamberlain's Examiner of Plays, there was the necessity to submit texts for censorship prior to performance. But the power of the Theatre Royal patentees was such that their reach, by virtue of the hegemonic forces they could mobilize to impose their patents, extended beyond the confines of Westminster and right into London hinterlands such as the area surrounding the Tower. Their power to halt spoken five-act drama in the case of the Coburg's *King Richard Third* will be referred to in Chapter 6, but they were also able to impose their will by forcing the authorities to impose the very letter of their patents. The battle for the Royalty's survival in the 1780s is a fascinating indicator of the problems encountered, and the strategies for evasion playhouses could employ, but the Royalty's case also illustrates the potential for growth in a local politicized contemporary drama which was

---

[1] See also Watson Nicholson, *The Struggle for a Free Stage in London* (London: Archibald Constable, 1906), ch. 5, 'The Royalty Theatre', pp. 98–123; Jane Moody, *Illegitimate Theatre in London, 1770–1840* (Cambridge: Cambridge University Press, 2000), 21–5.

otherwise effaced by the powers of the Royal theatres. In the late 1780s and early 1790s the much-harassed Royalty managed to present a highly distinctive repertoire aimed at mobilizing public support for their case.

The idea of opening further playhouses to complement those in the West End kept recurring in the late eighteenth century as London's population expanded. The Royalty Theatre, which opened in 1787, was probably the first major test of the resolve and resources of the Royal theatres to commit themselves to enforcing their privileges despite the public appetite for having drama closer to home. Something of the nature and longevity of the Royalty's struggle, however, can be indicated by the mid-1790s publication of *Considerations Upon How Far The Present Winter And Summer Theatres Can Be Affected By The Application To Parliament For An Act To Enable His Majesty To License, As A Playhouse For The Summer Season, The Royalty Theatre, In Well-Street, In The Liberty Of The Tower Hamlets* (1794). This pamphlet makes the apparently perfectly reasonable suggestion that the East End Royalty would open when the West End Royal theatres were shut. The Royalty Theatre put forward its case by saying that it expected to draw its 'constant audiences' from the East End of London, far away from the Drury Lane area, gathering its catchment in 'Wapping, Limehouse, Shadwell, Poplar, Blackwall, Mile-end, Stepney, Bow, Hackney, [and] Stratford' (p. 14). The licence was refused.

This was actually the second incarnation of the Royalty Theatre, the previous one having been built by the ex-Drury Lane actor John Palmer, opening in June 1787. A later commentator wrote that the Royalty (off Wellclose Square) was 'remote from the West End', 'inconvenient and mean in all its approaches', and 'fixed among the low traffickers of Rosemary Lane, and the miserable populace of Saltpetre Bank': in other words, the Royalty was a playhouse which directly catered for that part of London's working population which lived distant from the environs of Drury Lane. In a doomed attempt to avoid the requirement to license himself with the local magistrates, 'that he might not be deemed to have acted "for hire, gain, or reward" [Palmer] dedicated the whole receipts of the [first] night, that is, the produce of a completely crowded house, to the funds of the London hospital [Whitechapel Road]'.[2] Benefit nights for local charitable causes were not uncommon at this time but this was a particular strategy Palmer used to attempt to evade closure. However, such charitable performances also served to consolidate the role of playhouses in local communities and were quite common. In 1813 the semi-amateur theatre at Peckham, south London, fittingly presented *Education or, the Noble Emigrant* 'For the Benefit of the Peckham National School'.[3] In the provinces in the 1820s, the Birmingham Theatre Royal substantially supported Birmingham's General Hospital.[4] These productions promoted a strong relationship between local communities and theatre. For example, at the Royal Coburg's prosecution for attempting to perform *King Richard Third*, the defence attorney, tried—without success—to get Chief Justice Abbott to agree that half of the Coburg's fine should be paid into the poor box of the Coburg's specific local parish of St Mary, Lambeth, rather than into the general Lambeth parish coffers.[5] More significantly on account of the support for a radical political co-operative it implied, in the same year the Coburg held a benefit night for the Philanthropic Institution based at the Queen's Head Tavern, Crown Court, Soho.[6] Nevertheless, the Royalty had attracted spoiling attempts even before it opened when the rumour was put about in the newspapers that the theatre was, in reality, a dissenting meeting house, a culturally revealing strategy for muddying already murky waters between the established Church and Methodism's opposition to acting.[7]

---

[2] John Adolphus, *Memoirs of John Bannister, Comedian* (1839), 154–6.
[3] BL Playbills, Peckham Theatre, Wednesday, 6 October 1813.
[4] *Theatrical John Bull* (Birmingham), 1 (3 July 1825), 42–3.
[5] PRO LC 5/164, fos. 75–6.
[6] BL Playbills: Royal Coburg, 4 June 1821.
[7] *A Review of the Present Contest Between the Managers of the Winter Theatres, the Little Theatre in the Hay-market, and the Royalty Theatre in Well-close Square. To Which are Added, Several Authentic Papers* (1787), 10.

The 1737 Theatre Licensing Act was apparently the most important piece of legislation but this does not appear to have been directly invoked very often. However, as John Russell Stephens indicates in *The Censorship of English Drama 1824–1901* (1980), theatres on the south side of the river operated under the licensing regime of the local magistrates rather than of the Lord Chamberlain (unlike those, such as the Olympic, on the Westminster City side of the Thames). Out in the English provinces, magistrates could be both powerful and uncompromising. Samuel William Ryley, in *The Itinerant, or Memoirs of an Actor* (1817), told of how in Bolton, Lancashire, his production had been closed down, forcing him to employ the local bellman to call in all the tickets sold. The only explanation he was given was that 'The boroughreeve say yo mun shut up th'stage play, or by ___ he'll mack yo.'[8] However, there were also other strategies for unravelling the magistracy.

When Thomas Dibdin became the first owner of the Surrey Theatre in Lambeth, London, he clearly thought it worth his while to smooth his way with the local magistracy. Thomas's father, Charles Dibdin, had himself encountered problems when he became house author and stage-manager at the newly opened Royal Circus. His *The Boarding School Breaking Up* (1782) was forbidden because 'there was so much prose dialogue in it' and his commissioning of a dance called 'The Quakers' composed by Grimaldi, the famous clown's father, was similarly interdicted because the magistrates thought it a 'keen satire levelled at the "Society of Friends"'.[9] When Thomas Dibdin came into contact with a certain Mrs Evance, wife of a Surrey magistrate, he wisely produced the French melodrama *Khouli Khan*, a play she had herself offered him for consideration with a view to performance at the Surrey. The next time the licence for the Surrey Theatre came up for renewal at Kingston Crown Court in 1822, not only was the licence renewed, but one of the magistrates, a

---

[8] Samuel William Ryley, *The Itinerant, or Memoirs of an Actor* (1817), vi. 218.
[9] R. Humphreys, *The Memoirs Of J. Decastro, Comedian ... Accompanied By An Analysis Of The Life Of The Late Philip Astley, Esq. ... Also An Accompanying History Of The Royal Circus, Now The Surrey Theatre* (1824), 15.

Mr Evance, gave Dibdin a letter testifying to his good character, quite a useful document to have around in the uncertain world of London entertainment.[10] If these were the day-to-day practices of negotiation necessary for skirting around the local magistracy, the problems presented by the Royal theatres in their guardianship of rights of royal patent were even more entrenched and much less capable of local manoeuvre. It was these forces the Royalty encountered.

The debate about royal patents was always really a covert argument about how *many* theatres could be opened rather than what *types* of play they could perform. It was this pressure which the Royalty Theatre had to negotiate and attempt to defy. In other words, the debate about London theatres was one about the role of capital rather than about the defence of artistic privilege. At any rate, the Middlesex magistrate who was the author of *The number of little Theatres already opened ... having greatly injured the Theatres Royal ...* (*c*.1808) seems to have been bemused and non-committal when his opinion as a legal consultant had been sought by the Royal theatres. By the time of the *Report from the Select Committee on Dramatic Literature* (1832), the Home Office was more confidently identified as the ultimate authority for the all of the country's theatres *not* falling under the jurisdiction of the Lord Chamberlain who, it was argued, answered to no one except the King.[11] The Select Committee's interviewee on this matter, Thomas Baucott Mash, at that time had already served forty-three years in the Lord Chamberlain's office as the Examiner's Deputy, so he had obviously clarified the collective role and memory of the office between the time of Larpent's and Colman's regimes. Eventually, the right of the royal theatrical patent was awarded a special (upholding) inquiry.[12]

---

[10] Thomas Dibdin, *The Reminiscences of Thomas Dibdin* (1837), ii. 148–53. 'Evance, Esq.' was a subscriber to Humphreys, *The Memoirs Of J. Decastro*, p. xii.

[11] *Report from the Select Committee on Dramatic Literature: With The Minutes of Evidence... 2 August 1832*, Parliamentary Papers (1831–2) vol. vii, question 11.

[12] *The Report Of The Lord Chancellor And The Other Judges To His Majesty On The Investigation Of The Subject Of The Different Theatrical Petitions Was As Follows* [19 Feb. 1831].

The conditions pertaining to theatre licensing were a veritable theatrical *ancien régime* on the part of the Royal theatres. They were jealous of their interests but otherwise corrupt, inconsistent, inefficient and intrusive. It is little wonder that by 1832 reform of the Royal Patent theatres had become a proxy for the country's general political reform. Indeed, because the targets were narrower and more specific (the privilege of Royal Patent, the monopoly of the Royal theatres, the role of the Lord Chamberlain, etc.)—and certainly more local and publicly accessible—the language of the one could easily be mapped over that of the other ('the Boroughmongers of the Playhouses', 'a Theatrical Oligarchy').[13] But Government was not in a position where it could sit by and do nothing. Just as the radical press expanded with changes in the demographies of literacy, demands for new theatrical spaces evolved with changes in the size of London's population and their places of resort.

The destruction by accidental fire of Covent Garden in 1808 and Drury Lane in 1811 only exacerbated debates about the shortage of London playhouses and riots at Covent Garden and a fiasco about the competition for an opening poem at Drury Lane only created greater disquiet. A Bill for Erecting and Maintaining a New Theatre for Dramatic Entertainments within the Cities of London and Westminster, or Liberties thereof (Third Theatre Bill) (1812) noted that 'the Population of the Cities of London and Westminster has greatly increased within these few Years, and it would be expedient and convenient ... that there should be an additional Theatre for Dramatic Representations' nearer to where Londoners lived (p. 1). By 1832, the *Major And Minor Theatres* pamphleteer could still note that, while the Royal theatres served up a fare of 'tiger hunts and dioramas' (p. 15), the seven principal non-patent theatres operated in a twilight world of legality even as they served

---

[13] Anon., *Major And Minor Theatres. A Concise View Of The Question, As Regards, The Public, The Patentees, And The Profession With Remarks On The Decline Of The Drama, And The Means Of Its Restoration To Which Is Added The Petition Now Lying For Signature* (1832) 13; Eugene Macarthy, *A Letter To The King, On The Question Now At Issue Between The 'Major', And 'Minor' Theatres* (1832), 10.

an (estimated) London population of one and a half million. These conditions of exclusion-within-participation are, of course, analogous to contemporary arguments about the franchise and taxation. As late as 1840, Edward Mayhew in *Stage Effect: or, The Principles which Command Dramatic Success in the Theatre*, still noted the pressure on London's theatrical space forced by an 'increase of population, and consequent natural necessity for additional places of amusement' (p. 20). Writing in 1827, Thomas Dibdin (ex-manager of the Surrey Theatre), counted twenty-two places of dramatic entertainment in London which, he said, 'amounted to nearly one for every letter of the alphabet'.[14] This sounds impressive but, in reality, because they operated under different seasonal arrangements, they were rarely all open at once and, in any case, his list includes places such as the well established private theatre, the Minor, in Catherine Street and a smaller stage at Bagnigge Wells which was little more than a glorified tea-garden. It was also the case that, as time went on, the winter theatres at Covent Garden and Drury Lane gradually began to increase the length of their seasons to the discomfort of their sister houses such as the summer season Theatre Royal in the Haymarket. Their complaint in their 'Extempore temporary Sketch', *Patent Seasons* (1820) complained that '"Patent Rights" ... [were] something more like—*private wrongs*' and brought their cast onto stage (and the ghost of Garrick out of his portrait) to protest 'Not a scat taken ... The fruit women must feed upon their Goosberrys & the Money takers keep their suppers in their empty tills.'[15]

The seemingly immovable obstacle of the Royal theatres' implementation of their rights and privileges, whose longevity has been outlined above, provides the context for the Royalty's struggle for survival in the 1780s. Significantly, Palmer's choice for one of his pair of first-night productions was Shakespeare's *As You Like It*. His

---

[14] Dibdin, *The Reminiscences of Thomas Dibdin*, ii. 401.
[15] Larpent 2166, *Patent Seasons An Extempore temporary Sketch*, Huntington Library, Calif.

friend Thomas Bellamy's notice of the opening of the theatre for the *General Magazine, and Impartial Review* in June 1787 included an engraving showing the interior of the theatre with the scene set for the storm scene in *The Tempest*, which was paired with *As You Like It* on the opening night.[16] The Royalty took its name from Palmer's argument in the *Case of Mr. John Palmer* (1788) that the theatre was erected within the domain of an area formally designated as 'the Royalty of the Tower of London' and that this implied 'he should not be restricted in giving entertainments in the higher walks of the drama'.[17] Before spending 'Fifteen Thousand Pounds and upwards' in construction costs, Palmer thought he had received legitimate authority from Earl Cornwallis, the Constable of the Tower of London, but this did not stop the attack of the patentees.[18] Nevertheless, it seems obvious that Palmer was perfectly well aware of the resonance of the title, and that it would be understood as it was meant, as a sure sign of his attempt to encroach on the rights of the Royal theatres. Even though Palmer was ruined (the theatre eventually burned down), such enterprises became part of an important cultural memory of the adversity and oppression provoked by the patent theatres.[19]

Revealingly, the only surviving copy of the *Case of Mr. John Palmer, The Renters and Creditors of the Royalty Theatre ... relative to Players of Interludes, and Persons keeping Houses of Public Entertainment* (1788) is located at the Public Record Office in a box of miscellaneous Government papers dating to the 1780s belonging to the Headquarters of the British Army in America, implying that the

---

[16] *The General Magazine, and Impartial Review*, June 1787, 49–53.

[17] Humphreys, *Memoirs Of J. Decastro*, 183–4.

[18] *Case of Mr. John Palmer, The Renters and Creditors of the Royalty Theatre, Occasioned by a Bill now before the House of Peers, for amending the Acts made in the Tenth and Twenty-fifth Years of the Reign of his late Majesty, relative to Players of Interludes, and Persons keeping Houses of Public Entertainment* (1788).

[19] His eulogist described Palmer's problems with 'the chicanery of law ... the collusion of the rival managers, assisted by pettifogging justices, [by which] his pecuniary interests were ruined': T. Harral, *A Monody On the Death of Mr. John Palmer, The Comedian. To Which is Prefixed a Review of his Theatrical Powers* (1798), 6.

document had strayed into the filing system of soldiers on station in North America, perhaps a bureaucratic remnant of Cornwallis's role in the wars against the Americans.[20] It may even be the case that the generous-hearted Cornwallis felt he owed some kind of debt of honour to Palmer because he later helped Palmer's close friend, the comedian Charles Lee Lewes, when, acting as Governor of Calcutta, he offered him a fund of 1,000 rupees after the East India Company had forbidden him to perform there.[21] The dispersal of memories of the plight of the Royalty was much wider than the acting community. Palmer's claim to have petitioned over seven thousand *householders* in Tower Hamlets (my italics, i.e. representative of rather more than seven thousand persons) is an early example of East End community activism where skills of organization and focus could easily be transferred from theatrical to political agitation.[22]

Fifty years later, in the run-up to the Reform Bill when anti-monopolist discourse was becoming a proxy for general political reform, it is significant that these lessons had not been forgotten. The anonymous 'Friend to "Fair Play and a Free Stage"' still remembered the Royalty's history (by then rebuilt as the East-London Theatre) when he addressed Robert Peel to argue against the power of the patentees.[23] These cultural memories ran back into the early eighteenth century and were certainly being recollected in the mid-1820s when the ongoing debate about the authority of the Royal theatres began. Writing in 1832, Thomas Dibdin thought

---

[20] PRO PRO 30/55/87, fo. 9792.

[21] Charles Lee Lewes, *Comic Sketches; Or, The Comedian His Own Manager ... The Whole Forming Matter Sufficient for Two Evenings' Entertainment; Originally Intended for the East Indies* (1804), pp. xxxi–xxxv.

[22] *Case of Mr. John Palmer, The Renters and Creditors of the Royalty Theatre, Occasioned by a Bill now before the House of Peers, for amending the Acts made in the Tenth and Twenty-fifth Years of the Reign of his late Majesty, relative to Players of Interludes, and Persons keeping Houses of Public Entertainment* (1788).

[23] A Friend to 'Fair Play and a Free Stage', *Letter To The Right Hon. Robert Peel, Respecting The Proposed Introduction Of A Bill, To Repeal So Much Of The Act Of 10th Geo.Ii.Cap.28, As Requires Notice To Be Sent To The Lord Chamberlain ... And Showing That The Consequence Of Such An Act Would Be, To Confirm The Monopoly Claimed By The Proprietors Of Drury Lane And Covent Garden, And To Enable Them To Annihilate The Minor Theatres* (1829), 7.

that the 'Royalty Theatre was the first instance of innovation which I recollect on the monopolies of the three Theatres Royal, and the three minor theatres of that day.'[24] Dibdin's comment reminds us that the Royalty was not only encroaching on the Covent Garden, Drury Lane and the Haymarket opera house but also on the newer Westminster theatres such as the Sans Pareil (later Adelphi), Sans Souci (later Lyceum), and Olympic. This is a good reminder of the distinct stratification and social differentiation between these various types of theatre and the communities they served. As if to signal the politically progressive ideals of East London, a previous playhouse on this site, known as Goodman's Fields theatre, was said to have had an oval ceiling painting over the pit showing the King 'attended by Peace, Liberty and Justice, trampling Tyranny and Oppression under his Feet.'[25] As will be shown in Chapter 5 concerning the radical culture of Spitalfields, such political attitudes were contemporary, local, and widely understood within the area's less affluent communities.

The economically impoverished nature of the Royalty's hinterland was widely acknowledged by contemporaries. One commentator, engaged in the seemingly endless battle to maintain the theatre's viability against the West End patentees, urbanely noted that, excepting the immediate inhabitants of Goodman's Fields, 'very few inhabitants of the East end of the Metropolis ... have the advantage of a carriage.'[26] A frequently repeated argument during this period was that the distant Royal theatres around Drury Lane were inaccessible to whole swathes of London's growing population, especially those living to the south and east. As this commentator

---

[24] *Reminiscences of Thomas Dibdin*, ii. 394. Dibdin's father, Charles, had taken over the management of the Sans Souci in 1794, when it was then being used as additional gallery space for the nearby Royal Academy: Charles Dibdin, *The Professional Life of Mr. Dibdin, written by himself. Together with the words of six hundred songs selected from his works* (1803), iv. 6.

[25] Folger T.a. 78, 21 May 1825, Folger Shakespeare Library, Washington, DC.

[26] *A Review of the Present Contest Between the Managers of the Winter Theatres, the Little Theatre in the Hay-market, and the Royalty Theatre in Well-close Square. To Which are Added, Several Authentic Papers* (1787), 50.

went on to argue, even hired Hackney cabs were beyond the locals' means and also at the practical limits of their range due to their slow progress. The various owners of the Royalty certainly took great care to treat their audiences with respect, one farewell address stressing that the theatre hoped 'To gratify the wishes of the East, | (Tho' London's lowest part, yet not the least).'[27]

The struggle of the Royalty Theatre to remain open in the late 1780s tended to polarize social attitudes concerning ideas of repression versus liberalism. The result was a mini-theatrical pamphlet war, yet again another proxy or rehearsal for debates based upon the discussion of similar principles which were to occur after the French Revolution. George Daniel (as Peter Pindar, Jr.) in his 'Poetical Satyrical Interlude' addressed to *The Plotting Managers* (1787), which was supportive of the Royalty, used the growing vocabulary of natural rights versus political and economic corruption to attack both the local licensing magistrates and the Royal theatres' haughty cartel of patentees: 'Thus leagued, we'll still our sov'reign Rights maintain, | And spite of all, Monopolists remain.' Realizing that the Royalty was frequented by 'the Inferior Class of People', Daniel also strove to argue drama's morally improving role, arguing (somewhat disingenuously) that 'those who now resort to the Alehouse, and drink till they disgrace Human Nature, would then spend their Shilling at the Theatre, and sit like rational Beings, at a Performance.'[28] According to the history of this period recollected by the Royal Amphitheatre comedian Jacob Decastro many years later, the patentees were using a 'hireling' magistrate ('their cat's paw in the business'), Justice Staples, who achieved a certain notoriety as 'the only magistrate which sanctioned and enforced their unprincipled and arbitrary views'. Several actors were indicted, including Charles Bannister (another comedian), with the hearings taking place locally

[27] *A Poetical Epistle; Being the Farewell Address of the Royalty Theatre, to its late beloved Master, John Astley, Esq.* (1807), 4.

[28] Peter Pindar, Jr. [George Daniel], *The Plotting Managers, A Poetical Satyrical Interlude: To Which is Prefixed A Letter to Lord S—dn—y, On his recommending the Suppression of the Royalty-Theatre* (1787), pp. vi–viii, 22.

in Wellclose Square at the King's Arms Tavern.[29] Of course, the medium of this debate, the pamphlet and counter-pamphlet, would be widened to a national scale in the anti-Paineite propaganda of the early 1790s.

The cultural importance of these debates about the freedom of the playhouses is that they anticipated the specifically political discourses concerning natural rights, privileges, and monopolies which became so apparent after the French Revolution. Their prototype was initiated in the pre-1790s debates about theatrical freedom. Debates about liberalizing theatre, because the objectives were specific, local, and thoroughly intelligible to common experience, provided useful templates for more profound discussions about the role of natural political rights in the early 1790s. What is significant is the extent to which the concerns and anxieties about the role of the impoverished inhabitants of areas such as the East End of London are central to the parameters of the discussions. In many ways, the lack of progress about theatrical freedom mirrored changes in the national political culture as the idealism of the 1780s and 1790s was transformed into the more dogged acts of repression beginning in the 1800s and reaching their height in the unrest of the late 1810s.

The most decisive attempt to close down the Royalty came in 1802–3. The theatre had been refused its local magistrates' licence for the 1802 season but, in the next year, when it was preparing to reapply, it became the subject of one of the first campaigns organized by the litigious Society for the Suppression of Vice, whose repressive origins dated back to William Wilberforce's 1787 Proclamation Society. Later, in the early 1820s, the Society for the Suppression of Vice gained much notoriety for its pursuit of Richard Carlile and his sister, Mary Jane, a persecution continued through the courts against one of Carlile's shopgirls, Susannah Wright.[30] The Society's intervention marked the opening of another front in

---

[29] R. Humphreys, *The Memoirs Of J. Decastro*, 183, 187.

[30] *Report of the Trial of Mrs. Susannah Wright, for publishing, in his shop, the Writings and Correspondences of R. Carlile; Before Chief Justice Abbott ... Monday, July 8, 1822. Indictment at the Instance of the Society for the Suppression of Vice* (1822).

the attempts to repress the Royalty. In place of arguments waged by the capital's defensive and monopolistic Royal Patent theatres, the Society for the Suppression of Vice sought to attack dramatic entertainment generally, but the Royalty's in particular, on account of the theatre's location in East London and its supposed effects on the local audience.

That there existed a long-term strategy of moral campaign is made clear from one of the Society's series of objectives laid out in the Revd. Thomas Thirlwall's pamphlet *Royalty Theatre. A Solemn Protest Against The Revival Of Scenic Exhibitions And Interludes, At The Royalty Theatre; Containing Remarks On Pizarro, The Stranger, And John Bull; With A Postscript* (1803), which warned local people, '2dly. That they may be apprized in time that a spirit of opposition is awake, and will be exerted at a future opportunity' (p. 5). Thirlwall's objections to Sheridan's *Pizarro* (Drury Lane, 1799) or—another adaptation of Kotzebue—Benjamin's Thompson's *The Stranger* (Drury Lane, 1798), together with George Colman the Younger's *John Bull; or The Englishman's Fireside* (Covent Garden, 1803) were principally concerned with the portrayal of the sexual morality of their heroines (*Pizarro*: 'a bold and sentimental strumpet'; *The Stranger*: 'an adulteress … in criminal commerce with her seducer'; *John Bull*: 'the daughter of an humble tradesman … suffers herself to be seduced by the son of a baronet').[31] These critical objections to the literary or moral aspects of contemporary drama were nothing out of the ordinary except that Thirlwall tied his remarks specifically to the Royalty's notoriety as 'the rendezvous of bawds and prostitutes, who, as soon as it is opened, make it their constant resort, and take lodgings in the neighbourhood for the convenience of their business'. Drawn along by the prostitutes were their pimps ('gangs of thieves and pickpockets, whom they engage for their bullies') making it 'unsafe for an honest man, or a modest woman, to walk

[31] Thomas Thirlwall, *Royalty Theatre. A Solemn Protest Against The Revival Of Scenic Exhibitions And Interludes, At The Royalty Theatre; Containing Remarks On Pizarro, The Stranger, And John Bull; With A Postscript* (1803), 6–7.

the streets after dusk in that part of town'.[32] The East London
location and the habitual association of theatres and prostitution
were powerful arguments to focus the attention of the Society's
moralistic movements, although it is not actually clear whether
Pizarro, The Stranger, and *John Bull* were actually performed at
the Royalty or whether, quite simply, Thirlwall's comments were
meant to be attached comprehensively to all dramatic entertainment
in Britain. However, the specific character of productions at the
Royalty was obviously deeply worrying to organizations such as the
Society for the Suppression of Vice.

What was it about the character of the Royalty repertoire that
the Society for the Suppression of Vice should wish to crush it so
earnestly? Immediately after its first night in 1787, the magistrates
had proscribed dramatic performances at the Royalty. The cultural
memory of this occasion was long-lived amongst the theatrical and
local communities, who still smarted many years later about the
generic restrictions subsequently enforced on the playhouse. As
the author of *A Poetical Epistle; Being the Farewell Address of the
Royalty Theatre, to ... John Astley, Esq.* (1807) put it, the 'powerful
confederated band' of patentees forced the Royalty to work under a
very restrictive licence:

> But [they] kindly suffer'd me t'amuse the town
> With dumb-shews, or a harlequin and clown;
> With tumbling, or burlettas, or a song,
> Or else with men who dance the slender rope along. (pp. 7–8)

Extraordinary though it may seem, with spoken drama proscribed,
and pantomime, rope-dancing, and song the only legitimate altern-
atives, this range of entertainments appeared to be no less worrying
to the Society for the Suppression of Vice, perhaps precisely because
they embodied popular forms such as the one-man interlude and
harlequinade.

---

[32] Thomas Thirlwall, *Royalty Theatre. A Solemn Protest Against The Revival Of Scenic
Exhibitions And Interludes, At The Royalty Theatre; Containing Remarks On Pizarro, The
Stranger, And John Bull; With A Postscript* (1803), 8–9.

Records of performances at the Royalty during this period are fairly thin but enough information exists to make it possible to deduce the reason for the Society's concerns. 'The Benevolent Jew' by C. F. Barrett was performed as little more than an extended song or song with comic spoken accompaniment of 'patter' and was described in the printed version as 'recited' at the Royalty Theatre. Such a 'patter' accompaniment was designed to test the edges of legality of the piece but 'The Benevolent Jew' also typifies the close relationship between the Royalty and its East End catchment. Barrett's song was published in a jest book, *Laugh When You Can; or, The Monstrous Droll Jester* (c.1795–8), printed by Ann Lemoine, a relative of the Spitalfields Huguenot apprentice rag merchant, itinerant bookseller, and copperplate printer, Henry Lemoine, who began the occultist *Conjuror's Magazine* in 1792 and whose 1790 edition of Robert Blair's *Grave* poem was printed by his fellow Spitalfields printer, Robert Hawes (discussed below).[33]

The publishing career of Ann Lemoine illustrates how a fugitive press, with a personnel at least partly consisting of women, was sustained because of the proximity of playhouses like the Royalty. Ann Lemoine, of Coleman Street to the west of Spitalfields, dabbled in both Gothic fiction, narratives of female criminals (Captain C. Johnson, *Lives of the Most Remarkable Female Robbers* (1801)) and sexual sensation imprints, including at least two reprints of *The Woman of the Town; or, Authentic Memoirs of Phebe Phillips … Well Known in the vicinity of Covent Garden. Written by Herself* (1801). Lemoine also published Gothic spin-offs from the theatres such as *The Water Spectre: or, Kitty o'the Clyde: A Romance* (1805), a threepenny chapbook printing sources and songs from Charles Isaac Mungo Dibdin's Sadler's Well hit of that name. *Laugh When You Can* not only gives a firm indication of Lemoine's sure sense of the popular tastes of her local audience, it also reconstructs a positive image of London Jewry. Lemoine would never have published 'The

[33] Ian Maxted, *The London Book Trades, 1775–1800: A Preliminary Checklist of Members* (Folkestone: Dawson, 1977).

Benevolent Jew' unless she had been confident of its profitable reception. Replacing the stereotype of the rapacious Jewish stock-jobber, Barrett's song makes its Jew figure a wealthy trader on the stock exchange, but someone who had been orphaned at the age of 9 and forced into the hard graft of selling pencils, sealing-wax, and 'pomatum' cosmetics in order to make his 'money galore'. Although Barrett gives him the stock accent of the stage-Jew (for example, he trades commodities on the '*Shange*'), the conclusion to 'The Benevolent Jew' explains the song's title: looking back on his life of hard work, 'I made that my plan, | To be honest and just to mankind, sirs, | Altho' I'm a Jew.' What is even more surprising is that 'The Benevolent Jew' concludes with what is almost a separate song furthering a specifically patriotic loyalist characterization for the benevolent Jew's generous persona, 'This is the place for me: | So long may GEORGE o'er England reign, | The Land of Liberty!'[34]

This representation of British Jewry is highly significant: first because Ann Lemoine's venture was obviously responding to a pre-exisiting, very positive, climate of reception for 'The Benevolent Jew' and, secondly, because its Royalty recitals would have introduced Barrett's patter-song to possibly thousands of theatregoers as well as the readers of Ann Lemoine's printed edition. Finally, the demography of the Royalty's East End catchment of Wapping, Limehouse, Shadwell, Poplar, Blackwall, Mile End, Stepney, Bow, Hackney, and Stratford makes the social level of its reception quite specific to the artisan 'low traffickers' and 'miserable populace' who formed the distinctly enlightened inhabitants of these areas. It is also true that, in a more general sense, British theatre necessitated revisionist, enlightened attitudes to Jewry: the late eighteenth-century comic actor Jacob Decastro, for example, was a Hebrew-speaking Portuguese Jew born in Houndsditch, London, who as a schoolboy 'got up' plays and farces in commemoration of the *puerim*, in the Jewish festival of *Haman*.[35] As with the deeper, much more explicitly

---

[34] *Laugh When You Can; or, The Monstrous Droll Jester ... To Which is added, The Benevolent Jew, as Recited at The Royalty Theatre* (c.1795–8), 59–60.

[35] Humphreys, *Memoirs Of J. Decastro*, 2–3.

radicalized culture of the Spitalfields Huguenot associates of Robert Hawes (discussed in Chapter 5), it is clear that in its attitude to Jewry, London's East End operated as a very distinctive plebeian public sphere.

Banned from producing spoken drama, the Royalty seems to have specialized in socially unconventional burlesques or burlettas. Francis Godolphin Waldron's *The Man With Two Wives; or, Wigs For Ever!* (1798) for the Royalty would clearly have outraged the Society for the Suppression of Vice since the plot of this farcical 'Dramatick Fable', scored for three voices, is based on the straightforward supposition of bigamy.[36] The printer in this case was the ex-London Corresponding Society activist Henry Delahay Symonds, a factor which establishes once again another well-defined connective route of solidarity between theatrical and artisan radical print culture. The narrative of *The Man With Two Wives* is quite straightforward in its presentation of the plot's comic dilemma: 'Old Wife' wants 'Husband' to get rid of his dark hair while 'Young Wife' wants him to get rid of his grey ('HUSBAND. Two wives I have, and can't please either, | With black and grey hairs can please neither: | One wishes that my hair were black; | Whilst t'other, but I fear, alack!' (p. 5)). The agreeable solution is to buy three wigs, one for each of them (hence the subtitle, *Wigs For Ever!*). It is quite likely that in East End London such mutually satisfactory marriages of convenience were not uncommon although they would hardly have met with the encouragement of the Society for the Suppression of Vice. In addition to these challenges to stereotypes of racial and sexual behaviour, there was a third element to the Royalty's productions which shows its ability to publicize its predicament.

The Royalty appears to have quickly capitalized on the measure of local feeling supporting its cause: after all, the local populace were

---

[36] Francis Godolphin Waldron, *The Man With Two Wives; or, Wigs For Ever! A Dramatick Fable; By F. G. Waldron. Set To Musick By Mr. Sanderson. And First Performed At The Royalty Theatre, Saturday, March 24th. 1798* (1798). It is possible that *The Man With Two Wives* derives (as was frequently the case) from an unacknowledged French source since, towards the end, the two wives send for their wigs from Britain (p. 11).

potentially losing a highly accessible theatre, so the Royalty quickly introduced into its entertainments an element satirizing the Royal theatres. These were printed, possibly for sale at the venue, in a run of pieces dating to *c.*1787–8 which give some indication of the Royalty's resourceful repertoire. The pieces they used, as was to be expected in Tower Hamlets, were perfectly tuned to its artisan audiences and could be used to mobilize the politics of their position. In its collection of 'Songs, Catches, Glees, Duets, &c.' performed at the Royalty Theatre and published as *The Catch Club* (*c.*1787), one of their untitled catches captures the idiom of the surrounding working-class area with its fear of debt and arrest by creating a satiric dialogue between a vagrant and his arrest ('A match') by an official debt collector (the 'catch-pole' of the song):

> Come, by boys, let's sing a catch.
> A match, a match, a match.
> Be ware of catch-poles,
> Warrants and dark holes.
> You're a vagrant; that's a fact.
> Stop, stop, let me look at the act.
> No; I'm a gentleman. I beg your pardon;
> You're only such in Covent-Garden.
> Oh! curse your odious exclamations.
> Let us sing,
> God save the king;
> And be loyal, in spite of informations. (p. 10)

The point of the song is that vagrancy was precisely the indictment the seventeenth-century statutes permitted as the charge against actors who fell foul of the privileges of the Royal Patent theatres. As the catch song points out, actors were 'only such' legitimate 'gentlemen' if they acted at Covent Garden or Drury Lane. The pledge of loyalty to the sovereign is notable in that it appropriately distinguishes between the duty of subjects to the monarch and the rather different feelings they may have about the monarch's representatives in the shape of the Royal theatres.

Particularly sinister is the reference to 'informations', the complaints—sometimes by real beggars or vagrants, as *A Very Plain State
of the Case, or The Royalty Theatre Versus the Theatres Royal* (1787)
indicated—which initiated the process of prosecution. Grimly, this
was a piece sometimes sung by Leoni, one of the few actors to be
named in *A Very Plain State of the Case* as a target of prosecution
and a reminder that, although singing in burlettas was permissible
outside of the Royal theatres, it was the playhouse itself which was
the target of their suppressive litigation. The historical importance of
the catch songs narrating these modes of prosecution and indictment
against the Royalty Theatre and other non-patent playhouses was
that the repressive role of prosecution 'informations' began to take a
rather different turn in the 1790s and into the 1810s when it became
clear that '*ex-officio* information' (anonymous sources) became an
instrument of Government oppression. In other words, as with the
mapping of the discourses of national political reform onto the
campaigns against the privileges of the Royal Patent theatres at the
end of the 1820s, the case of the intimidation of the Royalty Theatre
became a kind of test-bed or laboratory for more vital confronta-
tions. The satirizing of 'informations' which began in Leoni's catch
song would later be paralleled in Peter Pindar's 1817 *Bubbles of
Treason* ('From *ex-officious* set us free, | Restore our wonted liberty,
| And give us meat and money!').[37] Rather chillingly, the reverse
must also have been true: the Government learned how to perse-
cute political radicals in the 1790s and 1810s from observing the
successes of the Royal theatres in regulating the playhouses in the
1780s.

If the songs were one vehicle through which the Royalty popularized its predicament, a much funnier piece recorded in *The Catch
Club* must have been the well known comedian Charles Lee Lewes's
adaptation of a celebrated comic piece known, after its originator,

---

[37] Peter Pindar, *Bubbles Of Treason; Or, State Trials At Large. Being A Poetical Epistle
From An Irishman In London To His Brother In Paris; And Containing A Humorous
Epitome Of The Charge, Evidence And Defence* (1817), 39.

as 'Hippesley's Drunken Man', which had a simple and formulaic structure but one which lent itself to topical modifications. It was exactly the kind of Bakhtinian heteroglossia capable of comically destabilizing the pomposity of the Royal theatres. The formula is simple: a drunken man, his speech slurred, first reads aloud and then comments on items he finds in the newspaper. Internal evidence about the closing of the summer theatre in the Haymarket and opening of the winter houses of Covent Garden and Drury Lane suggests that Lewes's adaptation related to Royalty performances in September or October 1787 or 1788. Lee Lewes probably kept to tried-and-tested jokes for much of the piece but, towards the end, he brings the Royalty's intimidation into his range of comedy: '[*Reads again*] "On Saturday next, the little Manger in the Hay-Market will shut-up his Theatre,"—well, that's tit for tat, he has done all he can to shut-up another Man's Theatre, and now he's obliged to shut-up his own'[38] Of course, the misread 'little Manger' (for manager) diminutively puns on the 'hay market' but the reference to attempts to 'shut-up another Man's Theatre' is a direct reference to the Royalty controversy where, no doubt, the Haymarket management with their summer licence colluded with the owners of Drury Lane and Covent Garden to stifle the East End venue.

A little further on in his version of 'Hippesley's Drunken Man', with more punning, Lee Lewes obliquely satirized the issue of the patentees' privileges: '[*Reads again*] "On Monday, the Theatre Royal Covent-garden will open with the Merry Wives of Windsor; or the humours of Sir John Falstaff,"—why that's apropos too, for they have been leaning upon a *false-staff* all along.'[39] However lamely it reads now, there can be little doubt that Lee Lewes's interlude

---

[38] *The Catch Club: A Collection of All the Songs, Catches, Glees, Duets, &c. As sung by . . . Mr. Leoni . . . at the Royalty Theatre, Well-Street, Goodman's-Fields: To which is Added Hippesley's Drunken-Man, As altered and spoken by Mr. Lee Lewes* (1787). 28. It is difficult to date Royalty editions reliably. The date given should be taken as the earliest possible date of publication.

[39] *The Catch Club*, 28.

appealed to the Royalty's audiences and was a 'favourite' piece there but, incidentally, not the least of its interest to the modern reader is its fully structured inclusion of a newspaper as an integral prop. The incorporation of a newspaper into the sketch, even in the impoverished area of Tower Hamlets, indicates the penetration of the press into working-class London by the 1780s.

These direct responses to threats of prosecution and closure were communicated to the Royalty's audiences via such pieces as the 'Drunken Man' and incorporated into an improvised programme of performances as the playhouse ducked and dived to avoid closure. Palmer's refuge in spoken stage recitations of Thomas Gray's 'Elegy in an English Churchyard' was a desperate measure to evade the patentees but he also successfully kept true to the playhouse's locality by having a benefit night for the charitable Marine Society, an important move in an area close to Thameside dockyard and shipping concerns.[40] The prolific playwright Arthur Murphy wrote an address for the Marine Society night which finished on an unequivocally loyalist note by having a '*back scene*' which '*discovers a view of the sea, a man of war with colours flying . . .— Then a procession of the Marine boys, with officers and sailors. The curtain drops to "Rule Britannia."*'[41] No doubt the Society boys, and perhaps even the officers and sailors, who paraded were the real thing, providing an important opportunity for the Royalty to consolidate its contacts with the local community.

Over the long term, such declarations of loyalty as the one envisaged by Murphy, set amidst the Royalty's struggles with patentee rights enshrined in seventeenth-century privileges granted by the monarch, helped fracture simple appeals to patriotism from the ruling class. Other productions at the Royalty such as *The Recruiting Serjeant* (*c*.1787) or *True Blue: or, The Press-Gang* (*c*.1787), however

---

[40] *An Elegy, Written in a Country Church-yard. A New Edition: As Deliver'd By Mr. Palmer At the Royalty Theatre, Goodman's Fields* (1787).

[41] *Songs, &c. in the Deserter of Naples; or, Royal Clemency: To Which is Added, An Ode to Friendship, A Tale from Baker's Chronicle, Address for the Marine Society, Mr. Lee Lewes's Farewell Address, and other favourite Pieces Performed at the Royalty Theatre* (1787), 13.

light-hearted, further alerted the local populace to realities: the powers of the authorities and their dependence on such lower-class districts as Tower Hamlets for their manpower.[42]

The capacity of the Royalty to dramatize its persecution through politicized drama was a facility it swiftly learned to deploy. The strategies of presentation which it developed in the mid- to late 1780s later became part of its repertoire when the time eventually came for it to reflect the much greater upheavals across Europe caused by the French Revolution. This repertoire became ever more sophisticated in its range and nuance. For example, the Royal theatres' threats of prosecution (and the actual imprisonment of John Palmer for vagrancy) were obliquely incorporated into the Royalty's *Apollo turn'd Stroller; or, Thereby hangs a Tale. A Musical Pasticcio* (*c.*1787). In *Apollo turn'd Stroller*, Apollo is kicked out of heaven at a drunken dinner of the gods and lands near a village where he hears a company of 'Strolling Players' rehearsing and publicizing playbills for their production, '*1st Play. (giving bills)* This night at seven, my lads, will be perform'd | Gibraltar siege—but not the fortress storm'd' (p. 6). The strolling players' cut-price and excerpted ('not the fortress storm'd') version of Frederick Pilon's *Siege of Gibraltar* (1780) farce is subjected to attempted suppression by the village gentry, Pan and Mysis, 'These vagrants we'll route with a mittimus, | Make them sing small as a tittymouse; | Informations shall harass them, | Warrants and Tip-staffs embarrass them' (p. 9).

In other words, the actions of Pan and Mysis with their 'Informations', harassments, and accusations of vagrancy in *Apollo turn'd Stroller* mirrors the real-life campaign of the Royal theatres against the Royalty. In another parallel with the Royalty's predicament vis-à-vis the patentees, Pan and Mysis try to enlist the local magistrate, Midas, to their cause: 'Why, Sir, some strolling vagabonds infest your

---

[42] *The Recruiting Serjeant, A Musical Entertainment, As it is Performed at the Royalty Theatre, Wellclose-Square* (1787); *True Blue: or, The Press-Gang. And the Story of John Gilpin . . . As Performing at the Royalty-Theatre, Wellclose-Square* (1787).

village, | Have hired a barn, and will the pockets pillage | Of all your tenants' (p. 17). At the end of *Apollo turn'd Stroller*, Midas reforms and sides with the strolling players, claiming Pan and Mysis have misled him ('this hint from good Apollo, | Convinces me I was,—a Justice Shallow. | The trade I'll leave, curse it, and its devisers, | My spite 'gainst you *arose from ill-advisers*' (p. 16). As the characters' names easily identify, Apollo is the romantic and successful god of the players and Midas the eventually friendly local magistrate invested with the power to turn their work into gold by permitting them to perform. The allegoric parallels between the predicament of the Royalty and those of the Strolling Players in *Apollo turn'd Stroller* were simple but effective.

No doubt it was the practice and experience gained in dramatizing the politics of its own dealings with the Royal theatres which gave the Royalty the ability and confidence to be able to present a Bastille pantomime in 1790 where the issues at stake were fundamentally European and ideological rather than the stuff of the local London politics of drama which *Apollo turn'd Stroller* presented. The 'dumb-shews, or ... harlequin and clown' interludes which the 1807 *Farewell Address* had noted as typical of the permissible fare at the Royalty Theatre proved surprisingly politicized in practice, especially in representing the confused beginnings of the French Revolution. The flights of fancy, mobility of scenery, and sheer malleability of persona typical of the harlequinades profoundly destabilized the conventions of literary drama. It was into a pre-existing context of so-called 'Bastille' plays in the form of harlequinades that the Royalty entered in the early 1790s.

Harlequin and Colombine were a minefield for the Lord Chamberlain to control because anything, and everything, could happen during their playing. For example, Examiner Larpent immediately marked as 'Forbidden' Covent Garden's 'revived' pantomime of *Harlequin Touchstone* when it was submitted to him in November 1789. Although no explanation was given for the suppression, *Harlequin*

Touchstone was typical of many dramas of the period in its sniping at the indolence of the legal and clerical professions:

> The learn'd Lawyer by good hap
> Now mounts the Bench to take his nap
> And priests grown rich who once were poor
> In fine Lawn Sleeves sit down and snore,
> While Inns [of Court] turn'd out, have nought to do
> But rub their Eyes, and cry Heigho—

More topically, the pantomime gestured towards ideological sympathy with Revolutionary France ('Oh, let the noble, rich and great | The poor man's griefs alleviate | Nor be the Yeoman or his Lord | A Slave or proud Dictator'), even if its Finale song was so clumsily worded as to be almost unintelligible:

> Augusta![France], Cordial friend and generous foe[.]
> With sympathizing heart Lutetia [Paris][,] see
> Thy Freedom pure as thy own Thames still flow[.]
> London, be happy, ever great and free.

Of course, such pro-revolutionary sympathies, mainly derived from distaste at France's politically repressive monarchy, were not at all uncommon in Britain before the execution of Louis XVI and the outbreak of war in 1793. However, appended to *Harlequin Touchstone*'s rather formulaic patriotic chorus ('Hail, England! Seat of Arms and Arts, | Freedom's enthroned in British hearts | . . . loyalty and freedom here are found') was also a 'Grand Spectacle' based on recent events in France at the beginning of the Revolution.[43] In London at this time there were at least three 'pantomimes' showing interpretations of '*Taking the Bastile*': at Sadler's Wells in north London, Astley's Amphitheatre in Lambeth, and the Royal Circus in Goodman's Fields, all of them well beyond the Lord Chamberlain's domain of control. Eventually, the East End Royalty would also

---

[43] *New Airs Songs & Dialogues &c Choruses in the revived Pantomime of Harlequin Touchstone* [19 November 1789], Larpent Plays, 851, Huntington Library, Calif.

produce a post-Bastille pantomime covering some of the unfolding events of the Revolution.

Henry Meister, a French visitor who saw all three 1789 productions, fully subscribed to several of the contemporary Bastille myths then circulating, which he thought had been 'collected with great discretion and moderation'. But he also noted that they had noticeably loyalist endings, the Bastille pantomimes closing with scenes of 'beautiful decoration representing Britannia seated in a triumphal car, holding transparent portraits of the *King and Queen of Great Britain*, which she offers for the homage of the audience'.[44] Nevertheless, as an indicator of the wider political atmosphere of those times, Meister added that the London 'print shops are besides full of caricatures relative to the transactions now going on at Paris'. It was probably the weight of this worrying topicality which led to the banning of *Harlequin Touchstone*. Its 'Grand Spectacle', although it referred to the events of 4 May 1789 during Louis XVI's procession of the Estates-General two months prior to July's storming of the Bastille, ensured Covent Garden's pantomime raised too many uncomfortable spectres about the swansong decline of the French monarchy.[45] Print shop caricatures were largely beyond the effective control of the courts but it is evident that, given the opportunity afforded by his jurisdiction, the Lord Chamberlain's office aimed to close down any attempt to portray the French Revolution on the stage.

If Larpent was sufficiently worried to prohibit *Harlequin Touchstone*, had the Royalty playhouse been within his jurisdiction, he would have been much more concerned about its 1790 entertainment combining a harlequinade *Pantomimic Preludio* with a spectacle of the Paris Federation of 14 July 1790.[46] The three London Bastille

---

[44] Simon Schama, *Citizens: A Chronicle of the French Revolution* (London: Viking, 1989), 389–94.

[45] Henry Meister, *Letters Written During a Residence in England* (1799), 29–30.

[46] *A Sketch Of The Entertainment, Now Performing At The Royalty Theatre, In Two Parts: Consisting Of A Pantomimic Preludio, And The Paris Federation. To which is added, The Popular French Music* (1790).

pantomimes of 1789 had been based upon reports found in Elysée Loustalot's *Révolutions de Paris* newspaper and it is likely, in view of the work's extremely documentary nature, that the same source was used for the Royalty's harlequin-Revolution spectacle.[47] The Royalty's *Pantomimic Preludio, And ... Paris Federation* consisted of two parts, a Harlequin and Colombine pantomime succeeded by scenes showing their visit to the Fête de la Fédération in the Champ de Mars, Paris, on 14 July 1790.

The first few scenes of the *Pantomimic Preludio* are in the form of a traditional harlequinade concerned with Harlequin's rejection as a prospective husband by Colombine's father, Pantaloon. Pantaloon's own choice of a husband for his daughter is a Spanish Don but 'Harlequin discomforts them all by his appearance, and making various uses of his power. At last, the servants, friers [*sic*], and the whole company, assist at the taking of him. He is deprived by them of his magic sword, and Colombine is left inconsolable for his loss' (p. 3). In the surreal empowerments which are ubiquitous in harlequinade, Harlequin and Colombine are then able to escape into the woods and, after adventures, are eventually married and reconciled with Pantaloon, whereupon 'Harlequin invites them to the Champ de Mars. End of the Preludio' (p. 8). This harlequinade 'Preludio' performs the important structural function of traditionalizing and universalizing rifts with paternal conformity, rewarding rebellion and conventionalizing subsequent reconciliation. The seamless nature of the closure of the preludio, when 'Harlequin invites them to the Champ de Mars', and the piece's reopening into the political materialities of contemporary revolutionary France, eases the transition of this English perspective onto troubled events across the Channel. Just as there had been three falls-of-the-Bastille in London, so too the theatres vied with one another. At the Royal Circus in Lambeth, they decided to follow their *Representation of the Destruction of the Bastile* with their own piece called *The Champ de Mars* which the comedian Decastro remembered as 'successful' until 'the houses began to thin'

---

[47] On Loustalot, see Schama, *Citizens*, 445–60.

as customers were sated on the Revolution or else the Federation news simply became stale.[48] Sadler's Wells also ran a two-part *The Champ de Mars; or, Loyal Foederation* until 18 July 1791.[49] However, it is clear from the Royalty's version that ideological explanation was deemed to be an integral part of the purpose of their performances.

From the closure of the first half's harlequinade onwards in the *Pantomimic Preludio, And ... Paris Federation*, there is a strong sense of wishing to present to the audience the different varieties of ideological innovation then occurring in France. The first scene appears to be set on an open road 'discovering many of the peasantry on their way to Paris'. When they see Harlequin's traditional costume, the French peasants declare 'the Clown's livery a badge of his inequality' and he is persuaded to change his clothes and don the revolutionary cockaded hat:

PEOPLE. But doff it all,
  For, great and small
  Are equal in this nation;
  Arms, titles, liv'ries, they
  Are for ever done away
  In a total annihilation.
CLOWN. Now, by the aid
  Of this cockade,
  I feel my liberation (pp. 8–9)

The apparently whimsical incorporation of the issue of Harlequin's traditional costume into the subject matter of the pantomime presents a strong sense of the revolutionaries' 'total annihilation' of rank and the levelling of 'great and small' until all 'Are equal in this nation'. Changing a political system is shown to be no more difficult than changing one's clothes ('by the aid | Of this cockade, | I feel my liberation'), and such a transformation, it implies, brings about a powerful sense of personal renewal. If, as must have been the case in view of the theatre's location in the East End, substantial parts of the

[48] Humphreys, *The Memoirs Of J. Decastro*, 126.
[49] BL Theatrical Cuttings, 49.

Royalty's audience were of the liveried servant class, the empowering significance of Harlequin's jovial transition from costumed clown to cockaded sansculotte would not have gone unnoticed.

'Thus equipp'd, | Of slav'ry stripp'd', Harlequin and Colombine set off for Paris to 'Attend the FEDERATION!' (p. 10). The author of the *Pantomimic Preludio, And . . . Paris Federation* employed a comic documentary style to portray quite specific events which happened in July 1790 when France was gearing itself up towards full-blown Revolution and accompanying Terror. A military drilling ground, the Champ de Mars, had been commandeered by the Revolutionary authorities as the Parisian venue for a national Fête de la Fédération that involved the National Guards taking an oath of allegiance, in this instance also to be witnessed not only by the Constituent legislators but also by Louis XVI himself.[50] For this event, the Champ de Mars had to be transformed from a parade ground into a festival site by excavating four feet of stony earth and rebuilding the spoil into a grand amphitheatre surmounted by an 'Altar of the Fatherland' and all approached via a triple-arched Arc de Triomphe. All of these reportage details were included somewhere or other in the Royalty's entertainment as they had also been at Sadler's Wells *The Champ de Mars; or, Loyal Foederation* ('Their zealous Activity in the Preparation of the Ground'). Indeed, Harlequin and Colombine are made eyewitness participants in the unfolding Revolution spectacles. In the Royalty piece, as Harlequin and Colombine approach the 'Environs of Paris' they are met by a rejoicing populace and they both join with ballad singers in singing an 'extremely popular' song whose words and music were reprinted for the London readership of the *Pantomimic Preludio, And . . . Paris Federation* ('The cruel Aristocracy | Ne'Er shed a tear at misery; | 'Twas that which caus'd our strife . . . | But now's arriv'd the happy day, | When all our sorrows fly away' (pp. 11–12). Singing of 'the rights of man' (a reference to the Declaration of the Rights of Man, July 1789) and of 'the proud Bastille's | Horrific dens and tort'ring wheels', praising

[50] See Schama, *Citizens*, 500–13.

Lafayette and the tricolour ('Vive le rouge, le blanc, le bleu'), they head off further into Paris. As the scene shifts to 'A street in Paris. The peasantry join the Parisians; and they dance indiscriminately to the ... Ça ira, Ça ira' (pp. 13–15). This is a reminder that, although within his jurisdiction the Lord Chamberlain's office could control the texts of songs figured to be offensive, they had no such control over music. Within the private sphere, for example, the drawing room harpsichord sonata *The Bastile* (*c.*1789)—although it included optional words—could use music's expressivity of an allegro 'Quick March expressing universal joy' at the fall of the Bastille before ending with a solidly affirmative andante grazioso. Designed by one 'Mr. Elfort' for drawing room performance by the harpsichord, the quieter predecessor of the piano, *The Bastile* sonata is a good contemporary indicator of the advanced popular sentiments of musically inclined middle-class families.

The point about the importation of French political songs into the pantomime, however, is that it allowed the Royalty's *Pantomimic Preludio, And ... Paris Federation* to emphasize the role of popular culture in embodying new revolutionary ideals. This is nowhere made more clear than in a scene showing a *poissarde* (a market woman speaking an abrupt Parisian dialect made notorious from their march on Versailles in October 1789), confronting a reluctant friar:

> Why loit'ring here, good frier [*sic*],
> Why not at the Champ de Mars?
> Exchange your useless beads,
> Your country serve with deeds;
> With spade in hand,
> Come take your stand,
> And work in the Champ de Mars.

As well as hinting at the future de-Christianizing tendencies of 1794, with documentary accuracy the *poissarde*'s belligerent song refers to the way in which, 'In social bands united', both high and low Parisians had mingled during June and July 1790 with spades and wheelbarrows to literally build and construct the Fête's triumphal spaces: the Royalty's *Pantomimic Preludio, And . . . Paris Federation*, included a scene showing 'The patriots . . . on their way to the Champ de Mars, carrying implements, &c. for the buildings there' (pp. 18–19). Finally, the pantomime ended with a scene portraying the climax of the festival itself where the king 'seated on the throne, erected by the people', gives an oath guaranteeing his honour and respect for his subjects, ending with a ceremony of consecration at the newly constructed altar. In Sadler's Wells's *The Champ de Mars; or, Loyal Foederation*, the converted parade ground was first shown in an unfinished state and then complete with its 'grand Triumphal Arches'.[51] Although his identity is not specified, the person who carried out this consecration was Bishop Talleyrand (the pantomime simply says 'a bishop'). The pantomime ends with words actually taken from a slogan beneath an image of Fame which stood on the festival platform ('Vive la loi, vive la nation, vive le roi'; pp. 21–2).

The Royalty's *Pantomimic Preludio, And . . . Paris Federation* gave a pretty accurate documentary of the events except for noting that, in reality, the whole of the proceedings were dominated by the political presence of Lafayette, especially when he took prime position at the altar to administer the federation oath. The Royalty representation, at least in its printed version, fails to mention him although it may well have been interpolated into their productions. Nevertheless, the Royalty's reportage of the continuing French Revolution, particularly with its characterization of an increasingly diminishing, subservient role for the monarch, is remarkably faithful in importing in an accessible and popular form some of the ideas and challenges being put into political practice across the Channel.

The transformation of the normal social divisions of labour represented in the *Pantomimic Preludio, And . . . Paris Federation*, allied to its anticlericalism and the incorporation of popular modes of levelling (such as politicized clothing and the singing of catchy revolutionary ballads) must have made the Royalty Theatre a deeply

[51] BL, *Collections Relating to Sadler's Wells*, vol. 2, 1787–95, newspaper cutting *c.*3 August 1791.

unsettling venue as far as the patrician classes of London were concerned. Not only did the Royalty in the early 1790s import French Revolutionary iconography in a form subliminally domesticated into the cosily familiar genre of the pantomime harlequinade, its other entertainments such as 'The Benevolent Jew' and *The Man With Two Wives* show that deep inside the working class boroughs of London's East End, entertainments were staged which challenged many cultural stereotypes. Furthermore, these representations were far beyond the reach of the Lord Chamberlain. When the Society for the Suppression of Vice targeted the Royalty in 1803, it was quite aware that the ad lib textual freedoms exhibited in works like 'The Benevolent Jew', *The Man With Two Wives*, and the *Pantomimic Preludio, And . . . Paris Federation* were difficult to police. The Revd Thomas Thirlwall in *A Solemn Protest Against The Revival Of Scenic Exhibitions . . . At The Royalty Theatre* particularly commented, in a general reference to contemporary comedy, that contemporary actors tended frequently to 'interlard their speeches, and supply the imperfections of their memory' with 'coarse profaneness and shameless blasphemies' 'by additions from their own prolific genius' (p. 7).

However, other than the aspersions on the morality of both the audience and actors, the principal objection Thirlwall made was about the effects the Royalty Theatre might have on the war effort. The hinterland of the Royalty was a centre of munitions manufacture at a time when in 1803 the country was alarmed by fears of invasion by Napoleon. Thirlwall knew that the 'East end of the town' was a 'hive of industry, where no man is presumed to have an idle hour'. His specific anxiety was a patrician nightmare of loose armaments workers seduced by theatre:

Suppose, at the present crisis, when the gunmaker has contracted to furnish, within a certain period, ten thousand stand of arms; that his numerous body of journeymen are called off from their work, by the sound of a trumpet, to see pass their shop windows a Company of dressed-up men, and boys, and girls on horseback, with the Taylor of Brentford, exhibiting his antic tricks amongst them.

Thirlwall's vision is of an East End threat to the very existence of the state during its 'present crisis', a threat which penetrates through to the industrialized processes of contract and schedule ('contracted to furnish, within a certain period'), a threat of theatricality destabilizing the workforce ('his numerous body of journeymen') through 'the sound of a trumpet', not the martial bugler's call to arms but, instead, a theatrical, unmilitarized 'Company' of inauthentic (even cross-dressed) 'dressed-up men'. What they are drawn to, as it passes by their '[work]shop windows', is a show of 'boys, and girls on horseback, with the Taylor of Brentford, exhibiting his antic tricks amongst them'.

What Thirlwall was describing was a street calvacade version of *Billy Buttons, or The Tailor's Ride to Brentford*, a famous horseback clown routine devised in 1768 by Philip Astley, owner of Astley's Amphitheatre.[52] Dickens refers to it in *Hard Times* as the 'highly novel and laughable hippocomedietta of The Tailor's Journey to Brentford', one of the horse riding acts advertised at 'Sleary's Horse-riding' pavilion (Book I, chapter 3). The basic formula of Astley's routine may still be familiar to modern circus-goers: the Tailor is a (skilfully) incompetent rider, who falls and is comically unable to re-mount his horse, gets chased by the animal, and (in some later manifestations) is helped by a circus 'stooge' placed in the audience, with similar results. (I remember my childhood amazement when the Tailor took off 'his' disguise to reveal a pretty young woman.) Whether Thirlwall was subliminally aware of it or not, Astley's original *Tailor's Ride to Brentford* was based on the tale of a tailor galloping to Brentford in order to be in time to vote for the radical Whig leader John Wilkes, in the controversial 1768 Middlesex election.

Of course, Thirlwall (surely a good candidate for the origin of Dickens's Gradgrind) makes it appear that the Tailor of Brentford's 'antic tricks' are a publicity stunt emanating from the Royalty Theatre (as perhaps it was). It may even be the case that the very Wilksite

[52] George Speaight, *A History of the Circus* (London: Tantivy Press, 1980), 24.

source of the Royalty's version of this 'hippocomedietta' was a deep psycho-manifestation of Thirlwall's anxiety about the theatre's political influence. However, what specifically vexed him was the possibility that 'one of these journeymen may express a wish to see this *fun*, and the rest of his shopmates, seeing the same curiosity, quit their shop to resort to this Theatre, and leave the master to lament over his heavy loss, and the serious injury to himself, to Government, and his country'.[53] Revealed here in Thirlwall's pamphlet is a remarkably structured set of anxieties about work and pleasure, class, capital, and nationhood, all revolving around a problem about the Royalty's place in East End popular culture. At the very least, Thirlwall's *Solemn Protest Against The Revival Of Scenic Exhibitions ... At The Royalty Theatre* is a common incarnation of a recurrent kind of stock Puritan disquiet, both about the stage and about 'this *fun*'.

Thirlwall was only one component in a greater moral and political movement co-ordinated by the increasingly comprehensive and interventionist Society for the Suppression of Vice. The importance of these organized and co-ordinated attempts to close down the Royalty Theatre is that they are indicative of an attempt to widen the regime of theatrical censorship and particularly to take the campaign into working-class areas. In the Royalty's case, the strategy was not simply to cut or excise scenes, songs, lines, or words from stage performances, as it was with the Lord Chamberlain's office, but rather to effect the wholesale closure of the medium of performance, the playhouse itself. Somewhere in the background one also senses the growth in the efficiency and organization of the ruling culture's means of coercion. The attempts to close the Royalty in the 1780s mobilized a sizeable, articulate, and creative local response in forms as diverse as Palmer's organized petitioning, pamphleteering, the writing of supportive odes, and, perhaps most

---

[53] Thomas Thirlwall, *Royalty Theatre. A Solemn Protest Against The Revival Of Scenic Exhibitions And Interludes, At The Royalty Theatre; Containing Remarks On Pizarro, The Stranger, And John Bull; With A Postscript* (1803), 9–10.

3

Theatrical Oligarchies: The Role of the Examiner of Plays

THE day-to-day excisions and (less frequent) suppressions of the drama submitted to John Larpent and his successor, George Colman the Younger, provides an evidential basis for the analysis of the workings of censorship in Romantic period Britain. The censorship of drama was a constant factor in writing for the stage in Westminster (meaning most of London as it then existed) as well as for the provincial Royal theatres outside of Ireland. There were two principal means by which official Government or local authority was exerted over the content and production of stage dramas. The first was by direct censorship of dramatic texts involving the reading and marking for excision of offensive passages or sometimes suppression of entire texts. The second means of censorship was through the exercise of local powers of regulation or intimidation offered through local magistrates or, as in the case of the Royalty, unelected organizations such as the Society for the Suppression of Vice. In addition, by a further paradox, the social mobilization of the patentees of the Royal theatres also tended towards advocacy of the closure of those playhouses which infringed their patent over five-act spoken drama. In other words, when deliberately socially networked, this pressure by the patentees was essentially a cartel constituted as a reaction to a perceived capital threat to the shareholders.

Effectively, this ensured that the only generic possibility allowable to the non-patent theatres was burletta. This is why various hybrid generic confections such as comic opera, spectacle, and three-act melodramas were the only products of those theatres existing outside of the royal patent. It was not a matter of choice. In other words, there was bipartite regulation: first of the texts, but also of the playhouses themselves. It is because control of play texts was exercised at the level of the single word, phrase, sentence, couplet, or lyric—or, on occasion, entire play—that the practice of censorship can be studied only by examining the individual textual interferences practised by the Lord Chamberlain. The picture that emerges for the period of the 1790s, a crucial decade of revolution, war, and social upheaval, is of a censorship which was domesticated, highly unpredictable, and totally dependent upon personal whim. The day-to-day working practices of John Larpent, as Examiner of Plays from 1778 until his death in 1824, reveals a bewildering, often contradictory, set of extraordinary decisions concerning excision and licensing.

Paradoxically, without their retention by the Examiner, many of the play texts would not have survived because, beyond his remit, only the more successful or notorious plays tended to find their way into print. Such, however, was the level of ignorant (or wilful) misunderstanding over the rights of ownership of the play texts submitted to the Lord Chamberlain that John Larpent's widow, imagining that she owned them herself, put the collection up for sale in its entirety. Luckily, they were bought (for £400) by John Payne Collier in 1832 who, expecting to find authors' manuscripts rather than copyists' drafts, thought them 'hardly worth the money' he had paid.[1] In other words, posterity came close to losing all the plays before 1824. From there, by the end of the nineteenth century, the Lord Chamberlain's play manuscripts up to 1824 had arrived at the Huntington Library, California. By contrast, Colman's manuscripts stayed with the Lord Chambelain and are now in the British Library. This level of administrative incompetence, bordering on corruption, typifies much of the atmosphere under which the London theatres had to operate during this era.

---

[1] John Payne Collier, *An Old Man's Diary, Forty Years Ago; For The First Six Months Of 1832* (London: Thomas Richards, 1871), i. 49.

In the midst of this confusion of official responsibility worked John and Anna Larpent. Indeed, John Larpent's role as dramatic censor was something of an unofficial cottage-industry conducted in the domestic setting of a Georgian living room.[2] In the early 1790s Larpent's wife, Anna Margaretta, contributed a significant input into individual decisions about theatrical censorship while the couple sat at their fireside in their home off Bedford Square surrounded by their children.[3] Of course, nothing disreputable is to be inferred from Larpent using his home as his office. Indeed, as will be described in Chapter 5, it at least had the virtue of allowing playwrights to know where he could be found, and so it was to Bedford Square, for example, that Thomas John Dibdin made his way in late summer 1800 when he discovered his politically sensitive *Two Farmers* for Covent Garden had been suppressed. Dibdin achieved no lifting of the ban but he was at least able to talk to Larpent. However, Larpent's use of his family home to carry out Government censorship removes any doubt that there was much in the way of checks or balances within the system, certainly nothing approaching the internal restraints on official conduct assured by a modern bureaucracy. Nevertheless, such bureaucratic procedures were current in other Government departments at this time, including areas which touched on the regulation of the theatre.

When Richard Ford in 1795, as described in Chapter 1, decided to put pressure on the New Circus management, his memorandum of instruction, commanding an official to visit the premises, was duly recorded in a Home Office copy book, a short entry amongst

---

[2] Larpent became Examiner of Plays in 1778: L. W. Conolly, *The Censorship of English Drama, 1737–1824* (San Marino, Calif.: Huntington Library, 1976), 34.

[3] For two fairly recuperative views of Anna Larpent, see Claire Miller Colombo, '"This pen of mine will say too much": Public Performance in the Journals of Anna Larpent', *Texas Studies in Literature and Language: A Journal of the Humanities*, 38:3/4 (1996), 285–301; John Brewer, 'Reconstructing the Reader: Prescriptions, Texts and Strategies in Anna Larpent's Reading', in James Raven, Helen Small, and Naomi Tadmor (eds.), *The Practice and Representation of Reading in England* (Cambridge: Cambridge University Press, 1996), 226–45.

several others on that page, all on completely different subjects.[4] The entry is almost certainly not in Ford's original hand but is the work of a scribe. However, the practices of George Colman (Larpent's successor) were even less well regulated in that, quite separately from returning manuscripts to the theatres together with his cuts marked up as Larpent had done, in the late 1820s Colman appears to have occasionally entered into a parallel correspondence with the theatres, a correspondence which was not collected or entered into a copy book (as was obviously Home Office practice as early as the mid-1790s), then to be preserved as part of the Lord Chamberlain's records.[5] The ultimate result of such arbitrary and individualistic sets of behaviour conducted over a long period was the confusion which is apparent on even a cursory reading of the *Report from the Select Committee on Dramatic Literature ... 2 August 1832* (1832) when witnesses, including Colman himself, had to be asked repeatedly to clarify the regulatory system to the Parliamentary committee.

The domesticity of theatrical censorship is one of the most remarkable features of British writing for the stage in the 1790s. The descriptions left in Anna Margaretta Larpent's diaries reveal not only fascinating glimpses into the domestic economy of late eighteenth-century London well-to-do family life, but also of Anna Larpent as an intelligent and influential helpmate to her husband in his official position as Examiner of Plays or public censor. It is not too broad a summary conclusion to observe that, throughout the early Romantic period, the censorship of serious British drama (of the five-act spoken variety typified by Shakespeare and

[4]   18 April 1795, HO 43/6.

[5]   Play manuscripts sent to Colman for censorship in his role as Lord Chamberlain's Examiner of Plays are collected in a sequence starting from BL Add. MS 42869. Examples of Colman's uncollected correspondence to theatres about censoring specific plays include, 6 January 1829 (*Caswallon, or the Briton Chief*), Folger Y.d. 483 (12); 5 November 1828 (*The Daughter's Vow*), Folger Y.d. 483 (11); no date (*The School of Gallantry*), Folger Y.d. 483 (10); 19 January 1828 (*The Haunted Inn*), Folger ART, vol. b19, Folger Shakespeare Library, Washington, DC.

other Elizabethan and Jacobean playwrights) was a practice almost entirely confined to the decisions of a husband and wife team whose duties and decisions were routinely administered from their drawing room.

With unconscious prophetic irony, in 1793 Anna described a typical summer's evening spent in the Larpent household, 'dressed dined . . . Evening walked till Tea. After which worked making John a waistcoat and Mr Larpent read loud a new Opera the Mountaineers. Supt. prayed & bed at 11.'[6] *The Mountaineers*, as it happens, was by the next Examiner, George Colman the Younger, but John Larpent's reading of it aloud in the living room while Anna Margaretta sewed their young son's waistcoat was intended to provide the means of, unofficially, including his wife's opinions in his censorship decisions. In the early 1790s, this was the normal mode under which stage censorship took place. Their control of plays appearing at the Royal Patent theatres, and of the minor theatres falling under the Westminster jurisdiction, was absolute. While Anna Larpent had no official role whatever, she clearly exercised a degree of influence from within the domestic sphere. Her diaries give a very full account of her role as unofficial assistant censor during the early 1790s.

A few days before the newly formed Association for Preserving Liberty and Property Against Republicans and Levellers began their surveillance of allegedly subversive taverns in Kennington and the harassing of such figures as the radical Holborn pamphleteer Thomas Spence, the Larpents were, in a similar spirit, cracking down on Covent Garden's proposed production of Richard Cumberland's innocuous comic opera *Richard the Second* (1792), which was refused a licence for performance.[7] Anna Larpent's diary provides a unique snapshot of the context for this decision and its complete immersion

[6] Diaries of Anna Margaretta Larpent, vol. i, 1 August 1793, Huntington Library, Calif.

[7] BL Add. MS 16922 fo. 12, 11 December 1792; Add. MS 16922, fo. 53, 12 December 1792.

in the unpredictable and casual workings of the British class system. It is worth examining the censorship process of *Richard the Second* in some detail precisely because it was far from being a high-profile case. And, in any event, Cumberland was already a long-established and successful playwright, very far from being a radical chancer or dramatic demagogue.

London in late 1792 was at the height of anti-Paineite loyalist agitation. British society was thoroughly polarized. For example, the impulsive actor James Fennell (then between work) discovered that John Reeves, the founder organizer of the ultra-reactionary Association for Protecting Liberty and Property Against Republicans and Levellers, was 'an old schoolmate of mine' and he became the organization's secretary, cheerfully 'signing under the name of "Moore"' in order to remain covert.[8] Despite her domestic responsibilities, Anna kept abreast of current affairs, conscientiously reading Paine's *Rights of Man* (1791/2). She was socially perceptive. A visit she made to an exhibition of Ozias Humphrey's crayon sketches of Calcutta while she was still in the middle of reading *Rights of Man* caused her to comment unfavourably on the 'pomp' and 'magnificence' of the city's high-living European colonists, 'how can Europeans used to such extravagance & grandeur accustom themselves to the privacy of their stations in England. I do not wonder they are so unhappy & insolent.'[9] Anna's concerns about the potentially corrosive effects on ideals of duty, when repatriated colonists returned from India, establishes her as a highly critical member of her class. As far as Paine was concerned she concluded when she finished the book, 'It is a Controversy I cannot in its full heat form a judgement on[.] Things are very wrong[.] how far these projectors will set them quite right is the Question.'[10] The operation

---

[8] James Fennell, *An Apology for the Life of James Fennell. Written by Himself* (Philadelphia: Moses Thomas, 1814), 330. Several documents signed by 'Moore' can be seen in BL Add. MS 16922.

[9] Diaries of Anna Margaretta Larpent, vol. i, 12 April 1792, Huntington Library, Calif.

[10] Ibid. 13 April 1792.

of British dramatic censorship was, to use a modern phrase, only 'a heart beat' away from Anna Larpent's influence and yet the ability of her husband (and herself, indirectly) to abort plays from their Bedford Square residence was final.

It is a consistent paradox about the way she thought and helped make decisions on matters of censorship that neither her evident high level of political understanding, nor her awareness of social modes of sensibility, stopped her abetting her husband in repressive acts. If anything, as an individual Anna Larpent was politically judicious by the standards of her social contemporaries. When the émigré Bishop of Montpelier came to see them in 1793, she obviously took seriously his verdict that the French Revolution had been caused by Voltaire, the *Encyclopédie*, and Rousseau ('a better intentioned Enthusiast') but preferred the judgement that the Revolution had been brought about by a nobility 'ill educated, without Energy' who 'corrupted others while they were corrupt themselves'.[11] Her programme of reading included novelists whose uncongenial political views she sought to remain detached from when giving an appreciation of their literary quality. Reading Charlotte Smith's *Desmond* (1792), she proceeded with her diary entry in her curious (but revealing as to her aspirations) mock 'literary reviewer' style, a style mixed with a sense of her own personal fulfilment in the process of reading the latest books, yet also sensitive to Smith's own difficult financial circumstances. Anna Larpent wrote into her diary: '"finished it" [i.e. *Desmond*] with a fine Imagination & Command of Language Charlotte Smith cannot write without Interest ... She is a wild Leveller. She defends the Revolution. She writes with the Enthusiasm of a Woman & a poetess.'[12] Nevertheless, these fine and discriminating literary perceptions appear to have been rendered redundant when it came to censoring drama for the public stage.

The manuscript of Cumberland's *Richard the Second* was censored by the husband-and-wife Larpent team on the very evening of the day of its dispatch from Covent Garden. The decision to declare

[11] Ibid. 22 January 1793.　　[12] Ibid. 14 August 1792.

its 'Licence Refused' was arrived at in similar circumstances to the household's usual domestic habits:

Mr Larpent read loud a Mss offered for Licensing An Opera Richard the 2d written by Cumberland it appears extremely unfit for representation at a time when the Country is full of Alarm, being the story of Wat Tyler the killing of the Tax Gatherer &C. very ill judgd [but the] poetry pretty & the whole really written with taste[.] supt & to bed early.[13]

Again, the separation of an appreciation of Cumberland's 'pretty' poetry and his good literary 'taste' from the text's overt political content is similar to Anna's comment on Charlotte Smith. Richard Cumberland was actually quite equivocal in his portrayal of Wat Tyler but it seems that even the very airing of such revolutionary subject matter was too much for the Larpents' to tolerate. Certainly *Richard the Second*'s opening in the armourer's forge of the rebel leader Jerry Furnace displays a vivid scene of clerical (though safely Catholic) drunkenness: 'Click, click, goes the Cann as it flies, | Wheel it round, Father Dominic cries, | By the Mass 'tis a Sin to be drunk; | If you want a jolly quest, | Recommend me to the Priest, | Merry, Monk, merry monk, merry monks!' The poll-tax gatherer, Ralph Rackum ('the Earl of Suffolk's varlet'), is pompous and officious but hardly an imminent danger to Furnace's daughter Rosamond whom he believes to be of 'taxable' age. Nevertheless, the wild Jerry Furnace ('By the Soul of the immortal Edward, if you do offer violence, I'll brain you like a Bullock with my Sledge') kills the tax-gatherer, whose death elicits a macabre comic comment from Father Dominic, 'he is, as I may say, a caput mortuum'. The piece glances at contemporary concerns relevant to May 1792's Royal Proclamation against seditious utterance ('If Master Gripe, the Lawyer, or Ralph Rackum ... heard you talk in that fashion, you'd have the sumpner in his Tawney Coat after you, so you wou'd. I tell, you Jerry, there is you and Wat Tyler and Jack Straw and others of your Cronies will prate yourselves into a Prison by and bye').

---

[13] Diaries of Anna Margaretta Larpent, vol. i, 8 December 1792; Larpent Plays, 963, Huntington Library, Calif.

For the Larpents, it was probably the final scenes of the opera which brought about the refusal of its dramatic licence for representation. Wat Tyler's speech against the poll-tax would have been considered an inflammatory example of demagoguery:

WAT TYLER. Did they, that tax our heads, make our heads? No; yet every scull amongst us, thick or thin, hard or soft, is cess'd by the Poll without pity or excuse. 'Tis the Luxuries & superfluities of life that shou'd be tax'd. Are our Noddles of that number? ... I grant you, there are some heads not worth the Cess that's put upon em, What then? Shol'd the tax imposed exceed the value of the thing taxed? It should not. Therefore do you see, down with the Tax-Gatherers, say I: We'll pay them after Jerry Furnace's fashion & none other.

JACK STRAW. True, most eloquent Tyler, and if we take off their heads, we take off their tax; so let no man say he is wrong'd by us.

Giving an indication of exactly contemporary fears for the relationship between Government office and radicalism, only four days earlier a Chatham collector of Stamp Duty had been prosecuted for selling copies of Paine's *Rights of Man*.[14] If this was not enough to make the Larpents jumpy, the opera's finale included a 'Chorus of Insurgents' ('Let us march, let us march, let confusion arise ... | Our gallant Wat Tyler, and brave Captain Straw | Let us free from our Taxes, & order & Law; | And when war is awaken'd, destruction's the word | And our March shall be trac'd by fire, famine & sword').[15] The level at which the Larpents responded by suppressive measures was motivated by more or less 'gut' feelings, visceral sensibilities that their superiors or social equals would be affronted or outraged and the lower classes energized out of passivity if they witnessed such things on stage.

That the Larpents' sense of the principles of censorship were clearly activated by very personal, even domestic, sets of values arrived at with loose reference to the current political climate can be judged from the responses to contemporary events recorded in Anna's diary.

---

[14] PRO HO 42/23. 116, 4 December 1792.
[15] Larpent Plays, 963, Richard Cumberland, *Richard the Second A Comic Opera in three Acts* (Covent Garden, 8 December 1792), Huntington Library, Calif.

On Christmas Eve 1792 the Larpents went to a meeting of a putative Epsom branch of John Reeves's Association for Protecting Liberty and Property Against Republicans and Levellers. The Larpents obviously found it a disquieting occasion ('We drove up & heard the Harrangers ... Mr Finch, the Government Member—told us so, of Alarm, French Troops, Republicans & Levellers that he made us shudder ... it was an odd scene ... we could only return to dinner').[16] Although their emotions were disturbed at the Association's vociferous fear-mongering, their Epsom visit conclusively establishes their involvement with reactionary political activity concurrent with John Larpent's role in public office as the Lord Chamberlain's Examiner. While this incident reflects the late eighteenth century's very different standards of civic probity, John and Anna Larpent were directly linked to practices of unpredictable patterns of Government-sponsored censorship which threatened to corrupt their notions of public responsibility. Larpent's role as official stage censor, together with this visit to the reactionary Association meeting, suddenly materializes corruption as a persistently recurrent problem within contemporary political culture. Although, as Kevin Gilmartin has noted, radicalism notably sustained its own figurative language of corruption, the underlying issues which created this language continued to be real enough.[17] Whatever principles of political propriety or morality the Larpents employed, their allegiance to loyalist activism cannot be in doubt.

A few weeks later, the Larpents were at the theatre again when news arrived in the playhouse of the execution of Louis XVI, which had prevented the British Royal Family's visit to see the play that night. Anna Larpent's composure was unsettled by public reaction in the theatre:

The Audience was Confused, most were agitated, others unfeeling yet scared from seeing others feel. The manager wished to stop the play—but

---

[16] Diaries of Anna Margaretta Larpent, vol. i, 24 December 1792, Huntington Library, Calif.

[17] Kevin Gilmartin, *Print Politics: The Press and Radical Opposition in Early Nineteenth-Century England* (Cambridge: Cambridge University Press, 1995), 14–17.

the house was too much disappointed at the Absence of the family to hear
further disappointment. The play was not given up. ye Curtain rose 'God
Save the King' sang. The effect was Awful. I never felt as I did at [that?]
moment—The play & pantomime went on without spirit—A thousand
Confused ideas rushed in my Mind—seemed to do so, in the minds of
most. These are wonderful times!!! May God protect us through them . . .
Returned home full of thoughts & conversations[18]

Incidentally, this eyewitness account of a momentous evening serves
as a perfect vehicle for understanding the role of theatre in contemporary society. To the audiences, the galleried strata of the theatre
not only enabled the otherwise highly differentiated social classes to
see each other; its spaces also allowed a point of individual reference for personal sensibilities and emotions. The feelings displayed
on this occasion encompassed uncertain stoicism ('others unfeeling
yet scared from seeing others feel'), the sharing of sublime fear
('The effect was Awful . . . A thousand Confused ideas rushed in
my Mind—seemed to do so, in the minds of most') and yet also
an apparent sense of an ideologically loyal and coherent national
community who began singing 'God Save the King'.

What needs to be remembered here is the cultural complexity of
the Larpents' agency in the control of drama. Their visit, however
unsettling, to the Epsom branch of the Association for Protecting
Liberty and Property Against Republicans and Levellers is a specific,
if not unsurprising, example of the collusion between a Government
office holder and a particularly disturbing manifestation of contemporary politics. Just how dangerous Reeves's, Association finally
became to the British constitution, and how ill-judged was the Larpents' brief connection with the Epsom branch of their organization,
can be estimated by the fact that just two years later Reeves was himself prosecuted for his pamphlet *Thoughts on the English Government*
(1795), which contained seditious imagery in which both Houses
of Parliament were compared to trees capable of being cut down

---

[18] Diaries of Anna Margaretta Larpent, vol. i, 23 January 1793, Huntington
Library, Calif.

and burned.[19] Living, as the Larpents did, through key events in western Europe and witnessing their reception in London and how their fellow subjects reacted, also helps us understand the turmoils and confusions they experienced. The problem, however, is that these understandable anxieties did not remain private or domestic concerns. Instead, by virtue of his office, John Larpent was able to project his personal traumas—impelled and supported by his wife—into an exacting and unpredictable control of English drama.

Unfortunately, as has been referred to above, one of the many literary casualties of the sensitively tuned emotions of Anna and John Larpent was the censorship of the mildly political comic opera *Richard the Second*. It is through the individual excision or suppression of dramas that the Larpents' true and absolute power was exercised. The disparity between the civilized domestic sensibilities of the Larpents and their powerful public exercise over the censorship of dramatic writing is striking. At church, Anna Larpent could feel that a printed fast-day sermon was too 'heavy, severe ... more scold than doctrine' yet she obviously quickly forgot her involvement in her husband's decision to ban *Richard the Second*.[20] After its refusal, Cumberland rewrote *Richard the Second* as *The Armorer*, which the Larpents went to see in spring 1793. It appeared on the same bill as *The Marriage of Figaro* ('which made us laugh–tho' I cannot approve the morality of it, & sometimes the ... [Squire] is too glaringly Indelicate'), but Anna Larpent obviously remembered nothing about the earlier incarnation of the night's 'new Opera' ('A very flat, uninteresting composition, the Music mixt & dull') except that on this occasion it had passed their official scrutiny.[21] For the Larpents it is difficult to escape the conclusion that theatrical censorship had become a

[19] A. V. Beedell, 'John Reeves's Prosecution for Seditious Libel, 1795–1796: A Study in Political Cynicism', *Historical Journal*, 36: 4 (1993), 810–11; David Eastwood, 'John Reeves and the Contested Idea of the Constitution', *British Journal for Eighteenth Century Studies*, 16 (1993) 197–212; John Barrell, *Imagining the King's Death: Figurative Treason, Fantasies of Regicide 1793–1796* (Oxford: Oxford University Press, 2000), 622–36.

[20] Diaries of Anna Margaretta Larpent, vol. i, 16 February 1794, Huntington Library, Calif.

[21] Ibid. 5 April 1793; Larpent Plays, 976, Huntington Library, Calif.

routine ingredient of their domestic life with Anna providing skills complementary to those of her husband ('Breakfasted . . . read an Italian Opera for Mr Larpent').[22]

The glimpses which Anna Margaretta's diaries afford of the day-to-day practices of dramatic censorship in the early 1790s reveal a haphazard, careless, unsystematic, highly personal monopoly of literary repression. As her young family grew up, she ceased writing about her contributions to her husband's work as censor. In spring 1795 she mentions dealing with 'various family concerns. Settled the weeks house bills worked all morning useful plain work, & very unwell low. murmuring. unhappy. wanting self command but I will try to conquer this nervous habitual Melancholy'. That evening they 'dressed dined . . . then drove out to see the Illuminations the Prince of Wales is married today! the crowd great but peaceable. The lights general but not particularly Elegant. The Theatre Covent Garden was the most so . . . Suffered all day dreadfully with the head ache.'[23] Perhaps these personal or domestic problems grew worse, or else were less capable of being alleviated by the attractions of their social round. In any event, by the late 1790s her comments on new plays had stopped altogether.

However much one may sympathize with an undoubtedly diligent and intelligent woman, the Larpents were representatives of an oligarchical society steeped in the patronage of public office. The roots and sinews of this apparatus stretched in unexpected directions. One day in spring 1794 she wrote in her diary of how an old man from Birmingham came to see her husband only to find him out. Nevertheless, she talked to him and pieced together his story. This 'Mr Carles' can now be identified as having been involved in the 1791 Birmingham loyalist riots which destroyed the house, laboratory, and library of the Unitarian dissenter Joseph Priestley. According to his account, Carles 'shewed himself a violent High Churchman &

---

[22] Diaries of Anna Margaretta Larpent, vol. i, 11 April 1795, Huntington Library, Calif.

[23] Ibid. 8 April 1795.

loyalist, for which the Dissenters vowed vengeance against him'.[24] Anna recorded how 'Government have rewarded his zeal by giving him the Clerkship of Privy Seal & Mr. Larpent the deputy's place which he holds for his Brother.'[25] As a part of a society with such elaborate networks of allegiance, deference, and reward (Larpent's brother was acutely in need of the post secured for him), the Larpents were particularly sensitive to the dramatic representation of faults relevant to their own class. Such criticism would be censored out of presentations at any Royal theatres.

In addition to their sensitivity to manifestations of political radicalism in drama, the Larpents were also suppressive of any suggestions in dramas which were critical of the ruling classes, even though this may have been at variance with their personal attitudes. At a play in 1795 attended by the Prince and Princess of Wales, she thought the Princess's figure 'made up, or rather I should say set off by dress', but were she 'Miss A or B' most people 'wd. not have noticed her'. She also thought her dull: 'She could not be amused not understand what past [*sic*] . . . Her countenance is pleasing when animated but one looks for the moment of animation to be pleased'. The Regent 'looks bloated, sadder, in short were he my footman with such a look—I should say he was drinking himself out of the world . . . his manner was not gracious, it was embarrassed, constrained not marked by attention to her or the Audience.'[26] Nevertheless, although the limitations of those in high social rank were plainly visible and well enough understood by such perceptive theatregoers as the Larpents, the powers of the Lord Chamberlain's Examiner of Plays ensured that their portrayal in the theatre was banned. The workings of the various complex elements of late eighteenth-century English social structure inevitably

---

[24] This person is Justice Carles, a loyalist allegedly forcibly ejected from the French Revolution dinner in Birmingham, 1791, which resulted in the anti-dissenter riots leading to Joseph Priestley's emigration to the USA; see Joseph Priestley, *Dr. Priestley's Letter to the Inhabitants of Birmingham* (1791), 8.

[25] Diaries of Anna Margaretta Larpent, vol. i, 19 March 1794, Huntington Library, Calif.

[26] Ibid. 20 April 1795.

resulted in collisions between finely differentiated spheres of rank and responsibility. The revelation through her diaries that so much of day-to-day censorship was conducted in a domestic setting bewilderingly destabilizes the possibility that the Larpents operated their censorship through some discernible set of principles. In the absence of any published criteria for censorship, and although irresponsible personal behaviour by aristocrats was clearly personally deplored by Anna Larpent, in 1795 her husband had no qualms in declaring as 'Prohibited from being acted', a manuscript entitled *The Whim A Comedy* for the Theatre Royal, Margate, a drama critical of the ruling class but written by the aristocrat Lady Mary Eglantine Wallace.[27]

Whatever the moralities or politics the Larpents were trying to defend or enforce, their powers were exercised at the level of the individual text. In the context of 1790s political culture, their decisions were not without immediate personal and social consequences for those involved in trying to perform plays. The reach of the Lord Chamberlain's powers into the increasingly fashionable south-east coast resort town of Margate is another reminder of how Larpent, without exception, censored all British Royal theatres outside of Ireland.[28] The author of *The Whim* was Eglantine Wallace, who quickly produced a locally printed edition subtitled *With an Address to the Public, Upon the Arbitrary and Unjust Aspersion of the Licenser Against its Political Sentiments* (1795). Intending it as a means of 'alleviating the sorrows of those afflicted by the pinching hand of Poverty—Sickness—or Oppression' (p. 3), Wallace made sure it was locally understood that it had been *Offered to be Acted for the Benefit of the hospital and Poor of the Isle of Thanet, But Refused the Royal Licence.* With both the social confidence and the financial means to produce her locally printed edition, Wallace included in its accompanying rebuttal a copy of her correspondence with the Marquis of Salisbury, the current Lord Chamberlain (pp. 5–6). Lady Wallace's location in

---

[27] Larpent Plays, 1093 [Lady Eglantine Wallace] *The Whim A Comedy, for the use of the Theatre Royal at Margate*, Huntington Library, Calif.

[28] Margate had been a Royal theatre only since 1786: Tracy C. Davis, *The Economics of the British Stage 1800–1914* (Cambridge: Cambridge University Press, 2000), 371 n. 28.

the minor aristocracy (her husband a baronet) did nothing to secure the play for representation. So sensitive were the unwritten codes that the Larpents interpreted and imposed, that membership of the ruling class did not confer the right of criticism of that class, at least not when that criticism was to be staged before an audience.

It is not difficult to appreciate the consternation the incident must have caused in Margate. The Theatre Royal manager had marked Larpent's copy as 'intended to be performed with all convenient speed', indicating that he assumed no problem was expected for its three-night run. In any event, Wallace 'gave it to be rehearsed . . . the house on its being announced, was overflowing, and those who were sent away, were not more disappointed, than those who squeesed [*sic*] in' (p. 4). With the audience already seated in the theatre they had to be told that, fearing for the loss of the royal patent, the piece would not be performed that night because 'the Licencer disapproved of the Piece as exceptionable' (p. 4). As it happened, the Theatre Royal Margate from its earliest beginnings was enmeshed in negotiating the cross-currents of patronage, plea-making, and the operation of covert societies common to late eighteenth-century England.

The Theatre Royal at Margate had developed from a stage set up in an adapted stable behind a local inn where it met opposition from a female manager, Mrs Baker, who formed her own company of actors until overruled by the site owner, who petitioned Parliament to build a new theatre with the coveted Royal Patent in 1786. While Sarah Baker literally transported her wooden structure to nearby Faversham, the *c*.400-capacity Theatre Royal Margate was opened in a ceremony 'attended by the free-masons of Margate, &c. in honour of Robson [an ex-Covent Garden actor] master of the Lodge, who sung several masonic songs, accompanied by a ban of music'.[29] Although Wallace may not have been too

---

[29] James Winston, *The Theatric Tourist; Being A Genuine Collection Of Correct Views, With Brief And Authentic Historical Accounts Of All The Principal Provincial Theatres In The United Kingdom. Replete With Useful And Necessary Information To Theatrical Professors, Whereby They May Learn How To Chuse And Regulate Their Country Engagements; And With Numerous Anecdotes To Amuse The Reader* (1805) 12–13.

worried for her economic future by being implicated in writing a banned play, she was fully aware of the subtle social aspersions created by Larpent's apparent 'right to affix odium to the reputation of any individual, by such unjust and injurious remarks' (p. 4). Wallace believed *The Whim* was deemed 'obnoxious from its Political sentiments' (p. 4) and as 'an apparent infringement of good order' which had been 'rejected on account of its Political sentiments' (p. 7).

The actual bureaucratic process of censorship seems not to have worked very efficiently. Wallace reported that 'the Piece had been presented to a Mr. Larpent, (who, I am told your Lordship has appointed to inspect all productions for the Theatre) and that he found no objections to it, if signed by a Patentee, and that it would be Licensed on Monday' (p. 5). As it seemed to have been passed, rehearsals went ahead, 'when a letter arrived, saying, that Mr. Larpent had objected to it from its exceptional sentiments' (p. 6). This fumbling incompetence was typical of Larpent's manner of operating, an approach which had more serious implications with his granting of a licence to the Adelphi's *Tom and Jerry* in 1821. This was why, unable to stop the notices of performance, the Margate audience assembled in the theatre. While some of Wallace's ire was reserved for the particular office of the Lord Chamberlain's Examiner ('did the Licenser permit more satire, more sentiment, and less ribaldry, *outré* pantomime, and folly, to appear under his auspices, it would be doing the State more service, than thus taking alarm at *The Whim*' (p. 14)), she also commented on the wider political and moral implications of such a 'despotic yes, or no' (p. 10).

The Whim was directed at expressing Eglantine Wallace's 'contempt for profligacy, injustice, or deceit, even if detected in a palace' (p. 9). Although it never employs caricature or ridicule, *The Whim* gently implied the existence of a morally corrupt gentry while stressing the positive role of duty and responsibility in ensuring the continuance of a just and stable society: 'A long list of ancestors,—large estates, and high sounding titles, are what are called Noble;—but reason, estimates the value of the man, not the splendour of his name; and looks up with disgust, to those, who under the influence of grandeur indulge atrocities and vices, which would render a plebeian an outcast from mankind' (p. 10). Her preface drew attention to the lessons learned from the French Revolution, where the 'System once adopted in France, that it was the Prerogative of the Nobles to be free from censure,—ridicule, or comparison, filled the honest mind with contempt, or hatred; whilst the Great, with haughty arrogance exulted indulgences, which would have been deemed crimes in their inferiors' (p. 13). Although this emphasis on the duties of rank and station was not particularly unusual in the age of Hannah More and Jane Austen, Eglantine Wallace is exceptional in promoting press freedom and uncensored drama as agents of a counterbalancing social satire: 'Happy! thrice happy, had the French Nation been! had the press, or drama, permitted those who were disinterested in the cause of honor and humanity, to raise their voice, to reprobate or ridicule their vices' (p. 13). She even dared ironize the liberalizing influence of Tom Paine: 'This reflection might have rescued them in time from vices, immoralities, and cruelties, which have finally hurled them from their fancied greatness, and deprived them of even the *Rights of Men!*' (p. 14). While Wallace obviously felt 'baulked in my charitable scheme' (p. 7), she was motivated to defend her playwriting in the printed edition since, to all intents and purposes, *The Whim* was now rendered unperformable.

At issue in Larpent's decision to refuse the licence was Wallace's avowed attempt to represent on stage a play showing how 'many of our great people are by their immoral and injudicious conduct destructive to the respectability and tranquillity of the community' (p. 15). It is only by turning to Larpent's excisions that one realizes the modest nature of Wallace's social criticism. The Examiner's verdict that *The Whim* was 'Prohibited from being acted' offered no middle-ground for negotiation. Although the offending speeches are clearly marked up in the licenser's copy sent to him by the Margate management, he appears to have erred on the side of official caution when considering the piece written by a woman who had, in the printed edition at least, made very clear her philanthropic aim of alleviating not just 'Poverty' and 'Sickness' but also 'Oppression' (p. 3). Typical of the excisions Larpent marked (indicated by shading here) is the following 'below-stairs' exchange between the two servants, Fag and Nell, employed by the genial Lord Crotchet:[30]

FAG. Lord Nell we shall so enjoy ourselves I shall have a Ball and Supper, the best wines. I shall make so pretty a Gentleman shan't I my Dear?

NELL. That you will, none of your degenerate wishy washy Fellows like our debauchee *Nobles* but a fine bold dashing Fellow.

Lord Crotchet, whose beliefs are both followed and understood by Fag and Nell, makes ancient Roman traditions of virtues and conduct his ideals. His 'whim' is to have a night of Saturnalia, an event which might have been locally still recognizable in Twelfth Night customs of 'misrule'. Nevertheless, it is extraordinary that Larpent excised the whole of the following speech:

CROT. there was then [in Roman times] due distinction of Personages— no distinction of Ranks the haughty Patricians and the proud Partisans were obliged to bend, for the Masters that day become the Servants of Even their Slaves, and heard with impunity them ridicule their Follies or execrate their Corruption.

Wallace's emphasis on the importance of individual responsibilities of behaviour ('due distinction of Personages') is shown in *The Whim* to have been learned by the servants who follow Crotchet's example. Again, Larpent cut their lines:

NELL. But I fancy our Nobles are not so good as the antients were.

FAG. I fear indeed many of them would feel the vengeance of their dependants for their Tyrannical Caprices before the day was over.

NELL. Ha! Ha! Ha! I cant help laughing at the sorry figure some of Our Luberly Great Men would cut if thus levelled.

---

[30] Larpent Plays, 1093, [Eglantine Wallace], *The Whim A Comedy, for the use of the Theatre Royal at Margate*, Huntington Library, Calif.

Extraordinarily, these cuts show that Larpent was not prepared to tolerate the representation on stage of deferential servants profiting from examples set by their employer, even when they themselves directly acknowledge their homespun belief in the status quo:

> NELL. And I for my part shall never in future repine, whatever my Situation sensible that if one will make the best of it, one may derive advantage even from other People's Whims; I wish not for my part to see the Order of things Changed but I wish every Body would remember as well as I do a Maxim I learnt at Mrs Reforms School never to let a flaw be long of Mending Else it would soon get incurable; for a stitch in time, saves nine—

The entirety of Crotchet's concluding speech was also cut, despite its loyalist language and the patriotic sentiment so obviously aimed at the well-to-do sections of the Margate audience:

> CROT. I shall never again give up even for a Day, the Duty of my Situation, But endeavour to Act worthy of those three Valuable Parts of Our Glorious Constitution. Who I hope will for Ages each distinctly discharge uncorruptibly their several Duties without encroaching on each others Prerogative So that the Name of Britons to the latest time, may be the Envy and Admiration of Mankind.

What is remarkable about the text of *The Whim* is that it falls so well short of being an exercise in coruscating wit or biting satire. Neither is it ideologically radical in anything that can be inferred from its political attitudes. Indeed, its political sentiments are, if anything, decidedly conservative-patrician mildly tinged with liberalism.

The reasons for the prohibition are obscure but may have something to do with the author's own tenacious personality coupled with some level of London-based concern about events in Margate. Home Office files show that in the summer of the previous year the authorities had been trying to trace a political extremist called Williams who was believed to be in hiding in Margate. Unusually, a Margate official had been summoned to the Home office department for consultation over the matter but had missed the

letter requesting his presence, forcing him to write a letter of reply
(and thereby placing concerns about Margate in the official records).
The Margate informant thought Williams 'may easily be trac'd' (a
clear enough indication of the level of local surveillance) but the
reporter also gave the name of another disaffected individual (the
dubiously named 'Smith') who 'seems very active here & talks in a
stile [*sic*] extremely inimical to Government'. In short, the informant
added that—having no nearer magistrate than Dover—'we have
too many persons among the Visitants who allow themselves large
latitude in conversations'.[31] While the idea of Margate being over-
run by revolutionary holiday visitors seems far-fetched to us, its
facilities as a port en route to continental Europe may have been
of concern to those in London. Crucially, the Margate informant
linked the activities of 'Visitants' 'inimical to Government' with
a recent incident in which the 'Treasurers Office' at the Theatre
Royal, Margate, had been 'burglariously entered by some Villain
or Villains' and for whose apprehension a handbill was published
and a reward offered.[32] The link between centralized London control and events in Margate concerned with the theatre is empirical
evidence of the crudely effective rudiments of Government poli-
cing operating in the 1790s and constituted in the departments of
the Lord Chamberlain and the Home Office. Whether such surveillance and control was ever more coherently implemented than
two separate departments responding to events on an ad hoc basis,
it is difficult to judge. Certainly, surprising though it may seem,
the necessary apparatus was already in place in seaside Margate
by 1794–5.

As far as her own political views were concerned, Eglantine
Wallace had every reason also to be wary of revolutionary disruption.
As an eyewitness of the first stages of the French Revolution, in her

---

[31] PRO HO 42/33. 25, 3 August 1794.
[32] PRO HO 42/33. 25, [handbill] *Robbery. Whereas the Office belonging to the Theatre,
was last Night between the Hours of Eleven and Twelve, burglariously entered by some Villain
or Villains, who broke open the Desk and stole the following Property: . . . Reward of Twenty
Pounds . . . Theatre Royal, Margate, Saturday, August 2, 1794.*

book *The Conduct of the King of Prussia and General Dumourier, Investigated* (1793)—published two years before *The Whim*—she described how in October 1789 she had been arrested in Paris by 'sixty National troops and sixteen Swiss guards' and accused of being an English spy.[33] After seven hours of interrogation (allegedly with a sword raised behind her head), she was released but had to pass through a drunken mob disguised by 'having decorated myself before I set out, with the tri-couleur ribbons' of the revolutionaries.[34] The chaotic military and civil circumstances of these times, living in the besieged town of Breda where she watched a tri-coloured Tree of Liberty planted in the market square, are presented as a judicious narrative of the problems of the royalist sympathizer General Dumourier but her account does not attempt to exaggerate the violence of the revolutionists.[35] Nevertheless, her skills as a writer should not be underestimated, nor her ability to adopt elusive personas. In 1794 she published a satirical *Sermon Addressed to the People, Pointing out the only sure method to obtain a speedy peace and reform*. Wallace's sermon, unlike most similar contemporary publications of its kind, does not specify either its location or its congregation. It is an exacting piece of writing, nicely poised as a series of ironic understatements: 'Sedition on the part of the people, is as much a breach of that contract, which is the very soul of the constitution, as if any other branch was to usurp despotic independent controul' (p. 11). Less equivocal, especially in the light of her own personal experiences, is her declaration, 'Look at France! And exult in the mild protection of your own government' (p. 18), but how does one read the following, written a year after a Suspension of Habeas Corpus:

What honest man would not rather place an extra degree of power in the hands of men who have proved disinterested faithful servants

[33] Eglantine Wallace, *The Conduct of the King of Prussia and General Dumourier, Investigated* (1793), 71, 129. On Charles Dumouriez at this time, see Simon Schama, *Citizens: A Chronicle of the French Revolution* (London: Viking, 1989), 684–9.

[34] Wallace, *Conduct of the King of Prussia*, 73.

[35] Ibid. 99–100.

of their countrymen! who have never in the smallest degree abused by an arbitrary act, that power which the wisdom of Parliament last year thought fit to give them? Who, I say, would not rather be at the mercy of such men, than become the bleeding, trembling slaves of a lawless mob? (p. 11).

What may also have alarmed Larpent, together with these two disconcerting works, was his knowledge of her Covent Garden play of seven years earlier, *The Ton; or, Follies of Fashion. A Comedy* (1788). Although it has been described as a failure, its production encountered malicious controversy precisely because of its satire upon upper-class society.[36]

Although rather a verbose play, rumours had gathered before its first night that *The Ton* satirized the manners and peccadilloes of several notable people, including the up-and-coming lawyer Thomas Erskine. Judging by her remarks in the Preface to the printed edition, it is possible Wallace first intended naming them directly in the production. According to her, the Covent Garden audience was filled with 'hissers' who had 'spread abroad, that it was filled with indecencies, and sent information to several Ladies who had boxes, that they had better stay away, as a riot was determined upon' (Preface, pp. i–ii).[37] The Prologue (written by herself) touched on the themes of both political reform ('While Reformation lifts her tardy hand | To scourge at length transgression from the land') and contracts of social duty owed by the aristocracy ('Who shall presume the rule of right to draw | For those who *make, enforce,* and *break* the law?') which are common to *The Whim* and *A Sermon Addressed to the People* (Prologue, p. i). While the exact import or register of *The Ton*'s topical allusions are now almost lost to us, the satiric intent

[36] 'The former [play, *The Ton* ...] was, in April 1788, acted in the Theatre Royal, Covent Garden, but was disapproved, and an attempt to reintroduce it also failed' (Charles Rogers, *The Book of Wallace* (1889), i. 87). However, a Dublin edition of *The Ton* was printed the same year as the London printing.

[37] The following is a good example of the play's comedy of manners: 'LADY RAYMOND. And it is quite bourgeois to countenance one's relations, except [the] equally fashionable' (Eglantine Wallace, *The Ton; or, Follies of Fashion. A Comedy* (1788), 29).

of the Prologue's conclusion is clear enough in its condemnation of metropolitan patrician mores:

> In London, happily, our zeal's more warm;
> Here live the great examples of reform:
> With pure disint'rest, each devoutly labours
> To mend, if not *himself,* at least his neighbours. (Prologue, p. i)

If it is the case that Larpent kept some kind of informal dossier or memoir on Eglantine Wallace, it is possible that he pre-empted her further commentaries on the upper classes by banning *The Whim* after his experience of having licensed *The Ton*.

It is striking how, in the 1790s, the dominant literary discourse of sensibility was entirely politically impotent to bring about alleviation of stage censorship. The production of *The Whim* for the charitable cause of '*the hospital and Poor of the Isle of Thanet*', with its implicit invocation of social benevolence, was insufficient to ensure that these Enlightenment virtues guaranteed a licence for performance. Instead, the actual practice of Larpent's censorship of British dramatic writing was unprincipled, without a coherent strategy of excision or refusal other than the gut feeling that the staging of contemporary social or political issues had to be prevented. Wallace had no problem in printing her play, complete with its polemical preface, but her difficulties in staging *The Whim* only serve to manifest the gulf between the political treatment of writing for the stage and writing employing the other literary forms. Wallace's true ideological sister is Jane Austen, yet the apparatus of censorship afflicted only the author of stage plays.

The workings of the process of dramatic censorship were continuously subject to the totally unaccountable principles of the Larpents. In April 1794 they received the manuscript of Edmund Eyre's (*four*-act) tragedy *The Maid of Normandy; or, The Death of the Queen of France* (1794) from the Theatre Royal, Bath. Anna recorded what were, in effect, their usual working arrangements for censorship: 'Evening worked Mr Larpent read loud a MSS Tragedy from a Country Theatre The Death of ye Queen of France, And the Maid of Normandy. A Strange, Absurd jumble of C. Cordel [*sic*] killing Marat.' Three years later, Eyre was still bitter at how 'the Lord-Chamberlain, by his prohibitory mandate, [had] consigned it to oblivion', although he clearly understood that it had been 'destroyed by the interference of a power, which no doubt was regulated by prudential motives'. As far as Eyre was concerned, 'that consideration silenced every murmur of discontent' and, indeed, his deeply conformist disposition is revealed in the avidly loyalist ideology of his satiric poetry.[38] However, such loyalism did not benefit the fate of his play for the Theatre Royal, Bath.

After John Larpent's read-through, the pair reached their verdict and retired to bed, deeming that the play was 'as devoid of poetry or judgement as it can be & highly improper just now were it otherwise. Supt at 10, prayed to bed at 11'.[39] One of the aspects of the play Anna particularly disliked was its sentimentality, what she called the 'ridiculous attempt at simplicity in the young King's Conversation, one part perfectly ridiculous' but especially where 'The Boy asks if God will take him on his knee & fondle him'.[40] Unfortunately, a copy of this 1794 submission of *The Maid of Normandy* has not survived in the Larpent collection, but their working practices in censoring this particular text can be closely followed from the copy surviving when the play was resubmitted (and again refused a licence) by the Theatre Royal, Norwich, in 1804.[41]

[38] Edmund John Eyre, *The Fatal Sisters; or, The Castle of the Forest: A Dramatic Romance, of Five Acts. With a Variety of Poetic Essays* (1797), p. vii.

[39] Diaries of Anna Margaretta Larpent, vol. i, 14 April 1794, Huntington Library, Calif. The manuscript of Larpent's copy of the play is not in the Huntington collection.

[40] Edmund John Eyre, *The Maid of Normandy; or, The Death of the Queen of France, A Tragedy in Four Acts; as Performed at the Theatre Wolverhampton* (1794): DAUPHIN. 'But, will he take me to his bosom, kiss, | And fondle o'er me, as my father did?' (p. 33).

[41] It is possible that the text retained in the Larpent collection and dated 7 May 1804 suffered some contemporary administrative error as to its dating, either during Larpent's lifetime or when it passed through Payne Collier's ownership, and that this manuscript is actually the one recorded by Anna Larpent in her 1794 diary entry. With the play having been refused at Bath in 1794, Norwich would have still been obliged to submit a copy for censorship in 1804. Nevertheless, it is difficult to reconstruct a scenario in 1804 which would have made the resuscitation of a ten-year-old tragedy about Charlotte Corday and Marie Antoinette topical enough for Norwich to have revived it. It is further perplexing that Norwich Theatre Royal did not save the labours of a scribe by submitting

The subject of the treatment of the Queen of France had always been presented as pathetic right from the time of Burke's *Reflections on the Revolution in France* (1791) and certainly Eyre's portrayal of the final 'Dungeon' scene emphasized her ill-treatment, showing the 'Queen discovered on the Ground. Straw & Hair dishevelled'. Eyre also devoted a generous number of lines to the Queen, enabling her to tell her own story in fairly lengthy speeches. Even the anti-republican ideological commitments of Charlotte Corday are modulated by personal grief for her dead fiancé ('When by the sev'ring Axe Alberto died [*weeps*] . . . | To avenge his murder, & my Countrys wrong . . . | To Act a deed, that will immortalize my name | What will they say of her, who scorning death | With Roman courage & heroic fire | Singly step'd forward to preserve her country'). In other words, *The Maid of Normandy* was filled with sentimental outpourings, a discourse of sensibility Eyre did not confine to royalty alone. Similarly, the crudely portrayed sound effects of the execution also attempt crude bathos: '[*Drums—The Queen led off—Scene a Front Street The Procession passes—Drums Scene. Scaffold & Guillotine Procession Enters. Queen Ascends—appears to pray—kneels—& at the moment she lays her head on the Guillotine the Curtain suddenly falls . . . The muffled Drums—continuing all the time & for some minutes after the Curtain falls.*]'[42] Such pathetic scenes were common in the visual print culture, to be found in such prints as Domenico Pellegrini's *The Dauphin taken from his Mother* (March 1794) or his *The Persecuted Queen hurried at the Dead of Night into a Common Prison* (March 1795).[43]

Obviously, it is extremely difficult now to reconstruct exactly what type of affront to political sentiment or emotional sensibilities the Larpents thought they were countering in Eyre's *Maid of Normandy*.

---

an amended printed text to Larpent by using one of the two printed editions available since 1794.

[42] Larpent Plays, 1413, Edmund John Eyre, *The Death of the Queen of France A Play in Four Acts*. Theatre Royal Norwich, 7 May 1804, Huntington Library, Calif.

[43] David Bindman (ed.), *The Shadow of the Guillotine: Britain and the French Revolution* (London: British Museum, 1989), cat. nos. 133, 134.

The suppression of Eyre's play signals the material implentation of an entire code of contemporary attitudes to Marie Antoinette which still remain to be recovered. Judith Pascoe's discussion of the context of Marie Antoinette's theatricalization in British culture seems to be quite compromised by the absence of *The Maid of Normandy* from her study.[44] The French Queen's commodification in contemporary British culture, signalled in Pascoe's chapter by Mary Robinson's incorporation of Marie Antoinette's self-dramatization and its contrast to Mary Wollstonecraft's prudent refutation of her theatrical power, seems to indicate a fairly stable set of attitudes towards the Queen, ones which were highly polarized but concretely grounded. Eyre's play, however, and its suppression by the Larpents, points to the much more complex underlying culture theatre had to negotiate.

Eyre's sentimentalization of the Queen is dramatized along predictable lines established by Burke, but *The Maid of Normandy* balances its empathy with the French monarch by having it preceded by the anti-republican interventionism of Charlotte Corday. On the basis of Pascoe's reading of Marie Antoinette's popular consumption as a role model either affirmed (as in the case of Robinson) or else denied (as in the case of Wollstonecraft), one might have predicted that Eyre's play would have been enthusiastically received by the Larpents, but that was not the case. Instead of welcoming Eyre's Marie Antoinette as a figure symptomatic of the dangers of revolutionary violence and the abuse of royalty, quite unpredictably Larpent suppressed the entire play. Larpent particularly excised those sections of Eyre's play relating to the suffering of the Queen, censoring these with as much enthusiasm as he did the passages relating to Charlotte Corday's role as anti-republican assassin. In other words, when presented with Eyre's dramatization of one of the age's most celebrated examples of suffering royalty, John Larpent decided to stifle *The Maid of Normandy*. It is evident that the Larpents thought the mere spectacle of European royalty being represented on stage as the subject of popular persecution

---

[44] Judith Pascoe, *Romantic Theatricality: Gender, Poetry, and Spectatorship* (Ithaca, NY: Cornell University Press, 1997), 95–129.

and domestic distress was sufficient to ban the play on the grounds of its appearing to be some kind of advocacy by materializing regicide on English playboards. At the very least, the ban testifies to the contemporary political potency of the theatre. However, it is also possible to localize the Larpents' fears into more topical manifestations of anxiety concerning royalty's relationship with the theatre.

In 1794 there was a stampede at the Theatre Royal, Haymarket, during which more than twenty people died. An unknown activist, perhaps within the London Corresponding Society, quickly produced an anonymous handbill drawing attention to how the King and Queen had continued to attend an array of functions, uninterrupted, including a 'Rout', a concert of 'Ancient Musick', and a visit to the Theatre Royal, Covent Garden. The handbill starkly contrasted the royals' continuance of their amusements after the deaths of English citizens ('it was *said* that THEIR MAJESTIES were not acquainted with it') with the period of official mourning declared after the execution of Louis XVI ('the avowed *Enemy of this Country*') during which 'Public Amusements' had been suspended. As the handbill rhetorically put it, 'Which of these Circumstances *ought* to have caused the most public Demonstrations of SORROW?' If plebeian sensitivities, directly reaching street level through the medium of handbills, were enraged at royalty frequenting playhouses, then the Larpents seem to have decided that staging the death of the Queen of France was too provocative in attempting to enlist the sort of sympathy declared wanting amongst the British monarchy for the dead Londoners at the Haymarket. The extent to which, at a formal level, Government was prepared to react coercively to such handbill agitation is proven by the placement of the unique surviving copy of this bill in the array of papers seized and collected as evidence by the Treasury Solicitor for the autumn 1794 treason trials of the London Corresponding Society leaders.[45]

In other words, as so often in this period, the overriding urge to repress dramatic representation on the public stage was not countered

---

[45] PRO TS 11/966 [handbill] *Theatre, Haymarket*, 17 February 1794.

by the presence of the late eighteenth-century aestheticization of sentimentality or sensibility. Instead, the day-to-day reactions and perceptions by the Larpents to the movement of politics became the chaotic cues for their repression of drama.

Keeping the lid on radicalism by seizing handbills about theatre was the Government's specific local intervention but managing the general representative contents of drama was the responsibility of the Larpents. With both ends of the spectrum of public expression policed, repression could be complete. Noticeable by their absence are the influences of the polite expressive genres of sensibility and taste readily found within the contemporary vocabulary of the dramatic or visual arts. Whatever their perceived force by virtue of their social distribution, sensibility and taste were inconsequential when it came to the exercise of dramatic censorship. With even the anti-republicanism of Charlotte Corday ('the Heroine of the North', as Eyre called her) being censored, *The Maid of Normandy* provides an unforgiving reminder that the contemporary politics of culture, even when elegantly proposed in Judith Pascoe's chapter, do not readily render themselves available for reconstruction.

Even if the cult of sensibility was unable (or unwilling) to engage with the problem of stage censorship, it seems certain Edmund Eyre's *The Maid of Normandy* found a provincial performance. The subtitle of *The Maid*'s imprint, *as Performed at the Theatre Wolverhampton*, suggests the identity of the venue, and Eyre's poem printed in 1797, entitled 'An Occasional Address, Spoken by the Author, at the Theatre in Wolverhampton, on the Night of his Benefit', seems to confirm both the playhouse and that Eyre stood on stage himself to declaim how '*We* to an English Jury trust *our* right! | And 'tis in them alone we rightly see | The grand Palladium of our Liberty!'[46] However, in the Preface to the published edition of *The Maid of Normandy*, Eyre could hardly be more explicitly

---

[46] Eyre, *Fatal Sisters*, 135. Eyre's comedy *Consequences; or, The School for Prejudice* (1794) was also performed at Wolverhampton (as well as Worcester and Shrewsbury), so it may be this benefit night to which his occasional poem refers. For other provincial plays in the same English Midlands region, see Ch. 9.

loyalist, saying that 'the subject of the present drama is founded upon Republican-Cruelty [*sic*]' and warning against 'Men, who hide their flagitious villanies under the specious title of Reformists'. For good measure he added, 'Such is the admirable Constitution of the English Government that no Nation in the world can pretend to a better model, and no People in the world may live more happy if they please.'[47] But this was not good enough for the Larpents because, of course, John Larpent also 'Refused' a production of *The Maid of Normandy* at the Theatre Royal, Norwich, ten years later in 1804.[48]

The suppressed *Maid of Normandy*, Cumberland's *Richard the Second*, together with the proven reach of both the Home Office and the censorship process into seaside Margate, are the censored texts of 1790s drama which reveal the microhistories of the day-to-day machinations of the political control of literature.

[47] Eyre, *The Maid of Normandy*, Preface. Errata list in the edition is dated 16 March 1794.
[48] Larpent Plays, 1413, *The Death of the Queen of France A Play in Four Acts*. Theatre Royal Norwich, 7 May 1804, Huntington Library, Calif.

4

Theatrical Subcultures: Fireworks, Freemasonry, and Philip de Loutherbourg

This chapter will examine the skills, networks of friendship, and common mentalities present within London theatrical subcultures prior to the French Revolution. It will be shown that republican ideologies, mystical spiritualities, and Masonic organization were already intricately distributed and connected through the metropolis's dramatic performance spaces. What emerges in this account is a demonstration of a skilled artisan public sphere capable of innovating and reinventing its range of symbolic practices through identifiable social communities connected with the economy of London theatre. The theatrical microhistories uncovered were involved in such things as the regular firework displays of London pleasure grounds, the use of Masonic imagery in the major theatres and all combined with active involvements in painting, the print trade and the period's wider relationship with print culture.

In 1773 David Garrick created a London sensation by employing the French scene designer and painter Philip de Loutherbourg. Their joint debut production was *A Christmas Tale*, a seasonal entertainment whose first night was at Drury Lane Theatre the day after Boxing Day in that year.[1] Although Garrick wrote the words, broadly based on Charles Simon Favart's *La Fée Urgèle*, the piece

---

[1] To get some idea of the atmosphere surrounding these entertainments, nearly sixty years later, see 'Christmas and the Theatre', in James Henry Leigh Hunt, *Leigh*

was constructed to fit a set of scenic designs which de Loutherbourg had created almost a year earlier.[2] Garrick's entertainment, with music by Charles Dibdin, appears to have been reasonably successful but mainly on account of de Loutherbourg's innovative scenic effects which, in turn, enabled de Loutherbourg to develop his Eidophusikon multimedia theatrical exhibit of 1781.[3] Nevertheless, both contemporary and modern criticism has largely bypassed *A Christmas Tale*. Garrick's most recent editors have commented that its 'total of nineteen performances is phenomenal for an entertainment devoid of character development and even common sense'.[4] Many contemporaries were hardly less sceptical. The *Westminster Magazine*, reviewing a condensed version performed as an afterpiece three years later, wrote that 'Though greatly shortened, it still contains nothing.'[5] However, what has never been investigated is the extent to which *A Christmas Tale* exhibits de Loutherbourg's quite specific spiritual interests typical of intellectual cross-currents within the range of occupational skills and mentalities associated within London theatre and print trades. *A Christmas Tale*'s confident and visually innovative transmission of Masonic symbolism is indicative of contemporary networks of skill and sociability existing in London's theatreland.

A Christmas Tale particularly reflects de Loutherbourg's own extensive interest in spirituality. The historically marked features of these spiritualities make them particularly recoverable by modern scholars because of their specificity. These metropolitan spiritualities were closely associated with the politicized role of alternative religions in contemporary London as typified in the kinds of radicalized millenarianism now increasingly familiar as the stuff of

Hunt's Dramatic Criticism, 1808–1831, ed. Lawrence Huston Houtchens and Carolyn Washburn Houtchens (New York: Columbia University Press, 1949), 254–5.

[2] Ralph G. Allen, '*A Christmas Tale*, or, Harlequin Scene Painter', *Texas Studies in Literature*, 19 (1974), 149–61.

[3] Sybil Rosenfeld, 'The Eidophusikon Illustrated', *Theatre Notebook*, 18:2 (1963), 52–4.

[4] Harry William Pedicord and Frederick Louis Bergmann (eds.), *The Plays of David Garrick* (Carbondale and Edwardsville: Southern Illinois University Press, 1980), ii. 349.

[5] Ibid. 347, quoting *Westminster Magazine*, October 1776.

contemporary counter public spheres with plebeian manifestations. De Loutherbourg's contribution of a pervasive Freemasonry to *A Christmas Tale*, which perhaps would have been entirely typical of artisan spiritualities of the later 1780s and 1790s, seemingly stands at odds with modern notions of David Garrick's urbanity and 'sterling reputation'.[6] However, while de Loutherbourg's personal politics cannot be readily deduced, he can clearly be associated with several strands of religious millenarianism common to radical activists in the London print trade. It may simply be the case that the political incarnations of millenarianism were not so clear-cut or as well defined in the early 1770s. The cross-currents between radical politics, millenarianism, and the theatre are typified in the complex networks of friendship, profession, and sociability linked to print culture represented by the likes of the Huguenot soldier and polemicist Major Peter Labilliere, the friend of Spitalfields typefounder and millenarian pressman Robert Hawes.

The rise of London's print trades and the capital's status as a major provider in the national economy of arts and luxury trades ensured that such networks prospered, even when attached to the more traditional professions of service in the empire's army and navy. The principal economic rationale of such circles of sociability, of which Freemasonry was a part, was that these mid-eighteenth-century networks and connections enabled professionals with employable skills, but little capital, to maintain levels of continued contact with each other to help ensure their success in the job market. Arguably, they were particularly vital to people such as the Huguenot Labilliere or the immigrant theatre workers de Loutherbourg and the firework maker and printseller Torré.

To the modern reader encountering it for the first time, *A Christmas Tale* may best be described as a kind of cross between Milton's *Comus* and Mozart's *The Magic Flute* (1791). Assuming that Garrick was

---

[6] For a rare Garrick foray into political satire and summary of modern criticism, see Phyllis T. Dircks, 'David Garrick, George III, and the Politics of Revision', *Philological Quarterly*, 76:3 (1997), 289–312.

not himself interested in mystical religions (although his Huguenot origins must have originally made him distinct from many of his polite contemporaries), it must be the case that the frequent allusions to Freemasonry in *A Christmas Tale*, and common to *The Magic Flute*, owe rather more to Philip de Loutherbourg than to David Garrick. In the 1760s and 1770s, Masonic lodges were occasional financial backers of entertainments at Covent Garden, the Haymarket, and Drury Lane.[7] By the time of Covent Garden's rebuild after the fire of 1808, the Prince of Wales, incongruously dressed as the Grand Master and accompanied by six Freemasons, laid the foundation stone with a silver gilt trowel accompanied by the Earl of Moira, the Deputy Grand Master.[8] Interest in Masonry in general was such that, within a couple of years of *A Christmas Tale*, William Hutchinson, the Barnard Castle, County Durham Freemason, had published his *Spirit of Masonry in Moral and Elucidatory Lectures* (1775) which, with the Grand Lodge's sanction, was intended to introduce the history and tenets of the Masons to the wider public and to help quell perennial fears as to Masonic loyalty.

In *A Christmas Tale*, an underworld of evil spirits ruled by the 'Bad Magician' Nigromant has to be defeated before the lovers Floridor and Camilla can find happiness. The escape of the inhabitants of the underworld occurs when the clown figure Tycho '[*Falls asleep and drops his wand; upon which, it thunders; the dens burst open, and various evil spirits of both sexes enter promiscuously, and viciously express their joy.*]' (p. 25).[9] The dramatic opportunities of such a scene are obvious. In the printed edition of the work, de Loutherbourg

[7]   Charles Beecher Hogan, *The London Stage 1660–1800* (Carbondale, Ill.: Southern Illinois University Press, 1968), 1398, 1477, 1548, 1725, 1912: *The Royal Slave*, 15 January 1768, Drury Lane; *The Orphan*, 1 February 1770, Covent Garden; *The Maid of the Mill*, 10 May 1771, Covent Garden; *King Richard III*, 20 May 1773, Covent Garden; 'Mason's Song', 21 September 1775, Haymarket.

[8]   Charles Isaac Mungo Dibdin, *History and Illustrations of the London Theatres* (1826), 18–19.

[9]   David Garrick, *A New Dramatic Entertainment, Called A Christmas Tale. In Five Parts. As it is Performed at the Theatre-Royal in Drury Lane. Embellished with an Etching, by Mr. Loutherbourg, 2nd ed.* (T. Becket, 1774), frontispiece.

included an etched frontispiece showing the den of demons clawing at their bars. However, *A Christmas Tale*'s main claim for a place in theatrical history lies in de Loutherbourg's introduction of new and extraordinary effects of scenery and lighting contrasting with orchestrated transitions of sound and colour. The principal features of these effects can be recovered both from the text and from the stage directions:

CAMILLA. I heard strange noises in the air; even now my eyes are deceiv'd, or this garden, the trees, the flowers, the heav'ns change their colours to my sight, and seem to say something mysterious, which is not in my heart to expound. [*The objects in the garden vary their colours.*] (p. 26)

According to Henry Angelo (who claimed Garrick hired de Loutherbourg at his father's instigation), the foliage changed from green to 'blood colour', by an effect produced by 'placing different coloured silks in the flies, or side-scenes, which turned on a pivot, and, with lights behind, which so illumined the stage, as to give the effect of enchantment'.[10] Amidst familiar gender stereotyping ('SONG. O the freaks of womankind! ... | No whims will starve in woman's mind' [p. 6]), the story uses these scenic effects to pursue a narrative redolent of magical imagery drawn from Freemasonry.

A typical example of such Masonic imagery would be the 'magical' revelation to the audience of talismanic words signalling the triple virtues of Freemasonry which occur when Camilla addresses Floridor at the beginning of the piece:

See, and behold! [*The laurel unfolds and discovers the words Valor, Constancy, and Honour, in letters of gold.*] You have prov'd your *Love* to me, by its unfolding at your request—Now read what is more expected from you. (p. 8)

A Christmas Tale then initiates a 'lovers' trial', activated by Camilla, which reiterates the triple nature of these heroic qualities as well as

---

[10] Henry Angelo, *Reminiscences of Henry Angelo, With Memoirs of his Late Father and Friends* (1828), i. 15–16; ii. 326.

the existence of a subterranean world of evil, finally leading—via the implementation of the three virtues—to Floridor's arrival at the desired goal of love and harmony:

CAMILLA. You have *Valour* to protect us;—it is you Floridor must deliver me from him [Nigromant]; *valor, constancy*, and *honour*, may subdue all evil spirits, and it is by them alone, you can only reach the summit of your wishes.

FLORIDOR. Then I will prepare for the trial. (p. 10)

The text repeats the presence of the symbolic number three ('FLORIDOR. I will but say three words, and then I'll come. TYCHO. If you have three words, the lady will have three thousand' [p. 7]), a figure heavily implicated in Masonic symbolism.

Such was the extent of the Masonic presence in London theatre that it seems likely some of this Masonic imagery came about through the influence of *A Christmas Tale's* musical composer, Charles Dibdin, who later went on to write a pantomime, *Harlequin Freemason* (1780), Covent Garden's circumspectly reverential burlesque on Masonry which similarly stressed such triple symbolism in both its opening glee ('Proportion, strength, and force unite | With ease and symmetry' [p. 3]) and also in its finale:

> Let three times three
> The signal of our plaudit be,
> While we toast to the King and Craft! (p. 7)

Dibdin's diplomatically modulated equation of 'King and [Masonic] Craft' was designed to pre-empt the traditional accusation of Freemasonry's divided or double civic loyalties but, of course, *Harlequin Freemason* of 1780 was written before the illuminati scaremongering engendered by Burke's *Reflections on the Revolution in France* (1791) and Robison's *Proofs Of A Conspiracy Against All The Religions And Governments Of Europe, Carried On In The Secret Meetings Of Free Masons, Illuminati, And Reading Societies* (1797).[11] Long after such

[11] Richard Northcott, *Charles Dibdin's Masonic Pantomime 'Harlequin Freemason'* (1915). On Dibdin's membership, see p. 10.

alarms had subsided, Dibdin's son, Thomas John (who was accepted into a Maidstone Lodge of the Freemasons in the mid-1790s) chose to end his first year of managing the Surrey Theatre in 1817 with a revival of *A Christmas Tale*.[12]

Remarkably, Garrick's *A Christmas Tale* contains several striking parallels with the well-documented Masonic allusions in Mozart's rather later opera, *The Magic Flute* (1791). These parallels occur through their plots centring on dramatized trials by fire, water, and air and the disguise of a female heroine in the character of an old woman. In *A Christmas Tale* Floridor's father, Bonoro (the 'Good Magician'), charges his son with a straightforward act of purification and filial obedience:

BONORO. Rise Son, and attend to me—some uncommon act of valor is expected from you.—Before I obtain'd your mother's hand, I conquer'd, and imprison'd these evil spirits, [*pointing to the Dens*] who molested the world in various characters: You are now upon *your* trial—What can so strongly demand your valor, as the destruction at once of your rival Nigromant, and the leader of these evil spirits? (p. 15)

Such trials of the lovers are common to both Garrick's *A Christmas Tale* and Mozart's *Magic Flute*. There are also further parallels. Floridor's search for Camilla and the destruction of the dens of the evil spirits require him to plunge into the 'fiery lake' (elemental fire and water) of Nigromant where he also finds (as a third—slightly 'hidden'—symbol of air) Tycho's rival Faladel transformed into 'a large Owl' (p. 59). Similarly, Tamino and Pamina in *The Magic Flute* pass through trials by fire and water and, just as Papagena is disguised from her lover Papegeno as an old crone in *The Magic Flute*, so too Camilla appears to Floridor disguised as Grinnelda, a toothless old woman ('Madam Nose and Chin' (p. 49)). To Leigh Hunt, writing in 1819, the 'once so celebrated' Masonic allusions of *The Magic Flute* were clear reminders of typical late eighteenth-century fashions of belief.[13]

---

[12] Thomas Dibdin, *The Reminiscences of Thomas Dibdin* (1837), i. 207; ii. 147.
[13] 'The Magic Flute', in *Hunt's Dramatic Criticism*, 214–18, 216.

Amidst this wealth of Masonic imagery, *A Christmas Tale* also stages a series of political, religious, and social satires in its parade of the dangerous evil spirits kept restrained in the prisons of Bonoro until they escape when Tycho falls asleep on guard duty (pp. 20–3). Even here Masonic imagery must have been fairly evident to theatre audiences: the *Whitehall Evening Post*, reviewing the first perform-ances, reported that the dungeons have 'talismans upon the doors' signalling that they were understood not be purely mundane places of imprisonment.[14] To an extent, the eight evil spirits have been designated according to residual notions of medieval vices (the most obvious of which is gluttony) but the figures are also commentaries on contemporary society; the Glutton, for example, is more widely representative of luxury ('I am a luxurious spirit; I lov'd eating and drinking a little too much'), a frequent target of eighteenth-century dissent. The age's prevalent anti-Catholicism is present in the first character to appear, the Jesuit whose (punning) '*cardinal* virtues' or ambitions make him into what Tycho calls a social 'cormorant'. Also present is the Gamester, perhaps like the Jesuit another corrupter of human potential and sublimity ('We lost good fortunes, by keep-ing bad company'). Elsewhere, the corruption of spiritual genius is represented in the figures of the Actress and Poet: the Actress turns prostitute ('TYCHO. An actress! what spirit's that? ACTRESS. A spirit to entertain the public, but quitting that for *private* practice'), while the Poet is an antisocial literary hireling ('I am a poetical spirit . . . here's a satire upon your neighbours, and a panegyrick upon yourself'). The final three categories, the Attorney, Statesman, and Woman of Quality, are much more sharply focused on their negative social roles, particularly in the case of the latter.

The Attorney ('A little mistake in practice only') is a frequent butt of eighteenth-century dramatic satire on account of the profession's legendary financial rapaciousness ('ATTORNEY. I am an *Attorney*, at your service. TYCHO. Not at mine, I beg of you') but the Statesman, quite noticeably, has been confined to Bonoro's dungeons because

[14] Allen, '*A Christmas Tale*', *Studies in* 154.

of tyrannical tendencies ('I am a political spirit, I had a soul of fire, that overleap'd all laws and considerations'). The final evil spirit is the Woman of Quality, which is where Garrick's social satire is particularly sharp, especially because her forwardness is rewarded by her being heard last:

W OF Q. Turn to me, Signior; I have a right to be heard first.

TYCHO. Then don't lose your right, I beg you—Who are you, Madam?

W OF Q. A spirit of quality!

TYCHO. And what are you in there for, Madam?

W OF Q. For being a woman of quality.

TYCHO. A woman of bad qualities you mean—Fye upon you! who ever heard of a bad woman of quality? this is *scandalum magnatum horrendissimum!* You are a foul weed, and ought to be pluck'd out from the fair garden of nobility!

Obviously, Tycho's comment 'who ever heard of a bad woman of quality?' is one heavily intoned with irony for an audience who would have readily accepted her placement in Bonoro's dens. A scene such as this in *A Christmas Tale* illustrates how social and political satire embodied within a Masonic framework could be imported into a vehicle as apparently devoid of contemporary commentary as a Christmas entertainment. Moreover, the social satire contained in Garrick and de Loutherbourg's *Christmas Tale* of the early 1770s represents an aspect of theatricalized Masonry which would quickly vanish once scares over international conspiracies of Masonic *illuminati* began to gather in the early 1790s.

Nevertheless, *A Christmas Tale* is both surprisingly representative and expressive of the gradually changing ideologies of natural rights and liberty already gathering pace elsewhere in Enlightenment Europe. If *A Christmas Tale* stops short of a fully articulated language of natural rights, even if the Woman of Quality's inverted 'right to be heard first' hints at their immanence in theatric discourse, the entertainment is perfectly ready to include the idea of Liberty as a term denoting a culturally valid meaning with specific political overtones. This is expressed both directly by making 'Liberty' both a mode of denial for the Evil Spirits during their confinement but also, after Floridor has recaptured them by destroying the castle of Nigromant and passing through his own trials, 'Liberty' also functions as a (quite literal) state of enlightenment bequeathed by Bonoro. In the first 'CHORUS of EVIL SPIRITS, from the Prisons', the prisoners sing 'Grant us still more—sweet liberty' (p. 12). When they escape, the same chorus sings 'We fly, we sink, and run, | From tyranny, | To liberty! | To liberty—again!' (p. 25). In the same way as nationalist rhetorics were defined within popular song, it is perfectly credible that embryonic formulations of the rhetoric of natural rights had similar nativities in the theatre.

Finally, towards the end of *A Christmas Tale*, Bonoro summarizes the enlightenment he has helped move them to achieve:

> Ye once most wretched of mankind,
> By tyrant pow'r and lust confin'd,
> From vice and slav'ry free,
> Come join our sports, and this way move,
> To celebrate their virtuous love,
> And your own liberty! (p. 76)

As a signal embodiment of this abstraction, the entertainment ends with the simultaneous freeing of women from Nigromant's seraglio (wherein Camilla has been held). This transition from sexual confinement to freedom is figured through de Loutherbourg's scenic effects, the stage directions requiring that the scene *'grows dark; flames of fire are seen thro' the Seraglio windows; all but Floridor quit the place shrieking'* (p. 67) until, finally, *'The Seraglio breaks to pieces and discovers the whole palace in flames'* (p. 68) after which *'the different characters of the Seraglio, Men and Women, and join in A GRAND DANCE'* (p. 76). Despite the unlikely vehicle of a seasonal pantomime, *A Christmas Tale* celebrates the attainment of personal and sexual liberty via the processes of Freemasonry.

The imagery of Freemasonry is obviously abundant in *A Christmas Tale*, and not simply as arcane allusions to Masonic rites; the presence of Freemasonry also acts as a device through which the construction of contrarious worlds of light and dark, good and evil, trials by fire and water structure and inform the entire entertainment. Charles Dibdin's own latent Masonry, evident from the later *Harlequin Freemason*, must have contributed something to *A Christmas Tale* but de Loutherbourg's interest was probably the paramount influence.[15] If the Theatre Royal Drury Lane in the 1770s seems an unlikely setting for such an explicitly Masonic entertainment with its nascent allusions to natural rights, the interests of de Loutherbourg exist within a much wider framework of contemporary millenarian and spiritual subcultures.

Many of the cultural meanings of these social confluences are only recoverable with difficulty but are indicative of the complexities of contemporary mentalities. The networks of belief, politics, and literacy are bewilderingly complex. For example, the Swedenborgian shorthand writer, Manoah Sibly—the man who transcribed the debates at the 1794 treason trial of the London Corresponding Society activist Thomas Hardy—also published a book totally devoted to determining, astrologically, 'The Nativity of that Wonderful Phaenomenon, Oliver Cromwell'. Presumably the link between being an aspirant dissenting shorthand writer and being an astrologist, in the case of Sibly, was defined within an ideological wish to locate Cromwell as a heroic political ideal ('all nations were his friends ... it was his own prudence, counsel, courage, and conduct, that carried him through').[16] Something of the inexplicable convergence

---

[15] De Loutherbourg made a number of paintings derived from *A Christmas Tale*; see Rüdiger Joppien, *Philippe Jacques de Loutherbourg, RA, 1740–1812, Kenwood, 2 June–13 August* (1973), Cat. 78, *Bonoro's Cell, c.*1773 (private collection); Cat. 79, *Floridor Fighting Nigromant and the Demons, c.*1773 (Musée des Beaux-Arts, Strasbourg); Cat. 80, *Mr Weston in the Character of Tycho Fighting the Evil Spirits* (British Museum Department of Prints and Drawings). At his death, de Loutherbourg still held one of his own paintings on the subject: Peter Coxe, *A Catalogue of all the Valuable drawings &c. of James Philip de Loutherbourg Esq R.A., 18 June 1812 ... And Extensive Library of Scarce Books* (1812), 'Paintings ... Lot 63 A Sketch on Paper, in Oil; the first Design for the Conflagration Scene in "The Christmas Tale"'. Copy in Victoria and Albert Museum, London.

[16] Manoah Sibly, *Supplement to Placidus De Titus; Containing The Nativity of that Wonderful Phaenomenon, Oliver Cromwell* (1790), 15–16. See also Manoah Sibly, *A Collection of Thirty Remarkable Nativities* (1789).

of such spiritualities is exemplified by de Loutherbourg's possession
of a copy of his brother Ebenezer Sibly's *A Key to Physic, and the
Occult Sciences* (1794). In other words, de Loutherbourg was part of
an almost irrecoverably intricate network of beliefs and mentalities
which can now best be defined by way of their temporal locations
rather than the true nature of their intellectual allegiances.

These complex links between Freemasonry, theatricality, and
other types of alternative subculture which may seem surprising to
the modern reader were thoroughly understood in the eighteenth
century. One mid eighteenth-century writer quite readily lumped
seventeenth-century prophetic Muggletonianism with the theatricalized qualities of Freemasonry, thinking of them as examples of only
the latest incarnation of the hidden practices of dissenting or pagan
worship. The Eleusine games and Bacchanalian revels, which it was
thought could be traced 'in several of our old Customs', were 'a Sort
of religious Farce' carried out 'among the Muggletonians; who, if
they are not belied, are in some Things Continuators of them'. The
adoption of disguising costumes was considered a common denominator, particularly because of the participants 'representing different
Personages, from what they are at other Times'. This anxiety about
inauthenticity is part of a more wide-ranging set of fears about
Masons which was gradually developing throughout this period,
particularly as the annual grand processions of Freemasons seemed
to incorporate into their iconography the tools and instruments
of skilled craftsmen artisans who gathered in 'nocturnal Meetings'.
These were perceived as costumed *'mechanical Masquerades'* bordering on *'mechanical Farces'* or, in other words, public displays of
an otherwise covert artisan community embodying covert religious
allegiances, theatricality, and Masonic rite linked to craft skills.[17]

The assimilation of Masonic theatricality, however, was widespread
enough for it still to be both respectable and unexceptional even

---

[17] A. Betson, *Miscellaneous Dissertation Historical, Critical, and Moral, On the Origin
and Antiquity of Masquerades, Plays, Poetry, &c. With an Enquiry into the Antiquity of
Free Masonry, and several other old Heathenish Customs* (1751), 30–1, 35–8.

in the English provinces of the pre-French Revolutionary period. For example, in Southampton in 1777, the theatre there played *The Temple of Virtue*, a benefit night Masonic ode performed in the form of an oratorio for the Concord Lodge of that city. Relations between the local Masonic lodge sponsors and the audience were obviously comfortable enough for the piece to end with the benefit actor's wife speaking a teasing epilogue dressed 'in the Character of a Free Mason's Wife' ('In circles most exact *you* deal; mere rote! | What circle's equal to our petticoat?').[18] In 1770s Southampton, trifling with the symbols of Freemasonry was received decorously but, by the late 1790s, Robison's and Burke's alarmism over covert illuminist societies had become so widely publicized that anti-Jacobin pamphleteers had to distinguish carefully between conventional Freemasonry—as it must have appeared in its manifestation in *A Christmas Tale*—and the brands of suspected illuminism perceived to be emerging on continental Europe. The title of the Birmingham-printed popular pamphlet *New Lights on Jacobinism, Abstracted from Professor Robison's History of Free Masonry. With an Appendix, Containing An Account of Voltaire's behaviour on his Death-bed, and a Letter from J. H. Stone, (Who was tried for Sedition,) To his Friend Dr. Priestley, Disclosing the Principles of Jacobinism* (1798) revealingly pulls together suspicions about the Enlightenment's propensity for atheism (figured here under Voltaire's deathbed conversion) as well as the links between popular sedition and Dr Joseph Priestley, who was forced to flee to America following the destruction of his Birmingham house by a Church and King mob in 1791. Significantly, *New Lights on Jacobinism* opened by declaring, 'Let not the Freemasons of England be alarmed at the title page, as they will not find in the following sheets, the secrets of their order revealed, nor any aspersions upon them; neither are they charged in the least with being involved in the impious Jacobin conspiracy against religion and government' (p. 5).

---

[18] *The Temple of Virtue, A Masonic Ode; As performed at the Theatre in Southampton, on Monday the 15th of September, 1777* (Southampton, 1777), 16.

New Lights on Jacobinism (a title suggestive of contemporary fears of a covert pan-European revolutionary movement as well as a destructive pun on conventional Masonic imagery of light and dark) is highly indicative of how, by the late 1790s, the public manifestation of Masonic imagery conducted in *A Christmas Tale* of 1773 had become politically dangerous. A 1790s production of *A Christmas Tale*, given the fear-mongering stirred up by Burke and Robison, would have been unthinkable, but the Surrey Theatre's 1817 revival shows that such alarmism quietened down after the end of the Napoleonic War.

Before that situation was reached, however, the implications of the kind of close reading of *A Christmas Tale* proposed here suggests the existence in the 1770s of both a tolerant cultural diversity and an elaborate repertoire of representational forms through which religious and radical political unorthodoxies could be expressed. The establishment of the dramatic validity of the counterpoised spiritual worlds in the play reflects the existence of materialized social movements which enable their theatrical representation. Clearly, the banishing of the dark forces of evil via the use of Masonic symbols could still be contemplated with equanimity. The remarkable specificity of *A Christmas Tale*'s demonstration of Freemasonry's historic mentalities makes it possible to trace the role of theatre and the broader kinds of liberal and radical dissent which later became unified in the radical politics of the 1790s.

However, part of the purpose of this book is also to go beyond close reading and to recover how different subcultures interacted with theatre, both politically and in the networks of belief amongst those who worked in the dramatic and allied trades. The links between metropolitan artisan culture and theatrical production were extremely close but also heavily involved in alternative spiritualities. The probable reason why such networks of belief, politics, and skill were so forwardly advanced in the theatrical trades was that drama relied so heavily on workable technologies capable of continued innovation. The growth in a type of theatre with a more visually stimulating emphasis quickly enabled skilled men from continental

Europe (whose first language might not have been English) to try their hand. The sorts of skills and beliefs they brought with them enriched London's culture but, revealingly, they are also indicative of the wide range of talents and practices included in the economy of the capital's dramatic life.

When de Loutherbourg came to London in 1771, he travelled with Giovanni Battista Torré, a pyrotechnicist and printer who directed the firework displays for several years at Marylebone Pleasure Gardens.[19] The Gardens themselves, along with Ranelagh and Vauxhall, were one of the great theatricalized public spaces of London. Like the theatres and circuses, Marylebone Gardens would have been subject to a common set of regulations enshrined in the 1752 Disorderly Houses Act. In any event, one easily gets an idea of how Marylebone Gardens was a place whose open air performances made it an assembly attractive to ordinary criminals already indictable under English common law, thereby adding a further twist to the Garden's involvement with London's judiciary. In 1771, the year de Loutherbourg arrived in London, one Harry Piddington had attended the Gardens 'to see that part of the entertainment called the Magnet' (readily identifiable as the poet and novelist Dorothea Du Bois's 'musical entertainment' of that title). Finding 'there were a great number of people stocked together to see it', Piddington was 'jostled about a good deal by the crowd' and had his £4, fish-skin cased, pocket watch stolen by one Charles Lyon (who was hanged).[20] Much as with the theatres, Marylebone's apparently genteel pleasure gardens drew to it both musically appreciative crowds and a share of London's criminal underworld.

---

[19] Disentangling the Torré family is problematic. However, there can be no doubt that the Torré family, as a group, were involved in ventures which included pleasure gardens, pyrotechnics, and print-dealing. For their relationship to print-dealing, giving a slightly different lineage from the one suggested here, see Timothy Clayton, *The English Print, 1688–1802* (London and New Haven: Yale University Press, 1997), 218, 304 n. 57.

[20] Dorothea Du Bois, *The Magnet: A Musical Entertainment* (1771); Charles Lyon, 23 October 1771, Michael Harris (ed.), *The Proceedings of the Old Bailey*, Ref. T 17711023-50, microform (Brighton: Harvester Microform, 1984) and www.oldbaileyonline.org.

Learning how to adapt to such conditions imposed by practices of common criminality and the regulation of public assemblies would have been important transferable skills for those seeking employment in the capital's theatrical spaces.[21] In other words, a good grasp of the workings of various legal texts and customary practices helped ensure the circulation of knowledges based upon the operation of abstract principles as well as crafts and trades. Torré's father was a watchmaker with an interest in alchemy.[22] The social proximity of this alliance of artisanal theatrical talents is an important aspect of the way in which the materiality of theatrical culture was mediated through close, potentially pan-European, networks of skilled men who were not only active in the contemporary labour market of the dramatic and visual arts, but who also shared domestic convivialities through friendship and a common interest in alternative religions. The production assistant for the lighting effects in *A Christmas Tale* was Henry Angelo, the swordsman, who had also supplied transparencies for two previous Garrick productions, *Harlequin's Invasion* (1759) and *The Jubilee* (1769).[23] Angelo's reminiscences, although written much later, paint a vivid picture of social domestic occasions involving de Loutherbourg's interest in magical tricks:

Many an evening have we been diverted with three clever men; Loutherbourg, with his fun and tricks, which were inexhaustible; and the two mechanicians, [John Joseph] Merlin and Jacquet D'Ross [i.e. Jaquet-Droz]; the former, who had superintended Cox's museum, was known for many year in this country, particularly when his mechanic exhibition was near Hanover-square.[24]

What is important in this snapshot of Henry Angelo's memoir is the evident sociability between de Loutherbourg and two other

[21] On the Disorderly Houses Act 1752, see Jane Moody, *Illegitimate Theatre in London, 1770–1840* (Cambridge: Cambridge University Press, 2000), 17; Marius Kwint, 'The Legitimization of the Circus in Late Georgian England', *Past and Present*, 174 (2002), 72–115.

[22] Christopher Baugh, *Garrick and Loutherbourg* (Cambridge and Alexandria, Va.: Chadwyck-Healey, 1990), 28–9.

[23] Pedicord and Bergmann, *Plays of David Garrick*, ii. 349.

[24] Angelo, *Reminiscences*, ii. 328–9.

'mechanicians' from the London popular shows which bordered on theatricalized entertainment, not to mention Angelo's own role as a sort of theatrical general tradesman. Angelo's recollection provides a tantalizing glimpse into an unorthodox strata of London's wider theatrical industry. It is also now possible to fit together the role of the Marylebone Gardens pyrotechnicist Giovanni Battista Torré into the framework of de Loutherbourg's development as both scenic designer and painter.

Once again, the common denominator linking Torré to de Loutherbourg is their probable sociability within networks of spirituality and theatre. Such incidences were not uncommon in late eighteenth-century London. For example, the Vauxhall Gardens oboist, the Freemason Redmond Simpson, successfully reinvented himself in the 1770s as a kind of Masonic musical impresario basing his influence on his connections with the Somerset House Masonic Lodge and the prestigious anniversary concerts at Freemason's Hall.[25] De Loutherbourg's mysticism is also a feature common to the pyrotechnist Torré's Marylebone Gardens musical collaborator, the Swedenborgian violinist François-Hippolyte Barthélemon. In turn, Barthélemon later sat on the governors' board of the charitable Royal Cumberland Freemason's School, founded in 1788 for the daughters of deceased and indigent Masons.[26]

That such commercial and artistic communities of labour operated via complex and interlinked networks of friendship and sociability, connecting the Theatre Royal Drury Lane with places such as Marylebone Gardens, can also be deduced from their productions. In August 1772 James Hook (the father of the *Killing No Murder* playwright Theodore), the musical director and general producer at Marylebone Gardens, featured firework displays as part of 'Mr Hook's Annual Festival' which portrayed, in flames, a 'Magnificent Temple' and

---

[25] Simon McVeigh, 'Freemasonry and Musical Life in London in the Late Eighteenth Century', in David Wyn Jones (ed.), *Music in Eighteenth-Century Britain* (Aldershot and Burlington, Vt.: Ashgate, 2000), 72–100.

[26] R. M. Handfield-Jones, *The History of the Royal Masonic Institution for Girls 1788–1974* (1974), 85.

'Cox's Museum'.[27] De Loutherbourg and his friends Torré and John Joseph Merlin, the superintendent of jeweller James Cox's Spring Gardens exhibition of mechanical models (the Cox's Musuem of the firework display), have clear friendship circles or communities of talent encompassing London's public shows and entertainments.[28] Marylebone Gardens was known to contemporaries as the French Gardens on account of its association with French refugees since the revocation of the Edict of Nantes, so someone like Torré would have found a natural home there. Marylebone Gardens also had quite exceptional links to Freemasonry. In 1763 'Brother Lowe' invited Masons to join in the chorus of the 'Fellow Craft's Song' and in 1764 the audience were invited to sing an 'Ode in Honour of Free-masonry'.[29] The extent of Torré's penetration into the hospitable groups of London's artistic culture was furthered by his commercial relationship with the printseller John Thane, of Market Lane near the Haymarket.[30] The practical mercantile determinants of these artisan networks also had their effect on de Loutherbourg.

In an anonymous 'Anecdotes of Mr. de Loutherbourg' which appeared in the *European Magazine* in 1782, the author writes that de Loutherbourg was learned

in the deepest and most abstruse points of mystics ... [and] was strongly attached to chemistry, [where] he found, by following the principles of nature, a method of preparing and blending his colours, unknown to other artists, by which they were rendered more vivid and durable, as one component part did not destroy the effect of the other.[31]

The immediate acquaintance of de Loutherbourg who was most likely to have acquired an advanced practical knowledge of chemistry was Torré, the Marylebone Gardens fireworks man whose father

[27] Alan St. H. Brock, *A History of Fireworks* (London: Harrap, 1949), 196.

[28] On Cox's museum, see Richard Altick, The *Shows of London* (Cambridge, Mass.: Belknap Press of Harvard University Press, 1978), 69–72.

[29] McVeigh, 'Freemasonry and Musical Life', 72–100.

[30] John Thomas Smith, *A Book for a Rainy Day: or, Recollections of the events of the Last Sixty-Six Years* (1845), 40.

[31] *European Magazine*, March 1782, 181–2.

was interested in alchemy.[32] In *A Christmas Tale*, the resolution of the plot is noticeably expressed in terms which draw on both Freemasonry and alchemy:

CAMILLA. And I am Floridor's, and Floridor's alone! [*Floridor starts and stands astonish'd.*] Behold the reward of thy *valor, constancy* and *honour*! the fire has try'd, and prov'd the value of the metal—come to my arms, my hero! (p. 73)

This purification through trials testing the triple Masonic virtues is here compared to the proving of metals. This metaphor in the play text's conclusion, with its allusion to the search for a purified metal akin to the alchemical 'Philosopher's Stone', was directly materialized in de Loutherbourg's paintings. The apparent metallic colouring of his paintings was quickly noticed by contemporaries.

John 'Peter Pindar' Walcot, in his poem on de Loutherbourg and his contemporaries, 'One More Peep at the Royal Academy; or, Odes to Academicians', satirized the metallic colouring of his paint formulas, describing how 'The poet ... endeavoureth to beat him out of his Belief in the Metalleity of general Nature.'[33] More recently Morton Paley has noted that the much commented-on 'peculiarities of de Loutherbourg's color combinations were deliberate', while Stephen Daniels has traced alchemical imagery in his later painting *Coalbrookdale by Night* (1801, Science Museum, London), arguing that de Loutherbourg evokes a counter-Industrial Revolution of metal working steeped in religious irrationalism.[34] John Gage in *Colour in Turner: Poetry and Truth* (1969) first drew attention to de Loutherbourg as a source for J. M. W. Turner's

---

[32] Torré's displays were very topical; see George Alexander Stevens, *The Trip to Portsmouth; A Comic Sketch of One Act, With Songs* (1773), 'You may bounce about like Torré's fireworks' (p. 10).

[33] John Walcot, *The Works of Peter Pindar* (1816) vol. iv; see also 'Learn, Loutherbourg, to thy surprise, | That grass and water, cows and skies, | Are *things* which Nature never makes of copper.'

[34] Morton D. Paley, *The Apocalyptic Sublime* (New Haven: Yale University Press, 1986), 61–2; Stephen Daniels, 'Loutherbourg's Chemical Theatre: Coalbrookdale by Night', in John Barrell (ed.), *Painting and the Politics of Culture: New Essays on British Art 1700–1850'* (Oxford: Oxford University Press, 1992), 195–230.

ground-breaking use of colour as well as colour's association in his work with mystical meanings.[35] To the diarist Joseph Farington, recording day-to-day conversations with de Loutherbourg in 1804, his opinions on colour ('Loutherburgh [*sic*] in conversation said ... that there are only *two original colours* viz: *Blue & Yellow*') were distinctive enough to be worth recording. Farington's *Diary* also makes clear the depth of de Loutherbourg's experience in understanding both contemporary pigments and how his methods compare with the techniques of the great northern European masters in managing the physical properties of the paint supplied to him from the colourmen.[36] However, de Loutherbourg's interest in both the 'chemistry' of colour, which the *European Magazine* had noted, and colour's physical properties, which tended to lead him to use pigment combinations with too much 'Metalleity', as Wolcot had put it, finds its most exact correlation with the work of firework makers of the eighteenth century who combined pyrotechnics with dramatic displays at places such as Marylebone Gardens.

For them, the search for a wider range of coloured flames appears to have been coincident with an interest in alchemy as a viable practical science. These qualities come together in the figure of Giovanni Battista Torré, de Loutherbourg's travelling companion when he arrived in London in 1771. As has been referred to above, Torré's father, a watchmaker and mystic, had already been in regular contact with 'Mr Luterbrook'.[37] Torré's work at Marylebone Gardens as the

---

[35] John Gage, *Colour in Turner: Poetry and Truth* (London: Studio Vista, 1969), 136–40.

[36] *Farington Diary*, vi. 2282, 28 March 1804; 'Loutherburgh talked with me abt. Process in painting.—He said that though Claude repeated the Colouring of his skies, going them over more than once yet it was in the lightest parts that He put on much body of Colour. He sd. Painters of the day make use of more kinds of Vehicles than those masters did. They, in his Opinion, painted with simple materials,—oils witht. Mixture,—no macgilps [*sic*].—He uses Poppy,—nut & linseed oil,—and Drying oil only for dark colours but never in skies and delicate parts ... He gets His [Turpentine] from Middleton. He prefers Legges white to Middleton's saying it is Whiter & purer.—He delights in Okers. The Flemings painted a White ground & then pummiced it smooth.—His grounds are laid by Legge with very little size' (vi. 2317, 8 May 1804).

[37] Baugh, *Garrick and Loutherbourg*, 28–9.

director of the firework displays was a cognate activity with London's other types of theatrical production. Economically, the firework shows were organized along similar lines to theatrical productions, with Torré dividing receipts at the door with the proprietor and having his own regular benefit nights.[38] Fireworks were a significant aspect of contemporary theatricals, implying the presence of a range of skilled pyrotechnicists both to make the fireworks and to arrange and supervise their display. By 1770, Ranelagh Gardens were heavily advertising their production of Isaac Bickerstaffe's *The Recruiting Serjeant* with featured '150 cases of brilliant Fountains, Roman Candles, Chinese Jerbs, Pots, d'Brians [and] Maroons.'[39] In the heavily overlapping types of concurrent dramatic activity and personnel in this era, the republican Edward Thompson's Shadwell adaptation, *The Fair Quaker*, at Drury Lane in November 1773 similarly displayed '£3.5s' of 'Fireworks'.[40]

Of course, fireworks themselves were also well established features of London's public political spectacles. The triumphant occasion of Ireland's conquest by King William in 1690 was celebrated by a 'Firework' and 'bonefires' 'Performd at the Charge of the Gentry' in Covent Garden piazza hard by the Theatre Royal, during which William and Mary's monogram was illuminated by fireworks in the dark recess under the classical portico of St Paul's, Covent Garden. A mezzotint print, by Bernard Lens II (1659–1725)—the essential component of representational amplification in late seventeenth-century politics—was promptly issued. The print provided a more permanent and distributable representation of this occasion in which an effigy of William's enemy Louis XIV of France had been hanged, drawn, quartered, and burnt in the middle of the piazza. As with de Loutherbourg's background and associates in the mid-eighteenth century, the artisanal skills found within Lens's contemporary London were based upon complex cross-currents of nationality,

belief, trade, and heritage: Lens's Dutch-born father, Bernard Lens I
(1631–1725), was himself an enamel painter and author of religious
tracts, while his son's early advocacy of the mezzotint technique
(one easily adaptable for the amateur artist) is a reminder that issues
of tonality—if not yet colour—were developing away from etching's dependence on line.[41] In this complex network of economic,
social, and artistic relations described above—all founded upon various emerging technologies—the issue of visual tonality, fireworks,
print-selling, politics, and religious belief all came to be connected within the sociabilities of these distinctive London theatrical
subcultures.

As far as the pyrotechnicists were concerned, the principal technical
endeavours of mid-eighteenth-century firework makers were directed
towards producing a wider range of coloured flame, an innovation
which would provide the kinds of tonality (mirrored in the emergence
of mezzotint in the print medium) lacking in contemporary fireworks.
The elusive ingredient which eventually revolutionized firework-
making in the early nineteenth century (although it had been
discovered as a possible component as early as 1786) was potassium
chlorate.[42] Until that time the leading practitioners, only a few of
whom committed their knowledge to writing—such as Lieutenant
Robert Jones, author of *Artificial Fire-Works, Improved to the Modern
Practice* (1766)—were limited to using mainly organic compounds
to add to the basic gunpowder. To create tinges of colour, the
firework makers added such things as 'meal powder', camphor,
Greek pitch, antimony, amber, and rosin.[43] This problem afflicted
even the most eminent pyrotechnic masters: a set of watercolour
drawings prepared by Torré for a display at Versailles in 1770 shows
a swathe of uniformly pale red flames cascading like a huge waterfall

---

[41] Antony Griffiths, with the collaboration of Robert A. Gerard, *The Print in Stuart
Britain, 1603–1689* (London: Trustees of the British Museum, 1998), 245, 263–4,
Cat. no. 213.

[42] Brock, *A History of Fireworks*, 156–60, 196–7.

[43] Robert Jones, *Artificial Fire-Works, Improved to the Modern Practice*, 2nd
edn. (1766), 64–5.

behind the clipped box hedges of the palace grounds.[44] As late as 1816 a pyrotechnicist named Angelo was obviously hard-pressed to list the formulae for constructing a few firework rockets which might be coloured as white stars, blue stars, and 'coloured or variegated' stars.[45] Knowing as we do that de Loutherbourg socialized with artisans who were connected to London's marketing of dramatic entertainment and exhibitions (mechanical as well as fine art), it seems fairly certain he would have discussed with companions such as Torré the use of chemical bases in pyrotechnics. Both men were knowledgeable about alchemy. Torré would have learned about it from his father's interests but de Loutherbourg also held an extensive and recondite collection of alchemical books in his library. At the auction of de Loutherbourg's library and paintings after his death, at least twenty books on alchemical subjects can be identified.

It is important to distinguish here the simultaneous existence of two apparently contradictory directions of belief and discourse centring on de Loutherbourg. First, what the *European Magazine* may have tactfully described as de Loutherbourg's interest in 'chemistry' very probably encompassed, as a mode of inquiry, the traditional philosophy of alchemy. Eighteenth-century discourses on these subjects overlapped, but de Loutherbourg's scientific or empirical interest in the chemistry and composition of colour was concurrent with his interest in alchemical philosophy and religious mysticism. The cognate fields of theatrical drama and firework displays meant that his contemporaries were encountering similar problems of enlivening visual dramatic presentations in pyrotechnics just as he encountered it lighting the theatrical productions.

[44] 'Alexandre-M.-Th. Morel/Jean-Baptiste Torré, 'Firework design for the marriage of the dauphin to Marie Antoinette' (watercolour, Brock Fireworks Collection, acc. no. P950001**.049), Kevin Salatino, *Incendiary Art: The Representation of Fireworks in Early Modern Europe* (Los Angeles: Getty Institution for the History of Art and the Humanities, 1997), plate 14.

[45] T. Angelo, *The Art of Making Fireworks, by Plain and Easy Rules* (1816?), 8–9. Angelo's first name is not known. On the title-page his identity is given as 'formerly of the Royal Laboratory, Woolwich'. It is conceivable that he is connected in some way with the fencing family of that name.

Although de Loutherbourg's library was collected over many years, the contents as sold in 1812 reveal an extensive interest in alchemy and mysticism. His collection included over twenty specifically alchemical works in French, German, English, and Latin, such as *Hermetischer Rosenkranz Chymische* (1747), *L'Ouverture de l'Escolle de Philosophie Transmutatoire Metallique*, Robert Fludd's *Mosaical Philosophy* (1659), and J. M. Faustij, *Compendium Alchymist Novum* (1706).[46] However, de Loutherbourg was also clearly interested in the Enlightenment's more empirically based scientific studies since his sale catalogue shows for disposal two *camera obscuras*, a telescope, a microscope, and a 'A capital electrifying machine, in a mahogany case, with lock and key; and Priestley's Introduction to the Study of Electricity, 4th edition'. It would not be surprising if de Loutherbourg's 'electrifying machine' was used for electrical healing therapies. Mysticism and Enlightenment technologies ran in parallel.

An interest in the development of these technologies (the pseudo-technology of alchemy included) and in religious mysticism is the common currency of the social and intellectual transferences implemented by their occupations within the London theatres and arts trades. It is known that de Loutherbourg's firework-making friend, Torré, directly influenced theatrical effects in Garrick's theatre by introducing a pyrotechnic 'licopodium' torch which simulated the flashing of lightning.[47] What is less easy to prove, although it remains a possibility, is that the innovative changes in coloured lighting at Covent Garden described in Henry Angelo's account of *A Christmas Tale* were also achieved by the use of some type of basic coloured firework similar to a slow-burning flare. Whatever the case, it is certain that Torré himself was also a part of an occupational culture which moved between the theatre, firework-making, and printselling, as well as between continental Europe and London. Torré had opened a scientific instrument shop (the 'Cabinet de Physique Expérimentale')

---

[46] Coxe, *Catalogue . . . Loutherbourg.*

[47] George Winchester Stone, Jr., and George M. Kahrl, *David Garrick: A Critical Biography* (Carbondale and Edwardsville: Southern Illinois University Press, 1979), 314.

in Paris in 1760 and went on to confer on his son, Anthony, the management of its London Pall Mall branch in 1767.[48] It is conceivable that the various scientific instruments in de Loutherbourg's possession at the time of his death came from this source.

Either way, an interest in such things as mechanical exhibitions or the retailing of scientific instruments, together with firework-making and some degree of religious or scientific mysticism, runs as a common thread through the intellectual and economic lives of Torré, de Loutherbourg, and their associates. A further influential factor, one which gathers this group together as creators of a culturally constitutive force, is their involvement with the print-selling trade. Whilst Torré's fireworks, or even Garrick and de Loutherbourg's stage productions, were fairly ephemeral in their nature, their involvement in the print trade stabilized and provided a capital permanence to their labours. Of course, de Loutherbourg was inevitably committed to negotiating his way through the London printsellers who provided him with a secondary market through the sale of engravings in order to give him an income and artistic profile reaching far beyond the possibilities afforded by selling individual paintings. In the 1770s, no doubt to diversify out of the arduous and dangerous work of firework-making, Torré had set himself up to trade with the printseller John Thane in Market Lane. Significantly, Torré was then joined by the Milanese emigrant Paul Colnaghi. Later, Thane and Torré transferred their premises from the Haymarket to a location in Pall Mall and then opened a new branch in the Palais Royale, Paris, in 1784 run by Colnaghi. Torré's publication of a set of engravings, *Caricatures of the English* (1775) by de Loutherbourg, with both French and English imprints, reveals an intention to penetrate both national markets. By the end of the next year, Torré and Colnaghi had established a profitable and long-lasting relationship with the eminent, and highly fashionable, stipple engraver Francesco Bartolozzi

---

[48] Donald Garstang (ed.), *Colnaghi, Established 1760, Art, Commerce, Scholarship: A Window onto the Art World—Colnaghi 1760 to 1984* (London: P. & D. Colnaghi, 1984), 16.

and, of course, Colnaghi's went on to become one of the great
London art dealerships of the nineteenth and twentieth centuries.[49]

This interchange of skills across these different industries should
not be underestimated. As well as his 'licopodium' torch, Torré reju-
venated the Marylebone Gardens presentation of firework displays
by including daring theatricalized entertainments on an ambitious
scale.[50] The most famous of these was Torré's scene of *The Forge
of Vulcan*, which began its performances in June 1774 in the season
following Garrick and de Loutherbourg's Drury Lane success, *The
Christmas Tale*. The contemporary antiquarian of popular culture
Joseph Strutt, in *The Sports and Pastimes of the People of England*
(1801), recorded personally witnessing *The Forge of Vulcan*. Strutt
wrote of how Torré 'introduced pantomimical spectacles, which
afforded him an opportunity of bringing forward much splendid
machinery, with appropriate scenery and stage decoration, whereby
he gave an astonishing effect to his performances'.[51] What is particularly noticeable is that these pyrotechnic shows included the use
of human actors moving (presumably quite dangerously) between
screens. In its initial versions, Torré's fireworks represented 'the
Forge of Vulcan, Under Mount Aetna; The Cavern of the Cyclops,
and Flowing of the Lava' with the actors portraying 'a Battle between
Mars and his attendant Warriors, against Vulcan and his Cyclops.
Vulcan, stimulated by jealousy, exerts his utmost efforts, and after
a furious contest, overwhelms his antagonist in the eruption of the
mount'.[52] In describing a related firework display depicting 'The
Descent of Orpheus to Hell', Strutt recalled that 'the flitting backwards and forwards of the spirits was admirably represented by means
of a transparent gauze artfully interposed between the actors and the

[49] Donald Garstang (ed.), *Colnaghi, Established 1760, Art, Commerce, Scholarship:
A Window onto the Art World—Colnaghi 1760 to 1984* (London: P. & D. Colnaghi,
1984), 16–17.

[50] Mollie Sands, *The Eighteenth-Century Pleasure Gardens of Marylebone* (London:
Society for Theatre Research, 1987), 86–107.

[51] Joseph Strutt, *The Sports and Pastimes of the People of England* (1801), 281.

[52] British Library, Marylebone Gardens collection of cuttings (shelfmark: 840.m.29),
dated 3 June 1774, fo. 23.

spectators'.[53] This type of theatricalized 'pantomimical spectacle', incorporating human actors dodging about between the banks of exploding fireworks, gives some idea of how fluid were the divisions between theatrical dramas with literary texts shown in theatres such as Drury Lane, and the settings of music and fireworks offered at Marylebone Gardens. Both places required recognizable communities of workers who exchanged and shared not only their skills but their beliefs. De Loutherbourg and Torré represent just one component of London's artistic culture incorporating such varied but complementary and transferable skills.

Just how broadly based this contemporary culture could become can be illustrated by the connection between the crafts already described and those of alternative medical regimens. Again, what is uncovered here is a set of pre-industrialized technologies fluently encompassing a bewildering range of skills and economic connections. The move into alternative spiritualized medical regimes, a diversification of their major skills, is an aspect of cultural behaviour common to this group of people in the trades attached to contemporary London theatre.

The Marylebone Gardens season beginning in the summer of 1774, the one which featured Torré's newly devised 'Forge of Vulcan', was the first to make use of the Garden's spa waters ('discovered last winter'), marketed to visitors as 'highly useful' for 'nervous and scorbutic disorders' and 'bilious cholics'.[54] Far from being a mere curiosity of eighteenth-century medicine, 'Marybone Spa' connects with yet another aspect of de Loutherbourg's interests. In the 1780s de Loutherbourg became associated with the then notorious Count Cagliostro who came with his wife to live, in secret, at de Loutherbourg's house.[55] Cagliostro was associated with both faith-healing and with Freemasonry. It is around this time, probably at Cagliostro's instigation, that de Loutherbourg completed eight

[53] Strutt, *Sports and Pastimes*, 282.
[54] BL, Marylebone Gardens collection of cuttings, 6 June 1774, fo. 23.
[55] Lucia, *The Life of the Count Cagliostro* (1787), 112.

watercolours (Torre Abbey House, Torbay) illustrating the Egyptian Rite of Freemasonry which Stephen Daniels has recently described as 'a sustained piece of subterranean theatre'.[56] When Cagliostro was eventually forced to flee the country, the de Loutherbourgs continued to accommodate his wife before travelling with her to Switzerland.[57] These events brought de Loutherbourg financial hardship, but one of his proposed solutions to their domestic plight was to form a trading partnership with Cagliostro which could benefit from their complementary talents: 'by making him a partner of what I earned from my painting, he by communicating to me everything that he knew and sharing the profits from his medicines'.[58] Nothing is known to have come of this partnership but the supposedly medicinal waters of 'Marybone Spa' form yet another part of that eighteenth-century spectrum of empirical and irrationalist science strongly associated with trades linked to luxury arts. For example, de Loutherbourg's friends John Joseph Merlin and Jaquet-Droz (the 'Jacquet D'Ross' of Henry Angelo's account, above), both made artificial limbs, invalid chairs, and an 'Oscillatory' 'Hygaeian' exercise chair which assisted 'the utility of swinging in pulmonary consumptions', a strange calling as Richard Altick has noted, but not one inconsistent with the wider interest in medical practices amongst this group.[59]

The cultural dynamics of these episodes were considerable. The medicinal Marylebone Gardens spa waters would have been both seen and sampled by thousands of people who also would have witnessed Torré's firework theatricals. The prosthetic limbs and therapeutic furniture offered for sale by Merlin and Jaquet-Droz must have been aimed at exactly the kind of affluent consumer

[56] Stephen Daniels, 'Loutherbourg's Chemical Theatre: Coalbrookdale by Night', in John Barrell (ed.), *Painting and the Politics of Culture: New Essays on British Art 1700–1850* (Oxford: Oxford University Press, 1992), 224, repro. figs. 7.20, 7.21. See also Joppien, *Loutherbourg*, Cat. no. 62.

[57] Lucia, *Life of the Count Cagliostro*, 122–3.

[58] Joppien, *Loutherbourg*, unpaginated.

[59] Altick, *Shows of London*, 72–6. On Merlin's Hygaeian Chair, see R. Humphreys, *The Memoirs Of J. Decastro, Comedian ... Accompanied By An Analysis Of The Life Of The Late Philip Astley, Esq. ... Also An Accompanying History Of The Royal Circus, Now The Surrey Theatre* (1824), 243–4.

which the later *Harlequin in his Element* also targeted with its Coade's stone and Hancock & Shepherd glass girandoles exhibits discussed in Chapter 6. The communities of trade, belief, and skill which these connections implicitly announce cut right across both the public and the private lives of contemporary Londoners.

There were riots outside de Loutherbourg's home at Hammersmith Terrace in 1789 when he began taking patients for prophetic healing. In Venice, Maria Cosway, artist and wife of the fashionable and successful painter Richard Cosway, sought de Loutherbourg's advice when their daughter was ill in 1791 and, according to some stories, Cosway himself had been in de Loutherbourg's house when it was threatened by a riotous crowd.[60] De Loutherbourg's library shows that he owned at least two books by the seventeenth-century medicinal alchemist Paracelsus (Theophrastus von Hohenheim) and one by Ebenezer Sibly, a late eighteenth-century medicinal mystic, herbalist, astrologer, and medico-sexual writer.[61] At this time de Loutherbourg was also associated with the Swedenborgian church in London, having been one of its founder members in 1778.[62] Although obviously absorbed in his mystical interests, de Loutherbourg seems to have taken care to situate his Hammersmith Terrace home in a neighbourhood also popular with successful theatrical people. On one side of him at No. 5 lived the actress Rosemund Mountain of Sadler's Wells and Covent Garden, while on the other side, at No. 15, lived one of the most prolific playwrights of the era, Arthur Murphy.[63] In

---

[60] Stephen Lloyd (ed.), *Richard and Maria Cosway: Regency Artists of Taste and Fashion* (Edinburgh: Scottish National Portrait Gallery, 1995), 67. Cosway's career moved from early dabbling in pornographic miniatures, alleged revolutionary sympathies, through to visionary hallucinations of Dante, Apelles, Charles I (on art), and Pitt: George C. Williamson, *Richard Cosway, R.A. and his Wife and Pupils* (London: George Bell & Sons, 1887), 39–42, 44.

[61] *Abrégé de la Doctrine de Paracelse* (Paris, 1724), *Aureum Vellus et Theophrasti Paracelci* (Hamburg, 1708), Ebenezer Sibly, *A Key to Physic, and the Occult Sciences. Opening to mental view, the System and order of the Interior and Exterior Heavens; the Angalogy betwixt Angels and Spirits of Men ... To which are added Lunar Tables, etc.* (c.1800): Coxe, *Catalogue ... Loutherbourg*.

[62] Baugh, *Garrick and Loutherbourg*, 48.

[63] Henry Austin Dobson, *At Prior Park and Other Papers* (London: Chatto & Windus, 1912), 95.

the middle of this careful professional positioning, de Loutherbourg
followed his interests in regimens of prophetic healing.

These communities are definable by the nature of their spiritual beliefs, their involvement in the theatre, and, not least, their
willingness to allow connections between their public and private
roles. Even before de Loutherbourg set up his healing practice with
his wife, as early as 1786 the Swedenborgian Benedict Chastan-
ier was using the columns of the *Morning Post* to advertise the
'Intellectual Treatment Of Disease By Sensations, Hitherto Called
Animal Magnetism' at his house in Tottenham Court Road.[64] In the
late 1780s de Loutherbourg similarly used his magnetic powers
in Hammersmith Terrace for 'prophetic healing' by 'influxes',
some of his cures being witnessed and affirmed in print by his
female follower, Mary Pratt.[65] This interest in occult medicinal
or prophetic regimens was also common to others in the London print trade as well as in the theatre. Around this time the
feckless actor James Fennell, who (although a loyalist himself)
later met Marat in Paris during the Revolution, combined his
interests in vegetarian pedestrianism alongside the electrical cures
he practised on children.[66] More generally, the modern historian
Gloria Flaherty has shown that elsewhere in Europe, the respected physician Johann Peter Frank (1745–1821), linked to the
University of Göttingen, was beginning to recommend attendance
or participation in theatre and the performing arts as therapies
to improve mental well being, as the Enlightenment relocated its
roots in ancient mystical practices connected to ancient traditions
of shamanism.[67]

---

[64] *Morning Post*, 18 May 1786.

[65] Mary Pratt, *A List of a Few Cures performed by Mr and Mrs de Loutherbourg
... without Medicine* (1789). De Loutherbourg later provided illustrations for S. J.
Pratt's *Sympathy, and Other Poems* (1807), which describes the social context of innate
sympathies whose origins are elemental and material as much as spiritual.

[66] James Fennell, *An Apology for the Life of James Fennell. Written by Himself*
(Philadelphia: Moses Thomas, 1814), 290–2.

[67] Gloria Flaherty, *Shamanism and the Eighteenth Century* (Princeton: Princeton
University Press, 1992), 103–4.

It is difficult to escape the conclusion that these were viable social and spiritual subcultures which created a network of personal relationships usually, though not invariably, carrying with them a set of economic determinants. While de Loutherburg charged nothing for his services, the unemployed ex-Swedenborgian and Society of Avignon *illuminé*, William Bryan, was forced to try to turn to paid prophetic healing after his return from France.[68] Bryan had traded in the 1780s as a copperplate printer and bookseller but, on his return from Avignon, he opened 'a shop as a druggist and vender [*sic*] of the patent medicines, at the same time dispensing as an apothecary, but on a different plan'.[69] Bryan's 'different plan' was to use prophetic powers to aid diagnosis, a calling suggested to him by an earlier training in medicine as well as by the noticeably physiological nature of his visionary experiences. He described how, when he was with patients, 'I could describe every symptom of their disease from *feeling it in my own body*; and such has been the mercy of the Lord, that it has instantly been communicated to my mind what to give, and I have even been ordered to say to them, *"this medicine will certainly cure you, by such or such a time you will be well"*; and this has accordingly happened.'[70] While de Loutherbourg left no account of his healing practices, Bryan's description serves to give a good idea of how he might have worked. William Bryan appears to have had no employment alternative but to turn to prophetic healing when work in copperplate printing dried up in the early 1790s.

In a similar way, although with less pressing financial imperatives, de Loutherbourg had sought to establish a trading partnership with Cagliostro involving medicinal regimens. This shifting between

---

[68] The issue of fees was controversial. De Loutherbourg was forced to emphasize this point, see *Mr. Lutherburg* [*sic*] *A true Copy of the Writing put up in his Room, where Patients wait, on Thursday, the second of July, 1789* (BL *Lysons Collectana*. C.191. c.16 vol. 1 (2), fo. 161). See also another newspaper cutting, fol. 162, 'Imposter Detected! A Caution to the Public'. On Bryan, see David Worrall, 'William Bryan: Another Anti-Swedenborgian Visionary Engraver of 1789', *Blake/An Illustrated Quarterly* (2000).

[69] William Bryan, *A Testimony of the Spirit of Truth, Concerning Richard Brothers* (1795), 29.

[70] Ibid. 30.

careers in response to different economic climates is a characteristic
of the activities of such artisans. For de Loutherbourg, however,
who was already a famous painter, the decision to practise prophetic healing signals a different embodiment of the duties of the
artisan entrepreneur, since whatever skills or gifts de Loutherbourg
possessed had to be integrated with his career as a painter. Of
course, the exhibition of a private belief in alchemy and mysticism, apparent from the contents of his library, came to be a
public practice when he opened his doors to prospective patients in
1789.[71] As also for de Loutherbourg's Swedenborgian and Behemist
friend Richard Cosway, London in the late 1780s was clearly a
place where religious beliefs alternative to mainstream Anglicanism
were broadly socially acceptable amongst the creative communities who sustained their livelihoods by catering for the captial's
luxury trades.

For example, William Bryan's career as both a copperplate printer
and prophetic healer illustrates how easily skilled artisans crossed
between religious mysticism and the necessary commercialism of
London's book and print trade. This route was traversed in another
direction by William Henry Ireland, who forms another fascinating
connection between London theatre, literary Grub Street, and the
visual arts. Ireland's father, Samuel, was an eminent engraver and
an amateur antiquarian with a taste for Shakespeare memorabilia.
Ireland, whose Shakespeare forgery of 1796, *Vortigern*, had a dis-
astrous opening night at Drury Lane, much like de Loutherbourg and
Bryan, needed to reinvent himself as his profession took new turns
and presented different opportunities. Indeed, it is Ireland's 'insider'
account of the workings of the late eighteenth-century London print
trade, allied to his own interest in drama, which helps us reconstitute
much of this social milieu.

Enriched by his knowledge of his father's experience as a highly
regarded engraver, William Henry Ireland wrote an extraordinary
satirical poem on the print selling trade, *Chalcographimania; or, the*

⁷¹ BL, *Mr. Lutherburg*.

Portrait-Collector and Printseller's Chronicle (1814), which presents a picture of London's market in old engravings and prints as a parallel world of deception, double-dealing, and forgery, one which he had inhabited himself as the 'discoverer' of Shakespeare's 'lost' tragedy, *Vortigern*. Ireland's *Chalcographimania* is an unflattering, but extremely well-informed, account of the history and demography of print-selling which touches tantalizingly on many of the personnel discussed in this chapter.

Writing in 1814, Ireland still remembered the (by then, long gone) firm of '*Th*[a]—*ne* and *T*[o]—*rr*[e]', the firework maker's Market Lane print-selling partnership, but his information was also of old enough vintage to denigrate the, by then, highly successful Colnaghi's ('sly *C*—*ln*—*ghi*') 'debut on the London *pavé* ... in the character of a *rat-catcher*', before his takeover from Torré and Thane.[72] In other words, as well as being an effective enough playwright (although, alas, *not* William Shakespeare), Ireland had an insider's knowledge of the gossip on London's art market which helps pull together the seemingly disconnected components of its artisan history. His snipe, in one of *Chalcographimania*'s notes, about Richard Cosway is heaped with knowledgeable satire: '*Mr. R*—*ch*—*rd C*—*sw*—*y*, *royally* denominated *Dirty Dick* ... whose eccentric brain, crammed with all the visionary chimeras of *Jacob Behmen*, *Swedenborg*, and other fantastic unravellers of fate ... is little better than a *Mother Shipton* in male attire'.[73] Not only did Cosway move in royal circles (and was frequently mocked for his fanciful and elaborate dress), Ireland knew about his mysticism as a follower of Jacob Boehme and Emanuel Swedenborg (rather more culturally significant figures than the spurious Yorkshire prophetess Mother Shipton). In other words, Ireland's account in *Chalcographimania*, written from the commercial motives of his own survival during a difficult career engendered by the fiasco of his *Vortigern* forgery, serves to connect

[72] William Henry Ireland, *Chalcographimania; or, The Portrait-Collector and Printseller's Chronicle, with Infatuations of every Description. A humorous poem in four books. With copious notes explanatory. By Satiricus Sculptor* (1814), 16, 90 n., 93 n.

[73] Ibid. 141 n.

and empirically confirm the materiality of the historicism which has been described.

De Loutherbourg's religious mysticism was probably as extensive as Cosway's but, because in the 1770s and 1780s he was so involved with different types of public theatricality, he was probably less able to shield his private beliefs from his clients. Nevertheless, when Cagliostro's notoriety became better publicized, de Loutherbourg must have squirmed when new revelations about his friend came to light in the Inquistion's interrogation published as *The Life of Joseph Balsamo, Commonly Called Count Cagliostro* (1791). Allegedly, amongst Cagliostro's papers had been found not only an account of his highly theatrical Egyptian ritual (pp. 101–7) but also a transcript of Cagliostro's 'pretended intercourse with spirits' in which Cagliostro sees 'Louth—g arrive' as an intimate of Cagliostro's role as Grand Cophta (pp. 143–4). Remarkably, de Loutherbourg's reputation was sufficiently strong for him to survive the revelation of his friendship with Cagliostro but, once again, the connections show how deeply embedded were quite varied spiritualities with London's luxury trades, even those dabbling in faith healing the populace.

Fireworks and theatre, the visual arts and medical healing, Freemasonry and the Royal theatres, all of these forms of expressivity are far more connected with each other than might at first be imagined yet the kinds of complex social networks outlined above are probably a typical characteristic of theatre in late eighteenth-century London. These demographies are formed from connections based on skill, commercial opportunity, and spiritual belief. Not only do distinctions between Enlightenment and counter-Enlightenment science break down, so also do other apparent demarcations between occupation, the public and private as well as differentiations between different discourse types and expressive repertoires.

What has been recovered in this chapter is only one kind of alternative public sphere which constituted a theatrical subculture. The basis of its ideological formation was the supposition of the continued viability of such independent counter-public spheres and their ability to support themselves financially through employment in theatre and its allied trades. For the most part they were, as has been shown, alternative theatrical belief communities whose material bases were usually, although not invariably, built upon links of skill and commerce. Intricate though such embodiments of artisan fraternity may seem, the most important dimension yet to be considered is that of politics. In the next chapter it will be shown how, superimposed upon many of the types of artisan community discussed above, were equally deep and complex networks of distinct political allegiance.

5

Political Microcultures: The Censorship of Thomas Dibdin's *Two Farmers*

THIS chapter is intended to establish the depth of radical political microcultures in late eighteenth-century London and to show how their ideologies and influences were sufficiently widely distributed as to reoccur in playwriting for Covent Garden Theatre Royal. The overall political movement described is that these contemporary ideologies, present in the impoverished East End, subsequently resurface at the metropolitan centre in Thomas John Dibdin's drama *The Two Farmers*, scheduled for acting at Covent Garden in early October 1800 during a period of food scarcity and rioting. The inclusion of an assertive black farm labourer in Dibdin's play (played, of course, by a white actor), would in itself have made *The Two Farmers* an exceptional drama for its moment but the piece is all the more exceptional because of the precise moment of its intervention. In the same way as earlier chapters have presented anthropologies of drama and its subcultures, this chapter will endeavour to show the persistence of a specific ideology, one which exhibits a fracture of expectations between radical and loyalist attitudes to land and the ownership of its productive capacities.

The temporal placing for a radicalized attitude to land within the metropolis is located within a particular political microculture of late eighteenth-century Spitalfields, one of London's highly specific urban, economic, and political spaces. This chapter traces the ideological consistency between radical Spitalfields and one of Covent Garden's most loyalist playwrights, Thomas John Dibdin.

That there exists a connection at all is, perhaps, surprising at first sight. Dibdin has been a particularly spectacular casualty of previous literary judgement, having been thoroughly lampooned in Leigh Hunt's influential essay 'Mr. T. Dibdin's Mock-Melodrama' written in 1808.[1] What denotes the successful distribution of a distinctive radical political ideology are the tell-tale markers of its reoccurrence within the discursive spaces of the dominant expressive culture. In the different print and writing cultures traced below, these recurrences are particularly easy to follow precisely because of their specificity to the Spitalfields area of London and to the great Theatre Royal protected by Royal Patent in Covent Garden. Spitalfields was defined by its boundaries in London's East End as being a by-word for poverty due to the decline of its weaving trades. By contrast, although lacking an obvious apparent connection with the degradations of Spitalfields, the Theatre Royal is a highly specific space whose major discursive events (its plays and songs) have been particularly well recorded because of the statuory requirement that its texts be licensed by the Lord Chamberlain.

The contention of this chapter is that political discourses supposedly situated at the margin are constitutive as well as illustrative, because they reappear at the centre. Throughout the discussion below, it will be noticed how frequent and commonplace are acts of censorship and repression. In eighteenth-century Spitalfields, a particularly resistive and nimble print culture often managed to evade Government and judicial surveillance and repression. Amongst the writers for Covent Garden or Drury Lane, there was little sign of a similar culture of defiance and, in any case, the economic implications for theatrical capital, as well as the routine textual modifications necessitated by circumnavigating the censor, resulted in co-operation with censorship. Nevertheless, it will be shown how closely integrated were the economic and political concerns of

---

[1] James Henry Leigh Hunt, *Leigh Hunt's Dramatic Criticism, 1808–1831*, ed. Lawrence Huston Houtchens and Carolyn Washburn Houtchens (New York: Columbia University Press, 1949), 10–14.

theatrical writing with the ideologies of those within the Spitalfields microculture.

Writing about plebeian symbolic expression, James Epstein has emphasized the fluidity of contemporary ritual cultural performatives (dinners, commemorations, toasting, processing) and how these were enactments within a social drama of meanings and roles often resisting straightforward articulation in writing or speech.[2] Their day-to-day enactment, which Epstein enumerates, provided much of the material basis on which formalized dramatic expression within the theatre could be fashioned, but plebeian culture was also extensively discursive and textual. Unlike the case with the Royal theatres, plebeian radical discourse within print culture adapted, re-formed, and redeployed themselves to suit wildly changing political conditions and persistent Government surveillance. The depth of the Spitalfields microculture forms the necessary discursive foundation for the theatrical culture which emerged later. Without this well-founded tradition of articulate radicalism and dissent expressed in print culture, theatre might have remained under the dead hand of the royal Patent Theatres, dependent on aristocratic patronage, deference, and political passivity but, as will be argued, in a time of crisis, marginal radical discourses resurfaced at the metropolitan centre.

The 'Master Book-Binder', bookseller, stationer, and printer Robert Hawes operated (save for one significant move to Croydon, south of London) from a number of premises in the Spitalfields area of east London from the mid-1760s through to the mid-1790s, at which time he disappears from view.[3] Hawes also owned a type foundry in London's Moorfields between 1775 and 1789, a crucial circumstance which not only explains his extensive use of elaborate fonts, innovative layouts, and typeset pictures but also

[2] James Epstein, *Radical Expression: Political Language, Ritual, and Symbol in England, 1790–1850* (Oxford: Oxford University Press, 1994) 149.

[3] David Worrall, 'Robert Hawes and the Millennium Press: A Political Micro-Culture of Late Eighteenth-Century Spitalfields', in Tim Fulford (ed.), *Romanticism and Millenarianism* (Basingstoke: Palgrave, 2002), pp. 167–82.

his ability to retain control of his productions.[4] Printing, politics, and typefounding were closely connected in the contemporary
London print trades. So embedded was Hawes in the culture of
the print trade that many of his outputs have yet to be catalogued
by the *ESTC*. As Paula McDowell has explained, we are only now
learning how to evaluate texts produced by eighteenth-century printers whose notions of authorship were extremely different from its
Romantic manifestations.[5] Hawes started his publishing career in
the 1760s when he was allied to Methodism before flirting with
Swedenborgianism in the early 1780s and then touching on the Uni-
versalism of the American Elhanan Winchester in the 1790s, before
becoming fully involved in the national issues of Paineite 'rights of
man' agitation around 1792. The last time his name resurfaces is as
an advocate of an early form of co-operative organization amongst
distressed Spitalfields weavers in 1796. The record of his presses gives
some idea of the demography of his working life although this is
incomplete because of the ephemeral nature of his imprints. Hawes
evaded, negotiated and innovated his way around contemporary
restraints on print culture while at the same time remaining within
definable London artisan communities as they passed through formu-
lations of natural rights towards agitation on behalf of Paine, Gordon,
and the backlash of early 1790s anti-Revolution organization.

Robert Hawes's roots were in a radical print culture of solid
independence, loud and vigorously individualistic. It is typical that,
before he disappears from view in 1796, the new cause to which he
became attached was one based in Spitalfields showing the beginnings
of a workers' co-operative aimed at combating the shortages caused
by the forestalling of grain in the wake of 1795 harvest failure. This
co-operative venture, founded within a distinctly plebeian sphere

[4] H. R. Plomer, G. H. Bushnell, and E. R. McC. Dix [sic], *A Dictionary of the Printers
and Booksellers who were at Work in England, Scotland and Ireland from 1726 to 1775*
(Oxford: Bibliographical Society, 1932), 120; Ian Maxted, *The London Book Trades,
1775–1800: A Preliminary Checklist of Members* (Folkestone: Dawson, 1977).

[5] Paula McDowell, *The Women of Grub Street: Press, Politics, and Gender in the
London Literary Marketplace 1678–1730* (Oxford: Clarendon Press, 1998).

of activity with the aim of facilitating an equitable distribution of foodstuffs and other necessities, is a significant precursor to the eruption of similar discourses concerning basic political economy in Dibdin's *Two Farmers*. The specificity (even simplicity) of their similar discourse concerns were put into representation at Covent Garden but were also available, earlier, in Spitalfields through the agency of the print culture centred on Robert Hawes.

The co-operative's beginnings can be found in *A True Description of the Real Causes and Principles of the British Fraternal and Philanthropic Community, United against Monopoly and Extortion*, a pamphlet printed at Hawes's press but written by Andrew Larcher who founded the society at a tavern meeting in Bethnal Green in early 1796. The names of Larcher's co-signatories strongly suggest the Huguenot populace of Spitalfields's notoriously impoverished silk-weaving industry.[6] The proposal to set up co-operatively owned storehouses of coal and corn is a significant development in the maturity of the radical movement out of Enlightenment natural rights agitation and into economic realities. Hawes also printed Larcher's *A Remedy For Establishing Universal Peace And Happiness, Against Universal Oppression, And Dangerous Tumults, Or, The Friendly Dictates Of Common Sense, To All Working People, Especially To The Silk Weavers Of London* ... ONE FIRMLY UNITED FRIENDLY AND PHILANTHROPIC SOCIETY OF FREE TRADESMEN. As well as the hint of millenarianism in its title, Hawes may also have welcomed the inclusion of Larcher's poem in *A Remedy* ('Go, plan of pure philanthropy, | Extend thy good to all mankind: | Go and chastise monopoly, | To feed the poor and lead the blind'). By the time of the publication in January 1797 of the society's constitution in *Fraternal and Philanthropic Policy, or Articles of the British Fraternal and Philanthropic Community, United against Monopoly and Extortion*, Hawes's name was missing from the imprint as, indeed, it is from the London trade directories for that year. It seems likely he died

---

[6] For a contemporary account of the area, see Daniel Isaac Eaton, 'Distresses of Spital Fields Weavers', *Politics for the People* (8, 16), Nov 1793, 110–14.

in 1796. The articles of the Community require payments into a 'friendly society' aimed at providing such things as pensions at 55, the education, clothing, and care of orphan children and the redistribution of weaving employment in times of hardship. In another revealing sign of the progressive impact of new attitudes on even the most stubborn 'old Jacks', female 'Sisters' were introduced as equal partners—provided they kept up with their payments.

As a fitting epitaph for a life spent immersed in print culture, radical politics, and dissenting religion deep inside one of London's poorest areas, Hawes would have been interested to know that a copy of his handbill *British Fraternal, and Philanthropic* COMMUNITY ('Fraternal Endeavours United for Reciprocal Advantages'), with his name proudly inscribed in the imprint as 'Printer to the Community', was forwarded for inspection to the Privy Council, a body similar in magnitude to today's Cabinet.[7] Even if he is unfamiliar to us today, the Government already had in its departmental files a considerable dossier of documents relating to Hawes and his lifetime in political activism.

The Fraternal and Philanthropic Community was a discrete response to a set of problems relative to poverty and subsistence. Hawes continuously advocated various political and religious ideologies through his publications. These discourses of millenarian, republican, and (almost) revolutionary socialism can all be located in eighteenth-century Spitalfields within this well-defined plebeian public sphere. They form the evidential basis for the depth, circulation, and longevity of two or three overlapping political ideologies. The political, economic, and social ideologies rehearsed by Hawes and his friends erupt in the drama of Thomas John Dibdin.

Polite English lyrical poetry has often been either complacent about the origins and distribution of national wealth or else resolutely triumphalist. For example, Richard Glover's 1739 poem *London: or, The Progress of Commerce* 'represents Commerce' (who 'is suppos'd on our invitation to choose England | for her chief abode, more

---

7 PRO P[rivy] C[ouncil] 1/34/90.

particularly London, our principal emporium, | as well as capital city')
as thriving in London: 'Fair seat of wealth and freedom ... | ... O
London: thee she hails, | Thou lov'd abode of Commerce.' Cornelius
Arnold's 1757 COMMERCE: *A Poem*, proclaimed a general national
fecundity: 'Hail, Commerce! fruitful hail! exhaustless Source! | Of all
that's great, magnificent, or good.' Even the rather more thoughtful
Ann Yearsley, in her 1796 poem *The* GENIUS OF ENGLAND ...
RECOMMENDING ORDER, COMMERCE AND UNION TO THE BRITONS,
asked '— Who ... | ... hails not Britannia's commerce?'

So how did we get from these statements of unbounded economic
optimism to this, two years later, in Thomas Malthus's *Essay on
the Principles of Population* (1798): 'Population, when unchecked,
increases in a geometrical ratio. Subsistence increases only in an
arithmetical ratio.' Or his even gloomier: 'the increase of wealth
of late years has had no tendency to increase the happiness of
the labouring poor' (chapter 16). Much of the answer lies in the
increased economic distress which came hard on the heels of the
1795 harvest failure, the immediate circumstance which prompted
Malthus to begin the *Essay*. The poor harvests of 1799–1801, the
period contiguous with the Spitalfields co-operative and Dibdin's
play, only accelerated the pessimism of Malthus's views. In *An
Investigation of the Cause of the Present High Price of Provisions*
(1800)—during which he refers to the out-of-print unavailability of
the *Essay on the Principles of Population*—Malthus wrote that he was

most strongly inclined to suspect, that the attempt ... to increase the parish
allowances in proportion to the price of corn, combined with the riches
of the country ... is, comparatively speaking, the sole cause, which has
occasioned the price of provisions in this country to rise so much higher
than the degree of scarcity would seem to warrant.

What is interesting is not so much Malthus's condemnation of the
Poor Laws but, rather, his apparently paradoxical view that the root of
the problem lies with 'the riches of the country'. In other words, the
national affluence which affords intervention into the market through
the Poor Laws serves to exacerbate the problems caused by high prices.

Not to put too fine a point on it, Malthus wrote in *An Investigation of the Cause of the Present High Price of Provisions* that

the whole of this deficiency, had things been left to their natural course, would have fallen almost exclusively on two, or perhaps three millions of the poorest inhabitants, a very considerable number of whom must in consequence have starved. The operation of the parish allowances, by raising the price of provisions so high, caused the distress to be divided among five or six millions ... instead of two or three, and to be by no means unfelt even by the remainder of the population.

Malthus's relative indifference to the short-term sufferings of the poor, although remarkable enough in its bluntness, should not deflect us from noticing that, in two years, he had moved from a subsistence argument to a prices or market forces argument.

There are a number of conclusions which may be drawn at this point. The first is that Malthus's cool estimation of the starvation of 'two, or perhaps three millions' of poor Britons marks the end of the eighteenth-century incarnation of civic humanism. The general argument of Malthus in the *Essay on the Principles of Population* was that the subsistence offered under the Poor Law had increased the propensity of people to marry younger which, in turn, gave rise to an unsustainable increase in population. As Malthus puts it in *An Investigation*, it is the 'parish allowances' which boost the prices of food for both rich and poor alike. Since Malthus was not encouraging the raising of allowances under the Poor Law (since this would bring about general distress to 'the remainder of the population'), the only inference to be drawn was that he was prepared to accept the death of two to three million people. Although coolly stated, Malthus's theory of economics did not cater for the poor who have bread prices lifted out of their reach because he had already objected to the raising of the Poor Law rates. The second point is that the Spitalfields co-operative project outlined in *A True Description of ... the British Fraternal and Philanthropic Community, United against Monopoly and Extortion* posits a collective answer to forestalling grain-hoarding farmers by placing reserves of food within the local community. While the efficiency of this remedy remained untested, the debate within the Spitalfields activists of 1796–7 made up a part of the responses to the food supply problems into which debate Malthus's writings were also aimed as interventions. In other words, the context of the arguments over the reality or fictiveness of harvest failures, plus the problems of maintaining a free market economy at a time when farmers were hoarding so as to force up the price of grain, were discourses which were already the subject of discussions amongst Spitalfields radical activists but also mirrored in Dibdin's *Two Farmers* written for the Covent Garden stage.

After the emollient implications of Malthus in his *An Investigation*, Thomas John Dibdin's *The Two Farmers* (1800) comes as something of a shock, a precise intervention opposed to Malthusian belief.[8] Dibdin's 'Musical Entertainment in two Acts' had been intended for performance at the Theatre Royal Covent Garden but was marked by the censor John Larpent as 'Withdrawn'. Evidently written and scheduled for October 1800, *The Two Farmers* came at the height of a combined harvest failure and alleged grain shortage which had brought about a crisis of national proportions and which was the subject of Malthus's discussions. The play was dated 10 October, scarcely three weeks after there had been scenes of acute unrest and rioting in London due to the shortages and high prices of bread, during which bakers were intimidated, houses attacked, and riotous crowds assembled in the Mark Lane corn market area. To quell and disperse the crowds, the Lord Mayor eventually had to call out two militia forces, the Union, Wapping, Limehouse and Ratcliffe Volunteers together with the South East District of Loyal London Volunteers.[9] The problem for Examiner Larpent was that Dibdin's piece featured as its principal villain a monopolizing and hoarding farmer bluntly named 'Locust'. Recalling the occasion over thirty years later, Dibdin described how (at the instigation of the Covent

---

[8] Larpent Plays, 1301, Huntington Library, Calif.

[9] David Worrall, *Radical Culture: Discourse, Resistance and Surveillance, 1790–1820* (Hemel Hempstead: Harvester, 1992), 42–7.

Garden management) he had gone to see Larpent at his home in Bedford Square in order to find out his objections. Larpent said that 'if the farce were to be acted, no respectable farmer would be able to pass through the streets lest people should cry out, "There goes an old Locust!"'[10] It need not necessarily be the case that Dibdin co-operatively 'withdrew' *The Two Farmers* even though that is how the Huntington copy is marked. Whoever was the scribe who wrote this on the wrapper, he also mistook Thomas John for Charles, his father, by attributing the play to 'C. Dibdin'.

At this point, it is timely to recollect that the dynamics of censorship ensure that a withdrawn play is not likely to resurface. Wealthy or well-connected writers such as Lady Wallace or Martin Archer Shee might contrive to have an edition printed but, without success in performance, an unperformed play by a comparatively unknown scion of a family of playwrights leads to the virtual erasure of the text, save for its location in the archive (although even here the provenance history of the Huntington's deposit of Larpent plays suggests that fate and good fortune played some part in the manuscript's survival). If censorship leads to literary speculation, as it tends to, one is forced to project the hypothetical reception of *The Two Farmers*. With Covent Garden playhouse holding about 3,000 people and supposing a two-thirds full house (perhaps a cautious estimate given that it was the beginning of the season), a modest five-night run for Dibdin's *Two Farmers* might have yielded a London audience of 10,000 people. In other words, 10,000 people who would themselves be aware of the rise in food prices, and possibly also of the bread and bakery riots in the Mark Lane area of the City of London, missed the opportunity of witnessing such a highly topical drama problematizing their very predicament about food shortages.

As well as being very topical, Dibdin's play also tapped deep-seated resentments within popular culture about the morality of farmers. For example, there was a long abiding memory of the 'Golden Farmer' executed at Newgate, a man named William Davis (1627–1690),

---

[10] Thomas Dibdin, *The Reminiscences of Thomas Dibdin* (1837) ii. 25.

whose case held almost legendary status commemorated in publications such as the chap book *The Surprising Life and Adventures of Robin Hood ... To which is added, The Wonderful Life of William Davis, Commonly called the Golden Farmer* (1805). Far from being a Robin Hood figure, Davis was alleged to have used his farming activities in Bagshot Heath, Surrey, as a front for highway robbery. As far as popular memory was concerned (confirmed by his notoriety metamorphosing into the name of a local tavern in Frimley by 1729), Davis's position as an affluent farmer was used to disguise his criminality: the implication being that many wealthy farmers were covert robbers of the people.[11] The ability of the metaphor of the 'Golden Farmer' to switch between being a specific reference to William Davis and yet a term used to encompass all farmers is not only a fascinating example of the fluidity of popular history but also an indicator of the cultural forces which must have impelled Larpent to censor *The Two Farmers*. The cultural dynamics of the near-legendary 'Golden Farmer' would have served to magnify, rather than diminish, the potency of Dibdin's representation of Farmer Locust.

The extent to which the notion of the 'Golden Farmer' highwayman continued to be embedded in contemporary popular culture is implicit in the success of Benjamin Nottingham Webster's later Boxing Day two-acter, *The Golden Farmer; or, The Last Crime: A Domestic Drama*, which ran successfully at the Royal Coburg, Sadler's Wells, Pavilion, Queen's, and Clarence theatres from 1832 to 1833. By the time of Webster's *Golden Farmer*, the worst days of Captain Swing agricultural unrest were over although corn prices after the 1831 harvest remained high but, in any case, unlike Dibdin's *Two Farmers*, Webster's piece did not fall under the jurisdiction of the Lord Chamberlain's Examiner (by then George Colman the Younger). However, the notion of the 'Golden Farmer' was still resonant enough in working-class circles for a treatise on agricultural improvement addressed to working men published in 1831 to take

[11] G. C. B. Poulter, '*Golden Farmer': The Inn and the Highwayman* (Camberley, Surrey: 1934).

the name as an innuendo to distinguish it from other types of agricultural writing. Edward Jarman Lance's *The Golden Farmer* drew on his experience as an auctioneer associated with the Mechanics' Institutes in giving 'Practical Operations of Husbandmen, To Enable them to Grow More Corn, and Increase the Employment of the Labourer'. In other words, the tension between farming and labour embodied in *The Two Farmers* remained as a continuing social fracture into the 1830s. As it happens, Lance's knowledge of the food shortages of 1800 give as succinct an account as any of the problems of that year, one still recollected over thirty years later.[12] As far as Dibdin is concerned, however, his experience of 1800 was a straightforward case of the censorship of a literary work.

Dibdin was perfectly aware that the late summer of 1800 was 'a season of monopoly and much artificial scarcity' and fully intended *The Two Farmers* to be a 'successful ridicule of monopoly' although, no doubt, the clarity with which he formulated this reminiscence from the hindsight of the 1830s may have been obscurer in this, his second year at Covent Garden.[13] At one level, *The Two Farmers* appears also intended to allude to the monopolistic position of the two Royal theatres since such restrictive practices were endemic to contemporary society: the farmers were merely imitating the practices of theatrical patentees. However, far from being a radical reformer, Dibdin himself came from a family of theatrical writers and dramatic entrepreneurs who were widely involved with the portrayal of loyalist attitudes in contemporary theatre. His father, Charles, was particularly well known for his ardently patriotic songs, typified by his uncompromising piece, *Britains Strike Home* ('the very first

---

[12] 'In 1800, a scarcity was experienced in England; we were then at war with half Europe; no corn could be obtained; a quarter of wheat was sold for 10*l*., the quartern loaf was 1*s*. 10 $\frac{1}{2}$*d*; orders in council were made that no puddings or pies were to be indulged in; no starch, nor hair powder, nor paste, nor distillation was to be made from wheat; the quantity to each person was regulated; barley flour was to be used with the wheat. Riots took place in London, August, 1800, on account of the high prices of provision' (Edward Jarman Lance, *The Golden Farmer, Being an Attempt to Unite the Facts Pointed Out by Nature, in the Sciences of Geology, Chemistry, and Botany* (1831), 47).

[13] *Reminiscences of Thomas Dibdin*, ii. 25.

word that you speak is your last' in his song 'A Welcome to the French').[14] Dibdin senior was receiving a Government pension for his loyalist efforts by 1803, so it is at first sight entirely consistent that his son's *Two Farmers* was projected to end with a finale comprising the entrance of two companies of Volunteers, the loyalist militias ostensibly raised to counter a possible French invasion but also, as has been seen, occasionally used in a domestic context.[15] They were long accustomed to receiving loyalist addresses from the stages of the Royal theatres such as Drury Lane, but the Volunteerists themselves were profoundly unpredictable in their allegiances.[16] Gillian Russell has explained the complex interaction between the Volunteers and notions of contemporary military theatricality, noting that Volunteers (who could not be court-martialled and, hence, were 'acting' at soldiery) may not have been unequivocally perceived as 'loyal'.[17] For example, in one comic song, 'Billy le Maitre', which was performed at the Royal Circus in 1809, Billy ('No Volunteer ever look'd smarter') drills on Kennington Common to impress his lover only to 'cut but a comical figure' and have to be relieved of duty ('Dear Col'nel, I pray, get me out of this fray, | My nerves are annoy'd by the rattle').[18] Russell's account of Volunteerists' taste for theatricality makes it is quite likely Dibdin envisaged the use of real Volunteerists in the finale.

Writing of the period around 1802, the fencing-master Henry Angelo, who had connections with the acting profession going back to the Garrick era, recalled that as well as coaching many actors in fencing, he also taught swordsmanship to the 'many gentlemen, pupils who rode in the City of London Light Horse

[14] Charles Dibdin, *Songs &c. In Britons Strike Home A New Entertainment of Sans Souci* (1803), 13.
[15] Gillian Russell, *The Theatres of War: Performance, Politics, and Society 1793–1815* (Oxford: Clarendon Press, 1995), 101–3.
[16] See 'Address to the Volunteers of Great Britain', 24 October 1794, included with an afterpiece by James Cobb, *The Glorious First of June*, first performed 2 July 1794, *London Stage*, 5 (1694), Larpent Plays, 2410, Huntington Library, Calif.
[17] Russell, *Theatres of War*, 50–1.
[18] *Fairburn's Laughable Songster, and Fashionable Quizzer, For 1809* (1809), 14–15.

Volunteers', whose magnificent horses and 'general appointments' of militia membership made the corps one which, for the 'wealth of its members, could not be matched by the whole world'.[19] In a local squib drama (*C*[oggesha]*ll Volunteer Corps. A Farce. In Two Acts*) written in Coggeshall, Essex, in 1804, the wife of a dandified, self-appointed lieutenant in the Volunteers ('My dear, would you think it, I am a lieutenant, a lieutenant 'pon honour . . . Lord, lovee! What an elegant figure I shall make') points out the highly self-conscious theatricality of the corps ('What the d—l, would make stage-player of me?').[20] In 1800 the invasion scares that would be prevalent in 1803 were distant enough for them to be able to indulge this theatrical foible of having real Volunteerists on the Covent Garden stage.

In any case, in the Irish Rebellion years of 1797 and 1798, Dibdin's brother, Charles Isaac Mungo Dibdin, had worked with veteran showman and ex-soldier Philip Astley who had already used 'live' soldiers to intimidate the volatile Dublin theatregoers at his Amphitheatre Royal when he fitted 'a large Sentry Box' in the middle of the Gallery complete with 'two soldiers; their firelocks and Bayonets projecting'.[21] Since the time of George II, Guardsmen had customarily stood duty at the Royal theatres subsequent to a backstage disturbance by a nobleman ('flushed with . . . streams of usquebaugh') during a performance of *The Beggar's Opera* at the Lincoln's Inn Fields theatre.[22] In the early 1810s at Sadler's Wells Theatre, Thomas's brother, Charles Isaac Mungo, wrote and produced two 'musical and military melanges', *Vittoria, or*

[19] Henry Angelo, *Reminiscences of Henry Angelo, With Memoirs of his Late Father and Friends* (1828), 268.

[20] An Inhabitant of Coggeshall, *C ____ ll Volunteer Corps. A Farce. In Two Acts* (Colchester, 1804), 9, 11.

[21] Charles Isaac Mungo Dibdin, *Professional and Literary Memoirs of Charles Dibdin the Younger, Dramatist and Upward of Thirty Years Manager of Minor Theatres*, ed. George Speaight (London: Society for Theatre Research, 1956), 24.

[22] R. Humphreys, *The Memoirs Of J. Decastro, Comedian . . . Accompanied By An Analysis Of The Life Of The Late Philip Astley, Esq. . . . Also An Accompanying History Of The Royal Circus, Now The Surrey Theatre* (1824), 195–7.

Wellington's Laurels (1812) and *The Battle of Salamanca* (1812), which mustered 'two very respectable lines of Infantry, properly armed and accoutred' in order to mount a staged bayonet '*pas de charge*, in miniature' simply by extending the usage of soldiery he was already employing within his theatre.[23]

No doubt to the consternation of Larpent (who had already marked up fairly extensive excisions), Thomas Dibdin at Covent Garden had proposed that the two Volunteer companies entered 'bearing a Banner inscribed "protection"'. In the context of October 1800's bread riots and the sentiments of Dibdin's play, there can be no doubt that the word 'protection' evoked not only a standard loyalist pledge by the Volunteer militiamen but also the 'protection' of the general populace against the real-life counterparts of the monopolizing Locust. Again, had it been represented on stage at Covent Garden, the audience could scarcely have missed the political paradox that the Volunteerists were offering their 'protection' not only against Bonaparte but also against hoarding farmers. Such a piece of theatre stages a formidable, and unexpected, fracture within loyalist ideology by forcing patriots to be both anti-Napoloen and anti-British farmer.

It is easy to predictively oversimplify the influence of the loyalist sympathies of Dibdin's family background. The kinds of loyalist ideology they espoused were steeped in a belief in the general munificence and plentitude of the British economy. As far back as the pantomime *Vineyard Revels; or, Harlequin Bacchanal* (*c*.1775) for Sadler's Wells, Charles Dibdin senior had composed songs conveying an obvious pride in the abundancy of the British harvest. Supplanting the 'foreign Vintage' of the grape, *Vineyard Revels*'s choral 'Hop-Pickers Song' celebrated beer, 'the full Measures' of the 'Rich Harvests of Corn' and the 'Flavour of Hops [which] crown the Juice of the Field' (p. 7). In a telling indication of just how far popular songs of the theatre helped define nationalist attitudes, Dibdin's Hop-Pickers

---

[23] *Memoirs of Charles Dibdin the Younger*, 107.

Song evokes not only the authentic appetites of rustic labourers, but it also defines beer drinking as an inherently British activity in contrast with the implicitly vinous and befuddled French:

> 'Tis the Liquor we love, 'tis the Juice we revere,
> 'Tis the Spring of our Courage, the true British Beer.
> Content with the Riches of Britain's fair Isle,
> Let the Subjects of Britain rejoice,
> May no foreign Vintage our Senses beguile,
> No Stream of the Grape have our Voice! (pp. 6–7)

In *Vineyard Revels*'s concluding chorus, an exact correspondence is made between the plentiful harvests of a fruitful Britain and the nation's consequent climate of political liberty: 'Hail! Happy Britain, favour'd Isle! | Where Peace and Plenty ever smile, | These are the Riches of the Free, | And such the Sweets of Liberty' (p. 8). Within this context of a British agriculture and polity continually celebrated for its 'Peace and Plenty', it is clear that his son's *Two Farmers* represents a surprisingly radical intervention. However, if this was Charles Dibdin's true loyalist position in the 1770s, T. J. Dibdin's father was himself also typical in exhibiting many signs of the contemporary social rift occasioned by the effects of monopolistic farmers during the 1800 grain crisis.

The ideological fracture occasioned by the 1800 harvest failures reached through to committed loyalists such as Charles Dibdin. In 1799–1800 Dibdin senior was engaged in preparing an illustrated tour book, *Observations on a Tour Through Almost the whole of England, and a considerable part of Scotland* (1801), which made several comments on the social changes of the era. In many respects, he comes across as straightforward reactionary, given, for example to long fulminations against such things as circulating libraries ('those drains, those common sewers'), but he was quite steadfast in his opposition to grasping farmers.[24] Dibdin found that the days of the humble farmer were gone, exchanged for farmers' 'airs, affectations, and caprice', and he dared anyone to explain to him 'in what way such extravagance can be maintained unless by monopoly, and its concomitants, forestalling and regrating'.[25] These comments are quite unequivocal in placing the blame squarely on the practice of hoarding grain in order to force up the price of bread. Rather like his son in the Finale of *The Two Farmers*, Dibdin senior fully subscribed to the notion of a natural fertility destroyed by a corrupt farming community, 'at the moment the blessings of heaven are showered upon these wretches, they almost seem exasperated against Providence for anticipating the necessity of bringing forward their hidden stores'. It is striking that Dibdin appears to have been personally prepared to confront farmers with these views during his tours, adding that 'I have received great pleasure in mortifying farmers upon this subject.'[26]

Given the views of his father on the subject of forestalling and regrating (practices of illegally controlling markets), Thomas Dibdin's *Two Farmers* is more understandable in the ways it combines traits of traditional loyalist values with evidence of emerging social rifts. By the time Dibdin was contemplating the piece, fractures in Volunteerist ranks had already broken out. At this juncture in the autumn of 1800, some of the Volunteer companies who had already been sent to disperse grain blockades or quell food riots had instead broken ranks and sided with the agitators. In particular, even the middle-class London Light Horse Volunteers underwent massive disaffections with resignations, zero recruitment, and repeated failure to turn up to drill (even for the King).[27] Conspicuous by their absence on parade, perhaps local Volunteerists contemplated treading the boards of the Theatre Royal Covent Garden. Whatever the

[24] Charles Dibdin, *Observations on a Tour Through Almost the whole of England, and a considerable part of Scotland* (1801), 135–43.

[25] Ibid. 287–8.   [26] Ibid. 290.

[27] Roger Wells, *Wretched Faces: Famine in Wartime England 1763–1803* (Gloucester: Alan Sutton, 1988), 121–32; 260–73, 270.

circumstances, it seems likely that Dibdin had friends who were Volunteerist sympathizers, perhaps even Volunteers themselves. In his piece for Covent Garden, *Harlequin's Tour; or, The Dominion of Fancy* (1800), Dibdin staged a song ('We'll count it victory to die') performed in the character of a 'Volunteer Officer' but which was contributed to him by a 'literary Friend to the Theatre', a Volunteerist poet, perhaps.[28]

The circumstances of the food crisis certainly gave a further dimension to Dibdin's stage directions for the finale, which specifies that the female chorus meet the Volunteers whereupon 'The girls exchange their arms for rustic implements, with which a general dance takes place'. In the precise contemporary registers of the early autumn of 1800 now recoverable, the exchange of 'arms-for-ploughshares' denotes not only anti-war sentiment but also an invitation for the Volunteerists to side with the populace in the provision and restoration of food supplies. Even on its own, this projection of an anti-war stance represented by the intervention of the domestic sphere into the national through the agency of women removing the Volunteerists' firearms and replacing them with the tools of agriculture, is a surprising theatrical finale projected for staging at the heart of the empire's capital during a time of war. Three years later, in 1803, John Cartwright Cross's *Our Native Land, And Gallant Protectors* for the Royal Circus mixed songs by 'steady Sam', uncertainly a soldier or civilian, at time when Napoleon's 'flat-bottom'd boats' threatened invasion and the piece also featured a song by an 'Officer of the Surry Yeoman Cavalry' ('Independent, no lucre our service secures, | . . . But the love of our country alone!'), but the whole spectacle was mixed with a substantial opening 'Rural Scene' of singing milk-maids and haymaking lasses.[29] In other words, the representation

[28]   Thomas John Dibdin, *Songs, Chorusses, &c. In The New Pantomime of Harlequin's Tour; Or, The Dominion of Fancy* (1800), 13.

[29]   John Cartwright Cross, *Songs, Recitatives, Chorusses, &c. in the New, Grand, Local, and Temporary Divertisement, Called, Our Native Land, and Gallant Protectors: Performed at the Royal Circus, For the First Time, On Thursday, June 23d, 1803* (1803), 7, 9, 12, 15.

of a unified nation ready to take arms against an invader was only credible if carefully supported by allusions to Britain's certain agricultural fertility.

Of course, the very presence of a character like Locust in the play is itself suggestive of the breakdown of the kind patrician civic humanist consensus which Malthus's theorizing elsewhere confirmed: 'haven't I been a useful man—passing my time in the honourable pursuit of agriculture, & keeping the profits of it all to myself? Dont I get all the farms into my hands, and the corn into my Granaries to prevent famine, and for the good of the nation?' The shaded passage traces Larpent's worried 'blue pencil' excisions but it is noticeable that the lines depend on an obvious irony which must have been clear to the audience, that farmers' full granaries are not intended 'for the good of the nation'. Of course, Dibdin was far from advocating radical political agendas. Both the Squire and, ultimately, the eventually reformed Locust speak up to restore confidence in the status quo. Nevertheless, the topicality of the issues contemplated in *The Two Farmers* led Larpent to cut virtually all of the Squire's concluding censorious homily to Locust: 'Let your future conduct repair the mischiefs your avarice may have occasioned. And let us commence our sports with a hope that the blessings we enjoy and the effects of honest labour may never be contracted by the sordid views of narrow minded monopoly.'

For his part, one senses that the Examiner of Plays, John Larpent, considered the very utterance of the word 'monopoly' to be disruptive of social cohesion at a time when there was tremendous uncertainty as to the true causes of high food prices. It is a pattern of behaviour in the censor, an extreme sensitivity towards establishing critical dialogue within the ruling class, which has already been described in Chapter 3. Within radical circles, the tradition became quickly established that the dearth was the result of forestallers and not of a genuine harvest failure. Recollecting these times in 1819, the radical journalist Richard Carlile in his *Republican* knew he could count on an assumed knowledge of this version of shortages during '1800, and 1801 [when] ... hundreds of individuals were starved even to death by a dearth of the necessaries of life which was proved afterwards to be only an artificial one: to be a dearth created by the murderous hand of monopoly.'[30] As far as Malthusian speculation is concerned, the subsistence theory elaborated in the 1798 *Essay on the Principles of Population* was starkly refuted in *The Two Farmers* where, far from presenting scenes of stricken harvests, poor weather or a ravenous population, the play had specifically begun with 'Scene 1st A rich Autumnal Landscape' giving onto a cheerful chorus singing 'Merry we seek the Harvest plain, | Merry we reap till day is done.' Dibdin's opening chorus of October 1800 decidedly makes it clear that, in his opinion, there was no bad harvest or naturally caused food shortage that year.

In consequence, it is difficult to estimate the loss to the credibility of Malthus's theory which would have been occasioned by its implicit critique before a large metropolitan audience at a time of crisis. Certainly, the economic analysis offered by Dibdin's abortive two-act 'entertainment' dramatizes cultural fractures inherent in earlier incarnations of Malthusian theory, which the political economist had urgently striven to modify in *An Investigation of the Cause of the Present High Price of Provisions* (1800). In Dibdin's play high prices are not caused by failed harvests but by grasping landowners. Even Locust, urging a tardy reaper, revealingly says 'To work, I say—Singing indeed with such a fine harvest in hand.' Ultimately, patrician investment in loyalty to the state has been undermined by forestallers and monopolizers, which was exactly the conundrum the senior politicians and judiciary had to resolve in the important contemporary case of the prosecution of the forestalling brewer Samuel Ferrand Waddington, discussed below.

However, the views represented in *The Two Farmers* were not particularly contingent on legalities or Malthusian theory because the play specifically details the harm done to the integrity of national loyalty and the disservice to the armed forces by selfish farmers whose scheming deceptions are betrayed by the general, commonsense

---

[30] Richard Carlile, *The Republican*, 10 (1819), 410–11.

observation that grain standing in the fields is plentiful. The play's representative sailor, Snatch, both celebrates Royal Navy blockading and, incidentally, affirms this natural plenitude:

At sea I've been laughing to see our enemies peeping out of their ports like so many Periwinkles from their shells, and drawing in their horns the moment a Gun could be brought to bear on them. On the Ocean I laught to see our flag fly and our trade flourish in spite of all the World, & on land, when the bounty of providence is spread over our fruitful fields to be sad wou'd be wickedness and ingratitude.

The sailor's articulation that 'the bounty of providence is spread over our fruitful fields' carries within it not only a minor register of the common ownership of 'our fruitful fields' but also an appeal to the validity of immediate scrutiny sanctioned by such a highly respected representative of the nation's military guardians: the sailor can see for himself that the fields are full of corn and that trade flourishes.

However, the part in Dibdin's *Two Farmers* which most clearly reveals its background in a contemporary popular culture which was rapidly assimilating liberal or radical ideals is the figure of Locust's farm labourer, an African ex-slave called Caesar. That Dibdin assumed the Covent Garden audience would readily accept as unexceptional the idea of a black man working on an English farm is itself revealing but what is most striking is Caesar's assertion of his possession of independent political and judicial rights equivalent to those of any English-born farm labourer. When Locust tries to strike him for not working hard enough, there ensues an exchange between Locust's automatic racial stereotyping and Caesar's swift delineation of the judicial framework potentially available for his protection as a black man working in England:

LOCUST. 'Phsa! all idleness . . . The harvest is a very serious business and if people come a field to cut capers instead of corn, what's to become of us? . . . what! I bid you do nothing You sable son of a sugar cane, if you tell me so, I'll kick you.
CAESAR. Top, Massa, top! Slave once, not now. Good Massa make Christian bring to great England. No Slave here—You pay, I worke—You kick,

I tell Massa *Kenyon*—he speak twelve men in a Box—dey take poor Negerman's [*sic*] part, & you kick black man no more, I warrant, Massa.

Caesar's invocation of the Chief Justice of King's Bench, Lord Kenyon, was highly topical in the autumn of 1800, so much so that the obviously alarmed censor marked it for excision. Once again Dibdin's censored entertainment uncovers a sharply topical reference to the issue of forestalling farmers.

Dibdin's play written in October 1800 came at the height of national controversy surrounding the final judgment expected to be delivered by Lord Kenyon concerning the protracted prosecution of the alleged forestaller, Samuel Ferrand Waddington, a case which was itself representative of the widespread concern raised at a national and popular level about the role of a moral economy in a time of food shortages.[31] In short, Waddington had already been convicted of forestalling grain in a lower court in Worcester in July 1800 but his testing of English common law necessitated Kenyon's final judgment at the beginning of the Michaelmas term in November 1800.

Legally, the issue was a landmark in defining the relationship between the rights of the farmers—to go to market when and whether they chose—and the rights of the consumer to have fair prices for food. It was a difficult and decisive case for adjudication between competing contemporary notions of natural rights versus civic duty. In many ways, Waddington's case embodies the national tensions which were the subject of critique by Malthus and intervention by both Dibdin and the London populace during their rioting. It is a remarkable piece of politicized theatre that Dibdin's black African ex-slave, Caeser, should invoke the protection of Lord Keynon on the eve of his anticipated judgment on the issue of forestalling farmers.

Dated to the first two weeks of October, and framed by both rioting and the impending Kenyon judgment, *The Two Farmers* could hardly have been more topical in its decisive presentation

---

[31] See Douglas Hay, 'The State and the Market in 1800: Lord Kenyon and Mr Waddington', *Past and Present*, 162 (1999), 163–94.

of contemporary popular opinions about grasping farmers whose agricultural language Dibdin seized upon for its obvious ironies:

[LOCUST]. I've a great deal of corn I mean to lock up out of the way and I just want a little thrashing.

LARRY. Lock up corn! then you must want threshing most damnably . . .

However, the character of Caesar also represents a crude but important post-colonial perspective on English political culture. Caesar's song swiftly encapsulates his own narrative history and mistreatment at the hands of, successively, buccaneers and Christian missionaries ('Buckraman steal me | From de Coastee Guinea | Christian Massa pray | Call me heathen doggee | Den I run away | Very much he floggee . . .') to which he adds a more traditional list of the professions loathed by the English poor, including the lawyer ('People den I saw | Go to Law so funny, | Dey take all the Law, | Massa all the money') and the doctor ('Hold him hand out so | And de fee dey givee | Dey be fool enough | Mass make great supee'). But, of course, it is the depth of assimilation of notions of judicial structure, independent juries, and natural rights which is so sharply defined in Caesar's prompt rebuttal of Locust. Dibdin's presentation of Caesar as an African ex-slave projects the strengths of his contemporary 'patriotic' discourses by contrasting them with the conventional formulations of loyalism now made visibly outmoded by the greed of Locust and made questionable or problematic when figured in the finale's Volunteer parade.

If British drama has lost an important piece of interventionist writing in the censorship of *The Two Farmers*, what should also not be overlooked is the implicit personal affront it caused to the sensibilities of a clearly politicized playwright. Not least, whatever happened in Dibdin's casting projections for the piece, the withdrawal of *The Two Farmers* must have affronted the author's sense of patriotic justice.[32] A glimpse of this can be judged by further contextualizing

---

[32] As well commenting in his memoir, *The Reminiscences of Thomas Dibdin, of the Theatres Royal, Covent Garden, Drury Lane, Haymarket &c. and Author of The Cabinet &c.*, 2 vols. (1827), the *DNB* also records his irritation at Larpent's objections.

The Two Farmers' place in Dibdin's works written both before and after the food crisis years of 1800–1. One year earlier (7 October 1799), his musical entertainment *The Naval Pillar*, which reflected topical proposals to build a national monument to Nelson, Howe, and other British naval heroes, had played successfully at Covent Garden. One commentator thought Dibdin's 'political squib' had just about enough 'pageantry to render … it a favourite with the old dotards, and children … who … generally constitute the major part the audience', but through it Dibdin also expressed the serious public duty of honouring dead British sailors by caring for their widows and orphans (BEN BOWSPRIT. 'And as for the monuments our countrymen may give us, we tars will never forget that they have built a lasting monument to their own honour, in providing for our wives and children', p. 18).[33] In other words, the violence done to posterity by the loss of *The Two Farmers*—save for its placement in the Huntington's Larpent archive—was not the only casualty of the act of censorship. A more immediate injury was done to the loyalist sensibilities of Dibdin himself, whose reverence for patriotic endeavour in a time of war he celebrated in *The Naval Pillar*, were undermined by the treachery of hoarding farmers one year later.

Despite the ephemeral nature of this genre of dramatic writing, works like *The Naval Pillar* are reminders that Dibdin's emotional investment in contemporary politics also enabled him to be a surprisingly perceptive commentator. Dibdin's social analysis is sufficiently perceptive to betray his awareness of the possible social rifts present in a contemporary Britain which had, by this time, already been at war for nearly seven years. *The Naval Pillar*'s pacifist Quaker, Habakuk (who 'isn't nobody's enemy', p. 14), and whose attendance on a sailor's sweetheart eventually proves harmlessly innocent, may have been a figure intended to denote subtle changes in contemporary cultural attitudes to war, or tuned to reflect some popular level of war-weariness. At the least, Habakuk's presentation

[33] *The Dramatic Censor; Or, Weekly Theatrical Report*, 26, 28 June 1800, 305.

is representative of commonplace social stresses within the ordinary population when husbands and lovers are away at war. However, *The Naval Pillar*'s choral finale, with its 'open view near the sea, a Pillar . . . discovered, inscribed to the memory of our Naval Heroes' (p. 24), also stresses the importance of maintaining 'The fruits of our Commerce round Liberty's shrine' (p. 27), a reiteration of the war's underlying economic objectives. Compared with another of his entertainments for Covent Garden, *The Mouth of the Nile; or, the Glorious First of August* (1798)—which celebrated Nelson's victory at Aboukir—the tone of *The Naval Pillar* is rather more muted and thoughtful.[34] Nevertheless, the sort of perceptive flair for reconstructing contemporary topics, which proved to be so visible in *The Two Farmers*, is also implicit in *The Mouth of the Nile* where (at least as detailed on the printed page) the piece's surprising representations include anti-French sentiments voiced through an Egyptian peasant, Michael, and a militarily cross-dressed sweetheart, Susan, who wants to follow her man into battle.

However much it was simultaneously prompted by the exigencies of playwriting to fit Covent Garden's busy schedule, there is plenty to suggest that *The Two Farmers* exemplifies a considered set of ideological positions concerning recent changes in British culture. Historically, the play was much more the victim of repression than any of Hawes's printing exploits in Spitalfields. Although Larpent might have been prepared to allow the play to be staged with the extensive cuts he had marked, Dibdin did not have the luxury of working within a social or economic vacuum. With a family to support and Theatre Royal patronage to consider, discretion must have proved the better part of valour.

---

[34] On *The Mouth of the Nile*, see *Reminiscences of Thomas Dibdin*, i. 219–21. Dibdin also recollected that Elizabeth Inchbald had appeared to object to the Quaker Habakuk in *The Naval Pillar* (whom Dibdin thought the 'fiddle of the piece') when she saw it in Dibdin's company. Inchbald was thinking that time of an imminent confusion of precedence concerning the Quaker family in her own forthcoming play, *The Wise Man of the East*, but it is evident that Dibdin appears to have assumed her objections were on the ground of religious sensitivity. Dibdin was paid £20 for the copyright: *Reminiscences of Thomas Dibdin*, i. 262–3, 77.

A contemporary guide to the London playhouses, in itself symptomatic of theatre's centrality in popular culture, poured scorn on Dibdin's lowly origins. *Crosby's Pocket Companion To The Playhouses* (1796) gives some indication as to how even such a well known theatrical family could become the victims of snobbery. Around this time, Dibdin senior had a side line in selling his songs from, as Crosby termed it, 'a shed' in the Covent Garden piazza. When he opened up larger premises a little further away, Crosby (who had been refused a memoir for his *Companion* by Dibdin) spitefully described it as 'a *shop*, we beg pardon, a *warehouse*, in the Strand'. As a further guide to the reception he might expect, despite his famous father, Crosby added in his guide that 'The town is again threatened with a similar production this winter; a ricketty cadet of the same house.'[35] In other words, Dibdin junior was struggling in a marketplace which would give him few breaks.

Through direct censorship and some understandable authorial timidity, the suppression of *The Two Farmers* was complete. When, at the instigation of the Covent Garden management, Dibdin sought out Larpent to confront him in his Bedford Square home, he got little response. Recalling the interview thirty years later, Dibdin recollected that 'Mr. Larpent would hardly deign to listen to a word ... he turned a deaf ear to all I could say.' Larpent represents the quietly repressive stranglehold of officialdom: aloof, unresponsive, unmovable. Apart from the loss to the literary canon, it is difficult to properly evaluate the consequences of censorship. For Covent Garden, there was some degree of inconvenience because the theatre's composer, John Moorhead, had written the music, it was already put into rehearsal and the two principal parts had been assigned. In addition, Covent Garden would have forfeited its licensing fee for the piece since Larpent had worked on it, marking it up for excision. Furthermore, not least, Dibdin lost the chance of the one hundred pounds copyright fee he had agreed upon.[36]

[35] *Crosby's Pocket Companion To The Playhouses* (1796), 104–5.
[36] *Reminiscences of Thomas Dibdin*, ii. 25.

However, since Dibdin was a frequent writer for Covent Garden, its exact cultural position and 'scene of writing' can be precisely determined. When grouped and considered together, it was quite an ideologically marked piece of writing: it defied Malthus and the farming community, vilified the practice of forestalling, condemned as unpatriotic the economic manipulators undermining the war effort, presented blacks as integrated into English political and judicial culture, and, finally, it barely stopped short of proposing armed Volunteers as enforcers of freeing-up food supplies. This play of 1800, intended for a Theatre Royal, dramatizes radical positions which were common to areas such as poverty-ridden Spitalfields. At a chapel in White-Row, Spitalfields (the thoroughfare later lived in by Robert Hawes), thirty years earlier the preacher Edward Hitchin had also condemned the forestallers and monopolizers, 'Notwithstanding the large demands for corn, our granaries are full. Now the hoarders of corn, those worst of thieves, as unmoved with the distresses of families, as deaf to cries, as blind to tears, as the senseless stone, can no longer starve the poor, and make a prey of their necessity.'[37] Such sentiments, once the province of the politicized discourses of Spitalfields, were now being expressed by a playwright working for one of the London Royal theatres.

Dibdin's play is an excellent reminder that this was a society undergoing enormous political change and transition during a time of war. As the historian of the 1800 food scarcities, Roger Wells, has remarked, Kenyon's judgment against Waddington marked 'a major change in government policy', proving that his 'serious conviction for profiteering had penetrated the highest levels' of contemporary society.[38] It is remarkable that the loyalist author of *The Naval Pillar* and *The Mouth of the Nile* was one and the same as the author of *The Two Farmers*. Elsewhere, it is possible to pick up the signals of such fractures being manifested but this time beyond the reach

[37] Edward Hitchin, *A sermon Preached at the New Meeting, in White-Row Spital-Fields, On Thursday 29 November 1759* (1759), 23.
[38] Wells, *Wretched Faces*, 87.

of the Examiner of Plays. At the Royal Amphitheatre in Lambeth in 1802, one of their most popular comic songs at the time of the Peace of Amiens condemned *'regrating'* and warned the 'glutton' farmer 'Mr. *sheep*' [*sic*] that the 'friends of John Bull, shall all *bite* at his *mutton!*' if *'monopoly* crops' forced the 'old *quartern loaf*' to two shillings. As with Dibdin's theatrical pieces, however, a distrust of the hoarders did not stop them also enjoying singing 'The Hero of the Nile' ('a true gallant tar, | Brave NELSON, LORD NELSON for ever!').[39] This dispersal into the favourite songs of popular culture helps define the context of many of the political attitudes also found in *The Two Farmers*. Dibdin's evident loyalism was obviously an ideological belief which included the presence of quite precise personal boundaries of deference. In 1800, those boundaries had been crossed.

[39] *The Words of the Most Favorite* [*sic*] *Songs, Duets, &c. Sung at the Royal Amphitheatre, Westminster-Bridge, and the Royalty Theatre, Well-Close Square* (Lambeth, 1802), 1–2, 9.

6

The Theatricalization of British Popular Culture: Queen Caroline and the Royal Coburg Theatre

THIS chapter examines the political use of theatricality by Caroline of Brunswick, the wife of the Prince of Wales, but estranged since 1796. This includes her political use of a private theatrical in the early 1800s and the implications of her decision to visit the Royal Coburg Theatre at the height of the so-called 'Queen Caroline affair' of 1820–1 following Caroline's triumphant return to England from voluntary exile to claim her right to be Queen when her husband became George IV in 1820.[1] Caroline's deliberate political use of theatricality is highly significant because although much of *Theatric Revolution* has been concerned with recovering plebeian or general contemporary cultural practices, no other British social role was constitutionally more elevated than that of the monarchy. With new playhouses such as the Olympic, Adelphi, and Royal Coburg opening since 1815, their availability must naturally have led her to consider how to incorporate these public spaces into her political campaigning against the Prince of Wales, who became Regent in 1811. It is not surprising, therefore, that the Prince Regent's consort, Caroline, projected the nuances of her acute political predicament within the context of the different types of theatre available to her. Before moving to discuss her visit to the Royal Coburg Theatre and the immediate context

---

[1] The most recent historian of the Caroline affair is Anna Clark, 'Queen Caroline and the Sexual Politics of Culture in London, 1820', *Representations* 31 (1990) 47–68.

of her appearances at the south-bank theatres, her extraordinary self-fashioning at a forgotten private theatrical will be examined.

When the Shakespeare editor (and forger) John Payne Collier was 'merely a lad', he was present at a private party attended by the Whig politicians R. B. Sheridan and William Windham. Collier was born in 1789 so the episode he related must have happened by the early 1800s at the latest (Windham died in 1810, Sheridan in 1816). If so, the location was probably Montague House, Blackheath (then on the south-eastern outskirts of London), where Caroline had lived separately from the Prince of Wales since 1798. Unknown to anyone except the hosts, there was to be one more guest at the party in addition to those already present. The layout of one of the rooms was arranged as if for a private house-party theatrical: 'a dark curtain was drawn across the end of the room, and . . . was at a signal drawn up'. When the curtain was pulled back, a female figure was 'discovered on a pedestal', feigning a statue. The identity of the figure, when she revealed herself to her surprised fellow guests, was Caroline, Princess of Wales the exiled and estranged consort of the Prince Regent. This drawing room scene with its carefully produced, highly self-conscious, allusion to the ending of *The Winter's Tale*, was considered 'very well managed', the 'effect of the lights behind the curtain on the female statue . . . extremely good'. Its political meaning, in the context of Caroline's relationship with the Prince Regent, was immediately apparent to the other guests: 'the understood inference was, that queen Caroline's situation was similar to that of the innocent queen of Leontes'.[2]

This elite private theatrical in front of a carefully selected audience is indicative of how the theatricalization of political issues functioned elsewhere in contemporary public culture. There was no embarrassment or lack of understanding on this occasion recorded by Collier: the context and the characterization were deemed perfectly apposite. The deployment of theatre for political effect was as soundly

---

[2] John Payne Collier, *An Old Man's Diary, Forty Years Ago; For The First Six Months Of 1832* (London: Thomas Richards, 1871) iii. 25.

understood by Caroline as it had been by her predecessors Elizabeth I or James I.

More than any other anecdote recorded in this book, Caroline's acting out of Hermione's statue role reveals the comfortable assimilation of explicit modes of theatricality into contemporary upper class social conviviality.[3] Not only was the theatricality of the Prince's consort unembarrassedly exhibited in the semi-public confines of the house-party, it was a deeply politicized piece of self-fashioning. As well as equating her own personal predicament with that of Shakespeare's Hermione in terms of a romantic tragic heroine, both pathetic and yet potentially re-empowered, Caroline's representation of this episode from *The Winter's Tale* took place as a single, early, moment during her projection of a developing public persona conveyed through the medium of theatricality.

During George's protracted (and ultimately abortive) divorce proceedings against her in 1820 through to his coronation in 1821, Caroline proved herself a grand manipulator of the genuine public esteem in which she was held.[4] The occasion of the crisis at which she was at the centre arose after her estrangement from the Prince of Wales in 1796 and voluntary exile from 1814. At the death of King George III on 29 January 1820, and the Prince Regent's accession to the throne, much to the King's consternation, Caroline planned to return to England and claim her place as Queen. After her triumphal arrival and journey to London in June 1820, the

[3] There was a contemporary fascination with Hermione as an example of distressed womanhood. Judith Pascoe draws attention to Sarah Siddons's use of a piece of lace once owned by Marie Antoinette whenever she performed the trial scene in *The Winter's Tale: Romantic Theatricality: Gender, Poetry, and Spectatorship* (Ithaca, NY: Cornell University Press, 1997), 95–7.

[4] On the background of Queen Caroline and its reception in popular culture, see Thomas W. Lacqueur, 'The Queen Caroline Affair: Politics as Art in the Reign of George IV', *Journal of Modern History* (September 1982), 417–66; Anna Clark, 'Queen Caroline and the Sexual Politics of Popular Culture in London, 1820', *Representations*, 31 (1990), 47–65; Anna Clark, *Scandal: The Sexual Politics of the British Constitution* (Princeton: Princeton University Press, 2003); David Worrall, 'The Mob and "Mrs Q": William Blake, William Benbow, and the Context of Regency Radicalism', in J. DiSalvo, G. A. Rosso, and Christopher Z. Hobson (eds.), *Blake, Politics, and History* (New York and London, Garland Publishing and Taylor & Francis, 1998), 169–86.

couple began lengthy divorce proceedings initiated by the King and culminating in Caroline's defence of herself at the bar of the House of Lords. The case against her collapsed. By this time, both the radical press—which had by then expanded sufficiently to be in a position to promote her cause—and widespread disquiet at the profligacy of the Prince, had resulted in Caroline's case reaching a national level of popular interest with mugs, plates, caricature prints, and political token coinage all adding to the dissemination of representations of the royal conflict. Caroline's own instinct for theatricality grew ever more astute as she reached a crisis in her relationship with the Prince. Part of her strategy of the deployment of public space on behalf of her cause was to make use of the minor theatres.

The minor theatres were specifically and categorically, *non*-Royal theatres but extremely popular with the artisan audiences who were amongst her most numerous and vocal supporters. It should be remembered that the overall political strategy of radical activists at the time was to issue (genuinely felt) support for Caroline at a moment when pro-Queen loyalism also happened to be the optimum strategic method of attacking George and the Tory Government (and also, incidentally, an opportunity for radicalizing women). Most of the time, carefully aided and advised by statesmen such as Alderman Wood and Brougham, Queen Caroline maintained a sure proximity with her subjects. She managed to convey a sense of her recognition of them as valid, worthy citizens of the nation, subjects who enriched her by the reciprocity of their empathy with her sufferings at the hands of the King, court, and Cabinet. Much of this was facilitated by her extraordinarily individualized replies to numerous 'loyal addresses' sent to her by communities unconnected with the nation's official civic bodies (who themselves tended to side with the King). Many of her responses were immediately reprinted as 'Answers of the Queen to Various Addresses' in even the most radical journals such as Richard Carlile's *Republican*.[5] In other words, Caroline's sense of

---

[5] See 'Answers of the Queen to Various Addresses', *The Republican*, 1, 8, 15 September, 20 October 1820.

there being a literate artisan community to which the vehicle of the traditional (usually conservative) 'loyal address' could be adapted, shows her awareness of the artisan or plebeian public sphere which the Surrey-side theatres represented. From the private theatrical of the drawing room, it was a small step to the newly emerging playhouses capable of being co-opted into her cause.

In view of this, Caroline's visits to London's Surrey-side minor theatres, the Royal Coburg and Surrey Theatres, were a deft political move. She could snub the Royal theatres but also maintain her links with artisan affection.[6] The visit by royalty is all the more remarkable given that even dramatic critics like Leigh Hunt never visited them in person but gleaned their information by reputation ('from what we hear of the Coburg and the Surrey, and have seen of the variety of printed dramas which have been sent us').[7] The definitive evidence for the popularity of Queen Caroline amongst these audience comes from the reminiscences of Thomas Dibdin who was, in 1820, the owner of the Surrey Theatre.

On the day in June 1820 when Caroline travelled up to London after her arrival at the coast on her return to Britain, there was already waiting an 'innumerable host, who had been expecting her all the afternoon', all lined up in the vicinity of the Surrey Theatre. Dibdin was confident of 'having the fullest house of the season' from such a ready-made audience. However, as Caroline passed the Surrey and crossed over Waterloo Bridge northwards into the capital, 'as many as could, followed the Queen over the bridge; and those who did not go into public-houses, I presume, went home'. Dibdin found that 'theatricals were out of the question' and his receipts 'were the worst of any night in the course of six years, being under fourteen

---

[6] George Bolwell Davidge, in evidence to the 1832 Parliamentary Select Committee, claimed that the Coburg had the 'working classes' mainly on Monday nights but, of course, he was trying to emphasise the playhouse's respectability, *Report from the Select Committee on Dramatic Literature: With The Minutes of Evidence ... 2 August 1832*, Parliamentary Papers (1831–2), vol. vii, statement 1270.

[7] James Henry Leigh Hunt, *Leigh Hunt's Dramatic Criticism, 1808–1831*, ed. Lawrence Huston Houtchens and Carolyn Washburn Houtchens (New York: Columbia University Press, 1949), 260.

pounds!!!' With his running expenses for the night at eight guineas, it was scarcely profitable. His financial grief ('anything but the jubilee sensations') was compounded by his already having turned down (in modern parlance) a 'futures option' from similarly over-optimistic 'Change-alley speculators' who had offered him a guaranteed price for the night.[8]

Dibdin's experience gives a fascinating insight not only into the economics of theatre management but also into the mass movements of the ordinary London populace drawn to the political spectacle of Caroline's royal progress. No doubt Caroline's route was determined with the same rigorous pre-planning of optimizing support as happened in virtually everything else she did.

Caroline eventually commanded a performance of *The Heart of Midlothian* at the Surrey Theatre but her similar night at the Royal Coburg was much more complex in its political implications because the campaign between the King and his estranged wife coincided with the latest stage in the patent theatres' attempts to suppress that particular playhouse.[9] In other words, the role of the theatre in the early 1820s was as a pivotal and defining public space in which were articulated a complex set of competing discourses surrounding commerce, print culture, monarchy and the popular politics of the street.

However, self-publicity was not the only cultural component functioning during the period of Caroline's visits because her appearances on the Surrey-side did not occur in a political vacuum. Not least, the principal constitutive factors affecting all playhouse discourses were the twin obstacles of monopolistic capitalism and censorship. Even on the south side of the Thames, there was no escaping the state's attempt to regulate the theatrical marketplace and Caroline's visits occurred at a time of crises within the new theatres as well as in her own personal life as consort.

In January 1820 the Coburg had been issued with an injunction by the Royal theatres because of their production of Cibber's adaptation

[8] Thomas Dibdin, *The Reminiscences of Thomas Dibdin* (1837), ii. 202–3.
[9] Ibid. 203.

of *King Richard the Third*.[10] The Coburg had advertised the play in their playbills as a work 'in 3 Acts, founded on Cibber's compiled Tragedy, from Shakespeare, interspersed with Music ... which will be called, *King Richard Third*'. The wording suggests that the three act structure, the emphasis on its 'compiled' nature and that it was 'interspersed with Music', were all valiant attempts to stress its proximity to burletta rather than to Shakespearian tragedy. However, the playbill itself also gave a clue as to why the Royal theatres' injunction against the Coburg's *King Richard Third* may have been quietly welcomed by the authorities. Given that popular feelings towards George, Prince of Wales, were never particularly warm, it is quite noticeable that the Coburg's playbills promised to feature in *King Richard Third* 'the Assassination of the Prince of Wales and Duke of York'.[11] Both the intention to stage the play and the playbill's association with an assassination of the Prince of Wales provide clear evidence that, at the very least, the Coburg was willing to seek a confrontational role.

There is also evidence that the minor theatres were able to pool their resources and work out strategies to outwit the Royal theatres' attempts to close them down. Within a few weeks of the first night of *King Richard Third*, John Saville Faucit, the manager of the West Kent Theatre, Greenwich, came to see Joseph Glossop, the manager of the Royal Coburg named in the indictment. Faucit wrote that he had come to appreciate that few 'Professional Gentlemen' (that is, lawyers) had experience of handling the legislation relating to theatre regulation and that he had recently found himself 'unfortunately ... compell'd to be my own Lawyer' during a recent closure attempt by local Methodists. Whatever the details of the action against the West Kent Theatre, Faucit had won the battle against his 'Powerful Assailants' and he was now offering his services to Glossop (on condition that his role remained anonymous because Faucit's wife, an actress,

---

[10] See also Jane Moody, *Illegitimate Theatre in London, 1770–1840* (Cambridge: Cambridge University Press, 2000), 41, 42, 133–4.

[11] BL Playbills, Royal Coburg, 27 December 1819.

had an 'excellent engagement at Covent Garden'.)[12] This ability to fight a common cause, to pool intellectual and material resources is a feature common to much of organized radicalism of the time.

The injunction against the Coburg was symptomatic of the theatre's place in the midst of a highly political contemporary popular culture. By the end of 1820 Caroline had undergone an arduous, but ultimately self-vindicating, arraignment at the bar of the House of Lords leading to the dissolving of George's divorce case against her in November. The battle between the patentees and the Coburg into which Caroline had stepped, largely following her personal agenda, exemplifies much of the complexity of how drama and the playhouses functioned amidst a rapidly emerging popular culture which embraced the affections of working-class people. In early 1821, despite popular adulation at both her arrival in England and the successful outcome of her divorce proceedings, Caroline temporarily gave up public appearances prior to George's long-delayed coronation scheduled for 19 July 1821. It could hardly escape being an uncomfortable and embarrassing time for the Queen but she soon began to figure the Royal Coburg in her campaigns against the King at a time when the case of the Royal theatres against the Coburg had yet to be concluded.

Some inkling as to the personal state of the tempers involved is gained from reports that, in May 1821, Glossop and James Winston, the acting manager of Drury Lane, were involved in some kind of public affray.[13] Nevertheless, this does not seem to have altered Caroline's decision. Neither does Caroline appear to have been put off by the increasingly specific politicization of the Coburg's repertoire. As far as back as July 1818, scarcely two months after it opened, the Coburg had played the anonymous *The Election; or, Candidates for Rottenburgh*, billed as a 'local extravaganza' (that is, based on a topical storyline), which featured the characters 'Mend'em (a Reforming

---

[12] Folger Manuscript, Y.c. 901 (1), John Saville Faucit to Joseph Glossop, 18 January 1820, Folger Shakespeare Library, Washington, DC.

[13] *The Cornucopia or Literary and Dramatic Mirror*, June 1821 92.

Cobler [*sic*])' and 'Stichloose (a Political Tailor)', perhaps allusions to the legendary ex-London Corresponding Society members Thomas Hardy and Francis Place.[14] During the summer of 1820 the Coburg had also begun a successful run for William Thomas Moncrieff's *Giovanni In the Country! or the Rake Husband*.

Moncrieff's *Giovanni In the Country! or the Rake Husband*, first performed in August 1820, was itself billed as 'a continuation' of *Giovanni in London*, Moncrieff's Olympic Theatre hit of 1817 based on the Don Giovanni story.[15] However, Moncrieff's subtitle, *the Rake Husband*, was almost certainly intended to create an allusion to the philandering Prince of Wales. Certainly, *Giovanni In the Country!* was deeply implicated in contemporary politics employing the sort of popular facetiousness which undermined the pomposity of the contemporary corrupt system. In Moncrieff's 'Bizzaro Entertainment' Giovanni sets out to be an MP; there are hustings, 'Harrangues', the canvassing of electors in a public house, and a victorious 'Election Entertainment'. The fictional name for the borough he stands for is (drunkenly) 'Lushington', but in *Giovanni in London*, upon their escape from Hades, Giovanni and Leporello had found themselves in the Borough, one of the most radicalized but impoverished areas of London, south of the Thames. In *Giovanni In the Country!* the allusion, when sung, makes the identity of the place appear geographically specific rather than generic: 'I'll put up for member, and stand for the Borough; | And, if I get in, I'll a Patriot prove! | Humanity's firmest friend, Tyranny's terror' (p. 11). Giovanni's running ticket as a radical patriot is also quite determinable ('I'll put up for the Borough; | ... I'll prove a Patriot thorough | ... For England and Liberty firmly I'll stand' (pp. 10–11)). It would have been obvious to most of the audience that Giovanni's stance

---

[14] BL Playbills, Royal Coburg, 13 July 1818.

[15] Ibid. 15 August 1820; W. T. Moncrieff, *Songs, Duets, Choruses &c.&c. &c. Sung in the New Comic Operatic Melo-Dramatic Pantomimic Moral Satirical Gallymaufrical Parodiacal Salmagundical Olla Podriadacal Extravaganza Bizzaro Entertainment ... Yclept Giovanni in the Country; or, the Rake Husband: as performed at the Royal Coburg Theatre* (1820).

as the Borough's radical patriot candidate was a teasingly satirical gesture complicit with the Coburg's audience, most of whom would have been unenfranchised and whose theatre was under threat from patentees they were powerless to depose.

True to the subtitle of the printed *Songs, Duets, Choruses &c.*, Moncrieff's burletta is certainly 'Parodiacal' but it is also familiar with the issues and the discourse of contemporary radicalism. In keeping with the much-publicized tribulations of Richard Carlile in 1820, Giovanni vows to 'keep up the Freedom of the Press. | None for Liberty | Shall stick up like me!' (p. 12). The musical settings for *Giovanni In the Country!* also lent themselves to radical political allusion. One of the song melodies was the 'Tyrolese Air to Liberty, arranged as a Glee'. But perhaps more significant as a piece of music is Giovanni's song urging the electors to vote. The setting is 'the Marseilles Hymn', the Coburg's anglicization of 'La Marseillaise', probably the most stirring anthem to have come out of the French Revolution.[16] Giovanni sings to the electorate's all-male franchise, urging them to vote for him but knowing that he has already charmed their wives ('Ye sons of Freedom, poll for Giovanni: | Hark! what numbers bid you vote. | Your wives, who dearer are than any, | Request for me you'll turn your coat'). Giovanni's rousing 'Marseillaise' song, nevertheless, is also surprisingly politically specific, repeating many highly contemporary Reformist discourses concerning Parliamentary corruption, taxation, court 'placemen', sinecurists and state 'pensioners': 'Shall hateful placemen, taxes laying, | With pensioners, a hireling band, | Rule o'er and represent the land, | While through the noses we all are paying?' (p. 13). The result is that Giovanni is elected, whereupon a chorus of 'The Females of Lushington' give him 'a Cap of Liberty'. Exactly how fine a line between sexual innuendo and political allusion has been traversed in a work like *Giovanni In the Country!* may be judged from the song's possible allusion to James Griffin's contemporary radical journal the *Cap of Liberty* (1819–20)

---

[16] Simon Schama, *Citizens: A Chronicle of the French Revolution* (London: Viking, 1989), 597–9.

as well as to the women of Lushington's outrageous *double entendre*, 'Oh, long may he our Member be!' (p. 14).

Such intricate political and cultural references recovered as an aspect of this type of historical anthropology of drama are revealing indications of the contemporary role of the playhouses and the context in which Queen Caroline made her visits to them. Scarcely recoverable now amidst such a rich field of allusion and innuendo is the dramaturgy of the plays. One piece of audience-participation that can be reconstructed is the cheering of the Coburg's crowd for Caroline. As is evident from *Tom and Jerry* (1821), Moncrieff's slightly later adaptation of Pierce Egan's *Life in London* (1820), there was a huge appetite for horse-racing scenes amongst the sort of audiences who went to the Coburg, so it is not surprising that *Giovanni In the Country!* included a horse-racing scene set at the 'Race Course at Lushington' where Giovanni enters his favourite-to-win, a horse called 'Caroline'. This scene portrayed 'Caroline against the Field', which Giovanni's Caroline wins.

Naming the horse after the female monarch may appear, at first sight, a rather questionable decision but, of course, in these scenes of 'Caroline against the Field' (or Caroline against the odds), there would have been obvious subtextual opportunities for the Coburg audiences to actually cheer loudly for Caroline and to make their connection with the progress of her case as it unwound outside the theatre. Given that British women tended to be hugely supportive of the Queen, it made perfect sense—without danger of embarrassment—for there also to be a scene showing 'Caroline for the Ladies Plate', the prize which Giovanni wins which may allude to the widespread female moral sponsorship of Caroline's cause. However the racing was actually staged, the editor of the *Cornucopia or Literary and Dramatic Mirror* evidently thought *Giovanni In the Country!*'s race-course scene 'particularly good' when he went to see it.[17] Other evidence of the popularity of the 'Caroline against the Field' scene in Moncrieff's play comes in the related semi-pirated,

---

[17] *Cornucopia or Literary and Dramatic Mirror*, September 1820, 10.

full-scale 'Hippodrame', or drama with horses, called *Giovanni in the Country; or, A Gallop to Gretna Green* (1820), which played at the Royal Amphitheatre. Although the Caroline allusions are gone, and the text is obviously subservient to the Royal Amphitheatre circus setting, *A Gallop to Gretna Green* illustrates how such popular shows and their reputation could percolate deep into the subculture of south London.[18]

If such political texts and subtexts were extraordinarily abundant on stage at the Coburg, it is also true that they were equally evident backstage. Given that the sort of politicization of theatre which *Theatric Revolution* is arguing was a key component of contemporary culture, it is not surprising that the people employed in the playhouses can be shown to be specifically political. Whether or not the Queen knew about the horse-racing in *Giovanni In the Country!*, there can be no doubting the vehemence of the pro-Caroline stance of the Royal Coburg's personnel. Virtually all of the Coburg's staff and actors were Caroline supporters. Twenty-five years later the comedian Joe Cowell (*Giovanni In the Country!*'s first Leporello—he claimed Moncrieff wrote the part specifically for him), recalled that everyone at the Coburg supported the Queen 'excepting good-natured, foolish old Lee, the stage-manager, Willis Jones, his father, who was the treasurer, and [the actress] Mrs. Waylett; [who] declared she thought the queen had acted very imprudently!!' On the night of Caroline's acquittal in November 1820, Cowell was due to act at the Royal Coburg before beginning a new contract at the Adelphi. He recorded that night, 'the excitement was terrific', and that the military had been 'ordered out, to intimidate the multitude by their presence, and . . . suppress any treasonable outbreak by the joy-intoxicated myriads who were

---

[18] *Giovanni in the Country; or, A Gallop to Gretna Green*'s co-author, William Barrymore, was himself a veteran manager of the Royal Coburg's opening in 1818 who knew the local audiences well. Perhaps *A Gallop*'s most striking moment is the Bailiff's knowing Cockney patter song ('My name is Sam Catch | And Lunnun is my quarters, | I tips the man, and tips the vife, | And sometime tips the daughters'), William Barrymore and W. Reeves, *Songs, Choruses &c in the New Comic, Melo-Dramatic, Hippodrome Entitled Giovanni in the Country; or, A Gallop to Gretna Green. as performed at Astley's Royal Amphitheatre* (1820), 7.

parading the streets, and rending the air with shouts of triumph.' Amidst this heady atmosphere, before a 'crowded' theatre, Cowell went on stage for his first role and 'without thought, in the fullness of my feeling, I proposed "Three cheers for the queen!" which was instantly given, with due dramatic precision, and responded to nine times by the audience, in a voice of thunder! All the actors rushed upon the stage, dressed and undressed.' Later that night, when all of London illuminated their windows with pro-Queen transparencies, Cowell rather mischievously 'assisted some hackney-coachmen to break old Lee's windows, and made him light up, in spite of the love he bears to George the Fourth'. For this episode, the Coburg management (the anti-Caroline Willis Jones was the treasurer, after all) tried to stop his pay. Later, Cowell recalled proudly that the 'queen's scourge' *New Times* journal had written that he was 'as illegitimate in my politics as I am in my acting'.[19]

In the midst of this popularity, it was a shrewd political move for Caroline to visit the Royal Coburg. Her visit was both a manifestation and a recognition of the political aspects of the Coburg's physical place amidst London's public spaces. Even the very name of the theatre was steeped in political meaning. Caroline would have been all too painfully aware that, right from its earliest inception when a vacant building plot was bought from the Royal Circus and before a single brick was laid, the Royal Coburg Theatre had been under the patronage of her son-in-law, Leopold, Prince of Saxe Coburg, the husband of her only child, Princess Charlotte.[20] Even after Charlotte died in childbirth in November 1817, to scenes of

---

[19] Joe Cowell, *Thirty Years Passed Among The Players In England And America: Interspersed With Anecdotes And Reminiscences Of A Variety Of Persons, Directly Or Indirectly Connected With The Drama During the Theatrical Life Of Joe Cowell, Comedian. Written By Himself* (New York, 1845), 48–9. On transparencies, see the contemporary popular antiquarian Joseph Strutt, *The Sports and Pastimes of the People of England* (1801), 'I do not know at what period Illuminations were first used as marks of rejoicing … transparent paintings, inscriptions, and a variety of other curious and expensive devices, these seem to be almost peculiar to the present age' (p. 279). Conversely, Dibdin, at the Surrey Theatre, reported that he 'did not receive half my nightly expenses' on the evening of the trial outcome, *Reminiscences of Thomas Dibdin*, 202.
[20] *Proposals for the Royal Coburg Theatre* (c.1817).

national outpourings of grief at her funeral, the Coburg's playbills continued to have printed on their masthead the legend, 'Under the Patronage of His Royal Highness Prince Leopold of Saxe Coburg'.[21] The Theatre's choice of Leopold and Charlotte as patrons was itself a clever manoeuvre to discomfort the royal patentees, but it was also a potentially political one. The 'Royal' Coburg was the south bank's mirror image of the Royal theatres on the Covent Garden side but the 'royals' referred to were the displaced Coburg dynasty, made defunct at the moment of Charlotte's death and forever removed from any chance of British succession. By memorializing this abortive monarchy, the Royal Coburg Theatre was placing itself within the local languages of popular culture as definitively anti-Hanoverian. Every Coburg playbill stuck upon a wall or posted in the press was a riposte to Drury Lane and Covent Garden and their royal protectors. The Coburg's naming was a subversion of the economic and political monopolies of the Royal theatres. Furthermore, as a space of public subversion, the Coburg was situated beyond the reach of the Lord Chamberlain's Examiner of Plays, whose authority stopped on the north bank of the Thames.

Such moves were part of a series of contingent interventions into the public and symbolic spaces occupied by contemporary theatre. These disruptive manoeuvres played out within the capital's symbolic and political economy do not appear to have compromised the underlying ideological independence of the audiences. It is instructive that the political symbolism of the theatre's choice of Saxe Coburg for its patronage eventually outlived its topical usefulness. Working-class attitudes towards royalty were highly provisional. The reverence of the public was always more enduringly directed towards Charlotte than it was towards Leopold. Within a few years of Charlotte's death, the sometime Shakespeare forger William Henry Ireland, in *Memoirs of a Young Greek Lady* (1823), was castigating Leopold's seduction of the 14-year-old Alexandre Panam, back in 1814. The melodramatic

---

[21] Stephen C. Behrendt, *Royal Mourning and Regency Culture: Elegies and Memorials of Princess Charlotte* (Basingstoke: Macmillan, 1997).

outrage Ireland evokes in his memoir, published by the radical pressman John Fairburn, is a useful reminder that the operative political condition was that offended plebeian sensibilities had made Leopold's appropriation expendable. This cultural dialetic was a fully structured aspect of the workings of contemporary politics: in exactly the same way as the apparently loyalist cause of Caroline was taken up by popular radicals as a cover for reformist and anti-regent agitation, so too the dubious intrigues of Prince Leopold could be paraded as an inherent flaw within a monarchical system.

From the time of the Coburg's opening in 1818, it is clear that the playhouse aligned itself as an anti-Regent theatre. When Queen Caroline chose to visit the Royal Coburg in 1821, the political implications of her act were intended not only to reactivate the popularity of Princess Charlotte, whose matrimonial surname was continued in the theatre's own title, but also to revive her own claims to share in the popular affection for her deceased daughter. As with her visit to St Paul's Cathedral, Caroline's actions were steeped in political symbolism. At least one modern historian has examined Caroline's relationship to London theatres at this time but the sensational politics of her visit to the Royal Coburg have been overlooked.[22] The overt reason for her visiting the Royal Coburg in July 1821 was to thwart Government publicity for the coronation of George.

A month before the coronation, the Royal Coburg presented *Marguerite! Or The Deserted Mother!* Within a week of the first performance, Caroline decided to go and see *Marguerite!* for herself. As with her private theatrical of the ill-treated Hermione in *The Winter's Tale* two decades or so earlier, Caroline was both personally inclined, and perfectly competent enough, to forge allusions between dramatic literature and contemporary politics. Conceivably the plot of *Marguerite!* held particular attractions for the Queen, involving as it did a suddenly deceased adult child, disinheritance, and a wicked

<hr />

[22] Christopher Murray, 'Elliston's Coronation Spectacle, 1821', *Theatre Notebook*, 25 (1970/1), 57–64.

uncle. No text of *Marguerite!* is extant (the Coburg did not need to send a copy to the Lord Chamberlain) but an extensive plot summary is given on the theatre's playbills.[23] The storyline of a breakdown in family trust, an attempt to purloin the estate of a bereaved mother, and the wicked role of her dead son's uncle, all conspire to portray the sort of dysfunctional family relationship which paralleled the acrimonious breakdown of Caroline's marriage, her bereavement as a mother, and her husband's attempts to thwart her right to be Queen.[24] Caroline's acute sense of deploying public space in the service of her own political symbolism is also a confirmation of the Coburg's political agency and of the role of theatrical space in contemporary politics. As had been the case in Elizabethan times, theatre could was still used in the Romantic period as an instrument of politics at the very highest level.

There is, however, one further aspect of *Marguerite!*'s command performance which must be considered because the topical context of the event intersected with a more legalistic set of concerns connected with the freedoms and privileges of contemporary stage expression. Caroline's trip to the theatre may well have been aimed at providing political and moral support for the Coburg in its hour of need. *Marguerite!*'s first performance was on 18 June 1821, Caroline's visit was made eight days later on 26 June. The day after her visit, Lord Justice Abbott finally delivered his judgment on *King Richard Third*.

The Coburg's legal problems were already fully disseminated into the plebeian public sphere. In early January 1820 the Coburg

[23] Authorship is indirectly attributed to John Howard Payne, the actor, poet, and correspondent of Mary Shelley, although it is probably more likely to have been an unattributed adaptation of a work by Julie Delafaye-Brehier. Amongst John Howard Payne's works for the Coburg around this time are *Thérèse or the Maid of Geneva*, 8 February 1821, from the French *Thérèse, ou, L'Orpheline de Geneva* by M. Victor; *Frederick the Great! And the Deserter! Or the Assassins of the Forest*, 19 February 1821; *Krastikan Prince of Assassins! or the Dreaded Harem*, 7 May 1821.

[24] BL Playbills 174 vol. 1, 1818–23, Royal Coburg, 18 June 1821. Caroline would also have seen that night, if she stayed, Moncrieff's short farce *Modern Collegians, or Over the Bridge!*, a work for the Royal Coburg based on the author's apparent spell in King's Bench debtors' prison, BL Add. MS 33964, fo. 299. Moncrieff managed the Coburg during 1819, just possibly at the time of *King Richard Third*.

published a playbill '☞ Appeal to the Public!!!' concerning the impending prosecution initiated by the Royal theatres for having presented what the Coburg curiously described its as 'rationalizing' version of Colley Cibber's adaptation of Shakespeare's *Richard III*. In its contemporary political context the term 'rationalizing' was particularly resonant. The playbill appeared at the height of Richard Carlile's judicial martyrdom which, five weeks later, he would describe in his *Republican* as the trial of ('The Society for the Suppression of . . .') 'VICE versus REASON'.[25] True to their instinctive sense of the political emotions their playbill might evoke, the Coburg made it clear that at issue was the Royal theatres' attempts to 'claim exclusivity to themselves . . . instituting a Monopoly'.[26] With a similar instinct for how politically charged words would 'play' to their overlapping audiences, the Coburg's choice of the term 'rationalizing' to describe their production of *King Richard Third* figures the event quite specifically into the political culture of radicalism during Carlile's promotion of atheistical Zetetic rationalism at a time when every issue of *The Republican* trumpeted Carlile's rationalist cause. This action against the Coburg for the infringement of the Theatre Royal monopolies has significant implications for understanding the role of the non-patent theatres and how the oligarchy of the patentees was resisted.

While this account has stressed the presence of the Queen's supporters at the Royal Coburg, it should be realized that many theatrical personnel in London were already engaged on one side or the other in the issue of the Queen's status, but they were not all pro-Caroline supporters. The comic actor Joe Cowell recollected that Robert William Elliston, then the manager of Drury Lane, sided with his '"friend, George the Fourth", as he always called him' and deliberately modified Drury Lane's playbills, 'omitting "et regina" at

[25] *The Republican*, 18 February 1820, 159. Carlile placarded his shop with a sign reading 'The Temple of Reason'. Daniel Isaac Eaton's premises in the early 1810s were called 'The Ratiocinatory'.

[26] BL Playbills, Royal Coburg, 10 January 1820.

the bottom . . . and leaving "vivant rex"'.[27] The playwright Theodore Edward Hook, a vigorous Tory activist, had already revealed himself as an apologist for Napoleon's treatment in exile in his lengthy, *Facts Illustrative of the Treatment of Napoleon Buonaparte in Saint Helena* (1819). As editor of the pro-Government *John Bull* magazine, in 1820 he had libelled Queen Caroline during a series of attacks on her and her cause.[28] Hook was also thought to be the compiler and author of the parodic *Radical Harmonist; or, A Collection of Songs and Toasts given at the late Crown and Anchor Dinner* (1820) which attacked not only the 1790s Jacobins, Thomas Hardy and the orator John Gale Jones, but also Thomas Watson (tried and acquitted for high treason in 1817) and a midget Spencean, Samuel Waddington ('Hail, imp of sedition!').[29] In other words, theatre and theatre personnel played prominent roles in the popular distribution of London's heatedly competing radical and reactionary discourses.

It must have been a daunting time for the Coburg because Lord Chief Justice Sir Charles Abbott had a formidable reputation. A host of contemporary radicals had come up before him at various times, representing in their court appearances the whole spectrum of radical politics from armed conspiracy (the Cato Street conspirators), blasphemy (Robert Wedderburn, the orator son of a slave), the new journal editors of radical print culture (T. J. Wooler, the pressman) right through to the beginnings of working-class female interventionism (feisty *Republican* shopgirl, Susannah Wright).[30] All

---

[27] Cowell, *Thirty Years Passed Among The Players*, 47.
[28] R. H. Dalton Barham, *The Life and Remains of Theodore Edward Hook* (Richard Bentley, 1853), 138–58.
[29] Theodore Edward Hook, *The Choice Humorous Works, Ludicrous Adventures, Bon Mots, Puns and Hoaxes of Theodore Edward Hook With a New Life of the Author* (1873) 24 n., 204.
[30] Erasmus Perkins [George Cannon], *The Trial of the Rev. Robt. Wedderburn, (A Dissenting Minister of the Unitarian persuasion,) For Blasphemy, Before Sir Charles Abbott, Knight, Lord Chief-Justice, and a Special Jury, in the Court of King's Bench, Westminster, The Sittings after Hilary Term, 1820; Containing a Verbatim Report of the Defence* (1820); *Report of the Trial of Mrs. Susannah Wright, for publishing, in his shop, the Writings and Correspondences of R. Carlile; Before Chief Justice Abbott . . . Monday, July 8, 1822. Indictment at the Instance of the Society for the Suppression of Vice* (1822).

of them suffered in his courts. The rumours circulating at the time
were that the action had been brought because the management of
Drury Lane insisted on their exclusive rights or else demanded a
reduction in rent. Alternatively, the Drury Lane lessors had the
option of prosecuting the illegitimate theatres: 'The latter was
preferred. The Coburg was first selected.'[31] Unsurprisingly, the
Royal Coburg was convicted at King's Bench of giving an illegal
performance.

The Royal theatres' chief prosecution witness, a disaffected Coburg
actor named Junius Brutus Booth, identified Joseph Glossop as
having caused to be rehearsed 'the character of Richard III in the
Cobourg Theatre'.[32] George Bolwell Davidge, the owner of the
Coburg at the time of the Parliamentary *Report from the Select
Committee on Dramatic Literature* (1832) gave evidence that they
had been fined two sums of £50 but, when asked whether he had
repeated the production of *King Richard Third* again, he answered
'Frequently', although he added that they had been threatened with
prosecution several times.[33] Oddly, of all the papers in the Lord
Chamberlain's archives for early nineteenth-century theatre, the
Coburg case is a rarity in that it records a legal judgment.

However, this specifically state-supported legal attempt at the
suppression of dramatic expression (actually the suppression of a
Shakespearian text) was not concluded by closure or inhibition.
Within a few weeks of Abbott's verdict, the Coburg was topic-
ally commenting on its position, uninterrupted. The circumstances
are worth outlining because they imply an enormous infrastructural

---

[31] A Friend to 'Fair Play and a Free Stage', *Letter To The Right Hon. Robert Peel,
Respecting The Proposed Introduction Of A Bill, To Repeal So Much Of The Act Of 10th
Geo.Ii.Cap.28, As Requires Notice To Be Sent To The Lord Chamberlain ... And Showing
That The Consequence Of Such An Act Would Be, To Confirm The Monopoly Claimed By
The Proprietors Of Drury Lane And Covent Garden, And To Enable Them To Annihilate
The Minor Theatres* (1829), 8.

[32] PRO LC 5/164. fo. 76, Rex v. [Joseph] Glossop, 27 June 1821.

[33] Davidge reported that the trial was held at the Surrey Assizes, Guildford, *Report
from the Select Committee on Dramatic Literature: With The Minutes of Evidence... 2
August 1832*, Parliamentary Papers (1831–2), vol. vii, statements 1212–13.

change in the cultural behaviour of London's working class. Whatever the financial pain implicit in Abbott's verdict, the slow tide was turning. Within a few weeks of the injunction, John Saville Faucit of the West Kent Theatre had offered his covert help. Queen Caroline's visit (however much undertaken to suit her own agenda) explicitly confirmed the Coburg's political agency during one of the most controversial episodes of early nineteenth-century British life. The social transformations occurring on the public stages of London's theatres appear to have prefigured the political changes in the franchise which took place in the latter half of the nineteenth century. Typifying this movement is the portrayal of local 'Cockney' characters pushing forward onto the stages of an excluded marginal theatre.

The Coburg began a run of plays which reflected social changes in its audience population as their economic activity increased and their deference was eroded. As Eugene Macarthy noted in 1832, 'to evade the penalties of the law, [the minor theatres] are sometimes in the habit of producing representations of local and other subjects'.[34] Disallowed, under threat of censorship and prosecution, to stage the 'national drama', the 'minor' theatres were obliged to move into areas of 'local' representation, that is, entertainments which addressed the topical and popular issues coinciding with the interests and aspirations of their audience catchments. Of course, such developments did not go unobserved or unregulated: their official surveillance is symptomatic of the social upheavals they reflected and engendered. Not only were these playhouses scrutinized by local magistrates or (where relevant), the Examiner of Plays, in the late 1820s it was specifically alleged that Astley's Amphitheatre and the Royal Coburg were kept under regular surveillance:

It is well known that police officers attend at those theatres during the whole of the performance; . . . paid by the [Theatre Royal] proprietors; that they report every morning to the Magistrates at Union Hall the closing time of the preceding evening, and whether or no there has been any

---

[34] Eugene Macarthy, *A Letter To The King, On The Question Now At Issue Between The 'Major', And 'Minor' Theatres* (1832), 6.

disorder or breach of the peace. These reports are entered in a book kept for that purpose.[35]

Amidst these restrictive conditions of production, the Coburg's one-act burletta *Crockery's Misfortunes or, Transmogrifications* (1821) exemplifies this staging of the unenfranchised, bringing their challenging perspectives to bear on London life in the wake of Justice Abbott's verdict.

Crockery's Misfortunes, produced in July 1821, is about changes in London newly apparent to Rowland and his Cockney servant, Crockery, upon their return to the capital after thirty years in India (or 'Hingy', as Crockery calls it). The 'Transmogrifications' (malapropped 'transformations') of the subtitle refers to the enormous amount of 'halteration' (p. 2) which has happened to London during their absence. Of course, Rowland's business in 'Hingy' is not only revealing of Britain's colonial empire but it also serves as a deliberately distancing perspective on London. Crockery's comments are all the more insightful in their effect simply because of his sense of London's strangeness. For example, in an interesting importation of the sense of modernity onto the 'minor' stages, the new gas street lighting (called for in Scene II's stage directions) provokes new sensations of smell: ('CROCKERY. Don't you smell a stench master? ROW. It's the gas, you stupid fellow. CROCKERY. Oh, dear, there vasn't no gash afor I vent to Hingy' (p. 4)). Crockery the Cockney is dislocated and alienated from his youthful environment: 'CROCKERY Master, do you know they've got a scaffolding up Saint Paul's—they say they're going to put a lamp a top to shew the cockneys their vay home' as he realizes he has now re-entered an aggressively mercantile capital already well forward in its 'March of Intellect': 'Then the sides of the houses are stuck full of bills, | About blacking, mock auctions and wonderful pills . . . | The play-bills have hard words vot I cannot speak, | And the organs play's nothing but Latin and Greek, | And—it's rain'd every day now for more than a week' (p. 5).

---

[35] A Friend to 'Fair Play and a Free Stage', 10.

Crockery's mixture of the exotic and the local, articulated in unabashed Cockney, mixes ignorance with knowingness, confidence with trepidation; after all, he's been all the way to 'Hingy' but is now returned to a commercialized, consumer oriented London whose walls are 'stuck full of bills' for 'wonderful' remedies. It is from this vantage point of enjoying modernity ('vat a vonderful place is this Lunnun'), even if *Crockery's Misfortunes* has barely edged into the 1820s, that gives added valence to Crockery's philosophical comments on the paradoxical influence of persistent *anciens régimes*, 'even Lambeth Marsh is haltered, for they've built a Cobourg playhouse there, vot the big play-houses want to put down' (p. 4).

The triumph of *Crockery's Misfortunes* is the triumph the Coburg itself because it was not 'put down'. Unsilenced, Crockery is both representative of the Coburg's Lambeth Marsh hinterland and yet also of its irrepressible speakers. Although confined, upon pain of judicially imposed financial penalties, to the unpromising genre of one-act burletta, *Crockery's Misfortunes* is representative of the Coburg's ability to evolve identifiable comic figures and to give them the opportunity for significant social comment. The laughter Crockery provokes was not only the downfall of the patents but also a harbinger of an ever wider political franchise. However skilful her manipulation of theatrical spaces, whether private or public, Queen Caroline had been dealing with a public sphere of greater magnitude than either her own personal circumstances or those of the monarchy she represented.

7

The Theatricalization of British Popular Culture: A General Historical Anthropology

THE steep social percolation of theatrical culture outlined in the previous chapter, from Caroline's *Winter's Tale* down to the throngs waiting to see her near the Surrey Theatre, or Joe Cowell breaking treasurer Lee's windows and getting the Coburg crowd to cheer the Queen, are all symptomatic of the centrality of London theatre and theatricality in contemporary popular politics. As has been demonstrated, the topical locus of Caroline and the Coburg was the site of a competing set of highly politicized dramatic discourses, even Cowell's delinquency being played out within the physically public spaces of the Coburg's backstage. This chapter serves to extend these particularized discussions of theatricality appearing in earlier sections of the book into a more general anthropology of behaviour, culture, and customary practice. If Caroline's private theatrical represented the apex of a social pyramid of the national taste for theatre, then this chapter will discuss the place of drama in the everyday lives of the Georgian-period British population. Beyond all doubt, theatricality was rooted in just about every imaginable sphere of contemporary life, permeating Georgian culture.

Theatre certainly operated as a highly effective interface between the Queen and the London crowd but if Caroline at the Coburg in 1821 presents a cross-section of the social gradient between monarch and populace, a wider study of theatricality in the period will reveal drama's pervasive cultural function. What follows is an attempt to reconstruct a general historical anthropology of contemporary theatricalized culture. Although the account given will sometimes linger uneasily between social survey and mere snapshot, it will attempt to give some idea of the range of mentalities, the economic determinants, and the usages of public and private spaces encompassed within the idea of theatre at the end of the eighteenth to the beginning of the nineteenth century.

At its most basic, the social appetite for dressing up (perhaps as fundamental as 'pretending to be someone else' in any definition of Western theatre) is best characterized in the contemporary economic field by the pastime of masquerading. Anthropologically analysed, the social gathering of the masquerade was not only a moment of courtship and intrigue but also of important conviviality. The masquerade's social importance is denoted by the presence in London of the masquerade costume warehouse or 'repository', not only depicted as part of the setting of Thomas Dibdin's *Harlequin in his Element* (1807) but whose shop window was also illustrated in the hand-coloured frontispiece to its printed edition.[1] Masquerading's continuing economic impact is recorded by such inclusions as the scene in Dibdin's *Harlequin in his Element*. Many elements of contemporary dramatic culture can be discovered in masquerading but such dramatized patterns of behaviour are best studied where it was materialized into more regularized forms of entertainment.

What follows is a structural study of the anthropology, sociability, and economic determinants of contemporary theatricality. It will move through a discussion of the theatre buildings, the audience, and the actors and then touch on subjects such as bailiffs and Methodists who appear to have been of equal concern to both the acting community and their audiences. The chapter will then branch

---

[1] T. J. Dibdin, *Harlequin in his Element: Or, Fire, Water, Earth, & Air* (Appleyards, 1807).

out into the more covert expressions of theatricality with particular emphasis on the culture of the louche drinking dens or 'song-and-supper' clubs of the late 1820s operating in the lee of the London theatres as well as their forerunners, the late eighteenth-century 'spouting clubs' where amateur actors at similar tavern venues displayed their enthusiasm for acting. These areas of sociable dramatics will be followed by an attempt to recover something of the culture of private theatricals, particularly the paedophilic tastes indulged in the country houses but also including the more rough-house private theatres of London's Soho and Camden and their later migration into the Penny Theatres for the destitute urban children of the early Victorian period. Finally, the underlying strength of the economic impact of theatre-going will be exemplified in an early example of 'product-placement' at Covent Garden.

As far as the theatre buildings themselves were concerned, they stood in the context of a commercially thriving, increasingly populous London. One writer in 1840 reckoned that London had 234 churches, 207 dissenters' chapels, 5,000 public houses, and 16 theatres, most of them in teeming proximity: 'Eight of them stand within ten minutes' walk of each other, on one side of the river; three on the other side, within five minutes; and the remaining five cast a dim enlightenment on the more unknown and barbarous regions of the metropolis.'[2] What this writer is describing are the components parts of a London which had grown into a metropolis. The principal distinction between London as a city and London as a metropolis is that the capital's emergence into metropolitan status arrived when the categorization of the traditional, readily identifiable centres of London (the West End, East End, St James's) were subverted by the presence of elements alien to them. Of course, some of this was simply a matter of urban growth, of more cultural variety assimilated into one well-defined area. The presence of new playhouses, as much as anything, served to define cultural change

---

[2] F. G. Tomlins, *A Brief View of the English Drama . . . with Suggestions for Elevating the present condition of the art, and of its professors* (1840), 58.

in the capital since, simultaneously, they accommodated the city's nightly audiences.

The West End playhouses, broadly definable as Drury Lane, Covent Garden, and the Haymarket, were thoroughly displaced from exclusively representing the imperial capital by their competitor neighbours, theatres such as the Adelphi, Olympic, or Lyceum, all of them (with the possible exception of the Haymarket a little further west) located within a few hundred yards of each other. Not only did these Westminster 'minor' playhouses not share the privilege of the Royal Patent, they had much more in common with the theatres in the metropolitan hinterland which similarly shared the stipulation of burletta (such as those on the Surrey side of the river, Astley's Amphitheatre, the Royal Coburg, and the Surrey itself) than they had with the principal Royal theatres. The East End, much suppressed, Royalty Theatre with its close proximity to the Tower of London, one of the capital's most ancient landmarks, acted as a further confusion or displacement of the notion of London's centre since the Royalty's persecution proved that historical association did not confer recognition. This cultural asymmetry (one which, of course, was not defined by the theatres alone), enhanced the recognition by Londoners that they were living in a capital which had multiple urban centres, a true metropolis. However late in eighteenth-century history one wishes to trace the formation of London as a metropolis, the capital's citizens—even their children—readily recognized the truth that the capital was a set of competing, even chaotic, locations.

The idea of London as a series of discrete spaces whose performative status could be removed from their temporal location had reached even into children's games, indicating an already comfortable reception in popular culture. An 1809 coloured etching, 'The Panorama of London, or A Day's Journey round the Metropolis, An Amusing and Instructive Game', showed fifty vignette views of London constructed as a spiral for children to identify.[3]

---

[3] Corporation of London, Record 27780.

The theatres were a key component in this symbolic dismember-ment of the capital city into its disaggregated constitution as the metropolis. The rougher south-bank playhouses were particularly unappetizing to many of those people who expressed elite views. The Royal Coburg was thought to be 'in one of the worst neigh-bourhoods, its audiences ... of the lowest kind', and the interior nauseating with 'vile odours arising from gin and tobacco, and bad ventilation'. There were even noticeable differences amongst the minor theatres, by the 1830s the Olympic Theatre adjacent to Drury Lane allegedly catered for a 'courtly audience', while the Coburg's was a 'porter-drinking one', the blended beer drunk by Smithfield market workers.[4] Such disruptions of expected cul-tural predictions, that a 'minor' theatre could become 'courtly' while another, half a mile away, could be equated with the labouring classes, typify the way in which London theatre embodied contemporary social fractures.

The physical proximity of audience neighbours was an extreme version of the politer, better regulated, conditions of London's churches, which were the only places where, on a regular basis, the social classes mixed at the level of being able to hear, smell, and spectate each other. George Wightwick remembered that it was the custom at Covent Garden and Drury Lane for a senior Bow Street officer to warn of pickpockets by appearing at the back of the crowd before the pit doors opened shouting '"Ladies and Gentlemen take care of your pockets! There's *one* in!"'[5] Plunging into the interior of London theatres, 'every person endeavours to enter first; the space is clogged; and pushing, screams, and execrations follow', the audience become 'stripped of the outward garments' because of the heat, and begin 'beating the floor with sticks, hissing, clapping the hands, and piercing whistles, with exclamations for "Musick"'.[6] Wightwick (who was 15 in 1817) remembered that at

[4] Tomlins, *Brief View of the English Drama*, 59–60.

[5] George Wightwick, *Theatricals 45 Years Ago* (Portishead, Somerset: 1862), 1–2.

[6] James Peller Malcolm, *Anecdotes Of The Manners And Customs Of London During The Eighteenth-Century Including The Charities, Depravities, Dresses, And Amusements, Of*

that time, before the introduction of gas lighting, 'the proverbial redolence of the play-house [was] that of orange peel and lamp oil' and that wax candles beautifully flattered 'the fully developed constellation of "young beauties"' looking down on the pit from the dress circle.[7] Even with the performance under way, in 1788 the manager of the Theatre Royal, Birmingham, offered a reward to anyone 'who will discover the Ruffians who have thrown, or shall hereafter throw, Bottles, Plates, Apples &c at the Actors and upon the Stage, during and after a Performance'.[8] Notoriously, the 3,000-seater capacity of each of the recently refurbished London Royal theatres made the actors barely audible. Some writers gave as the 'hacknied but unanswerable cause of this decay of dramatic originality, the enormous size of the two principal London theatres'.[9] In one of his Grub Street works written long after his Drury Lane Shakespeare forgery, *Vortigern*, William Henry Ireland experienced the 'slamming of box-doors, and boisterous uproar . . . in the galleries, that every attempt at hearing proved fruitless', an audibility problem mainly associated with Drury Lane and Covent Garden but not confined to those places. At the 'minor' Lyceum Theatre during a performance of *Romeo and Juliet* (presumably while it was home to Drury Lane after their fire of 1812) Ireland also experienced 'a general row, which was most methodically kicked up upon this occasion, by a succession of sounds from every part of the house', in other words a social tendency for noise—making it and hearing it—to become a casualized aspect of theatre-going.[10] In

---

The Citizens Of London During That Period; With A Review Of The State Of Society In 1807, 2 vols. (1810), ii. 408–9.

[7] Wightwick, *Theatricals 45 Years Ago*, 3.

[8] John E. Cunningham, *Theatre Royal: The History of the Theatre Royal Birmingham* (Oxford: George Ronald, 1950), 42.

[9] *The Modern Stage. A Letter To The Hon. George Lamb, M.P. On The Decay And Degradation Of English Dramatic Literature: With A Proposal For The Encouragement Of Composition For The Stage, By The Legislative Protection Of New Pieces; So That They Might Be Produced In The Provincial Theatres, Or Otherwise Published, With An Adequate Reward, Independent Of The Caprice Of Arbitrary Judges* (1819), 8.

[10] W. H. Ireland, *Something Concerning Nobody, Embellished with Fourteen Characteristic Etchings* (1814), 164, 168–9.

this context, customs of social deference appear to have been largely abandoned. It is difficult to escape the conclusion that, whatever the norms of behaviour outside the theatres, such standards were largely abandoned as inappropriate and impossible to enforce once inside the playhouse.

This is quite an important point because it shows that the meeting of various social subcultures were embedded within contemporary experiences of theatre-going. While one might escape the sight, sound, or smell of other social groups in the vicinity of one's residence, such collisions of the classes (literally elbowing, arguing, and pushing amidst several hours of close physical confinement in the pit or gallery) became exaggerated in the theatre. By contrast, places of public worship were more orderly modes of demographic fragmentation as chapels or synagogues vied with the buildings and congregations of the established religion's churches. The function of the playhouse was, quite singularly, to act as a physical containment or compression of disruptive social forces. One hardly needs to formulate a New Historicist or Foucauldian perspective to realize that, on a nightly basis, this is what happened in the Georgian theatre.

These public spaces circumscribing such potentially eruptive forces were themselves extremely fluid and lacking in standardization, very much the residue of an early modern culture. To understand theatricality in this period as configured in a built environment of public and private spaces, the modern notion of architecturally magnificent proscenium-arched theatres with pits, galleries, box-lobbies, and professional actors has to be largely abandoned. The standards of refined, rebuilt, and refurbished interior infrastructure set by the Covent Garden and Drury Lane are quite misleading as a general guide to Georgian theatres, even those elsewhere in London. The theatrical disposition of the populace extended far beyond modern concepts of conventional theatre.

Acting spaces were far more provisional than might be expected, and far more geared towards relationships with the quite varied commercial enterprise typical of the beginnings of modernity. The self-styled 'Unfortunate Son of Thespis', Edward Cape Everard, recalled that in the 1770s, only 'two miles from London Bridge', he performed to full houses in a tiny playhouse which would have been recognizable from Elizabethan England. The China-Hall Theatre, a wooden building with a 3-foot high brick base, having 'a wooden kind of sentry-box for the money-taker', was set in a china dealer's tea garden as a type of mini-Vauxhall Gardens where the location was primarily established as an outlet for the sale of ceramics, 'wines, cyder, ales &c'. There, with the future tragedian George Frederick Cooke, he played (possibly only two-handed) scenes from *King Lear* before the place was closed down by magistrates, allegedly following a conspiracy by local Methodists (who were also thought to have burned down a rival mini-theatre at the nearby 'St Helena's' tea gardens).[11] In the mid-nineteenth century, the comedian Peter Paterson recalled his time playing *The Castle Spectre* inside a fairground booth near a 'manufacturing town', playing it as 'the shape of an essence [of the original]... in twelve or thirteen minutes', scenes which 'in regular play-house ... [would] take nearly three hours'.[12]

Paterson subtitled his memoir *Confessions of a Strolling Player* and, indeed, early modern theatre's origins in strolling players were still in evidence. The inn-yard setting of many provincial theatres had scarcely died out by this period. In remote areas such as Laxfield, in Suffolk, the tumbler and 'pantomime' James Pack remembered performing as a child on a 'stage erected near a public house', having been more or less press-ganged by adults exploiting his tumbling skills.[13] In Andover, Hampshire, until the late 1780s the theatre used 'a large malt-house' as its premises but, even when it moved, it was

[11] Edward Cape Everard, *Memoirs Of An Unfortunate Son Of Thespis; Being A Sketch Of The Life Of Edward Cape Everard, Comedian* (1818), 74–8.

[12] Peter Paterson, *Behind the Scenes: Being the Confessions of a Strolling Player* (Edinburgh: D. Mathers, 1859), 74–88.

[13] James Pack, *Some Account Of The Life And Experience Of James Pack, Late A Celebrated Actor, In The Pantomime Department, At ... Drury Lane ... But Now, By The Grace Of God, A Disciple And Follower Of The Lord Jesus Christ* (1819), 12.

only to a thatched barn in the yard of the Angel Inn.[14] In many of these buildings the tell-tale signs of literary culture must have served as almost postmodernist quotations grafted onto the vernacular architecture of provincial commerce. In the early 1800s the theatre at Edmonton, Middlesex, was but a barn 'recently erected' although it was adorned with a classical lyre over the main window, while the theatre at Maidstone, which had a bust of Shakespeare on its frontage, shared its only access door with a fruiterer's shop.[15] Even in royal Windsor until 1793 the self-designated Theatre Royal, 'literally a barn' holding some 250 people, was situated a mile from the town 'in a dirty farm yard'.[16] Nevertheless, the book from which most of these details about contemporary provincial theatres derives, James Winston's *The Theatric Tourist* (1805), is itself indicative not only of the growth of theatricality but also of the widespread occurrence of acting as a trade allowing (or necessitating) great flexibility in the working life of the actor. *The Theatric Tourist* gave many quite specific commercial and contractual details for each theatre (such as comments on location, type of audience, the manager's principles of sharing of benefit nights, terms of employment), all of which were aimed at prospective employees as much as an avid public wishing to collect the book's coloured plates.

This demography of human movement, each one a personal exploit or narrative increasingly recorded in the burgeoning appetite for actors' memoirs, is quite paradoxically related to the provisionality of the built structure of the theatres. Even in Wych Street, adjacent to Drury Lane and the Strand, Philip Astley's newly built Olympic Pavilion, which first opened in 1807 for 'stage and equestrian performances', had a '*conoid*' shaped roof of 'block tin' (a tin roof) to create 'a strong vibration of sound in the music which was to

---

[14] James Winston, *The Theatric Tourist; Being A Genuine Collection Of Correct Views, With Brief And Authentic Historical Accounts Of All The Principal Provincial Theatres In The United Kingdom. Replete With Useful And Necessary Information To Theatrical Professors, Whereby They May Learn How To Chuse And Regulate Their Country Engagements; And With Numerous Anecdotes To Amuse The Reader* (1805), 9.

[15] Ibid. 46, 49.   [16] Ibid. 54.

accompany the entertainments'.[17] In other words, the contemporary following for drama and acting was a much more substantial cultural activity than the material construction of its buildings might suggest.

Much of the materiality of the theatres rests in our knowledge of the recoverable lives of the theatregoers themselves. At its most basic, even the boisterous atmosphere of the theatres provides clues to the social class of the audiences. The sizes of the audiences are also unpredictable. While both Covent Garden and Drury Lane had capacities of some 3,000 people as spectators of the canonical five-act dramas which were their privilege, Peter Paterson's recollection was that his twelve-minute *Castle Spectre* at country fairgrounds in the Birmingham area 'accommodated a thousand people' in 'a very large tent' with 'additional canvas'. At one shilling and sixpence per spectator (playing eight times a night) they 'reaped a golden harvest—not less ... than two hundred and fifty pounds'.[18] Paterson's memoir implies (based on his estimate of nightly takings) that the audiences for the excerpted *Castle Spectre* were about the same as (or slightly larger than) the average audience settled reasonably quietly into their seats and boxes at the Royal theatres. Of course, the principal difference between any Theatre Royal and any theatrical booth was that it reached right into the heart of the local community.

Reconstructing the Georgian audience is something of the Holy Grail of theatre studies. Some of the clearest evidence for audience composition comes from lists recorded by legal authorities at moments of disturbance or tragedy. Marc Baer's *Theatre and Disorder in Late Georgian London* (1992) says that 62.2 per cent of the OP riot audiences whose details were taken at their magistrates' hearings were clerks, tradesmen, or higher (such as professional men or gentlemen).[19] However, Baer's fairly remote use of Government

---

[17] R. Humphreys, *The Memoirs Of J. Decastro, Comedian ... Accompanied By An Analysis Of The Life Of The Late Philip Astley, Esq. ... Also An Accompanying History Of The Royal Circus, Now The Surrey Theatre* (1824), 102–4.

[18] Paterson, *Behind the Scenes*, 100–1.

[19] Marc Baer, *Theatre and Disorder in Late Georgian London* (Oxford: Clarendon 1992) Ch. 7: 'Who were the OPs?', table 2, pp. 135–65.

records makes his account misleading on the details. Examination of the King's Bench papers in the Public Record Office shows that those arrested during the OP disturbances probably included a greater proportion of labourers than Baer allows except that, very often, their cases were subsequently dismissed because a 'True Bill' (a case to answer) was not found by the court.[20] The arrested rioters included Cheapside shopmen, Hackney coal merchants, footmen in livery, Shadwell brewer's clerks, a Soho 'respectable tradesman' and a journeyman currier.[21] Unnoticed by Baer was also George Soane, 'The son of Mr. SOAME [sic], the architect, in Lincoln's-Inn Fields'. Sir John Soane's son, who went on to become the author of Drury Lane's *Masaniello, The Fisherman of Naples* (1825), a drama about seventeenth-century insurrection, was charged with causing a 'riot and disturbance' by 'hissing and hooting during the performances'. He was bound over with sureties of £50 for his future behaviour.[22] Also present at the riots was the ex-London Corresponding Society leader Francis Place (although he committed no offence). Place provides a good example of how various private and political lives were intertwined around this location of London's theatreland. He had been born on the south side of Drury Lane Theatre and, in the early 1820s, began a long relationship with Louisa Simeon Chatterley, a Covent Garden actress who made her debut in *She Stoops to Conquer* in 1821. In his *Autobiography*, Place also recalled that part of the committee of the 1798 incarnation of the London Corresponding Society, by then distanced from him, were arrested under the Suspension of Habeas Corpus in Craven House, Wych Street, rooms which he recalled as subsequently rebuilt as the Olympic Theatre.[23]

---

[20] For cases against five labourers where a true bill was not found, see PRO K[ing's] B[ench] 10/56/18. See also PRO KB 10/56/13–21; KB10/56/41; KB10/56/43-5.

[21] *The Covent Garden Journal* (1810), 23 Sept 1809, pp. 307–8; 12 October 1809, p. 312; 13 October 1809, p. 316; 18 October 1809, pp. 324–5; 19 October 1809, pp. 325–6; 31 October 1809, p. 329.

[22] Ibid. 13 October 1809, p. 316.

[23] *The Autobiography of Francis Place (1771–1854)*, ed. Mary Thale (Cambridge: Cambridge University Press 1972), 23, 176, 258.

Francis Place conforms to the overall measure of respectability which accompanied the OP riots, typified by the celebratory dinners of mutual condolence and admiration attended by both the Covent Garden manager, John Kemble, and by Francis Place. Balancing this, of course, is the presence in 1800 of someone like James Hadfield, the severely head-wounded ex-soldier who fired shots at King George from the pit of Drury Lane. Hadfield was clearly deranged and hallucinated about such things as building a house in White Conduit-fields and living there as God (with Satan living with him as a companion curiously employed as a cobbler). Several witnesses drawn from the theatre staff and that night's audience contributed evidence during Hadfield's trial for high treason. The occupations of the witnesses included, besides members of the theatre's orchestra, a Smithfield oil and colourman, a hairdresser, two silver-spoon makers, a major in the army, and one woman of no given occupation.[24] Again, the picture is of a predominantly skilled, artisanal audience but even some of the OP rioters incurred indictments for sedition. During the agitation around Covent Garden Theatre, John Lambert, a printer, and James Perry, a gentleman, were indicted for printing and publishing the words '"What a crowd of blessings rush upon one's mind that might be bestowed upon the country in the event of a total change of system!—Of all monarchs indeed since the Revolution the successor of George the Third will have the finest opportunity of becoming nobly popular."'[25] Their indictment is definitive evidence of the presence of a radical print culture with interests in the progress of the Covent Garden rioting.

Not only do the extreme examples of OP and Hadfield show that the theatres were recognized as appropriate and suitable vehicles for political expression, they are reminders that social exclusivity or segregation of the classes was an impossibility within these spaces. The surprisingly political experimental nature of these public spaces

---

[24] *The Trial of James Hadfield, At the Court of King's Bench, Before Lord Kenyon, on the 26th of June, 1800, for High Treason in Attempting the Life of the King on the Fifteenth of May, Last* (Newcastle upon Tyne, 1800).

[25] PRO KB 10/56/12.

is perhaps no better indicated than in what one eyewitness later recollected as the 'strange mixture of whimsicality and distressing circumstance' which characterized the OP riots.[26] In short, it is as if the London theatres of the 1800s were a kind of laboratory for both revolution and reform, a theatre of paradox which encompasses both the regicide of Hadfield and the reconciliatory dinners of Place and Kemble.

It has been shown that the discounting from Baer's account of uncharged detainees undermines some of his conclusions but the grim index of bodies at fatal accidents cannot be misconstrued. Re-examining such events today gives a better idea of the social composition of contemporary audiences. On 15 October 1807 a stampede took place at Sadler's Wells Theatre during a performance of one of its water spectacles, *The Ocean Fiend, or, The Infant's Peril.* In the confusion, eighteen people died. According to the account of the manager, Charles Dibdin, a brawl involving two drunken brewer's servants and two women caused members of the audience to shout 'A Fight! A Fight!' which was mistaken for the words 'A Fire! A Fire!'[27] Details about the deceased were given by the witnesses who identified the bodies for the subsequent coroner's inquest (held at the nearby Sir Hugh Myddleton's Head public house). In the stampede, seven men, seven women, and three children died along with another male whose age was not known.

Caught in the grim snapshot of the melee, the evidence of the audience composition is a definitive sampling of the Sadler's Wells audience that day. Despite the probability that young adult males would be amongst those most likely to escape and survive, the average

[26] Charles Isaac Mungo Dibdin, *History and Illustrations of the London Theatres* (1826), 20–2.

[27] Charles Isaac Mungo Dibdin, *Professional and Literary Memoirs of Charles Dibdin the Younger, Dramatist and Upward of Thirty Years Manager of Minor Theatres*, ed. George Speaight (London: Society for Theatre Research, 1956), 92–6. There are a number of prints of the incident including *A View of the Confusion at Sadlers Wells occasioned by the false alarm of Fire On Thursday Night Oct. 15, 1807, When, 18 Persons lost their lives* (G. Thompson, 43 Long Lane, Smithfield, 1807). See also Dennis Arundel, *The Story of Sadler's Wells, 1683–1977* (Newton Abbot: David & Charles, 1978), 80–3.

age of the deceased men is scarcely 21. Similarly, the average age of the seven women (who died perhaps because they were more likely to stumble and be crushed on account of their long skirts) is barely 20. There is no clue as to the location of the bodies in relationship to the theatre but the close grouping of the ages of the young adults, and their even division between the sexes, strongly suggests that Sadler's Wells was visited as a venue for socializing with friends, perhaps as part of the practice of courtship (only one of the women was described as married). Of the children, two were aged 11 and the other was aged 9. John Ward, one of the 11-years-olds, was described as an unemployed errand boy. Other details can be teased out. At the inquest, the mother of the deceased 11-year-old, Benjamin Price, told the hearing that she and his younger sister had been at home during the performance when the little girl suddenly had a vision of her brother in their kitchen. The mother then 'hastened with a friend to Sadler's Wells, where she found her son a corpse'. Quite apart from the element of superstition (and the parent's apparent credulity of the child's testimony), it is interesting that since no father, relative, or family friend is mentioned, Benjamin Price must have been at Sadler's Wells without supervision.[28]

The occupations of the Sadler's Wells deceased (where they are given) are also fascinating, but quite different from the mainly male defendants thrown up in the OP riots two years later at Covent Garden. Perhaps the person most closely conforming to the stereotype of the early-modern female playgoer was Caroline Twitcher, described as 'a woman of the town' (or prostitute) whose body was identified by a Swedish sailor from HMS *York*. Three of the men, and three of the women, have no given occupation but, although the young child John Ward was dutifully recorded as an unemployed errand boy, these omissions may simply reflect an inconsistency in the coroner's practices. Elsewhere, as a significant clue to class origin, the trade of the father was given. The occupations referred to are: prostitute, wheelwright, apprentice cabinet maker, porter, servant, carver

[28] The possibility that he worked in or around Sadler's Wells cannot be ruled out.

and gilder, two labourers' daughters, and the son of a looking-glass maker.[29] Overall, this suggests a slightly lower-class social ranking for the Sadler's Wells deceased compared with the arrested OP rioters. In addition, perhaps skewed by the two labourers' daughters, the prostitute, and cabinet maker's apprentice, the economic status of the audience at Sadler's Wells must have been significantly lower than that of the average Covent Garden OP rioter. The presence of children in the Sadler's Wells stampede may also be significant as indicating particularly elusive strata of the Georgian theatre-going audience (who had perhaps even entered the theatre unseen). Studies of fires and other disasters in late Victorian British music halls, which benefited from an improved coroner's bureaucracy, confirms that the age and gender profiles of victims of the Sadler's Wells stampede are broadly consistent with the later period, with children forming a sizeable audience grouping and the female adults likely to have been young, single, and in employment.[30] Although the evidence of the death toll is statistically inconclusive, the inescapability of the bare facts remains as an unequivocal record of who went to Sadler's Wells that day and remains as a tantalizing trace of Georgian theatregoers.

If such were the audience, the actors themselves seem to have lived similarly precarious lives, especially with regard to their economic circumstances. Some fell in and out of employment purely as a result of their own shortcomings. In the late 1780s and early 1790s, an educated, well-connected actor like James Fennell could quite literally walk into Edinburgh (Fennell was a keen pedestrian vegetarian), land a major part in *Othello*, and cause a series of well documented riots and disturbances concerning actors' rights of role-swapping, before making his way to Covent Garden until, feeling 'piqued against the managers', starting up the *Theatrical Guardian* journal (which

[29] *Dreadful Catastrophe* [Sadler's Wells, Thursday, 15 October 1807], BL shelfmark Crach I. Tab. 4.5. 4/3/1.

[30] Dagmar Höher, 'The Composition of Music Hall Audiences, 1850–1900', in Peter Bailey (ed.), *Music Hall: The Business of Pleasure* (Milton Keynes: Open University Press, 1986), 73–92; see also Tracy C. Davis's chapter 'Industrial Regulation and Safety'', in her *Economics of the British Stage 1800–1914* (Cambridge: Cambridge University Press, 2000), 70–114.

'I continued ... for several weeks, and, as usual, gave up') and then going on to Revolutionary France where he met (unremarkably) Marat in Paris.[31] Nevertheless, not everyone was as sure-footed or self-confident as Fennell. The dangers to actors of imprisonment under the provisions of the (originally Elizabethan) statutes of vagrancy were still in force. In the late 1800s, a Middlesex consultant magistrate employed by the Royal theatres confirmed the validity of the vagrancy act 10th Geo. II c. 28 of 1737.[32] John Palmer of the Royalty Theatre was committed to Surrey gaol as a vagrant under this act on 9 November 1789 because of his infringement of speaking rather than using the burletta form (he had been both the manager and the fictional hero Henry du Bois in their production of John Dent's *The Bastile*).[33] *The Dramatic Scorpion* (1818) satirized 'drama's strolling crew' with their 'caravan' of properties 'Cramm'd full of thunder! rivers! castles! trees! | Trumpets! lamps! daggers! flags! And "bread and cheese"'.[34] In the late 1780s or early 1790s, the Aberdeen Methodist minister Alexander Kilham, during a controversy with the comic actor Charles Lee Lewes over the staging of Cibber's Molière adaptation, *The Hypocrite*, recalled that once in Malton, Yorkshire, he had been instrumental in having fourteen out of an itinerant band of thirty 'hunger-bitten' ('Potatoes had been their principal diet') actors 'committed to the house of correction' after warrants were issued by local magistrates.[35] Vagrancy was always on the edge of the actor's

[31] James Fennell, *An Apology for the Life of James Fennell. Written by Himself* (Philadelphia, 1814) 306–8, 327.

[32] *The number of little Theatres already opened ... having greatly injured the Theatres Royal ...* (c.1808–10).

[33] Edward Wedlake Brayley, *Historical and Descriptive Accounts of the Theatres of London* (1826), 71. Dent's play was often referred to under the title *The Destruction of the Bastile*.

[34] John Philip Kemble, *The Dramatic Scorpion. A Satire, in Three Cantos, With Explanatory Notes* (1818), 17, 19.

[35] Alexander Kilham, *The Hypocrite Detected And Exposed; And The True Christian Vindicated And Supported: In a Sermon Preached From A Passage In A Play-Bill, December 15, 1793, In The Methodist Chapel In This City. With A Reply, In an Appendix, To A Paper Signed Civis, Concerning Dancing. And A Postscript, With Remarks, On The Mr. Lee Lewes's Answer* (Aberdeen, 1793), 47–8.

life, not only as an ever present legal threat but also an economic condition determined by the unpredictability of acting which carried its legacies into old age. In 1787 the ex-Sadler's Wells singer Mrs Brown died in the workhouse having been turned out of cheap lodgings kept by the notorious Black-boy-alley 'fence, or receiver of stolen goods' Lydia Hall. Although Brown was once 'a public toast, and afterwards in keeping by a nobleman', Hall had turned her out of doors where she was forced by her 'misfortunes to pick up bones about the streets ... when incapable by illness to walk, and after lying three days in a shed was removed to the parish workhouse'.[36]

Within the popular chapbook culture of the early 1820s, however, the riches-to-rags biography was subjected to its reversal in a trajectory of rags-to-riches. The revolution in manners exemplified in Pierce Egan's *Life in London* provided the context for a kind of female freedom retold in *The Lady of Pleasure and Fashion ... Mary Morris, The Chaunting Beggar-Girl, and Strolling Actress* (*c.*1821). In this *faux memoir*, Mary's expulsion (for being too pretty: 'Rachel's beau ... did what any of his sex would have done ...') from the protection of her guardians (who, pointedly, have implicitly slave-owning interests in Barbados) begins her advance in the theatre (suitably, in *The Clandestine Marriage*). Instead of prostitution, however, Mary Morris finally retires ('for I was now nearly thirty') to Dawlish in Devon, very much in control of her life and with a rich husband: 'Harcourt is not a bad husband, he has his faults; he says I have mine,—no doubt, yet our matrimony is different from that of a virtuous couple, recriminations will burst forth and annoy us.'[37] At a period of rising activism by the Society for the Suppression of Vice, the marital equilibrium founded on a balance of mutual sin

---

[36] Newspaper cutting, 24 December 1787, BL *Collections Relating to Sadler's Wells*, vol. ii, 1787–95.

[37] *The Lady of Pleasure and Fashion. Being the Remarkable Adventures of the Celebrated Mary Morris, The Chaunting Beggar-Girl, and Strolling Actress. Displaying Vicissitudes of Low and High Life, As Led by a Beautiful Girl; Through the Metricious Arts of Seduction, Intrigue, and Cyprian Amours* (*c.*1821), 12, 13, 17, 28.

marks a strong contrast to the pressures of the dominant culture. If theatrical emancipation was far from being the reality for theatre workers themselves, then the print subculture, with its attractive hand-coloured etched frontispieces, projected the possibility of a future for women which combined the fanciful with the honest. Revealingly, the theatre is the agent of social elevation and material advancement. In particular the sixpenny *The Chaunting Beggar-Girl, and Strolling Actress*, was appealing to exactly the type of readership who would have been likely to have seen the actresses in the theatres and to reflect on what they both saw in the playhouse and read in the chapbook.

Alongside these fictionalized accounts many real actors, such as the Drury Lane tumbler James Pack, lived out their whole lives between extremes of success and poverty. The extraordinary details of Pack's life have come down to us because of his religious conversion in 1814, after which he wrote *Some Account Of The Life And Experience Of James Pack, Late A Celebrated Actor, In The Pantomime Department, At . . . Drury Lane. . . But Now, By The Grace Of God, A Disciple And Follower Of The Lord Jesus Christ* (1819). Pack's career in tumbling encompassed extreme hardship, working the agricultural fairs across East Anglia westwards to the Welsh Borders before finding a weekly income rising from £6 at the Royal Circus up to £22 per week at Richmond Theatre in a concurrent engagement he held with Drury Lane. Pack was born to an East Essex militiaman father in Sudbury, Suffolk, where he learned tumbling from itinerant fairground mountebanks and experienced the childhood visions and dreams which must have confirmed his later religious conversion. Soldiers in both Sudbury and the garrison town of Colchester were never far from the extraordinary scenes of his childhood ('One of the cavalry then lying at Sudbury would often form me into a cap, and would parade the town with me on his head') and it was amongst a troop of East Anglian showman horseriders ('Samwell's . . . the same kind as Astley's') that he became 'well accomplished in the art of tumbling, though very young'. It was a career of incredible physical hardship. Much of Pack's narrative is simply concerned with him trudging the roads between fairs, often in conditions of extreme poverty and deprivation, or 'rambling for support', as he called it. In one incident, the horseriding and tumbling troop he belonged to were so impoverished that 'Our dog was starved, and his skin was taken off and sold to pay the turnpike on our way to Billericay Fair.' Tumbling and horsemanship showmen took him to the agricultural fairs of Nottingham, Bristol, Birmingham, Norwich, Worcester and, eventually, to London's famous Bartholomew Fair. Pack seems to have been a small-framed, very agile man, but the personal dangers of his work were immense: 'Four or five times have I done a wonderful flight head downwards, nearly or quite ninety-nine feet, excepting once, escaping unhurt. Four times I was thrown a back somerset from a painted monument, supposed to be twenty-six feet high, having nothing to catch at but the solid stage.'[38] Pack's brief *Life* recounts a totally vanished world, one which must have been fast disappearing even as he wrote his memoir.

Throughout the drama of this period, the image of the debtors' prison or pursuit by the bailiff is ubiquitous. Its popularity probably implies that it was a concern of equal consequence to both the actors and the audience. The actor James Fennell's story is typical. In the late 1780s, falling on hard times, he sold his clothes, went to London, was arrested for debt, was thrown into prison until bailed, then obtained an acting engagement at Richmond enabling him to remain solvent.[39] Even someone as successful as the playwright and manager Charles Mungo Dibdin, fairly late in his career in 1819, spent time in King's Bench Prison for debt.[40] The whole of W. T. Moncrieff's *Frankenstein* spin-off farce, *Frank-in-Steam, or, The Modern Promise to pay* (1824), was concerned with a plot based upon how Frank-in-Steam is 'over head and Ear in debt' and has to turn to body-snatching to stave off the bum-bailiff.[41] Around 1819, Moncrieff himself had spent some time in King's Bench debtors' prison, writing a collection

[38] Pack, *Life And Experience*, 16–19, 21, 26.   [39] Fennell, *Apology*, 286.
[40] C. I. M. Dibdin, *Professional and Literary Memoirs*, 126.
[41] W. T. Moncrieff, *Frank-in-Steam, or, The Modern Promise to pay* (1824), BL Add. MS 42869.

of poetry, *Prison Thoughts* (1821) and *Modern Collegians; or, Over The Bridge. A Half Hours Comic Sketch Before Dinner . . . As Performed At The Royal Coburg Theatre, October 9th 1820* (1820), the latter being a piece perhaps seen by Queen Caroline on her visit to the Coburg and drawing on his gaol experiences.

The rules of incarceration for London debtors were quite complicated but held special advantages for actors in that, under the King's Bench 'Rules' for debtors, prisoners were allowed to leave the gaol for short periods within well-defined geographic restrictions. Notably, the Surrey-side location of King's Bench, hard by the Royal Circus, allowed actors who might normally have played only Covent Garden or Drury Lane to have the freedom to leave the gaol for short periods and to resume acting in local theatres such as the Royal Circus which fell within range. This is how it came about that in 1789 John Palmer (late manager of the Royalty) was engaged to perform the solo George Alexander Stevens's *Celebrated Lecture on Heads* (1766), the forerunner of Charles Mathews's *At Home* (1818), before going on to take a leading role in *The Destruction of the Bastile* (1789), also at the Royal Circus. When he was prosecuted for this role, it was the vagrancy act (ever lurking behind actors) which ensnared him, sufficient to confine him, as Jacob Decastro recalled it, in the 'County Bridewell, St. George's Fields, now Toulmin's soap manufactory'.[42] It was widely thought that the politically sensitive nature of the latter piece, plus the influence of the Royal theatres, led Lord Chief Justice Kenyon to modify the King's Bench 'Rules' to exclude all places of public amusement and, at the same time, also the taverns and public houses which had formerly been open to the prisoners.[43]

The harsh nature of these experiences led to many notable characterizations, particularly of the bailiffs and of the culture of bribery they encouraged. William Barrymore's (with William Reeve)

---

[42] Humphreys, *Memoirs Of J. Decastro*, 125.
[43] Ibid. 122, 126, 134; Brayley, *Accounts of the Theatres of London*, 71.

'hippodrame' *Giovanni in the Country; or, A Gallop to Gretna Green* (1820) for the Royal Amphitheatre had the chillingly comic cockney bailiff, Sam Catch:

> Now ven that I does nap my man
> I says to Prison you must go, Sir,
> He says it's a thing I do not like
> It is so very low, Sir,
> *(Spoken)* Vy then, says I, if you don't like to go to prison you
> can go to my house . . .
> But—if you—he knows vat I vas going to say—so without any
> further ado, he slips a ten pound note into my hand . . .
> I do this now and then a second time,
> But never on the third, Sirs,
> For if they then, don't pay the bill
> I always cage my bird, Sirs,
> Thus I get vell paid by both
> The plaintiff and defendant
> And I that vas a poor man once
> Am now quite Independent. (p. 7)

King's Bench prison, which housed debtors as well as other types of criminal, was a very visible presence even from the time of the childhoods of the personnel of the 'Surrey-side' theatres adjacent to some of south London's most depressed neighbourhoods. The comedian Jacob Decastro recalled in the 1820s that to the south front of the Royal Circus lay a 'large waste of ground' from where 'in our infancy we have often stood at the Circus gate, and seen the people go into and come out of the King's Bench Prison and the Borough of Southwark'.[44]

As well as bailiffs and prison, 'Methodists' were also perceived as an ever-present danger to players. Edward Cape Everard, as related above, thought the China Garden Theatre had been closed down by Methodists and a similar mini-playhouse burned at their instigation. The reality was probably a little more complicated than

---

[44] Humphreys, *Memoirs Of J. Decastro*, 138.

Everard's allegations. John Larpent was widely assumed to have Methodist leanings. In part this supposition fitted neatly with the well-documented attempts by Methodists (which have been referred to above) to suppress theatrical entertainment but it was also a persistent belief which survived his death. The *Newgate Monthly Magazine* of 1824, for example, wrote that the late Larpent was 'a biggotee Methodist' and explained his suppression of parts of Hook's *Killing No Murder* as all part of his attempt to 'prohibit every thing from being represented, which, in the least, tended to bring sectarianism into ridicule'.[45] However, others differed. The Quaker moralist Lindley Murray, quoting Hannah More's *Strictures on the Modern System of Female Education*, let theatre-going remain a matter of private judgement.[46] Henry Angelo even claimed that the comic actor Edward Shuter was a follower of the Methodist George Whitefield and helped support the Methodists' Tottenham Court Road meeting house. Indeed, Angelo also maintained that Whitefield had 'been a player himself at one period of his life' and encouraged his congregation to attend Shuter's benefit nights.[47] But general beliefs about the anti-dramatic disposition of Methodists persisted. Writing thirty years after his own brush with them, William Thomas Moncrieff recollected how his *Tom and Jerry* had been attacked by 'the Actors' old rivals, the Methodists', who 'distributed the whole of the stock of the Religious Tract Society at the doors of the [Adelphi] Theatre—in vain ... denounced *"Tom and Jerry"* from the pulpit'.[48] The proximity of social interchange which this chapter has emphasized as a part of the strength of theatrical culture could also have a reverse effect. Provincial groups of itinerant players were clearly occasionally subjected to various attempts at local coercion to desist.

---

[45] *Newgate Monthly Magazine, or Calendar of Men, Things and Opinions*, September 1824, 78–9.
[46] Lindley Murray, *Sentiments of Pious and Eminent Persons on the Pernicious Tendency of Dramatic Entertainments, and other Vain Amusements* (1823), 4th edn.
[47] Henry Angelo, *Reminiscences of Henry Angelo, With Memoirs of his Late Father and Friends* (1828) 341.
[48] W. T. Moncrieff, *Selection from the Dramatic Works of William T. Moncrieff* (1851) iii, p. vi.

In the 1790s, for example, the Aberdeen Methodist minister Andrew Kilham had predictably sought to close down an itinerant band of actors performing Molière in the city, but his actions brought the actors to his chapel, no doubt as silent intimidation, and he had to have the conviction to preach whilst 'Most of the Play-actors were present' sitting before him in the congregation.[49] Such encounters no doubt also contributed to providing the theatre with its material allowing it to mount a counter-campaign. The fulminating harangues of a 'Methodist Parson' ('I am no velvet-mouth preacher; I scorn your lawn sleeves') was a stock character in George Alexander Stevens's frequently played *Lecture on Heads*, which has him expounding against theatres: 'the Devil [is] among the Players! The players, they play the Devil to pay.—The play-house is Satan's ground, where women stretch themselves out upon the tenter-hooks of temptation.—Tragedy is the blank verse of Beelzebub;—Comedy is his hasty pudding; and Pantomime is the Devil's country dance.)'[50] Stevens's *Lectures on Heads* was much-developed and improvised upon by individual performers as time went on, a factor which increased its cultural reach, but Stevens's portrayals are also of interest in showing how such 'one-man shows' characteristically blurred the distinctions between authorial texts and their relationship with the audience: 'With one eye he looks up to Heaven, to make his congregation think he is devout, that's his spiritual eye; and with the other eye he looks down to see what he can get; and that's his carnal eye; and thus with locks flowing down his face, he says, or seems to say, or at least, with your permission, we'll attempt to say for him'.[51]

---

[49] Alexander Kilham, *The Hypocrite Detected And Exposed; And The True Christian Vindicated And Supported: In a Sermon Preached From A Passage In A Play-Bill, December 15, 1793, In The Methodist Chapel In This City. With A Reply, In an Appendix, To A Paper Signed Civis, Concerning Dancing. And A Postcript, With Remarks, On Mr. Lee Lewes's Answer* (Aberdeen, 1793), p. iii.

[50] George Alexander Stevens, *The Celebrated Lecture on Heads; which has been exhibited upwards of Two Hundred and Fifty successive Nights* (1766), 8.

[51] Ibid.

The persistence of such caricatures became a deeply embedded feature of popular culture and commanded some measure of credibility as anticlericalism became more focused after the late 1810s. The subcultural impact of anti-Methodist representations may be glimpsed in the popular appetite for Robert Taylor's blasphemous sermons delivered in 1830–1 at Richard Carlile's Rotunda, Blackfriars, a galleried, theatrical space which later became a music-hall (and where Dan Leno's parents performed). Dressed in clerical robes at the Rotunda, Taylor could irreverently refer to Jesus as a 'May-bug' or 'cockchafer', the latter an innuendo having a particularly salacious meaning in the context of bawdy songs published in William West's discreet mini-sized collections such as *The Flash Songster and Cockchafer* or *The Nobby Songster* which emanated from the 1830s 'song-and-supper' clubs of the Coal Hole, Fountain Court, and the Cyder Cellars, Maiden Lane.[52]

The constant trafficking between theatre and general popular culture is difficult to demarcate reliably but the presence of the symptoms of a cultural transfer are hard to miss. One of the points of merger, of transferral, between stage and street comes in the forms of these post-performance London drinking dens. The 'song-and-supper' clubs were venues where theatre, literature, and the popular culture of the street met together in clouds of speech, song, alcohol, and tobacco. The geographical proximity of these drinking dens to the theatres is illuminating. For both actors and audiences alike it was just a quick step to come out of the stage door or exits of the theatres and to finish off the evening in a 'song-and-supper' club. In turn, hard by the clubs were the low printing houses which supported them. Rather like the producers and sellers of the playbills, the presses set in surrounding alleys and passageways, such as Russell Court, lived off the passing trade of the theatregoers. These disorderly houses were recollected in the parts of Thackeray's *Pendennis* set in the Back Kitchen of

[52] *The Devil's Pulpit*, 1:1, 4 March 1831, 11. Taylor's sermon had been preached at the Rotunda on 7 November 1830. On William West's bawdy songs imprints, see George Speaight, *Bawdy Songs of the Early Music Hall* (Newton Abbot: David & Charles, 1975), 10–11.

the Fieldings Head tavern. William West, the printer of *The Flash Songster and Cockchafer* and *The Nobby Songster, A Prime Collection*, worked from 1823 at premises in Wych Street just opposite the Olympic Theatre.[53] The songs West collected would have been those still featuring at the 'song-and-supper' clubs enabling him accurately to describe them as 'now Singing at Offley's Cyder Cellar: Coal Hole &c.' The aristocratic taste for these rough houses attracted the likes of Lord Byron and the great Theatre Royal tragedian Edmund Kean, as well as penniless scholars.[54] Offley's and the Coal Hole stayed open well into the night after the nearby theatres closed; indeed the Offley's Cyder Cellar entrance was conveniently situated exactly next to the stage-door of the Adelphi Theatre. At another nearby drinking establishment, Renton Nicholson, the editor and landlord of the Garrick's Head, Bow Street, learned enough about these clubs and their frequenters to write extensively about them in his *Autobiography of a Fast Man* (1863). A lot of the aristocratic 'slumming' of the late 1810s and early 1820s can be traced back to the impact of hits such as Moncrieff's Olympic success *Giovanni in London* (1817) or his popular burletta, *Tom and Jerry, or Life in London* (1821) for the Adelphi. The covert street 'Flash' slang of the criminalized classes which created so much popular fascination in *Tom and Jerry*, in their turn, were incorporated into bawdy songs such as 'The Swell Coves Alphabet' included in *The Nobby Songster*.

At this level of the culture of the street and stage it is not easy to differentiate between the originators of a genuinely popularized culture and those who simply catered for its tastes. It looks not likely to be the case that glossaries of slang were created only for the benefit of patrician theatregoers anxiously dumbfounded by the argot of *Tom and Jerry* but that venues like the Coal Hole and Offley's Cyder Cellar were the genuine interface between theatricality and anarchic London life.

---

[53] Speaight, *Bawdy Songs*, 10–11.
[54] Archibald Haddon, *The Story of the Music Hall from Cave of Harmony to Caberet* (London: Cecil Palmer, 1924), 5.

Someone who moved between both worlds was the journalist and playwright Pierce Egan, who said that he balanced his drunkenness at the Cyder Cellar with visits to picture galleries, to 'make amends for it'.[55] According to J. Ewing Ritchie, whose *The Night Side of London* (1857) is an eyewitness account of this culture, people went to these places because they 'thought it a fine thing to view those distinguished men maudlin, or obscene, or blasphemous, over their cups'.[56] They were places, quite literally, of social upheaval and moral irreverence. The 'song-and-supper' clubs even spawned their own specific art form, the *improvisatore* performance. This involved the improvising of songs composed upon the spot. The most famous of these *improvisatores* was the loyalist playwright Theodore Edward Hook, who usually performed at Offley's. Renton Nicholson's *Autobiography of a Fast Man* (1863) records one of Hook's songs, a set of spontaneously composed verses about the gambling habits of his drinking companions, replete with 'flash', 'slap-up Corinthian' language.[57]

Nicholson's book was obviously an opportunist piece of writing intended to cash in on London's low life but there are startling indicators of the authenticity of the criminalized subcultures he pictures. For example, one of the people Nicholson knew as a frequenter of one these places in the early 1830s was George Ruthven of Bow Street, whom he describes as an 'inveterate' gambler.[58] Whether Nicholson knew it or not, Ruthven was not just a Bow Street runner but also a Government informer and infiltrator whose covert operational name was 'George Williams' when he had spied for the Home Office during much of the 1810s.[59] The incidental presence of George Ruthven in the text of Nicholson's *Autobiography of a*

[55] Pierce Egan, *Show Folks!* (1831), 47.
[56] J. Ewing Ritchie, *The Night Side of London* (1857), 101.
[57] Renton Nicholson, *Autobiography of a Fast Man* (1863), 70–3.
[58] Ibid. 88.
[59] For an example of his infiltration of a political society, see PRO TS 11/204/875 (ii) fo. 899, 18 December 1816. See also David Worrall, *Radical Culture: Discourse, Resistance and Surveillance, 1790–1820* (Hemel Hempstead: Harvester, 1992), 104.

Fast Man provides conclusive empirical evidence of the interchange between an official culture which persisted in the surveillance of working-class life and the semi-theatricalized revelry of the 'song-and-suppers' in all their vigorous moral anarchy.

The premeditated theatricalization of the private self into public space appears to have been a pervasive social habit. If Caroline's representation of Hermione is a constrained example of projection into a limited public space, far more assertive and bewildering was a young Bunhill-row druggists' assistant 'who, in naval uniform, addressed the pit at Covent Garden Theatre' during the 1809 OP riots, having 'assumed the dress, manners and language of a naval officer' and then proceeded to harangue the audience, requesting them 'to join with those on the quarter-deck, meaning the pit, and they would make the admiral of the new prices strike or knock under . . . "D—n my eyes, my lads, if we can get within our grappling irons fair-weather Jack [Kemble], we will bring him to book."'[60] As Marc Baer has shown, at the OP riots such conscious but elaborate interventions were all part of a wider cultural repertoire involving the physical occupation of public spaces.[61]

The social elaboration of theatricality, of everyday life lived as a performance, is at one end of the spectrum exemplified in the 'song-and-supper' drinking dens. Another part of this spectrum is represented by elaborate political hoaxing such as the trail of false clues plotted out by urban ultra-radical Spenceans at the 1817 Bartholomew Fair where they tried to convince the Government that they were about to stage an uprising on a similar scale to the Spa Fields rising of 1816. At the Harp and O.P. ('Opposite Prompter') or P.S. ('Prompt Side') taverns (the latter also called Kean's Head) in Russell Court, Pierce Egan recalled elaborate hoaxes played upon 'stagestruck' youths who were brought to the tavern under the impression that they were being 'formally introduced

---

[60] *Covent Garden Journal* (1810), 17 October 1809, pp. 322, 324.

[61] Chapter 8, 'Audiences as Actors', in Marc Baer, *Theatre and Disorder in Late Georgian London* (Oxford: Clarendon Press, 1992), 166–88.

to the ... proprietor of a country theatre' and then duped into getting onto a table to recite Shakespeare.[62] Their fooling, at the very least, is an indicator of the popularity of actors and acting amongst random members of the public. At a more personal level, hoaxing could also take the form of incorporating London's astonishingly varied commercial life into elaborate practical jokes structured and engineered so as to take place in real time.

Perhaps the more notorious of these was the so-called Berners Street Hoax of 1810, an immense trick carried out by the larger-than-life figure of the playwright Theodore Edward Hook. Upon some real or imagined pretext, Hook constructed a series of messages to London tradesmen requesting goods, samples, or services to be sent to a certain Mrs Tottingham or Tottenham of 54 Berners Street. At a pre-determined day, beginning early in the morning but continuing throughout the morning, afternoon and evening, Hook caused to be sent to 54 Berners Street an avalanche of tradesmen supplying goods and services. These included chimney sweeps, six men bearing an organ; barbers, wine porters, wig makers, mantua-makers, opticians, coal-merchants, linen drapers, furniture men, portrait painters, surgeons, fishmongers, and butchers. In addition, Hook told the Governor of the Bank of England that a fraud was about to be committed at Berners Street, and he also managed to lure to the house the Duke of Gloucester and the Chairman of the East India Company.[63] The end result was that Berners Street was completely congested by goods and traffic causing mayhem and disruption to the normal business of the area. It may well be the case that the examples of theatricalization so evident in the OP riots engendered Hook's boldness to carry out the Berners Street Hoax. With the tradesmen (not to mention Mrs Tottingham) unwitting actors in a scene directed by Hook, the episode was an audacious piece of remote direction-by-proxy. At the very least, Hook's hoax

---

[62] Egan, *Show Folks!*, 27. See also Pierce Egan, *The Life of an Actor* (1825), 43 and its plate by Theodore Lane, 'House of Call for Actors'.

[63] R. H. Dalton Barham, *The Life and Remains of Theodore Edward Hook* (Richard Bentley, 1853), 52–6. See also *The Times*, 28 November 1810.

is a vivid reminder of the sheer number of trades and professions which could be mustered, using nothing more than a horse and cart, to converge into one place at one time. Whatever the origin, Hook's hoax shows that the occupation of a highly theatricalized public space was well within the range of possibilities available to contemporaries.

Only slightly more structured are the examples of theatricality found in the so-called 'spouting clubs' which ran from the mid-eighteenth into the beginnings of the nineteenth century.[64] As with the 'song-and-supper' clubs of the 1820s and 1830s, the expression of theatricality was deeply embedded into social conviviality. Gillian Russell has shown that popular lecturing bordered on theatricality, 'the power of theatre as an enactment of the possibility of self-transformation had always had a political meaning in eighteenth-century culture, explaining in part the suspicion of amateur acting, especially that of the male lower orders'.[65] The suggestion of deviance or social disorder was embedded in the contemporary fascination with both the spouting clubs and the 'song-and-supper' clubs which shared similar tavern venues and were extremely popular with young men. They swiftly became associated with the type of disorderly behaviour which Arthur Murphy's farce *The Apprentice* (1756) was meant to 'repress, by timely ridicule, a passion then growing to excess among the younger branches of the commercial community; that of assembling in spouting clubs'.[66] In 'The Spouting Club', a

[64] On these contexts, see Iain McCalman, *Radical Underworld: Prophets, Revolutionaries and Pornographers in London, 1795–1840* (Cambridge: Cambridge University Press, 1988); Gillian Russell, '"Keeping place": servants, theater and sociability in mid-eighteenth-century Britain', *Eighteenth Century: Theory and Interpretation* (Texas Tech Univ., Lubbock), 42:1 (2001), 21–42.

[65] Gillian Russell, 'The Sociability of Romantic Lecturing', in Gillian Russell and Clara Tuite (eds.), *Romantic Sociability: Social Networks and Literary Culture in Britain, 1770–1840* (Cambridge: Cambridge University Press, 2002), 123–44, p. 138.

[66] John Adolphus, *Memoirs of John Bannister, Comedian* (1839) 25. John A. Thieme notes that London spouting clubs declined in popularity after the 1770s although he does not note their transmogrification into working-class private theatres of the 'song-and-supper' clubs of the 1820s and 1830s, 'Spouting, Spouting-Clubs and Spouting Companions', *Theatre Notebook*, 29 (1975), 9–18.

poem written in 1759, the writer recalled a ten-strong police raid on such a club, detailing such things as how makeup was improvised by burning wine bottle corks to provide smooth-faced young men with beards ('The cork | Intruded swift in the candle's blaze | Is nigrified, and marks th'aspiring youth | With whiskers bold'). A noticeable feature of 'The Spouting Club' is its obvious awareness of how the 'rants elaborate' of these young actors affected their self-esteem, with the audience's reaction positioning them relative to the group:

> He ended; but the tribe
> Withhold the grasp'd-at-banners of applause.
> Then down he sits, with woeful aspect dull.
> But strait emerging from a sea of thought,
> He swallows hasty the salubrious stream,
> And re-inthrones his abdicated soul.[67]

To some extent, the tavern spouting clubs were always disreputable although some amateurs made them their debut platform for later acting careers. Thomas Bellamy, writing the life of the comedian William Parsons nearly forty years later, recalled that the venues where two of his actor contemporaries had first 'set up their standards theatrical, were the Bird Cage in Wood Street, and the Horns in Doctor's Commons:—places ... of a far more respectable description than that which attaches to the spouting clubs of the present day'.[68] The spouting clubs also provided other kinds of opportunities.

Although the first black man did not act on an English stage until 1825 (at the Royal Coburg), Julius Soubise, the son of a Jamaican slave, was brought back to London around the middle of the eighteenth century and performed Shakespeare in the spouting clubs.[69] This 'uncommonly smart and intelligent little Mungo' was taught elocution by the elder Sheridan, swordsmanship by Henry

---

[67] Malcolm, *Anecdotes*, ii. 208. This poem seems to be the same one quoted as 'The Picture of a Spouting Club' in Thieme, 'Spouting, Spouting-Clubs and Spouting Companions', 9–18.

[68] Thomas Bellamy, *The Life of Mr. William Parsons, Comedian* (1795), 8.

[69] Julia Swindells, *Glorious Causes: The Grand Theatre of Political Change, 1789 to 1833* (Oxford: Oxford University Press, 2001), 72 n.

Angelo, and became a favourite of Garrick's. Having 'studied the speeches of Othello ... [he] declaimed at the spouting clubs, with mighty applause'.[70] As well as these progressive racial attitudes achieved by the socially loosening cultural affects of acting, where a public rather than private self is unthreateningly staged and contained, spouting clubs overlapped with other types of venue where speech and theatricality remained the basis of the entertainment. The straightforward speech-making of the political debating clubs which first became popular in London during the 1790s continued into the early Victorian period. The caricaturist Theodore Lane used to visit the Harp tavern in Russell Street, Drury Lane, to draw and observe 'spouting youths, anxious to become actors'.[71] J. Ewing Ritchie listed the Belvidere in Pentonville and the Horns in Kennington, as well as the Temple Forum and Coger's Hall in Shoe Lane.[72]

Such venues may have helped increase working-class confidence and articulacy but perhaps more typical were their more louche incarnations. Ritchie described in *The Night Side of London* a visit to a 'Judge and Jury Club', perhaps an even more louche type of entertainment where the visitors, as the name implies, acted out real or imaginary court cases. Although Ritchie was scarcely forthcoming, the one he described (revealingly held in the upper room of a hotel) gave ample opportunity for sado-masochistic and trans-sexual deviancy. With over a hundred people present, Ritchie claimed that 'witnesses were examined and cross-examined, the female being men dressed up in women's clothes, and everything was done that could be to pander to the lowest propensities of depraved humanity'.[73]

As far as the history of London subcultures is concerned, it is important to notice that some of the spouting clubs, such as the one for 'stage-stricken heroes' based at the Jacob's Well tavern in the Barbican, were places where political radicalism and acting probably

[70] Angelo, *Reminiscences*, i. 446–52.   [71] Egan, *Show Folks!*, 47.
[72] Ritchie, *The Night Side of London*, 90–8.   [73] Ibid. 76–82.

overlapped. Writing in 1828, Henry Angelo took care to recall his memories of the Jacob's Well of around 1790 as being 'harmless in its pursuits, and only to be ranked amongst the multifarious clubs, ycleped *Choice-spirits, Humdrums, Good-fellows, Free-and-easys*, and a catalogue of others, where spouting, speechifying, singing, drolling, mimicking, and sing-song, kept the parties perhaps from worse amusements'. Angelo's verbal sketch gives a good idea of the activities and how they were arranged:

There was a president, who from a rostrum knocking with his ivory mallet, hoarsely bawled, 'Will any gentleman favour the company with a speech, a recitation, an imitation, or a song?' Half-a-dozen candidates for fame, in each department proposed, started up; when the moderator, from his lofty seat, decided who was first to his legs. The party then retired, a bell was rung, the curtain was raised at the end of the room, and the spouter or singer making his bow, commenced his part.

It may also have been experiences at the Jacob's Well that prompted Angelo to give a less respectful recollection of the black man Soubise, where he witnessed the audience's derisive laughter at 'the representation of Othello, *solus*, by a man of colour, the son of a West Indian planter, newly imported, whose thick speech and phraseology might have better fitted him for *Massa Mungo*, in [Charles Dibdin's] the Padlock'.[74] Nevertheless, by the late 1810s the Jacob's Well, Barbican, had become closely associated with the organization of physical force revolutionary Spenceans. As such, it was put under regular surveillance from the Home Office where, for example, a spy noted that around 290 angry protestors turned up in late August 1819 to agitate about the Peterloo Massacre. Intriguingly, given the apparent connections between public speaking, the Jacob's Well, and the black man Soubise, it is revealing that after Peterloo another Jamaican son of a slave, the Spencean orator and leader Robert Wedderburn, was found haranguing the tavern crowd at the Jacob's Well along with another black man.[75] Henry Angelo's wish

---

[74] Angelo, *Reminiscences, and Friends* (1828), i. 284–7.
[75] Worrall, *Radical Culture*, 146, 161; PRO HO 42/193.97, 23 August 1819.

to stress the respectability of the tavern when he wrote in the late 1820s no doubt reflected his misgivings about the continuities of the highly racially mixed, politically radical, working-class culture he had experienced there when he was younger. Again, as with the spy George Ruthven frequenting the gambling dens recorded by Renton Nicholson, the Jacob's Well of the Peterloo era had been thoroughly infiltrated by Government spies. Clearly, spouting club acting, political speech-making, and racially mixed working-class association were culturally widely dispersed in early nineteenth-century London and were deeply worrying to those who identified themselves with the patrician class.

Delving still further into the underworld of Romantic period theatricality, one comes across the astonishing realm of the private theatre. Tracy C. Davis has noted that as early as 1811 there was a proposal to create a theatre in the parishes of Marylebone or St George's which opened three nights a week on a subscription basis. While the proposal was at least partially aimed at circumventing the jurisdiction of the magistrates and Lord Chamberlain, its 50 guinea to 100 guinea rates strongly implied that the proposed playhouse was aimed at a genteel, affluent audience.[76] The plans never came to fruition but the impetus behind the proposal is helpful in indicating the strength of London demand. However, the subsequent pent-up market forces unleashed a very different set of private playhouses from the type imagined in the 1811 proposal. These were theatrical spaces far removed from the country house soirées of the young Jane Austen at Steventon rectory, spaces which completely outflanked the rules and censorship of the Lord Chamberlain's Examiner of Plays. Austen's negativity towards private theatricals in *Mansfield Park* (1814), although the subject of intense recent discussion, may have been coloured by the rise of the more dubious metropolitan private theatres.[77] Written in 1827, Thomas Dibdin's *Reminiscences*

[76] Tracy C. Davis, *The Economics of the British Stage 1800–1914* (Cambridge: Cambridge University Press, 2000), 232–2.

[77] Paula Byrne, *Jane Austen and the Theatre* (London: Hambledon, 2002); Penny Gay, *Jane Austen and the Theatre* (Cambridge: Cambridge University Press, 2002).

discussed the similarity between the 'old club' at Jacob's Well, Barbican, and the array of 'regular private theatres' which currently abounded on the fringe of London life. Dibdin listed existing private theatres in Tottenham Court Road, Berwick Street, Commercial Road, John Street, Wilmington Square, Kennington, Regent Street, Wych Street, and Temple Bar. His criticism of them was not only concerned with their 'incalculable mischief to public morals' but also with their role in depressing the wages of actors by 'inundating the theatres with pretenders at low salaries', bringing hardship to the theatrical fraternity by 'depriving the families of respectable and fairly-established regular practitioners'.[78] By their very nature, the metropolitan private theatres are difficult to recover because they so often existed in a twilight world of legality. Although Sybil Rosenfeld in her *Temples of Thespis: Some Private Theatres and Theatricals in England and Wales, 1700–1820* (1978) briefly indicates their existence, the metropolitan private theatres were on an unrespectable par with the song-and-supper and Judge and Jury clubs which mixed indistinguishably with other types of low life 'free-and-easy'. Dibdin's aspersion on their 'incalculable mischief to public morals' was a comment frequently made. In the early 1800s, one writer of a guidebook, *A View Of London, or, The Stranger's Guide Through The British Metropolis*, counted seventeen private theatres in London, adding that

it would be no rash censure to denominate them nurseries of vice and dissipation since tradesmen, with their wives and daughters, are thus initiated in all the arts of affectation, and become heroes and heroines in proportion as their imagination is heated; insomuch, that they too often neglect their business, to commit to memory their part of the dialogue for the next night's exhibition.[79]

Such criticism correlates with the Society for the Suppression of Vice's attempts to close down the Royalty Theatre in 1803 where,

---

[78] *Reminiscences of Thomas Dibdin*, ii. 394–6.
[79] *A View Of London, or, The Stranger's Guide Through The British Metropolis* (1803–4), 86.

again, one of the more explicit fears is of the harm to commerce engendered by theatre-going.

The effects of private theatre on sexual morals was also a concern to many contemporaries. In 1801 Richard Graves's chapter 'Theatrico-Mania: An Essay on the Rage for Private Theatrical Exhibitions', as well as commenting on the generalized tendency for theatricality to undermine traditional class divisions and moralities ('so fond are we of every thing theatrical, that our young ladies of rank … are now taught to emulate the dancers of the stage [and to introduce] the voluptuous morals of the French nation'), he also took occasion to criticize the opportunities for sexual indiscretions at country house theatrical parties because 'the *private* apartments in noblemen's and gentlemen's houses, where the young people retire to change their dresses and the like, have been productive of more than one intrigue, and elopements, and improper marriages'.[80] Graves's disquiet, however, went deeper than that: he voiced his concern about the role of grammar school theatricals in inculcating sexual deviance. What worried him was that, owing to the all male environment, 'some of the boys must necessarily be metamorphosed, for the time, into the other sex'. His own attitudes were, themselves, quite complex: saying that 'though I have been rather pleased with the partiality of a fond mother, delighted to see what an handsome girl her booby son would make', he added, 'to me [it is] a disgusting sight'.[81]

Paedophilic tastes played their part in these theatrical spaces on the edges of the mainstream. Although he was closely associated with the more stable and successful of the 'minor' theatres, W. T. Moncrieff's *Actors Al Fresco* (1827) for Vauxhall Gardens no doubt made use of very youthful actresses to sing in his 'The Boarding School Play', a short sketch depicting Christmas holiday theatricals ('Then, dull learning, girls spurn; | The whole school-room they turn | To a theatre gay, | For the breaking-up play'). From these cues,

---

[80] Richard Graves, *Senilities; or Solitary Amusements: in Prose and Verse: With a Cursory Disquisition on the Future Condition of the Sexes* (1801), 63–4.
[81] Ibid. 62.

Moncrieff developed a mixture of innuendo (based on word-play on the names of popular actors) and homoerotic implications amongst the schoolchildren, perhaps also glancing at their suggestive clothing or costume:

> Each miss, then, feeling Young and Kean,
> Makes the lesser scholars' hearts tremble;
> And struts and frets upon the scene,
> Like Siddons, O'Neill, Kean, and Kemble;
> Now melting, and now in a fury.
> Hose and doublet they wear.[82]

Moncrieff seems to have followed up this theme in his song 'Beauty Was A Little Girl', which quickly accelerates the female child from innocence to knowing provocation ('She mov'd so meek, and look'd so shy, | None, then, saw mischief in her eye, | Nor dream'd that youths for her would die'). Again, presumably some of the dramatic interest in Moncrieff's song arises from the portrayal of her sexual development from 'Beauty was a little girl,— | Heighho! Heighho! | Pure and lovely as a pearl' to adult knowingness: 'Beauty's now a woman grown, | ... Looking like a rose full-blown, | ... Weaving still for hearts a snare, | She seems to cry, with saucy air, | Come, and kiss me,—if you dare.'[83] Over twenty years earlier, it seems almost certain that the 14-year-old 'Young Roscius', Willam Henry West Betty, about whose looks it was written that 'Female beauty cannot afford any thing more sweet than his smile', was a favourite of adult male audiences for similar reasons. In an account published by John Fairburn of a December 1804 performance by Betty at Covent Garden, the theatre was described as quite transformed by the adult males who had come to see the 14-year-old: 'The pit had a dark and dismal appearance; scarcely a female had courage to venture into it. It was of course, almost exclusively

---

[82] W. T. Moncrieff, *Songs, Duets, Trios, Choruses, &c.&c. in Actors Al Fresco; or, the Play in the Pleasure Grounds; (an Occasional Vaudeville) First Produced at the Royal Gardens, Vauxhall, 4th June, 1827 ... To be had only in the Gardens* (1827), 5–6.
[83] Ibid. 6–7.

occupied by men, and did not afford that pleasing variety which it usually exhibits.'[84] Of course, the role of children in the theatrical entertainment was quite different from what it is today. Charles Dibdin, who built and managed the Royal Circus, Blackfriars Road, which opened in 1782, ran it as an equestrian arena. One-third of the profits for the venture were detailed to be paid to the chief rider, Charles Hughes, 'for his performance and breaking horses'. Alongside this expenditure, Dibdin employed nearly twenty children, apparently as ballet dancers, all of them currently indentured to Giuseppe Grimaldi as ballet apprentices. Although Dibdin probably did this to keep down costs (an unsuccessful attempt since he spent time in the King's Bench prison *c*.1783), it is likely he also had an eye to the attractiveness of the children, despite the considerable physical danger to which they were subjected by their inevitably close proximity to horse-riding entertainment.[85] When Dibdin unsuccessfully applied for a licence to local magistrates, the *London Chronicle* reported that it was intended there would be 'near 50 children of both sexes, from six years old to 14 … [who] were intended to act speaking pantomimes, operas, medleys, drolls, and interludes'. Devastatingly, the *London Chronicle* added that 'horsemanship … was only intended to be served up as a dessert'.[86] While waiting precariously between different kinds of licensing arrangements, Dibdin still continued with his shows but met opposition from the parents of his child actors, particularly about Grimaldi, against whom 'criminal accusations were preferred' and the local magistrates ordered 'a compleat investigation into the morals and conduct of the place'.[87] The morality of those involved is doubly in doubt since Dibdin makes it quite clear that he entered

[84] John Fairburn, *The Life of Wm. Henry West Betty, The Celebrated and Wonderful Young Roscius: Containing the Particulars of his Theatrical Career, His Education, Character, & Abilities; Together with an Impartial Account of his Astonishing Performances on [sic] the London Theatres* (1804), 27, 30.

[85] Charles Dibdin, *Royal Circus Epitomized* (1784), 4–6.

[86] Quoted in Robert Fahrner, 'The Turbulent First Year of the Royal Circus (1782–1783)', *Theatre Survey*, 19 (1978), 155–70.

[87] Charles Dibdin, *Royal Circus Epitomized*, 29.

into a firm contract with the fathers of at least three of the children he employed via Grimaldi.[88] In other words, by only lightly inferring the probable intentions of those involved, it looks quite likely that equestrianism was only a front for a show which featured the display of children under the age of 14.

The private theatres in the great houses afforded even more opportunities for the exercise of paedophilic tastes. In 1782 William Beckford, the author of *Vathek*, helped stage a private theatrical pastoral at Queensbury House, Charles Street. Beckford's lengthy accounts leave no doubt that the whole event was staged because of his interest in the 'ravissant' scenes of 'not less than twenty or thirty blooming girls and boys appearing together at one time on the stage'. His lingering descriptions over their 'coral lips', their 'tender colouring—those evanescent tints' of the all-teenage cast is orchestrated into the narrative of paedophilic delectation. Even during the rehearsals, Beckford relates how they had finished one day with a 'prodigiously gay supper (quite an orgy), after the innocents (one excepted) had been prudently dismissed to their couches'. The reason for keeping the 'one excepted' behind is not discussed but Beckford frequently sought to validate his own desires by transposing them into an imagined collusion with the audience, as if they equally shared his tastes: 'You cannot imagine how many "potent grave and reverend Signors" are on the "qui vive" to witness this charming expansion of buds and blossoms'. Beckford took care to deliberately oversee their stage makeup precisely in order to preserve the possibilities of sexual fascination in the children: 'Among the Figurantes were some of the most nymph-like ethereal Creatures you ever beheld—pale and interesting; for I entered a strong protest against rouge ... Some indiscreet, gloating stares from the Satyrical part of the audience covered many lovely cheeks with blushes'. Once again, Beckford not only notices that the way pastoral has been cast and directed arouses the 'Satyrical' interest of the audience but he also ascribes his own feelings as the shared experience of others. Not

[88] Ibid. 6.

least, Beckford also hints that the children also play, through their blushes, some part in knowing provocation or acknowledgement of their sexual role.[89]

If such private theatricals in the great English country houses allowed the patrician class to indulge their peccadilloes, back in the metropolis the range of private theatres admitted a much wider range of audiences and participants. The link between juvenile acting and private theatres was later sustained in the 'Penny Theatres' or 'Gaffs' recorded in James Grant's *Sketches in London* (1838), an account written when they had only been in existence some five or six years. The Penny Theatres are a sort of interim between the earlier adult private theatres described below (which dated in that particular incarnation to the late 1810s or early 1820s) and the taste for juvenile acting which may have arisen with the fame of 'Master Betty'. The surprising thing about the Penny Theatres was that, while their owners were impoverished adults, the audiences were described by Grant as being preponderantly male children aged between 8 and 16 years. In just about every respect, the Penny Theatres were the social inversion of the house-party private theatricals of the type orchestrated by Beckford. Whereas the aristocratic theatricals featured children who were materially cosseted, even if sexually seduced, the Penny Theatres were places of resort for children turned out of the family home for the night by their parents. Police raids were not uncommon because the Gaff boys were frequently associated with street crime and burglaries. Grant thought that there were between eighty and one hundred Gaffs, located in down-at-heel London East End areas in Ratcliffe Highway, Mile End Road, St George's Fields, the New Cut, King's Cross, and the west end Marylebone. He estimated that their nightly audiences were around 24,000 persons on account of their custom of holding several 'houses' each night. The theatres themselves were roughly built with exposed roof joists and brickwork but the performers seem to have

---

[89] J. W. Oliver, *The Life of William Beckford* (London: Oxford University Press, 1932), 109–16.

all been adults. With handwritten playbills, and the audience sitting
on hard benches, the Penny Theatres were rough enough but they
necessarily led to very naturalistic styles of acting ('"It's so like—jist
the thing—that's the very way she goes on at home"') with frequent
interruptions and conversations between performers and audiences.
The plays themselves were often based on 'local' topics such as
murders or other types of crime and although Grant remembered
a much-truncated version of *Othello*, the pieces were often written
especially for the Gaff venues, featuring such works as *Greenacre, or
The Murder of Carpenter's Buildings, The Blood-stained Handkerchief*,
and *The Red-Nosed Monster, or The Tyrant of the Mountains*.[90] Not
least, the Penny Theatres as a phenomenon are suggestive not only
of the appetite for theatricality which, by the end of the century,
would transform itself into the music-hall of the East End, but they
also indicate the existence in the earliest parts of the century of the
obscure role of children as theatre-goers.

Some of the most sustained records of the existence of the adult
versions of the private theatres of the early 1820s come in the form of
an irregular 'Private Theatricals' feature that ran for some time in the
Rambler's Magazine, or, Man of Fashion's Companion. The dubious
venues of Soho and Camden noticed in the *Rambler's Magazine*
provide extraordinary documentary evidence for the coincidence
of a taste for theatricals merging with that of contemporary semi-
criminal London subcultures. It seems that the same rules governing
the independence of private property which secured the big country-
house theatrical parties from legal intrusion (even though Beckford's
memoir suggests it may have been well merited), also protected their
lower-class imitations in London's seedier streets.[91] This meant that
they were free to perform spoken drama in much the same way that
country-house parties might mount a performance of Shakespeare.

[90] This account is drawn from James Grant, *Sketches in London* (1838), ch. 5, pp.
161–92.
[91] Sybil Rosenfeld is aware of these lower-class private theatres, but touches on them
only fleetingly, *Temples of Thespis, Some Private Theatres and Theatricals in England and
Wales, 1700–1820* (London: Society for Theatre Research, 1978), 8.

Legal authorities, such as magistrates, do not appear to have been interested in their theatrical exhibitions except in so far as their premises threw up separate criminal cases such as embezzlement. Instances of apprentices rifling their masters' cash tills to pay their acting fees, and a reference to private theatres in the Olympic's *Two More Slaves; or, The Escape from Brixton* (1822), both incidents discussed below, indicate that the London private playhouses were strongly associated with crime but were not otherwise directly subject to suppression. Arguably, their presence in London even allowed the authorities some leeway in offsetting the draconian instincts of the Royal theatres. Indeed, the rise of a range of private theatres in London indicates better than anything else the existence of a commercially viable, but unsupplied, popular demand for drama. The movement into these ventures of owners seeking to exploit their customers testifies to a subculture of theatricality which had arisen as a direct result of the Royal theatre monopolies and their litigious propensities to suppress public theatres in the capital.

Into this vacuum emerged a range of activities, some of them with loose connections to radical politics and the popular press. The *Rambler's Magazine* was run by the shadowy figure of George Cannon, the acquaintance of P. B. Shelley who, in his short-lived journal the *Theological Inquirer* (1815), had first published *Queen Mab* to a wider circulation so that the *Rambler's* was well positioned to court pornography and blasphemy through its well-connected links with urban radical Spenceanism.[92] The *Rambler's Magazine* (by 1824 it had become simply the *Rambler or Fashionable Companion*) also made a speciality in semi-pornographic frontispieces as well as, increasingly, luridly full reportage of rape and adultery cases, evidently culling its reports from provincial as well as the metropolitan press. The *Rambler's Magazine* was very much the product of a distinct plebeian public sphere in the sense that it often directly addresses the sort of raffish urban coterie that modern

---

[92] Iain McCalman, *Radical Underworld: Prophets, Revolutionaries and Pornographers in London, 1795–1840* (Cambridge: Cambridge University Press, 1988), 208–10.

readers might most readily recognize from Pierce Egan's *Life in London* (1820) or its various *Tom and Jerry* spin-offs, although the magazine itself pointedly did not adopt the ready-made 'swell' Corinthian language of Egan's works. Indeed, the beginning of the *Rambler's* in early 1822 virtually coincides with Moncrieff's hit of *Tom and Jerry* at the Adelphi in December 1821 so that it is particularly interesting that it remained more or less immune from the wave of fashion for criminalized languages that the play's success created. One may infer that, being thoroughly the product and expression of a pre-existing plebeian public sphere, the *Rambler's* felt no need to ape the newly studied but fashionable street argot which abounded in *Tom and Jerry*.

In other words, the *Rambler's Magazine* exposure of the private theatres of working-class London throws remarkable light on the existence of a properly plebeian public sphere of print culture, politics, and theatricality.[93] In a piece entitled 'Private Theatrical Conspiracy', the first issue of the *Rambler's Magazine* claimed that, in setting up the 'Private Theatricals' feature, it was adopting into its columns an abortive attempt by a 'junto' of 'two conductors and ... understrappers' who had hoped to establish a cheap theatrical magazine intended 'to contain copious criticisms on private theatricals'.[94] This in itself is quite revealing because it demonstrates the increasing proximity between ultra-radicalism and theatre: even the austere Richard Carlile would eventually succumb to the opportunities afforded by the Rotunda layout to present Taylor's *Swing, or, Who are the Incendiaries?* Furthermore, it particularly provides evidence of the close connections between political radicalism in London and the taste for the kinds of private theatricals to be discussed below. What followed in the ensuing months of 1822 was a series of brief comments and anecdotes on several private theatres, a list which (with the exception of the one in Berwick Street) is completely different from Thomas Dibdin's

[93] Much of the contextual framework is laid out in Kevin Gilmartin, *Print Politics: The Press and Radical Opposition in Early Nineteenth-Century England* (Cambridge: Cambridge University Press, 1995).

[94] *The Rambler's Magazine, or, Man of Fashion's Companion*, 1 February 1822, 57–9.

unofficial census of 1827. The *Rambler's Magazine* printed brief notices of plays appearing at the private theatres of Berwick Street, Rawstone Place, Wilson Street, and Francis Street in Newington.

Very little, if anything, is known about these places. Partly because of its confidence in addressing its own public sphere directly, the distinctively 'knowing' language of these reviews only obliquely sheds light on events in the theatres themselves. Pierce Egan recollected that in the 1810s Berwick Street 'was well known in theatrical circles' except that 'injudicious applause given by friends' led to false encouragement and failed careers, but his memoir is important in stressing the sociability and conviviality of amateur acting.[95] A pirated piece presumably taken from one of Charles Mathews's shows included a sketch about the Berwick Street theatre, a comic narrative which ended in a raid by the watchmen and the arrest of the participants.[96] Conditions must have been a long way removed from even the roughest of the established 'minor' theatres. One London private theatre was 'formerly a cow-house' while the Berwick Street theatre had a pit of 'bare earth'.[97] A notice of the Rawstone Place Theatre's production of *The Castle Spectre* commented on the fact that the leading lady 'fainted away' and 'as usual, the conclusion of the piece was adjourned'.[98] Some of the theatres were evidently fitted up with basic theatrical properties since another Rawstone Place production (of *Wallace*), mentioned the problems experienced with the curtains which caused 'several skirmishes among the audience'. The evening ended with 'children squalling, women roaring, and a general row occasioned by the audience making an attempt to carry the stage by storm' (again, the presence of children is a good indicator of the gender and age structure of these types of theatre). At the Berwick Street theatre, this would not have been too difficult as the stage was

[95] Egan, *Show Folks!*, 26.

[96] *Entirely New Entertainment. Mathews in America; Or, The Theatrical Wanderer: A Cargo of New Characters, Original Songs And concluding Piece of the Wild Goose Chase, Or the Inn At Baltimore* (1823), 9–13.

[97] Kemble, *Dramatic Scorpion*, 11 n., 12 n.

[98] *Rambler's Magazine, or, Man of Fashion's Companion* 2 January 1822, 80.

only fifteen inches high.[99] The evening *Wallace* was performed, the anonymous reviewer mentioned that the audience was 'principally composed of hackney writers, and scribes of the lowest order' who had assembled there to see their friends 'behind the curtain'.[100] In other words, the private theatres were places not only where friends gathered together to appear as both actors and spectators but, moreover, in the rough playhouses such as Rawstone Place, an essential component of the evening was that the actors paid to act.

Perhaps no other single factor demonstrates the cultural reach of drama in this period or its ability to percolate down through society than the willingness of 'hackney writers, and scribes of the lowest order' to pay to act. To satirists, the private theatres served only to endanger the morals of 'the shop-girl and, fancy dress-maker' who took the roles. John Philip Kemble's misogynistic description of an overweight shop-girl playing Juliet ('Two bulky legs her beauteous figure grace, | And rolls of fat adorn her brawny face; | Thick as she's high ...') were figured as part of a predictable trajectory of ruin 'after imperfectly waded thro' some dozen novels and amatory epistles, betake themselves to the private stage'.[101] Here, amongst 'Berwick's tag-rag crew' a 'victim lies' 'By *thee* seduc'd'.[102] Private theatres were being opened by unscrupulous entrepreneurs who not only offered an acting space but also sold the roles. During a performance of *Pizarro*, 'a great commotion was observable among the audience, occasioned by the appearance of a person, who is famed for making benefits at the theatres, by selling the characters to wretched would be actors, for most extravagant prices'. As the review concluded, 'this worthy has been frequently heard to say, that he did not want good actors, but those who would dub up [*sic*] a large price, and if they did that, he would not care a d—n whether they butchered the characters or not'.[103] Kemble, in

---

[99] Kemble, *Dramatic Scorpion*, 12.
[100] *Rambler's Magazine, or, Man of Fashion's Companion*, 8 January 1822, 81.
[101] John Philip Kemble, *The Dramatic Scorpion*, 14 n.
[102] Ibid. 15.
[103] *Rambler's Magazine, or, Man of Fashion's Companion*, 16 January 1822, 82.

The Dramatic Scorpion, recorded that the usual procedure was to announce a 'general sale' of roles by auction at which 'the characters are named, and the highest bidder becomes the purchaser'.[104] The *Rambler's Magazine* purported to receive correspondence from several people involved with the organization of the private theatres, with one writer claiming to reveal the identities of nearly two hundred 'private performers, with their real, as well as assumed, names — their occupations and addresses, as well as those of their employers'.[105] One of the most intriguing correspondents claimed to be 'the proprietor of three minor theatres, and two "preparatory barns" for green-horns to study in', presumably his ownership of the former being a spoof but the latter referring to private theatres under his control. He complained to the *Rambler's* that he had lost his paying actors because their 'masters have inspected their tills' or, in other words, apprentices and shopworkers had been caught financing their amateur acting careers by stealing money from their employers. In any event, this 'Timothy Buskin's' address, in Hopkins Street, Soho, was an authentic enough location, the narrow thoroughfare having been the place where in 1820 Robert Wedderburn's hayloft blasphemous chapel was run as the ideological wing of the Cato Street conspiracy.[106] It may have been Wedderburn's imprisonment for blasphemy in May 1820 which both vacated the venue and led to its ready-made local audience transferring its tastes from atheistical preaching to amateur acting.

These working-class private theatres obviously existed in a twilight world of legality where would-be actors were ripped off and where the organizers absconded with the money. John Philip Kemble, the by no means neutral author of *The Dramatic Scorpion* (1818), alleged that at one private theatre Shakespeare's *Richard III* had been played by 'a reputed swindler' playing alongside his mistress.[107] Their

[104] Kemble, *Dramatic Scorpion*, 16.

[105] *Rambler's Magazine, or, Man of Fashion's Companion*, 13 February 1822, 130.

[106] *Rambler's Magazine, or, Man of Fashion's Companion* (1822), 177. On Hopkins Street, see Worrall, *Radical Culture*, 165–84.

[107] Kemble, *Dramatic Scorpion*, 11 n.

illegalities were even well enough known to contemporaries to find mocking portrayal on the stages of the 'minor' theatres. The Olympic Theatre's *Two More Slaves; or, The Escape from Brixton* (1822), a 'Burlesque Parody' of John Howard Payne's Covent Garden hit, *The Galley Slaves*, contained a scene set in Brixton gaol (then notorious for its newly opened treadmill) which featured a character called 'Amateur' who had been locked up for embezzling the takings from a private theatre in Camden Town:

> I am not Actor Sir; only an Amateur
> Last week at Camden Town to pass away
> Our winter's night, we tried a private play,
> Took money at the Door, which was a rarity,
> But pocketed it ourselves, & called it charity.
> 'The Wheel of Fortune' was the play we fix'd on,
> But that you see is chang'd to Wheel of Brixton;
> The after-piece was better nam'd you'll say,
> For that was to have been the 'Devil to pay'.[108]

The Wheel of Fortune, like *The Devil to Pay*, were both established repertoire pieces for the minors which had originated in the patent houses. For the most part, the private theatres tended to present the best pieces from the minor theatres, itself an indication that theatre-going crossed fluidly between the two types of venue, but with perhaps amateur actors wanting to try their hand at the big hits. In this way, burlettas such as *Who Wants a Guinea*, James Kenney's *Raising the Wind*, George Colman the Younger's *John Bull or An Englishman's Fireside* and *The Heir at Law*, *The Poor Gentleman*, as well as the prolific William Thomas Moncrieff's *Rochester* and *Tom and Jerry* were all presented. It was also a not inconsiderable asset of the private theatres that, unlike the minors, they could give legal performances of Shakespeare with *The Merchant of Venice*, *Richard III*, and *Othello* all finding performance at the sort of dubious rough playhouses described in the pages of the *Rambler's Magazine*.

---

[108] Larpent Plays, 2322, Huntington Library, Calif.

The Soho and Camden private theatres were remarkable places exemplifying the growing alterity of working-class culture. They emerged out of several sets of material factors. One was the resistance to the opening of new theatres in London because of the cartel operated by the Royal theatres. Secondly, they became, for the same reason, the only venues where, unchallenged, spoken drama could be performed, even though one must assume they were excerpting rather than doing the full texts. Thirdly, the recovery of the (admittedly scant) evidence of their endeavours reveals the full integration of the private theatres into a context of plebeian culture both in its print forms, as in the *Rambler's Magazine*, and in its oral forms, as in *The Wheel of Fortune*. Finally, the plebeian private theatres present an inversion of capital relationships between actors and audience. In the plebeian private theatres it was the actors who paid the highest prices, not the spectators. This unexpected and innovative set of economic relationships between theatres and audiences was a continuous feature of the social role of the playhouses in this period.

The proliferation of both the Penny Theatres of the 1830s and the metropolitan private theatres of the early 1820s suggests that there existed a strong relationship between theatricality and commercial enterprise. The mid-eighteenth-century spouting clubs, as well as the 1820s private theatres featured in the *Rambler's Magazine*, both relied on catchments of paying actors as well as audiences. The Penny Theatres were objects of social exclusion save for visitations by, on the one hand, the new breed of journalists from the radical press or, on the other, morally impelled visitors who saw the public organization of private theatricality as socially subversive. Despite this, they were quite significant components in the theatrical economy. It is remarkable that the spread of London 1820s theatrical culture was able to encompass both the grandeur of the royal command performances as well as the apprentices and hackney writers who scraped together their own (and their employers') money to piece out their theatre-going. The kind of private or semi-impoverished aspects of theatricality discussed so far gives little indication of the enormous role of theatres in the London economy. In part, the expansion of interest in drama can be gauged by the number of new journals with titles such as the *British Stage, and Literary Cabinet*, the *Dramatic Magazine*, the *Mirror of the Stage; or, New Dramatic Censor*, the *Cornucopia or Literary and Dramatic Mirror*, as well as provincially based journals such as Birmingham's *Theatrical John Bull*.[109] As may be judged from the expansion in the number of biographies and autobiographies of actors appearing at this time, there was obviously a growth in all kinds of theatrical memorabilia and anecdote.

However, nothing quite so forcefully indicates the presence of theatre as an economic factor in consumerism than the existence of entertainments such as Thomas John Dibdin's two pantomimes *Harlequin in his Element, or Fire, Water, Earth, & Air* (1807) for Covent Garden, and *Melodrame Mad! Or The Siege of Troy* (1819) for the Surrey Theatre. If London's fugitive private theatres represented both opportunities for the theatrical entrepreneur (and an inversion of the normal expectation that actors appearing to a paying audience earned wages), *Harlequin in his Element* and *Melodrame Mad!* present an altogether more conventional—if no less remarkable—relationship between the economic roles of theatre and public. Both pieces illustrate that London playhouse audiences were perceived by manufacturers and financiers, as well as by theatre managements, to be economically active consumers and that the theatre stage was an established space where luxury products could be introduced to theatregoers. In the case of *Harlequin in his Element*, London's role as a manufacturing centre is highlighted. By 1819, however, Dibdin's *Melodrame Mad!*, with its references to the newly invented Velocipede bicycles and the Sun and Norwich insurance companies, showed surprising perspicuity in reflecting the subtle economic changes already slowly transforming London from its traditional role as a manufacturing centre to a modern capital

---

[109] See James F. Allerton and John W. Robinson, *English Theatrical Literature 1559–1900* (London: Society for Theatre Research, 1970).

based upon individual mobility and intellectual or financial property. Such transitions, made quite explicit at the Surrey, heralded the development of London towards its early twentieth-century status. Melodrama, the bicycle, and the various fire insurance offices featured in Dibdin's 1819 piece, mark a qualitative transformation, a movement in popular theatre which was receptive towards the capital's increasing concern with intellectual property and social mobility as it developed during the nineteenth century. It is a notable distancing away from the eighteenth century's heritage of harlequinade, clowning, and manufactories, all of which had been evident in his Covent Garden pantomime little more than a decade earlier.

Harlequin in his Element comprised a series of scenes whose painted backdrops portrayed a range of the city's commercial life. What is unusual is that specific, branded, shops and manufactories were depicted on stage. By the 1820s, even provincial Birmingham featured pantomimes such as William Thomas Moncrieff's *Harlequin and the Flying Chest* (1823), staging his Drury Lane production complete with 272 foot moving dioramas of the 'Quarries at Oreston' and the building of the Plymouth breakwater, ensuring that the representation of the country's economic life became a familiar aspect of theatre-going.[110] However, *Harlequin in his Element* is an unusual pantomime in advertising specific goods and services. In part, a tradition of shopkeeping scenes in English harlequinades can be traced back to seventeenth-century French pantomimes incorporating an underclothier's and a confectioner's stalls.[111] *Harlequin in his Element* combined its pictures with commerce by having scenes showing London as 'a distant prospect of the Metropolis in which the West towers of the Abbey are most perceptible' together with a moonlight river scene with 'A timber yard on the banks of the

[110] *Theatrical John Bull* (Birmingham), 1, 5 June 1825, 20; for the Plymouth breakwater diorama, see David Mayer, *Harlequin in his Element: The English Pantomime, 1806–1836* (Cambridge, Mass.: Harvard University Press, 1969), fig. 16.

[111] R. J. Broadbent, *A History of Pantomime* (London: Simpkins, Marshall, Hamilton, Kent & Co., 1901), 181.

Thames' and 'sailing boats ... which have a most beautiful and picturesque appearance'. This combination of the picturesque and the
mercantile went together with other scenes representing a complete
order of national social harmony during a time of war. For example,
in an episode set in an anonymous village, the

scene is enlivened by the entrance of an old blind soldier, drawing an
hand organ, and attended by his son. ... While he is singing, the villagers
are bestowing their charitable benefactions on the old soldier. Among the
groups that surround him, are three sailors. Harlequin enters, and by a
touch of his wand, transforms the organ into the model of a man of war.
The music strikes up Rule Britannia, and the sailors give three cheers.

The pantomime's depiction of wartime solidarity with its heroes,
together with pride in London's commercial prowess, sit comfortably
together. Using the same formula love story as many other pantomimes, such as the Royalty Theatre's *Pantomimic Preludio, And ...
Paris Federation* (1790), the incidental harlequinade is comprised of
the Columbine figure resisting her guardian's, Sir Feeble Sordid's,
attempts to marry her (whereupon the gods of the four elements
create a Harlequin for her protection). In other words, running
alongside the scenes of social and patriotic duty lies the story of the
rejection of familial authority.

What makes *Harlequin in his Element* so extraordinary, however,
are scenes in a glass factory, a paper mill, and a manufactury of
artificial stone used to make garden statuary.[112] In at least two
of the three scenes, the pantomime showed not only the process of
manufacture but also exhibited the wares produced and displayed
them on the Covent Garden stage as scenery, objects placed as if
ready for sale. In the scene set in 'Hancock & Shepherd's Cut Glass
Manufactory' there was shown 'a superb and curious temple of cut
glass—on each side are hung girandoles, chandeliers, lustres, &c. of
various dimensions, richly ornamented'. At 'Code's Artificial Stone

---

[112] Jane Moody also comments on the inclusion of shop scenes in harlequinades,
Illegitimate Theatre in London, 1770–1840 (Cambridge: Cambridge University Press,
2000), 218–21.

Manufactory', in Lambeth, there was a picture of the exterior of the building, while the interior scene showed 'masons ... at work. Busts, effigies, &c are scattered about. In the front are two pedestals. On each is an Egyptian sphinx.' The printed edition published by Scales added the comment that 'The exhibition of stone work ... was received with much applause.' As well as these London manufacturers who were able to advertise their premises, the scene set in 'Dodd's Paper-Mill, at Cheyney, near Rickmansworth' in rural Hertfordshire showed the mill 'surrounded by picturesque scenery, and ... a wood'. In other words, urban manufacturers are shown taking their place in a national economy of luxury goods which still maintained its undefiled pastoral origins. The depiction of luxury products, goods, and services (other scenes were set in a 'Trunk-Maker's' and outside a dyer's shop) are revealing of London's economic role as a provider of fine manufactured goods.

There is a degree of self-conscious literary reflexivity involved in the portrayal of the different trades. For example, at a scene set in a bookseller's, the owner is 'accosted by a poet of wretched appearance, with a manuscript' while, in another part of the same scene, a printing press used to print a reward poster for the capture of the Clown is shown alongside a 'large play-bill' advertising Thomas John Dibdin's *Five Miles Off, or, The Finger-Post, A Comedy in Three Acts* (1806) and Theodore Edward Hook's *Catch Him Who Can: A Musical Farce, in Two Acts* (1806), two other shows then running at Covent Garden. Of course, in addition, the Clown role (often played by Joseph Grimaldi) could also be drafted into these scenes for simple comic effects: in the glass manufactory scene, 'One of the men shews Columbine the method of blowing glass through a tube; the Clown, ever busy snatches one of them from the furnace, and begins to imitate the man, when two globes of red hot glass rise the end next to his mouth and fasten one on each cheek.'[113]

---

[113] The details are drawn from *Scales's Edition. A Description of Harlequin in his Element, or Fire, Water, Earth, & Air. A New Popular Pantomime Performing with Universal Applause, At Covent-Garden Theatre* (1806) and *Airs, Chorusses, &c. and A List*

These scenes from *Harlequin in his Element* demonstrate the significance to the London economy not only of the manufacturers and providers of luxury services but, perhaps more importantly, their relationship with the Covent Garden audience who are clearly perceived as potential consumers. Unsurprisingly, implicit throughout *Harlequin in his Element* is the buoyancy and optimism of London as a commercial centre, a producer of excess wealth which, in a time of war, could be redistributed via acts of benevolence to the needy old soldier organ grinders of England.

This pantomime's singular importance, however, lies in its creation into visual spectacle of much of Neil McKendrick in *The Birth of a Consumer Society* (1982) has otherwise noted as being relatively neglected by modern historians of the revolution in consumerism in the late eighteenth century: Covent Garden's display materializes commerce's increasing competition for the surplus income of the capital's population.[114] That *Harlequin in his Element* of 1807 is an unusually early theatrical outing for consumer goods is evidenced by a glass-blowing exhibit which featured nearly twenty years later at the Smithfield Fair where one Holden, wearing a glass wig, sold penny tobacco pipes and threepenny teacups in a caravan.[115] In turn, as Lorna Weatherill has noted, the display of luxury goods in places like the Covent Garden area was mirrored by the audience's opportunities for ostentation and social assembly.[116] In particular, the manufactories represented in *Harlequin in his Element*, like the insurance offices in Dibdin's *Melodrame Mad!*, signify a particularly rich and complex network of economic relations articulated between

---

of the Scenery, in the New Comic Pantomime, called Harlequin in his Element, or Fire, Water, Earth, & Air. As Performed At the Theatre Royal, Covent-Garden Theatre (1806).

[114] Neil McKendrick, 'Commercialization and the Economy', in Neil McKendrick, John Brewer, and J. H. Plumb (eds.), *The Birth of a Consumer Society: The Commercialization of Eighteenth-Century England* (London: Europa Publications, 1982), 9–196, esp. 29–31.

[115] Thomas Frost, *The Old Showmen, And the Old London Fairs* (London: Tinsley Brothers, 1874), 299, 301.

[116] Lorna Weatherill, *Consumer Behaviour and Material Culture in Britain, 1660–1760* (London: Routledge, 1988), 79–81 and pl. 6.

commercially opportunist theatre managers and an aspirant audience, the latter apparently content to have their entertainment laced with consumer products ready for purchase.

The scene set in the 'Cut Glass Manufactory' is implicitly supported by a material economy fully represented in the pantomime. Hancock & Shepherd's onstage display of 'girandoles, chandeliers, lustres, &c'. is commodified by the stage directions requiring the Clown to be 'left in darkness' when Sir Feeble Sordid and Columbine leave the stage.[117] This gives the opportunity for Harlequin to goad and torment the Clown by bringing on 'two bronze statues, each representing boys ... animated' by teasing him with the light from the 'three lustres with lighted candles' which they hold before leaving him 'in darkness; not knowing whither to go ... he gropes his way out'. Clown then returns 'and endeavors to relight the lustres'. The whole of this stage business is obviously intended to project the role of Hancock & Shepherd as manufacturers of lighting equipment but this is not the limit of the network of economic relations implied. Earlier in *Harlequin in his Element*, an evening scene '*near London*' included 'an oil shop, over which is written, Thump, Oilman' in which the next episode takes place.[118] The presence of Thump's shop indicates the fuel with which Hancock & Shepherd's girandoles, chandeliers, and lustres were illuminated. In other words, *Harlequin in his Element* represents a complete cycle of goods and services constituting a viable market economy for consumer goods.

Other features of *Harlequin in his Element* similarly demonstrate a well developed material economy by incorporating it into its action. The scene in 'Code's Artificial Stone Manufactory' portrayed a business located in Lambeth, not far from Astley's Amphitheatre, which issued its own illustrated catalogues of 'Statues, Vases, Bustos' for use in gardens and buildings as early as the 1790s.[119] Coades also produced ornamental facings and finishings for public and

[117] *Scales's Edition. A Description of Harlequin in his Element*, 19.
[118] Ibid. 1806 15–16.
[119] *Coade's Gallery, Or, Exhibition in Artificial Stone* (Lambeth, 1799).

private buildings in London and provincial England so *Harlequin in his Element* was simply an extension of their merchandizing, developing their normal factory exhibition gallery into this early example of 'product placement'. As Maxine Berg has recently pointed out in connection with the production of luxury and semi-luxury commodities in eighteenth-century England, the economic significance of goods such as the manufacture of artificial stone resides in their assignment as an imitative process mimicking the more expensive Portland stone and, thereby, situating Coade's stone as a field of consumption occurring within a social process of emulation and aspiration.[120] In other words, the commercial motives underlying the spectacle of Coade's stone are indicative of the behavioural strategies of both an aspirant consumer culture and its suppliers.

The harlequinades may seem surprising barometers of national prosperity yet they mirror significant changes in the capital's economy. Places like Dodd's paper mill were part of a growth in the mechanization of paper-making following Nicholas-Louis Robert's 1798 invention of a machine for making continuous sheets of paper, a process which had quickly been introduced into Britain after further development in 1804 by Brian Donkin for Henry and Sealy Fourdrinier's more commercially successful machine. By the middle of the nineteenth century, apart from Dodd's mill at Cheyney, there were a clutch of Hertfordshire paper mills in the Rickmansworth area. Of course, the real benefit of such mechanization was a reduction in costs to the consumer, a transition of industrial technology directly leading to the development of a mass popular press in the second quarter of the nineteenth century.

However, it was the mirroring of other developments in the national economy which is most surprising. Nearly fifteen years later, Thomas Dibdin's *Melodrame Mad! Or The Siege of Troy* (1819) for the Surrey Theatre, showed in its veritable '*Anachronasmatic, Ethic,*

---

[120] Maxine Berg, 'New Commodities, Luxuries and their Consumers in Eighteenth-Century England', in Maxine Berg and Helen Clifford (eds.), *Consumers and Luxury: Consumer Culture in Europe 1650–1850* (Manchester: Manchester University Press, 1999), 63–85.

Epic Melange', scenes featuring France's new Velocipede bicycles and a classical Laocoon together with the fall of Troy, and all dramatized through the agency of fire insurance companies. In *Melodrame Mad!* the flames of Troy are extinguished by the intercession of the insurers when Jupiter calls up onto the stage an assembly of various contemporary insurance company fire brigades, fire fighters, their engines, and fire-hoses:

> JUPITER. Enough of fire and sword—your wrath restraining,
>> Too much of this may prove too entertaining.
>> Troy I've destroyed to please that angry elf *(pointing to Pallas)*.
>> And I'll restore it now to please myself.
>> Quick Phoenix! Norwich! Sun! and Hand-in-Hand,
>> Bring forth your engines—Patrons understand,
>> That if our follies are not past endurance,
>> We hope you'll kindly pardon our *Assurance*. (p. 41)

The product placement element was made perfectly precise by the whole scene then changing '*to a beautiful allegorical palace of safety and the Arts* [created] *by Insurance*', with the fire engines magically transformed to '*pedestals*' surmounted by the '*Genii of each Fire-office*' (p. 41). The '*Genii*' are the fire offices' wall plaques, metal plates fixed to properties covered by fire insurance. The companies named in *Melodrame Mad!*, Phoenix, Norwich, Sun and 'Hand-in-Hand', are still largely recognizable. The Sun insurance company (later Royal Sun Alliance) was established in 1710 and later acquired the Phoenix Assurance Company (established 1782). The Hand-In-Hand Fire and Life Insurance Society dated back to 1696 (later trading in England as Commercial Union) making it only slightly younger than the Norwich Fire Office, begun in 1680 which is still trading under the Norwich name. What the Surrey Theatre's *Melodrame Mad!* of 1819 faithfully portrays, especially in comparison to Dibdin's *Harlequin in his Element* of 1807, is the local economy's gradual move away from a manufacturing base towards London's gradually acquired status as an international financial centre. The commodification and trading of virtual assets such as insurance risk would become an important aspect of the capital's role in the consolidation of empire.

Harlequin in his Element, like *Melodrame Mad!* in its thoroughly commercial motivations, its confidence in reflecting the audience's social, political, and material aspirations—together with its sure judgement of the economic power of consumers—presents theatricality at the opposite end of the spectrum to that which, contemporaneously, involved Princess Caroline's private theatrical of Hermione's statue in *The Winter's Tale*. Caroline's was a private showing, *Harlequin in his Element* intensely commercial. In one edition of the pantomime, the specific naming of Hancock & Shepherd has been dropped while that of Code's stone-ware and Dodd's paper mills has been retained. Not only does this suggest that economic relationships were capable of being changed but the edition's vigorous frontispiece etching of the famous clown Joseph Grimaldi, in the role of the Watchman in the Tin Shop scene, is a reminder of the ability of such comics to draw large audiences.[121]

Between them lies a spectrum of china-garden theatres, penny 'gaffs', spouting clubs, song-and-supper clubs, and the semi-legal metropolitan private theatres. Frozen out by the power of the Royal theatres, constantly negotiating the powers of local magistrates, evading surveillance and raids, Georgian theatricality represented a series of definitive encounters between the private and public lives of the population. Above all, theatricality was social, convivial, and manifested itself as a series of separate but overlapping public spheres, part-plebeian and part-patrician. The social and demographic cultural range of theatricality and its ability to percolate right across society through private theatres, harlequinades, and paedophilic experiments, all make concentration on Shakespeare and the five-act 'national dramas' seem both redundant and remote to the lives of the contemporary population.

---

[121] *Harlequin in his Element; Or, Fire, Water, Earth, & Air; A Favourite Pantomime. As Performed at The Theatre Royal, Covent Garden* (London: Appleyards, 1807–8 [*sic*]). This edition is in Beinecke Library, Yale University.

8

Political Dramas: *Harlequin Negro* and *Plots and Placemen*

By the late 1810s drama was the primary literary form mediating between the British people and national issues. It may seem surprising that it was not the novel or poetry—or even the period's growing journal and newspaper press—which occupied this role. The playhouses, like their mirror images the churches, reached audiences drawn from all the social classes without the necessity for literacy. The role in communication of audible rather than literate communication should not be underestimated. Any random sampling of the songs performed on the stage in the years around 1800 will show that national attitudes, particularly emphasizing the determined progress of the war but also the general success of the sailors in the navy, were served up night after night, obviously to great applause. Nevertheless, the concurrent growth and circulation of print culture from the 1790s onwards, particularly within the plebeian sphere, is a significant enabling factor in the deployment of drama, a change which amounted to a transition in the material basis of the national infrastructure of public expression. Events such as those detailed in the next chapter, surrounding the 'real-life' case of the murder of Mary Ashford in May 1817, coincide with the beginnings of a new breed of semi-national weekly radical journal. In short, the decade of the 1810s not only marks a notable turning point in the history of the radical press, it also coincides with a surprising degree of sophistication in dramatic writing.

In part, the growth of the press in the late 1810s came in response to the vacuum left by the demise of the *Political Register* upon William Cobbett's decision to go to America at the outset of the March 1817 suspension of Habeas Corpus. *Sherwin's Weekly Political Register*, which aimed to fill the place of Cobbett's *Register*, had begun in March 1817, Sherwin's collaborator being Richard Carlile, who then went on to edit *The Republican* in August, 1817. Similarly, T. J. Wooler's *Black Dwarf* began publication in January 1817, a month before the first issue of William Hone's influential *Reformists' Register and Weekly Companion*, Hone himself also being that year famously put to trial for his *Political Litanies*. More importantly, this moment is also indicative of a turning point when it is possible to think of a sufficiently economically dispersed, yet ideologically collectivized, plebeian public sphere which enabled the formation of a critical mass of radical print politics the Government was unable to repress.[1] By contrast with the 1780s and 1790s, the dominant characteristic of the late 1810s radical press was that its leading pressmen had the ability to transmute themselves from one publication to another, abandoning and re-creating journals supported by the ebb and flow of an ideologically committed structure of family and kinship.

The kinds of conjunction discussed later in this chapter between the radical press and the usages of dramatic form suggest that there had long existed a culturally appropriate relationship between radical pressmen and the stage. Despite the asymmetric relationship between radicalism and the theatre (productions in theatres by radicals were effectively ruled out by the Lord Chamberlain's censor or, beyond his remit, the powers of the local magistrates), an interest in theatrical forms was a constant presence in radical culture. As John Barrell has recently shown, mock playbills were a familiar part of the symbolic repertoire of radical satire.[2] For example, in the early 1790s

---

[1] The key work in this area is Kevin Gilmartin, *Print Politics: The Press and Radical Opposition in Early Nineteenth-Century England* (Cambridge: Cambridge University Press, 1995).

[2] John Barrell, *'Exhibition Extraordinary!!': Radical Broadsides of the Mid-1790s* (Nottingham: Trent Editions, 2001).

Richard 'King Killing' Lee published a single-sheet mock playbill, *By General Desire . . . On the Grand Theatre at St. James's, An Entire new Pantomime, called the Royal Vagabonds* (*c*.1791) and followed it with others in the form of spoof 'Benefit' nights with elaborate generic descriptions ('*Grand Ballet Pantomime*'), the introduction of stock characters in new guises ('*Harlequin Impeacher*') and puffed-up promises ('*a Sublime and Animating Spectacle*').

Nor was this incorporation of theatrical tropes solely a feature of the 1790s. Playbill hoaxes or, at least, the use of playbills with overtly political content continued after the end of the Napoleonic War. At the Gosport theatre in October 1816 officers of the 28th Regiment, 'Under the Patronage of Col. Brown', mounted a benefit performance of James Boaden's *The Voice of Nature* (1803) and published their playbill, which was forwarded to the Home Office. The play's moral narrative was based on the Judgement of Solomon, inoffensive enough perhaps but the regiment's playbill warned of how 'cruelty, aided by power, may for a time oppress . . . the hour must arrive, when justice will assert its right'. It continued that the play's subject presented 'a most striking LESSON TO KINGS' and showed the necessity of 'having laws with an even balance, [to] distribute alike to THE RICH AND POOR'.[3] This troop of disaffected or shortly to be disbanded infantry officers had little to lose; the authorities must have been worried about how the playbill reflected the state of unrest endured in the army during a period of economic distress. While the Lord Chamberlain and the local magistrates could control and suppress civilian theatres, confronting a regiment of soldiers on the verge of de-mob and half-pay must have been a formidable experience to contemplate.

The lack of spaces for public performance ought not to disguise the existence of an already well-developed relationship between dramatic form and radical politics. For example, in the 1790s James Ridgway's relentless publishing of Tom Paine's works, and thereafter on behalf of other causes such as the 1793 Scottish seditionists and the 1794

---

[3] PRO HO 40/9. 506; 25 October 1816.

LCS treason trials, was interspersed with his occasional publication of drama. At the end of the decade, his efforts came to be financially rewarded by the success of Sheridan's adaptation of Kotzebue's *Pizarro* which ran through at least twenty-seven impressions in Ridgway's 1799 edition. Typifying the way he worked, that same year Ridgway also found time to publish ('for the Benefit of the Men in Confinement') *An Account of the Rise and Progress of the Dispute Between the Masters and Journeymen Printers* (1799) detailing the trial proceedings of five Farringdon printers sentenced to two years in Newgate for union combination and conspiracy. Such is the complexity of interaction between printer and public, text and society, war and events that, as Gillian Russell has shown, a few years later speeches from *Pizarro* were identified as marking loyalist positions.[4] This kind of complex political 'afterlife' of Ridgway's politics and the plays he published should be borne in mind when considering the printing context of the Ashford case in the next chapter. In other words, in the Georgian period, there was an intimate but economically quite complex relationship between radical politics and popular drama.

One of the most remarkable unperformed dramas of the post-Waterloo years was the pseudonymous 'Zachary Zealoushead's' closet drama, *Plots And Placemen, Or Green Bag Glory, An Historical Melo Drama, In Two Acts ... As performed at the Boroughmongers' Private Theatre* (1817), a play text published as a pamphlet with little suggestion that it was ever intended to be acted. Its publication is definitive evidence of how extremist branches of contemporary ultra-radicalism found expressive possibilities in dramatic form. This chapter will show how the writing of drama—and sometimes its performance—was deeply connected with extreme radical politics. In particular, it will be shown that the main two dramas forming the focus of this chapter, Furibond, or, *Harlequin Negro* (1807) and

---

[4] Gillian Russell, *The Theatres of War: Performance, Politics, and Society 1793–1815* (Oxford: Clarendon Press, 1995), 54–9. Russell gives 29,000 copies as the first edition of *Pizarro* (p. 54).

Plots And Placemen, are intimately connected to each other. Although written from polarized perspectives, they were the products of writers deeply implicated in the most hardened sections of the battle for contemporary political freedom. *Harlequin Negro,* performed at Drury Lane, is the work of James Powell, a Government mole who successfully infiltrated and betrayed the London Corresponding Society in 1798. The anonymous closet drama *Plots And Placemen* was written in support of a group of Spenceans who, by the time of its writing in early 1817, were either imprisoned or under persistent Government surveillance. This chapter contends that these two works, along with the other plays discussed here, present definitive evidence for how drama was the premier genre of choice for political activists during the period's turbulent politics.

Plots And Placemen is closely connected with a highly identifiable group of extreme, physical force, ultra-radicals. While the true identity of the pseudonymous author 'Zachary Zealoushead' cannot be positively identified, the choice of surname, 'Zealoushead', gives some idea of the (slightly self-conscious) nature of the politics involved. One possibility for the author's identity is the shoemaker poet Robert Charles Fair, who (as referred to in the Introduction) had submitted an unsuccessful opening address poem for the Drury Lane reopening competition of 1812. However, it is possible to be much more positive about many other factors about this drama. The printer of *Plots And Placemen* was Arthur Seale of Tottenham Court Road, who had intimate connections with the extreme radicalism of the early 1800s when he was under frequent surveillance and sometimes dangerously implicated with both Thomas Evans and Colonel Edward Marcus Despard, who was executed for treason in 1803.[5] More than any other material feature of the play, Seale's role in its print production marks its intimate connection with the most extreme politics of the first two decades of the nineteenth century.

Plots And Placemen is a satire on the suppression of radicalism featuring many familiar Romantic period villain figures such as

---

[5] PRO T[reasury] S[olicitor] 11/939/3362; HO 48/12. 171, 23 October 1803.

Lord Castlereagh ('Callouswretch'), Lord Sidmouth ('Proudmouth') and Lord Ellenborough ('Lord Justice Lawall') aided and abetted by the Prince Regent ('His Imperial Highness, the Chinese Viceroy of the Green Isles'). The 'Incidents of the Piece' can be specifically dated to events occurring between December 1816 (the date of the Spa Fields rising) and April 1817. The characters include several of those subsequently put on trial for high treason as the Spa Fields ringleaders, including the apothecary Dr Watson ('Dr. Leadem'), the lame shoemaker Thomas Preston ('Tom Cordovan'), and John Hooper ('Jack Hatchway'). Also featured in the drama is the Government spy and *agent provocateur* John Castle ('Jack Tower') and (as the Dramatis Personae puts it) assorted 'Placemen, Pensioners, Sinecurists, Boroughmongers, Contractors ... Officers, Conspirators, &c.' Despite the play's specificity about dates, *Plots And Placemen* actually encompasses events up to June 1817 because it also includes references to John Oliver, the notorious 'Oliver the Spy' of the Derbyshire Pentridge Rising (p. 15). It is this unparalleled intricacy of reference to topical revolutionary politics which makes *Plots And Placemen* one of the most significant pieces of writing to emerge from a newly developing plebeian public sphere enabled by an autonomous print culture.

Significantly, not listed at all in the Dramatis Personae are two characters who actually appear in the penultimate sixth scene of the drama, 'Vanse, Sen.' and 'Young Vanse'. These names are simple anagrams for two prominent Spencean activists, Thomas Evans senior and his son Thomas John Evans, who had both been implicated in the Spa Fields rising of 2 December 1816. The rising itself, which only succeeded in wreaking one night's havoc in the Minories and Tower Hamlets area of London, was the outcome of a sustained and thoroughly ideological Spencean programme of resistance. Amongst the post-war Spenceans, Evans senior was the movement's most accomplished advocate, a role he continued to play until he disappears from public records (and official surveillance), having managed to avoid implication in the Cato

Street conspiracy of February 1820. The afternoon and evening of the rising followed a series of inflammatory speeches made by James Watson and his namesake son at a well-attended public meeting on the Spa Fields. After the rioting the authorities quickly arrested and charged Hooper, Watson, and Preston with high treason. A fourth person, the later Cato Street conspirator Arthur Thistlewood, was also charged but his name is unaccountably absent from *Plots And Placemen*. Although interrogated, the authorities were unable to charge Thomas Evans Snr. but both he and his son were arrested and imprisoned early in 1817 as soon as the Suspension of Habeas Corpus Bill had been passed by Parliament.

The role of the two Evanses in plebeian print culture is well established but it is their appearance in the elaborate satiric play text of *Plots And Placemen* which confirms the proximity between plebeian radical culture and dramatic form. Exactly how close this relationship actually was borders on the bizarre. Thomas Evans senior had already been imprisoned once before, under the 1798 suspension of Habeas Corpus, when he and several other members of the newly formed Society of United English (essentially an ultra-radical group splintering from the latest incarnation of the London Corresponding Society—of which Evans was then Secretary) were arrested in 'the George Publick House', Clerkenwell.[6] The United English had close associations with the United Irish, a factor underlined by the role in both these groups of Colonel Despard, a powerful politically disaffected figure with a background in Caribbean colonialism who was eventually tried for high treason after an abortive London coup attempt and executed in 1803.[7] The mole who triggered Thomas Evans's arrest in April 1798 was James Powell, the Government spy

---

[6] On the context, see Iain McCalman, *Radical Underworld: Prophets, Revolutionaries and Pornographers in London, 1795–1840* (Cambridge: Cambridge University Press, 1988), 11–16. The list of those arrested at the George is at PRO PC 1/41/139.

[7] See Peter Linebaugh and Marcus Rediker, *The Many-Headed Hydra: Sailors, Slaves, Commoners, and the Hidden History of the Revolutionary Atlantic* (London: Verso, 2000), 248–86.

whose *Furibond, or Harlequin Negro* (1807) for Drury Lane will be the subject of the second half of this chapter.

Tracing James Powell's career as spy, translator, and dramatist involves taking a journey into some of the most complex day-to-day manoeuvrings concerning the Government's surveillance and suppression of radical activism. Powell's namesake father was a friend of London Corresponding Society activist, Francis Place. It was through these family links that Powell junior probably managed to infiltrate himself into the heart of what was, by then, the second phase of the London Corresponding Society following the 1794 treason trials when it had regrouped itself around a core of Spencean opportunists led by Thomas Evans senior. By this time, a more physical force ideology was being promoted, especially in connection with its United Irish links. Place later described Powell junior's involvement with Evans's group as that of being 'their coadjutator'. Although James Powell senior had been dead 'some years' by 1798 (according to Place), it is possible that either Place's connections, or those of Powell junior's, with the pre-1794 executive of the London Corresponding Society were instrumental in connecting Powell's son with Henry Delahay Symonds, the London Corresponding Society pressman who published his two early closet dramas, *The Narcotic and Private Theatricals*.[8]

Powell's role amongst some of high-profile contemporary incidents connected to our understanding of this period may be quite significant. According to the modern historian Marc Baer, Powell junior was also a Government informer during the 1809 OP riots.[9] He may also have figured as one of a small network of spies controlled from London who may have met up with the possible informer poet William Wordsworth during his residence in Germany in 1799.[10] Powell certainly knew James Walsh, the infamous 'Spy Nozy' who

[8] BL Add. MS 27808, fo. 93.
[9] The assertion about Powell's OP role is in Marc Baer, *Theatre and Disorder in Late Georgian London* (Oxford: Clarendon Press, 1992), 94. I have not been able to confirm this fact from the evidence Baer provides.
[10] Kenneth Johnston, *The Hidden Wordsworth* (London: Norton, 1998), 847–51.

had dogged Wordsworth and Coleridge in the Quantocks in 1797.[11] Long after Powell took advised exile in Germany, bankrolled by the Government, his controller, Sir Richard Ford of Bow Street magistrates, was still turning up 'some old Stuff of J[ames].P[owells].'s' amongst his papers on the surveillance surrounding the arrest of Colonel Edward Marcus Despard.[12] Francis Place was closely involved in the events surrounding Evans's arrest in 1798 when he had attempted to forestall the Government swoop he knew would be coming. Remarkably, Place remained totally ignorant that the source of the Government's security information was Powell.

When Evans, Benjamin Binns, and several others were seized in April 1798 in Clerkenwell, Place recalled in his *Autobiography* that 'on Evans was found a copy of a test and another in a different form was found under the table, where it had been thrown by Powell'. The 'test' was an oath of allegiance, an illegal and potentially highly incriminating document (similar evidence was enough to hang Despard five years later) whose apparent disposal at the moment of arrest was cleverly worked into Powell's mini-drama of subterfuge. The United English had already elaborated itself into a printed set of *Declarations, Resolutions, and Constitution of the Societies of United Englishmen* and structured itself around a 'Baronial' organization which held beliefs such as that the Society would hold no distinction of religion (an important point of commonality in view of the United Englishmen's' links with the United Irish).[13] Place's narrative makes it clear that he was ignorant of Powell's true role but, a few days later, he took pity on him when he 'came to me almost in a state of despair', letting him stay in his own home (as a sure place where the authorities would not look) and finally making Powell (Place was a tailor) 'a suit of half military cloaths' as well as providing safe passage to Harwich and escape to 'Hamburgh'.[14] Of course,

---

[11] Nicholas Roe, *Wordsworth and Coleridge: The Radical Years* (Oxford: Clarendon Press, 1988), 249–51, 257–62.

[12] PRO PC 1/3117 [part A], 28 Nov [1803] [Ford to Moody].

[13] PRO PC 1/41/139.

[14] BL Add. MS 27808, fo. 92–4.

Powell's despairing deportment in front of Place after he had (as it seemed) only narrowly escaped arrest with Evans was all a ruse. Place obviously had a low opinion of Powell: he knew that his wife ('a woman of the town') had already left him and that he was then living off his widowed mother, but what he cannot have known was how incomplete was his knowledge of the man he had helped escape.

Powell had actually taken care to leave a false trail behind him by going to Yarmouth rather than to Harwich, as he had told Place. The difference is a significant one because stationed at Yarmouth on Government secret service was special agent, 'Spy Nozy', James Walsh. Walsh had been sent to Yarmouth to assist the local Customs Office in providing surveillance of the Yarmouth–Hamburg *Duke of York* ferry which was believed to be assisting the passage of United Irishmen by standing off the English coast and disembarking its passengers into local fishing boats so that they could land unobserved.[15] Hamburg's importance was that it was a free port providing a meeting place connecting the United Irish with their French collaborators, an episode in Anglo-Irish history perhaps typified by the role of Wolfe Tone in mounting the abortive French-backed invasion of Ireland in 1797. What emerges from Powell's correspondence to Sir Richard Ford, now filed amongst Privy Council papers, is that—rightly or wrongly—Powell thought himself to be a more significant Government spy than James Walsh: 'Being personally known to Mr Walsh here by my real name I was under the unpleasant necessity of placing some confidence in him but I am convinced he is a good fellow & no harm will arise from it.' Powell's wariness of Walsh suggests that it was the former, rather than the latter, who was the leading Government agent in Yarmouth. Again, the role played in Yarmouth surveillance by the Customs Office, which was the background of his father, must have eased Powell's passage in the town and provided him with authority and friends in the locality. His entire complicity in Government business seems to be verified by his giving 'Presents to

---

[15] Roger Wells, *Insurrection: The British Experience, 1795–1803* (Gloucester: Alan Sutton, 1983), 35–6.

the Steward of the Ship[,] Servants at Inn[,] Necessary things which Mr Walsh told me I must take on Board besides paying the Captn.' Such gifts might be customary practice but, quite possibly, they were gifts given to maintain local surveillance in Yarmouth and the ferries. Furthermore, it is clear that Powell had already been detailed to follow up surveillance of United Irish activity when he arrived in 'Hamburg'. He mentions Walsh having put him onto 'George Orr a united Irishman with whom I was very intimate with in London [who] sailed from here to Hamburg a fortnight ago'. Powell hoped to use this contact 'to get among the Irishmen immediately'. In other words, Powell's activities were part of a continuing role of infiltration, passing from one group of activists to another, from the LCS to the United Irish. Not least, something of his standing in the world of espionage can be estimated by his astonishing submission of £27 7s. 2d. as his accommodation and travel expenses for getting from London to Yarmouth.[16]

With Powell playing an important role in infiltrating the LCS and United Irish, his subsequent writing career (no doubt supplementing his espionage pay) gives a unique insight into the relationship between writing for the stage and some of the most extreme revolutionary politics. Although Powell initially anticipated being only 'two or three months' in Hamburg, he probably stayed there longer, certainly long enough to become highly literate in German.[17] Assuming Powell returned to Britain in the early 1800s (perhaps after Despard's execution in 1803), he knew the German language well enough to publish London translations of two novels by Augustus Lafontaine (*Rudolph of Werdenberg* (1805) and *The Village of Friedewalkde: or, The Enthusiast* (1806)), as well as a translation of Veit Weber's *Wolf; or, The Tribunal of Blood* (1806), the latter being part of Powell's own project to establish a complete translated edition of Weber's novels. It was in the context of re-establishing a literary career after the inconclusive closet dramas *The Narcotic and Private Theatricals* (*c.*1793) and these translations from the German, that

---

[16] PRO PC 1/41/138, 28 April 1798.   [17] Ibid.

Powell embarked on writing a play whose history is almost as complicated as his career as a secret agent.

Powell's Preface to his drama *The Venetian Outlaw, His Country's Friend* (1805), a three-act adaptation of Pixérécourt's *The Man with Three Faces*, was mainly concerned with manuscript acceptance problems with Drury Lane (as noted in Chapter 1) but it also provides some clues as to Powell's whereabouts after Hamburg. He says that he first saw Pixérécourt's play 'at Audinot's Theatre at Paris, during the late peace', that is, during the 1802 Peace of Amiens, and that he delivered his completed manuscript adaptation to Drury Lane at the 'latter end of November' 1803 (p. iii). Despard had been hanged in February 1803 and, although Powell's own part in his downfall must have been minimal, he may not have felt it was safe enough to return to England until then (although, in any case, Place continued ignorant of his role in the 1798 arrests).[18]

Under difficult circumstances, Powell manipulated his social contacts as best he could. Powell's original recruitment into espionage probably came about because he and his father had been employed in the London Customs House, as made clear in Powell junior's styling himself 'of the Custom House' in the imprint to *The Narcotic and Private Theatricals* (1793).[19] Francis Place knew Powell's deceased 'father had been a clerk in the Custom House a man of property', and it may have been these connections which gave Powell junior the opportunity to take up spying at a time when the Customs offices were at the forefront of the Government's organization of the surveillance of British harbours and ports.[20] Place was actually quite naïve on this issue and failed to register the danger. Like press gangs, bumbailiffs, hangmen, and informers, 'excise and custom-house officers',

[18] J. Ann Hone gives the date of Powell's return as 1802 but agrees that he returned after the Peace of Amiens. She also notes that he made several trips back to London but does not identify him as a playwright, *For the Cause of Truth: Radicalism in London, 1796–1821* (Oxford: Clarendon Press, 1982), 63.

[19] James Powell, Snr., had been appointed as Customs Collector at Exeter but he may no longer have been there when Place knew him, BL Add. MS 3289, fo. 134, 17 September 1755.

[20] BL Add. MS 27808, fo. 93; Wells, *Insurrection*, 35–6.

were firmly on the list of the 'Distresses of the Nation' identified by contemporary radicals.[21] It is also looks likely that after the 1809 OP riots (during which Powell may have acted as Government informer), he sought refuge from London and was employed in the Customs House, Cowes, whence he wrote, mysteriously, that he was on 'Special Service'.[22] In the context of Powell's spying activities, *The Venetian Outlaw* is a remarkable piece. Although it had effectively been stolen (or, more likely, the author's identity simply lost) by the Theatre Royal Drury Lane, it was, nevertheless, 'performed almost verbatim from the first manuscript' Powell had originally delivered.[23]

The basic storyline of *The Venetian Outlaw* is that Vivaldi has been outlawed from Venice but returns to covertly meet his servant, Spadillo, and to seek his assistance in infiltrating a conspiracy by Count Orsano to assassinate the Doge. Vivaldi successfully halts the conspiracy, receives the Doge's profound thanks and, quite naturally, obtains his complete reinstatement into Venetian society (as well as getting to marry the girl he loves). It is not difficult to imagine that Pixérécourt's original version of *The Venetian Outlaw* profoundly affected Powell when he saw it in Paris in 1802 because its plot must have so nearly mirrored what he hoped might have been his own role in saving Britain from internal conspiracy. The play contains relatively few statements of political ideology although, at one point, Spadillo the servant says that 'Unanimity between the governor, and the governed, is the true basis of power; where such is the foundation, a pillar will be raised to Justice, Peace, and Happiness, which no foreign foe can ever batter down' (p. 10). It is impossible to know how far Powell subscribed to such ideals of political perfection but, when Spadillo and Vivaldi are first reunited in the Doge's garden, the

---

[21] *Address to the People, On the Distresses of the Nation, Stating the Causes, Effects, and proposed Remedy; also an Examination of the Letters of the Rt. Hon. G. Rose, and the Rt. Hon. G. Canning, in Answer to the 19,000 Memorialists of Bolton* (1816), PRO HO 40/9. 302.

[22] BL Add. MS 2776, fo. 94, 20 March 1810, James Powell to George Rose.

[23] James Powell, *The Venetian Outlaw, His Country's Friend. A Drama, in Three Acts, Now Performing at the Theatre Royal, Drury-Lane, with unbounded Applause ... Altered from the French of A. Pixiricourt* (1805), pp. iii–iv.

situation must have echoed many experiences in Powell's own life as a secret agent: '*SPAD. Speak softly, my dear unfortunate master. Have you forgot that we are surrounded every where by spies and informers? That the walls themselves are evidence to indiscreet actions? [He looks cautiously round to see if any person is near them, then runs hastily to Vivaldi.]*' (p. 19). Such anxieties and special precautions must have been regular features of Powell's operational life.

The plot of *The Venetian Outlaw* may also have evoked deeply embedded memories from Powell's past. One scene he surely would have recognized from his own experience is where 'Orsano gets them to swear an oath' in which 'All [the conspirators] form a half circle, their left arms entwin'd together ... with their right hand holding their naked swords plac'd on that of Orsano' (pp. 38–9). Powell had been present in that obscure Clerkenwell tavern seven years earlier when Thomas Evans had been arrested in possession of a written oath or 'test' which Powell himself may have helped contrive in order to incriminate the United English. More conclusively, the whole scheme of *The Venetian Outlaw* demands that Vivaldi infiltrates Count Orsano's conspiracy against the Venetian head of state, a situation exactly paralleling Powell's infiltration of Evans's United English. A few years later, Despard's coup attempt would have solidified the image in Powell's mind. Whereas Powell had feigned histrionic despair in front of Francis Place to maintain his cover story, his fictional substitute, Vivaldi, converts *The Venetian Outlaw*'s ending into the play's moment of triumphant melodramatic denouement. Having assembled Orsano and the other conspirators in the presence of the Doge, Vivaldi appears poised to carry through the assassination when he suddenly reverses the ambush and calls for the guards to arrest them.

VIVALDI. You see Doge, both you and the state are in my power. [*To Conspirators*] Well, worthy friends, I expected no less from your courage, and you shall now receive the reward due to your valour. [*turns coolly round*] Solders seize!—[*He appears to direct his Orders against the Doge, when suddenly he changes his Attitude, and adds rapidly pointing to the Conspirators.*] These Wretches. (p. 74)

At this point he unfastens his disguise, the conspirators are arrested, Vivaldi is revealed as the subtitle's 'Country's Friend', and his
outlawry is over. Amongst the most attractive features of melodramas like *The Venetian Outlaw*, with its breathless finale, is that
such sudden reversals fall comfortably within the generic expectations of the form. In addition, the play's actual performance
('almost verbatim' with Powell's translation), must have given him
a profound sense of self-validation as Drury Lane echoed to the
applause of Vivaldi's vindicated heroism and the character's loyalty
in adversity.

The Venetian Outlaw, His Country's Friend projected onto the
stage of Drury Lane an international spy's frustrated desires for
recognition and political validation. He was even able to use his
real name on its imprint because he was so deeply placed as
a mole that he was never challenged. His feigned escape from
arrest gave him a cast-iron alibi with an easily verifiable source
in the veteran London Corresponding Society member, Francis
Place. The complex intersection of real-life espionage and fictional drama in *The Venetian Outlaw* provides an extraordinary
example of the coincidence of espionage, playwriting, and acting. Quite incidentally, it also records one individual's chance
encounter with Drury Lane's incompetent, if not downright deceit-
ful, management.

Whatever problems Powell had in 1805 with Drury Lane, by the
end of 1808 he must have found some kind of *rapprochement*. This
may have been helped by his spy master Sir Richard Ford's links to
Drury Lane. Ford was not only the chief Bow Street magistrate from
1800 until his death in 1806 but he also played a highly pivotal
role in communicating and controlling the foreign and domestic
espionage system, and Powell's letters from Yarmouth were probably
addressed to him. In the late eighteenth century Ford's father, James,
had held a major capital interest in the Drury Lane theatre and,
whether Ford junior inherited these financial interests or not, Sir
Richard was socially well connected to the theatrical world both as
the friend of R. B. Sheridan and as the lover of the actress Dorothy

Jordan.[24] Ford must have been fully involved in Powell's movements in 1798 because the panicking Francis Place, worried about Despard and Evans's hijacking of the London Corresponding Society in the name of the United English, contemplated acting with other London Corresponding Society moderates to 'to stop their proceeding by communicating to Mr. Ford the Magistrate at the Treasury who and what they were and what they intended'.[25] In other words, it looks as if Place knew of Ford's role in domestic surveillance and wished to defuse the extremism of the London Corresponding Society before it reached a critical, potentially treacherous, point. As it turned out, Powell was already keeping Ford regularly informed. It is possible that the sociabilities of these close links between Ford, Place, and the apparently innocuous Powell, survived Ford's sudden death in 1806 because, notwithstanding Drury Lane's alleged plagiarism of *The Venetian Outlaw*, by Christmas 1807 Powell's pantomime *Furibond; Or, Harlequin Negro* (1807) was put into production.

Furibond; Or, Harlequin Negro was first performed at Drury Lane on 28 December, 1807.[26] Few notices of it exist, save for one review which recorded not only that the production had been lavished with 'liberal expenditure' but that it had experienced unusual problems because of its scenery 'frequently failed in the working', leading to cries of '"Off, off"'. Apparently *Harlequin Negro* was, as the reviewer put it, 'in every way a *bastard*'.[27] Nevertheless,

---

[24] Clare Jerrold, *The Story of Dorothy Jordan* (London: Eveleigh Nash, 1914), 106, 160; Baer *Theatre and Disorder*, 94. On the way Ford has been underestimated by historians, see J. Ann Hone, *For the Cause of Truth: Radicalism in London, 1796–1821* (Oxford: Clarendon Press, 1982), 69–70.

[25] BL Add. MS 27808, fo. 92.

[26] See Larpent Plays, 1533, 19 December, 1807; only the covering title, 'The New Comic Pantomime', is given, Huntington Library, Calif. The printed highlights were sold at the performances, James Powell, *Furibond; Or, Harlequin Negro. The Songs Choruses &C. With A Descriptions Of The Pantomime. As Performed At The Theatre Royal, Drury-Lane. Monday, December, 28th* (1807). A MS inscription in the BL copy attributes this pantomime to Powell and to 'Male'. Powell's authorship is consistent with his other dramatic writings. A payment of £ 25 to 'Powell for Pant' is in BL Add. MS 29710, fo. 377r. A payment 'By Agr for Pant' of £ 25 was also made to 'Moyle', fo. 388v.

[27] *The Monthly Mirror*, 3 (1808), 45–6; Sybil Rosenfeld, *Georgian Scene Painters and Scene Painting* (Cambridge: Cambridge University Press, 1981), 171.

it must have been moderately successful, running as it did for twenty performances.[28] On its first night it was paired with the traditional Christmas season entertainment, *George Barnwell*; at other times it ran in tandem with pieces such as Matthew Lewis's *The Castle Spectre*.[29]

By any standards *Harlequin Negro* is an extraordinary work (not least as a baffling choice for a Christmas season entertainment). The manuscript sent to Larpent (who approved it without excision) is actually a much abbreviated version of the printed edition but even the latter collapses into paraphrase much of the most interesting-sounding dialogue. In the printed version, the character Furibond is quite quickly dismissed from the action of the pantomime, the first half of which takes place in a 'West Indian' 'Coffee Plantation', perhaps Powell's imagining of one of the chief Caribbean coffee-growing areas of Dominica, Jamaica, or St Lucia where up to 20 per cent of the islands' slave population were employed in coffee production.[30] The timing of *Harlequin Negro* was perfectly attuned to 1807's abolition of the slave trade.[31] Drury Lane's decision to run it sometimes paired with *The Castle Spectre* which featured Lewis's sympathetically portrayed characters, Hassan and Saib, may be the theatre's attempts to reflect the topicality of abolition.

The eponymous Furibond is '(*an Enchanter*) who resides on the Island' and is also the suitor of Columbine, the traditional leading female role in pantomime. However, Columbine is 'disgusted at his addresses'. Her father (the harlequinade's Pantaloon figure) is Sir Peevish Antique, 'a celebrated *Antiquary*' who is visiting 'his possessions in the West Indies' which include the coffee plantation. Having 'arranged his affairs, [Sir Peevish] prepares to return with

[28] Or for twenty-eight performances, *The History of the Theatres of London . . . Being a Continuation of Victor's and Oulton's Histories, From the Year 1795 to 1817 Inclusive* (1818), i. 151–2.

[29] BL Playbills, 18 January 1808.

[30] James Walvin, *Fruits of Empire: Exotic Produce and British Taste, 1660–1800* (Basingstoke: Macmillan, 1997), 45.

[31] James Walvin, *Slaves and Slavery: The British Colonial Experience* (Manchester: Manchester University Press, 1992), 88–100.

his Family to his residence in London'. The second half of the
pantomime is located in London after the family's return and is
also the part principally concerned with transformations typical of
harlequinade. In Examiner Larpent's manuscript version, the pantomime envisaged showing Furibond's demiurge, Maligno, promising
his master that 'my spells shall gain thy just reward' when they plot
to follow Sir Peevish back to England. This subplot may well have
happened in the Drury Lane production but the printed version is
so much abbreviated into highlighting the more marketable 'Songs
Choruses &c.' that it may simply have been narrative omitted from
the published abridgement. The coffee plantation setting and Sir
Peevish's ownership of West Indian property is a natural location for
the portrayal of slavery. As James Walvin notes, 'By the late eighteenth century no one doubted, when they discussed plantations,
that they meant *slave* plantations'.[32] In *Harlequin Negro*, the departure of Sir Peevish for London provides the cue for the expression
of contemporary liberal or abolitionist attitudes exemplified in the
treatment by Slave Driver of a character simply called Slave. The
Slave role is particularly important because this character is later
transformed into Harlequin and magically transported to England
by the island's benevolent demiurge, Benigna.

A rare literary feature of *Harlequin Negro* is its presentation of
potential miscegenation concerning a white woman's love for a negro
male. The pantomime's leading female character, Columbine, specifically rejects Furibond's courtship, 'disgusted at his addresses', on
account of her having previously 'conceived an inclination for a Slave,
who is a servant on SIR PEEVISH's Estate' (p. 10). In other words,
Columbine, the white daughter of the colonialist Sir Peevish Antique,
selects a black slave as a potential lover, a bond finally sealed with
all the customary fidelities subsumed in *Harlequin Negro*'s pairing
of Harlequin (after his transformation from Slave) and Columbine
in the harlequinade tradition. *Harlequin Negro* is quite specific that
Columbine has 'conceived an inclination for a Slave', a factor which,

[32] Walvin, *Fruits of Empire*, 141.

not unexpectedly, appears to lead to the victimization of Slave by the Slave Driver. When the Antiques have departed for England, Slave enters carrying a basket 'which he throws down—and expressing sorrow at the departure of Columbine throws himself down in despair' for which action he is then punished by Slave Driver, who 'rebukes him for idleness—and strikes him'. Slave is then dragged off, bound to a tree, and punished further by Slave Driver, at which point a serpent appears ('Fair Benigna' in disguise) to save him. The Slave Driver and others threaten the serpent with their working tools so Slave hides the serpent in a basket, at which point she reveals herself to him as Benigna. Oddly in view of her intervention to save Slave from Slave Driver, Benigna then expresses 'her gratitude for the protection he has given her, [and] grants him the election of different characters'. Slave chooses to become Harlequin and, transmuted by the power of the harlequinade conventions, gains the ability to pursue his love for Columbine by next being magically transported to England. However, in a simple setting out of national abolitionist idealism, before he departs for England, Harlequin 'supplicates for the emancipation of his brother slaves, who appear in chains dragged on by the Driver'.

Drury Lane's staging of emancipation by the transformation of Slave into Harlequin is an arresting trope. Whatever Powell's moral shortcomings, this *coup de théâtre* is a vivid moment of empowerment changing the oppressed black Caribbean slave into a gorgeously costumed comic hero. The liberty realized in the Slave's transformation into Harlequin is both naturalized and domesticated through its pantomime setting. Predictably, this initiates the broader signification of *Harlequin Negro*, that it will be a celebration of British abolitionist principles as well a private, interracial love story employing the stereotypes of harlequinade. To reinforce the British role, at this point, 'Britannia appears in the clouds—with the Genius of Britain &c. attending—at the sight of which the chains fall off the slaves—who kneel in thankfulness and depart in great glee'. An exposition of the advantages of British liberalism are then breathlessly pursued in the harlequinade: in the next scene, Harlequin finds himself in 'Greenwich Park, With A View Of London' upon which 'the Fairy informs Harlequin she has now brought him to the Land of Liberty' (pp. 10–11). The emancipation of all the slaves on Sir Peevish's West Indian coffee plantation, together with the transformative appearance of Britannia with the Genius of Britain, all conform with the projection onstage of a reforming imperial power energized by ideals of justice and sensibility.

What is perhaps surprising is the level of political sophistication achieved through the apparently unpromising vehicle of pantomime. In practice, an evening at a Royal theatre might often contain both pantomime and spoken drama. Jeffrey N. Cox and Michael Gamer's *Broadview Anthology of Romantic Drama* (2003) reminds us that, on a single night at Covent Garden in 1789, it was possible to see 'grand serious-pantomimic-ballet' of *The Death of Captain Cook* (1789), George Colman's *Inkle and Yarico* (1787), and Thomas Shadwell's *Don Juan; or, The Libertine Destroyed* (1736).[33] This mixing of pantomime and speech drama was the privilege of the Royal theatres but even there, not only was it permissible to bill onto a single evening's entertainment both a serious mainpiece and a pantomime afterpiece, their monopoly over speech still allowed them to irritate the censor. In an 1825 letter to Members of Parliament (printed but only privately circulated), the new Examiner of Plays, George Colman, revealed that it was not unknown for the Lord Chamberlain's office to put pressure on the Royal theatres when they billed certain dramas considered to be politically sensitive: 'Who will dispute that the [Thomas Otway] Tragedy of Venice Preserved [1681] was not prudentially suspended, in times of the greatest ferment?—who will say that the representation of King Lear should not have been discontinued, during the lamented affliction of our late revered Sovereign'.[34] The fielding of pantomimes

[33] Jeffrey N. Cox and Michael Gamer (eds.), *The Broadview Anthology of Romantic Drama* (Peterborough, Ont.: Broadview Press, 2003), p. xv.
[34] George Colman, *Observations On The Notice Of A Motion To Rescind Certain Powers Of His Majesty's Lord Chamberlain* (1829), 3. I have not yet been able to identify which particular playhouses, at which dates, were subjected to these pressures. King George III's first episode of mental illness had occurred in 1765 with a longer period of affliction beginning in 1788. Privy Council records include a draft proclamation

in tandem with, or in place of, such coerced plays provided both contingent and non-contingent unregulated opportunities to comment visually on current affairs. At certain times, pantomime would have been an attractive option to both the patent and the non-patent playhouses. Writing about these practices, David Mayer in *Harlequin in his Element: The English Pantomime, 1806–1836* (1969) has noted that pantomimes such as the Adelphi's *Who Kill'd the Dog; or Harlequin's Triumph* (1822) commented directly on the poaching wars while Thomas John Dibdin's *Harlequin and Mother Goose* (1806), Charles Dibdin's *Fashion's Fools* (1796), and Henry Woodward's *Harlequin's Jubilee* (1770), revived for Sadler's Wells in 1814, all satirized the army.[35] Indeed, pantomimes were quite often openly billed as including political commentary. A few months before the French Revolution and with the anniversary of 1688 still topical, the York Theatre Royal pantomime, *The Vision of an Hour*, was billed as concluding with 'the Rising of Harlequin's Temple, With an Apotheosis of King William III of glorious and immortal Memory'.[36] Earlier, productions such as Philip de Loutherbourg and John O'Keefe's *Omai: Or, A Trip Round the World* (1785) for Covent Garden, had brought together a team which pushed the boundaries of pantomime and provided a model for its development in the Regency period. *Omai*'s use of painted scenery dropped onto the stage, together with a range of other dramatic devices (including the technically difficult rapid lighting changes first encountered in *A Christmas Tale*) were emulated in Powell's Drury Lane pantomime thirty years later. Although the conventions of Columbine's disagreement with the Pantaloon figure (Sir Peevish), and the travails of the lovers impeded by the spiteful Clown figure (Slave Driver) were observed, *Harlequin Negro* similarly made use of innovative dramatic technologies.

of thanksgiving for the King's recovery written at the end of 1789 and showing that Government offices were concerned with the issue, PRO PC 1/18/19.

[35] David Mayer, *Harlequin in his Element: The English Pantomime, 1806–1836* (Cambridge, Mass.: Harvard University Press, 1969), 204, 276.

[36] Playbills, Theatre Royal York, 21 May 1789.

One of the more curious scenic details of *Harlequin Negro* was its use of several types of 'Transparency'. Transparencies, in their eighteenth-century meaning, were back-lit paintings, in this case in the form of painted stage scenery which could be dropped into position, perhaps bringing about the production problems referred to in the *Monthly Mirror* review.[37] James Powell seems to have envisaged quite advanced use of these devices, particularly as a means of conveying political allusions.[38] When the Slave saves Benigna, she asks him if he would like any favours granted. In reply, '*The Slave complains of his black complexion*' to which she responds by presenting before him a transparency of Narcissus. The negro promptly rejects this image of this possible version of his self because she has placed on its attainment the precondition of excluding him from 'powers of the mind':

BENIGNA. What, art thou weary of thy sable hue?
  I can on one condition that remove,
  Such are the terms;—thus fair Narcissus view,
  An object only to himself of love.
  She waves her wand.
[*A TRANSPARENCY APPEARS,*
Representing Narcissus admiring himself in a Fountain.]
  Wilt thou the beauties of the mind forego,
[*The Slave expresses dislike.*]
  I knew thy manly nature would say no.
  The slave asks for power. (pp. 13–14)

The Slave's request for power is itself a revealing, telling response to his enslavement and exploitation on Peevish's coffee plantation but Benigna is quick to give this a political manifestation and to point out the dangers of misrule:

BENIGNA. For power!—and doe ambition swell thy breast,
  Try if thy wish obtain'd would make thee blest.

---

[37] 'Transparent paintings ... seem to be peculiar to the present age', Joseph Strutt, *The Sports and Pastimes of the People of England* (1801), 279.
[38] One commentator claimed that *Furibond*'s limited success was entirely due to 'skills of the scene-painter' *The History of the Theatres of London*, 152.

[*She waves her wand.*
A TRANSPARENCY APPEARS,
Representing a Tyrant tramping on a Subject.
The Slave turns away with horror.] (p. 14)

In *Harlequin Negro*, the black man is also given a swift series of lessons in becoming a citizen or public subject. After Slave's 'horror' at the tyrant, he is shown a mitigating scene of social benevolence:

BENIGNA. Well may'st thou turn thee from the cruel scene,
   'Tis gone. —
[*Waves her wand,*
A TRANSPARENCY APPEARS.
Representing Harlequin relieving distressed objects.]
   View now what thou might'st have been.
   Dispensing comfort to the opprest with grief,
   Heavens instrument of general relief.
[*The Slave in Raptures.*] (p. 15)

The Slave's responses to love of the self, political tyranny and benevolence show how *Harlequin Negro* idealizes the emancipation of slaves into fully socialized political beings. The imperial role of Britain as liberator of slaves then follows after '*Harlequin supplicates for the emancipation of his fellow Slaves who appear in chains*' and Benigna departs to allow Britannia to descend from the skies to show that 'England shall stamp the blest decree, | That gives the Negro *Liberty*' (pp. 16–17) and the scene shifts to Greenwich Park, the seat of London's maritime power.

From the West Indian coffee plantation to Greenwich Park, *Harlequin Negro* unselfconsciously applauds the liberal virtues of imperial power, implying that negroes can safely be assimilated into the values of empire as a part of the continuities of British history ('From Alfred's oak, our fleet then rose, | The nation's shield, the dread of foes; | And to this day that brave decree, | Secure the Briton's *Liberty!*' (p. 12)). Slave's transformation into Harlequin even allows the pantomime to skirt over the racial problem of his union with Columbine. And because this is all comic harlequinade,

Powell ended with a curious clowning scene showing Gaffer Gray and three travellers, a scene equally complex in ways equivalent to Powell's representation of race (although parts of it were omitted from the actual production).

Although 'Gaffer Grey' was a traditional broadside ballad, its importation into *Harlequin Negro* further politicizes Powell's Christmas pantomime.[39] In this scene, Gaffer Gray and the travellers are homeless vagrants, seeking hospitality at Christmas. In a move expressing anxieties so frequently represented in the drama of this period, Gaffer Gray and the travellers are suspicious of the charity offered by figures from the professions. The 'jolly' Priest 'often preaches | Against worldly wishes, | But ne'er gives a mite to the poor' while the Lawyer, 'Warmly fenc'd both in back and in front', is a threatening magistrate who will 'soon fasten his locks, | And will threaten the stocks, | Should he evermore find me in want, | Well-a-day!' The solution to these mendicants lies, perhaps predictably, in the traditional hospitality of the Squire's house where 'fat beeves & brown ale' in the Christmas 'Season will welcome you there, for 'his merry new year, | Are all for the flush and the fair' (pp. 19–20). Despite the constraints of its Christmas seasonal form, James Powell pushed *Harlequin Negro* to remarkable lengths, attempting to provide a symmetry of structure between the privations of the West Indian slaves and the poor British homeless.

Powell may have been a dangerous informer, deeply infiltrated as a mole into the London Corresponding Society, the Societies of United Englishmen and United Irish during a period covering a suspension of Habeas Corpus, a rebellion in Ireland, and the threat of invasion from France, but his pantomime *Furibond; Or, Harlequin Negro* provides a number of challenges to the politics of critical interpretation. Deeply reprehensible though Powell may have been as a person, *Harlequin Negro* successfully incorporated much that was common to contemporary radical idealism. *Harlequin Negro*

---

[39] For a contemporary reprinting, see the broadside *Great Sea Snake, and Gaffer Grey* (*c*.1800).

problematizes the notion that mentalities demonstrating repress-ive loyalist activism, of the most despicable kind in Powell's case, were not able to exist within discourses normally associated with abolitionist politics.

Furibond; Or, Harlequin Negro's production also crucially prob-lematizes the cultural role of drama written during this period. With his infiltration into London radicalism set to continue for three or four more years, before finally settling around the 1809 OP riots and his apparent escape to the Custom House at Cowes, Powell is an enigmatic figure. Yet though Powell has been neglected in modern times as a literary figure, his contemporary cultural signi-ficance was disproportionately great. Assuming average audiences of around 2,500 per night (a three-quarters full house) during its twenty (or twenty-eight)-night run at Drury Lane, *Harlequin Negro* would have been seen by around 50,000 people. As a piece of drama produced from within the murkiest depths of contemporary London anti-radicalism, its cultural impact may have been much more immediate, direct, and dynamic in its effects on its audi-ences than journals such as the *Edinburgh Review*, which printed only 7,000 copies per issue in 1807.[40] If nothing else, *Harlequin Negro* shows that drama was a natural and accessible literary form to contemporary activists at the forefront of the political upheavals traversing Britain.

While Powell's pantomime represents a complex manifestation of progressive liberal politics articulated by an extraordinarily reaction-ary author, Zachary Zealoushead's *Plots And Placemen, Or Green Bag Glory, An Historical Melo Drama, In Two Acts . . . As performed at the Boroughmongers' Private Theatre* (1817) presents a reverse perspective on the political use of dramatic form. *Plots And Placemen* voices the views of the men Powell had been paid to help suppress because, between 1798 and 1817, there were many continuities amongst the

---

[40] Lee Erickson, *The Economy of Literary Form: English Literature and the Indus-trialization of Publishing, 1800–1850* (Baltimore: Johns Hopkins University Press, 1996) 77.

personnel of London's revolutionary politics which James Powell's spying was intended to betray and send to an uncertain fate. The Thomas Evans seized in the George public house, Clerkenwell, in 1798 on Powell's information is the same man who features as the character 'Vanse, Sen.' in *Plots And Placemen*. Imprisoned once again in 1817 under a suspension of Habeas Corpus, he would eventually be freed, uncharged. It is a telling vindication of the stamina and persistence of these contemporary ultra-radical ideologies that not only did Thomas Evans pass his political convictions to his son, Thomas John Evans, but also that their ideology had survived despite the best suppressive efforts of Powell and the Government.

The personnel of radical politics, especially during the era of mass political meetings harangued by figures such as Henry 'Orator' Hunt or the semi-professional radical orator John Gales Jones tended to be 'larger than life' figures who shared fervent views alongside vivid personalities. Nearly a decade later, a contributor to the *Theatrical John Bull*, a journal based around the Birmingham Theatre Royal, noted that during the theatre's 1825 summer closed season, when it was used for social functions, two 'snob-looking personages' appeared at a masquerade dressed as 'Preston and Little Waddington'. As a result of his 1817 treason trial, plus the publication of his biography in that same year, Thomas Preston ('Thomas Cordovan' in *Plots And Placemen*) achieved a kind of notoriety which had both reached the provinces and stood the test of time. Similarly, Samuel 'Little Waddy' Waddington, his Spencean printer and placard-bearing associate, must also have caught the attention of the Birmingham populace. This is a reminder that the city was clearly embracing the linguistic transformation of local popular culture engendered by Pierce Egan's *Life in London* (1820) and the Birmingham performance of Moncrieff's *Tom and Jerry* (1821) whose 'abundance of Charleys [night watchmen] . . . reminded us forcibly of All Max in the East'.[41]

---

[41] *Theatrical John Bull*, 31 July 1825, 75–6.

This complex relationship between popular culture and radical politics was strongly related to local associations with theatricality. If Arthur Seale, the author of *Plots And Placemen,* was also its printer (a common enough practice at that time for jobbing pressmen), then it is possible to be certain about his most local theatre. Seale's nearest theatre would have been the Regency Theatre in Tottenham Street, just round the corner from his own premises in Tottenham Court Road. The piece's subtitle, ... *As performed at the Boroughmongers' Private Theatre,* not only satirizes the restricted status of the Houses of Parliament as a forum for public debate but also alludes to the exclusive domain of upper-class private theatricals and restrictive repertoires of the Royal theatres which the Regency countered. As will be noted in Chapter 9, the Regency playhouse had itself evolved out of such a private theatre. If Seale visited his local theatre in early 1817 he would have found such things as an improving astronomical lecture illustrated by 'a grand Mechanical Exhibition' mixed in with the burlettas or pieces such as John Fawcett's 'abolitionist serio-pantomime' about a runaway slave, *Obi; or, Three Finger'd Jack.*[42] This appetite for self-improvement is a consistent feature of early nineteenth-century artisan history but the Regency's programme is also a reminder that education may have been encountered alongside theatrical entertainment.

This dual interest in ideological improvement and dramatic expression is typified by the rare snapshot we have of Evans senior's reading. When the two Evanses were imprisoned in 1817, the authorities also seized the elder Evans's pocket book containing an inventory of his library dated by its owner back to 10 March 1809. The objective of this confiscation was not official interest in Evans's reading habits but, rather, a stray entry concerning 'Expences for London Paris Sept 1809 [£]7–15'. [43] Quite fortuitously, as a by-product of the

[42] BL *Playbills, Regency Theatre, Queen's Theatre, 1817–32,* 25 Feb 1817; Jane Moody, *Illegitimate Theatre in London, 1770–1840* (Cambridge: Cambridge University Press, 2000), 88.
[43] PRO HO 42/168. 338.

Government's anxiety to locate a possible international conspiracy, Evans's impounded inventory of some fifty-odd volumes preserves an extremely rare, possibly unique, example of an ultra-radical artisan's library from this period. In so far as some editions can be tentatively identified, the collection suggests a fairly wide set of interests. A liberal reformist interest in poetry is suggested by *Odes, by George Dyer, M*[ary] *Robinson, A*[nna] *L*[aetitia] *Barbauld ... &c. &c* (Ludlow, 1800), Evans's copy perhaps coming to him via its London bookseller and ex-London Corresponding Society and Newgate detainee, Henry Delahay Symonds. Evans's links to the United Irish were reflected in the anonymous *The Exile of Ireland! Or, The Wonderful Adventures and Extraordinary Escapes, of an Irish Rebel Officer ... Written by Himself* (*c*.1805) and typical radical interests in *philosophe* rationalism were represented in Nicolas A. Boulanger's *The Origin And Progress Of Despotism, In The Oriental, And Other Empires, Of Africa, Europe, And America* (1764). Amidst these works, apart from copies of Shakespeare's *The Winter's Tale* and *Julius Caesar*, there is just one identifiable contemporary play text, *Safe And Sound; An Opera In Three Acts* (1809) by Theodore Edward Hook, a writer later strongly associated with loyalist satires such as *The Radical Harmonist; or ... Songs and Toasts given at the late Crown and Anchor Dinner* (1820).[44]

That Evans read works of popular literature is a little surprising given that such records of him as exist promote the idea of a somewhat austere, ideologically driven, political activist. Perhaps like the Zetetic rationalist Richard Carlile, who opened up the Rotunda as a theatre, the role of literature in the lives of these ideologues needs to be re-evaluated. The depth of radical culture's familiarity with drama, however, can be judged by examining the range of plays and poetry parodied in *Plots And Placemen*, from which it is evident that wide literary interests coexisted with extreme radicalism. For example, if

---

[44] Theodore Edward Hook, *The Choice Humorous Works, Ludicrous Adventures, Bon Mots, Puns and Hoaxes of Theodore Edward Hook With a New Life of the Author* (1873), 204.

Seale is a possible candidate for authorship of *Plots And Placemen* as well as being its printer, he approached it with a background steeped in his own experience of arrest and surveillance since 1800, while in 1817 Seale remained close enough to the alleged Spa Fields conspirators to take a crucial role in acting as their defence witness.[45]

At every point, *Plots And Placemen* is self-consciously aware of contemporary literary culture. Indeed, in several ways, it is indicative of the existence of a plebeian, specifically literary counter-culture in the late 1810s, a true working-class public sphere inverting elite cultural standards and importing new types of literary hero espousing new ideologies.

At its most basic level, however, *Plots And Placemen* is constructed out of a variety of literary parodies such as the piece's rather predictable concluding parody of 'Rule Britannia' ('Rule Corruption! Rule the knaves,— | For Britons shortly will be slaves') which obviously drew on a long-established tradition of challenging or satirizing the national patriotic deity. But its involvement with the contemporary literary scene was probably accelerated by the example of Robert Southey, the Poet Laureate whose *Wat Tyler: A Dramatic Poem* had been pirated in early 1817. Southey has a considerable role in *Plots And Placemen*, figuring in the piece as the court 'Poet' who appears in a 'Magnificent Saloon' (p. 20) to conclude a regal entertainment ending with the parody of 'Rule Britannia' and during which scene the 'Poet' makes a long speech parodying John Ball's address to the mob in *Wat Tyler*. Nor was this the piece's only involvement with contemporary literary figures.

In the Prologue, the Castlereagh figure declares that 'C[oleri]dge and S[ou]th[e]y' and the editor of *The Times* will defend his views. Their turncoat status is much vilified. The Southey figure leads a grand procession in the 'Magnificent Saloon' where his renunciation of his youthful radicalism is turned into a heraldic device: 'After him [came] a banner bearer, with the Poet's arms richly emblazoned—the

[45] David Worrall, *Radical Culture: Discourse, Resistance and Surveillance, 1790–1820* (Hemel Hempstead: Harvester, 1992), 109–13.

arms, field Or, a viper biting a file; crest, camelion; supporters, a blacksmith and a ragged priest—the motto, which is in *heathen greek*, means "My boyish errors are renounced"' (p. 21). Behind Poet enter two servants who process carrying a box 'on which is inscribed Coleridge's "Lay Sermons, defence of the Bourbons and the Holy Inquisition, &c."' (p. 21). This pairing of Coleridge with Southey is politically aligned with the next part of the procession which comprises 'a crowd of Sinecurists, Pensioners, and Boroughmongers, dragging an immense Iron Cage . . . in which is *suspended*.. a roll of Parchment, with the words "Habeas Corpus Act" on it' (p. 21). With its elaborate pun on the '*suspended*' Habeas Corpus Bill, and its allusion to Wat Tyler the blacksmith, *Plots And Placemen* was typical of the voluminous derision in which both the Government and the Poet Laureate were held but what makes the piece historically significant is its projection of a counter-Poet Laureate, a visionary plebeian poet in the Miltonic mode named the 'Prisoner' or 'Conspirator' (p. 16).

What is particularly interesting about *Plots And Placemen* is that it can be so accurately located within the highly marked and specific ideologies of a group of London Spencean radicals. Their radicalized inversion of the court 'Poet' contrasts a plebeian literature with the reactionary figures of Coleridge and Southey and implies the emergence of a new poetics. 'Prisoner' or 'Conspirator' is a plebeian voice presented as the author of 'The Loss of Freedom, A Poem, Book the First' which parodies Book One of *Paradise Lost*. In the piece's simple structure of parallel incident, *Plots And Placemen* ends with Southey's triumphantly repressive parody of 'Rule Britannia' but this is preceded by the conspirator poet whose epic poem 'The Loss of Freedom' is read aloud by Canning with the intention of ridiculing these 'doggerel rhymes, seditious, blasphemous' (p. 17). Canning's role as the speaker is an unavoidable device to allow a reading of 'The Loss of Freedom' but it also ironizes Canning's role as a satirist working on the *Anti-Jacobin Review*.

Plots And Placemen's own contextualizing of the capture of the 'Prisoner' 'Conspirator' indicates that it assumed the presence of an already radicalized print culture. This conspirator poet had been seized 'Within a mile of Manchester's fam'd town'. In the immediate context of this group's mid-1810s Spenceanism, the location in a northern industrial town attempts to establish a connection between metropolitan radicalism and the renewed sense of a possible northern grouping which the June 1817 Pentridge Rising in Derbyshire had blazoned. In contrast to the well-funded opulence of the Southeyean poet, the conspirator poet has been arrested in 'a mud-built hovel' along with nine or ten other conspirators. The manuscript of 'The Loss of Freedom' is said to have been found on a table amidst an incriminating 'heap | Of Cobbett's trash, pen, ink an paper', a probable reference to Cobbett's *Address To The Journeymen and Labourers of England* published in February 1817.[46] It is significant that the poem manuscript is visualized by the author of *Plots And Placemen* as lying in the hovel physically alongside not only Cobbett, but also 'pen, ink an paper', the very materials and tools of poetic inspiration and political response. Written from deep within this very specific extremist ultra-radical culture, the relationship between the new radical press and poetry could hardly be more vivid.

The poem itself is inevitably truncated since it is contemptuously read by Canning but it was clearly an impossibility to merge it with any pretence to dramatic form. The extract Canning reads out consists of some twenty six lines beginning:

> Of Pitt's first horrid Councils, and the cause
> Of that unhallowed war, whose impious rage
> Brought want into our land, and dire distress,
> With loss of Freedom, till Reform's grand sway
> Restore us . . .

The passage is sufficient to sketch out a typical radical post-war position indicating a long memory of the war's origins with Pitt and

---

[46] See PRO HO 42/162. 214 for how Government sought legal opinion about whether to proceed with a prosecution of *Address To The Journeymen and Labourers of England*.

the ensuing social deprivation caused by the long campaign and the subsequent economic distress felt urgently in 1816–17. Canning's reading is then apoplectically interrupted by the Ellenborough figure (modifying *Othello*), 'It's all a lie; "an odious damned lie; | Upon my soul a lie ..."' There then follow two short ripostes by the Prisoner ('Most haughty, proud, and ignorant placemen, | My most oppressive and unlawful Judges, — | That I did write that Poem and compose it, | It is most true; true I'm a Reformer ...' (p. 18)) before Ellenborough confines him to a dungeon because of his 'purposed guilt | And treason 'gainst the state' (p. 19)). *Plots And Placemen*'s parodying of *Othello* and other plays by Shakespeare may reflect the general social context of continuing antipathy between illegitimate drama and the Royal playhouses. Jane Moody has noted how there was a steady stream of highly provocative adaptations of Shakespeare at the beginning of the nineteenth century, including the Royal Circus's 'Grand Ballet of Action' version of *Macbeth* in 1809 and John Poole's *Hamlet Travestie* of 1810, which had a continuous production and publishing popularity.[47] Plebeian, parodic versions of Shakespeare would have been considered part of the repertoire of republican discourses Spenceans could co-opt to further their aim of overturning the state.

There are two things of importance to note in the appearance of the Prisoner poet in *Plots And Placemen*. The first is that, structurally, the Southeyean poet's identification with the ruling class is made absolute enough in *Plots And Placemen* to mark out the Prisoner poet's role as both oppositional and adversarial. Although bonded by the common use of the English literary register, the court poet speaks from within the discourse of the 1817 rediscovery of Southey's *Wat Tyler*, an allusive literary device highly suggestive of corrupted poets and weakened ideals. By contrast, the Prisoner poet speaks the politically unambiguous language of the seventeenth-century Commonwealth republican John Milton.

More importantly, however, the Prisoner poet's appearance in *Plots And Placemen* is a definitive moment when a highly specific

---

[47] Moody, *Illegitimate Theatre in London*, 129–41.

and identifiable group of metropolitan ultra-radical activists figured an epic Miltonic poet as one of their leaders. *Plots And Placemen* envisages a coexistivity between the social role of literature and the role of direct political intervention. Additionally, because this Prisoner poet figure occurs within a pamphlet indisputably situated within a plebeian public sphere, the work fictionalizes the Prisoner poet rather than fictionalizing its own commitment to revolutionary political change.

This marks an important reversal in the social role of literature in the Romantic period since the piece's origin in a Spencean collective emblematizes that, while dramatic and poetic writing was a pre-existing condition of those ideologies, its specific literary formation was not sublimated in an ascendant, predictive or prophetic substitute for political action. The Spencean group centred on Seale and the Evanses does not use poetry or drama as a vehicle for the Romantic displacement of revolutionary endeavour. The actual lives of this group surrounding Seale and Evans were spent in closer political conflict with authority than their texts fictionalize. Literature is, therefore, a reduction, not an inflation, of their political experience.

The personnel contained within the particular Spencean group associated with *Plots And Placemen* should not be politically under-estimated. They were deeply engaged, over a long period of time, in a number of overt and covert endeavours aimed at bringing about revolutionary political change in Britain. Their investment was far from being dependent on the socially tenuous role of poets to inspire or activate their tactics. It is significant that P. B Shelley's notion of poets as the 'unacknowledged legislators of the world', made in 'A Defence of Poetry' which he began writing is 1820, was preceded by the construction of the radical conspirator epic poet within *Plots And Placemen*, the product of a highly politicized and specific print culture with a strong relationship to physical force activism. Of course, while clearly intended as a closet drama, there can be no question that if it had been submitted to anywhere within the Lord Chamberlain's remit, it would have been refused a licence. One tantalizing possibility is that the Spenceans may have read it aloud at their meetings because

'Part of the Poem of Watt Tyler' had been read out at the Mulberry Tree tavern, in London's Moorfields, that March.[48]

The Government spy who recorded the reading out of Southey's *Wat Tyler* was symptomatic of the proximity of *Plots And Placemen* to the implications of other types of contemporary repression articulated in Scene 3. In this extraordinary scene which portrays the imprisonment without trial of the Evanses, Thomas Evans ('Vanse, Sen.') is described as '*pacing backwards and forwards*' in his dungeon. He soliloquizes about his predicament until '*A Flute is heard*', played by his son, Thomas John Evans, who was also confined in Horsemonger Lane gaol but kept in another cell. '*Young Vanse is* [then] *heard to sing the following Song*'. The appearance of the Evanses in *Plots And Placemen* is a specific example of how an alternative radicalized print culture could employ its presses to celebrate and sentimentalize a strand of politics mainly having currency amongst the working class. The deep-seated radical credentials of the real-life Thomas Evans are no better corroborated than by a letter sent from the radical pressman William Hone to Evans senior just subsequent to Spa Fields. The letter not only reveals Hone's business association with the Evanses but also Hone's remarkably considerate caution in not wishing, by proposing to publish part of Evans's millenarian Spencean pamphlet *Christian Policy the Salvation of the Empire* (1816), to put Evans into any further danger of Government persecution.[49] While Evans was hardly nationally notorious, he does occasionally figure in contemporary commentaries such as *Choice Cabinet Pictures; With a Few Portraits Done to the Life* (1817), printed by the veteran printseller and pressman S. W. Fores, which ironically refers to Evans's confinement 'on *suspicion of being suspected of a crime*' (p. 34).

Although *Plots And Placemen*'s notion of an imprisoned father separated from his flute-playing son who resides in the same gaol seems to sentimentalize their predicament, the legal circumstances

---

[48] PRO HO 42/162, 280.

[49] 'You may not be desirous that the [Spencean] Plan should be thus publicly noticed at this juncture'. BM Add MS 50746, fo. 1, William Hone to Thomas Evans, 13 December 1816.

ironized in both *Choice Cabinet Pictures* and *Plots And Placemen* are
a fair approximation of what actually took place. Although arrested and imprisoned on 8 February 1817 under the terms of the
suspension of Habeas Corpus, ten days later the Evanses had still
not been charged but were brought before both Lords Sidmouth
('Proudmouth') and Ellenborough ('Lord Justice Lawall') for further questioning. A further week later, Evans complained, when
questioned once more by Sidmouth, that neither his petition to the
House of Commons (meant to be sent via Sir Francis Burdett) nor
a letter to his solicitor had yet been delivered. On 10 March, much
as portrayed in *Choice Cabinet Pictures*, Sidmouth told him that
'the Examinations were now brought to a point which had led to
a Determination to commit him on a suspicion of High Treason'.
In other words, there was insufficient evidence to charge him. These
details, gleaned from the files of the Treasury Solicitor, show that
there was little or no inflation or hyperbole in this scene in *Plots
And Placemen* since the records show that father and son were,
indeed, usually confined and questioned separately.[50] Again, all this
suggests just how closely related the play is to perspectives current in
contemporary metropolitan ultra-radicalism.

The extent of the work's immediate alterity to canonical writers
such as Scott in *The Field of Waterloo* (1815) or Southey in *The
Poet's Pilgrimage to Waterloo* (1816) can be judged by the text of
'Young Vanse's' song, which not only refers to the decisive battle as a
blemish on the national honour and a restoration of tyrannic power
('Thy Country's *stains* record | The triumphs of *Duke W—ton* |
The slaughters of his sword! | The deeds he did, the fields he won,
| The *Tyrants* he restored!'), but which also goes on to wish that
the defeated French might revenge themselves ('Though though art
fall'n brave *Marshall Ney*, | *Thy wrongs thou wilt bequeath*, | *The
valiant men who fought with thee*, | Will soon revenge thy death').

It is also possible to correlate much of the political sentiment
of *Plots And Placemen* with other contemporary expressions of

50 PRO TS 11/204/875 (ii), fo. 893.

antithetical political feelings which were the subject of suppression. The lukewarm reception for Wellington's great victories evident in *Plots and Placemen* was a sentiment which provoked Lord Chamberlain's Examiner to refuse a licence for the Lyceum Theatre to perform the anonymous farce *The Duke's Coat; Or, The Night After Waterloo* (1815).[51] Once it had been *Interdicted By The Licenser Of Plays*, as the printed version's subtitle put it, its author rather disingenuously admitted that, after all, the piece derived from a French source. There was an enormous degree of official sensitivity to the preservation of Wellington's reputation. What appears to have particularly incensed Larpent was a lack of deference to the Duke. The play's main plot device, mistaken identity leading to the arrest of a French innkeeper near the battlefield, merely revolved around the innocuous comic punch-line, 'Yes, I am not the Duke—only the Duke's Coat' (p. 30). Both *The Duke's Coat* and *Plots And Placemen* are useful examples for how unperformed, or closet, drama was the only viable option for making such criticisms in dramatic form.

This move towards print as the supplement of performance is a factor of literary production entirely brought about by political constraints operating on those dramas whose presentation it was anticipated would fall within the jurisdiction of the Lord Chamberlain's office. The case of James Powell's playwriting in *The Venetian Outlaw* and *Harlequin Negro*, with their intricate ramifications for how we understand the relationship between contemporary politics and drama, is a reminder that the role of the Examiner of Plays added a further layer of unpredictability to the craft of dramatic writing. The importance of a work such as *Plots And Placemen* is not simply that it emerges as a text produced from within a highly identifiable group of ultra-radical extremists with specific ideological agendas linked to a well-developed plebeian press network, but that it also had a role of cultural mediation between dramatic writing and a theatre which was itself the subject of state suppression.

---

[51] *The Duke's Coat; or, The Night After Waterloo: A Dramatick Anecdote; Prepared For Representation on The 6th September, At The Theatre-Royal, Lyceum, And Interdicted By The Licenser Of Plays* (1815).

9

Crime, Theatre, and Political Culture: *The Mysterious Murder* and *The Murdered Maid*

THE alleged murder of a 20-year-old gardener's daughter, Mary Ashford, in a flooded Warwickshire sandpit in 1817 provides a particularly rich example for how melodrama functioned during the Regency period, circulating in the plebeian public sphere described in the last chapter and articulated by use of this expanding print culture. In particular, the Ashford case illustrates the complex interaction in late-Georgian Britain between metropolitan and provincial regions, print culture, politics, gender, theatricality, and the legal system. Although much of *Theatric Revolution* is at pains to describe the political and cultural complexity of theatre subcultures based upon London, this chapter will outline how the less visible connections between the capital and the provinces, by the time of the late Regency, were so extensively supported by a new print culture that incidents in provincial England could initiate a complex set of cultural relations at the metropolitan centre in which drama played a significant role.

Ashford's death and the two trials of her alleged murderer, a local bricklayer named Abraham Thornton, not only inaugurated a set of textual and symbolic exchanges reaching back into the Gothic relics of legal precedent, but also revealed how dramatic writing was positioned within an intricate structure of sexual, legal, class, and print politics. It is precisely because the case was plebeian and provincial in origin, as well as initially restricted in national influence, that it serves as an excellent indicator of the social function of contemporary drama. Incidentally, Ashford's murder also reveals the emerging force of 'public opinion', newly mechanized by increasing industrialization of the national economy and paralleled by an independent, decentralized, print culture such as that discussed at the beginning of Chapter 5. Richard Carlile's highly influential *Republican*, for example, began publication in August 1817, only three weeks after the first trial of Ashford's alleged murderer.

Out of Ashford's death arose a number of publications dealing with the developing consequences of the case. These include several pamphlets, a couple of 'hot-pressed' maps of the murder scene and, not least, two extraordinary three-act plays, *The Mysterious Murder* (1818) and *The Murdered Maid* (1818), written and printed in the English Midlands. Two further plays, performed for London audiences, William Barrymore's *Trial by Battle; or, Heaven Defend the Right: A Melodramatic Spectacle* (1818) and John Kerr's *Presumptive Guilt, or, The Fiery Ordeal* (1818), were clearly founded on the case's extended legal consequences. Evidence for the actual performance of the first two plays is thin but what is not in doubt is their proximity to a debate within popular print culture.

Recovering the circumstances of performance in Georgian provincial England is, at best, patchy. Over twenty years earlier, as discussed in Chapter 3 in relation to its suppression, there had been a London printed edition of Edmund John Eyre's tragedy *The Maid of Normandy; or, The Death of the Queen of France* (1794) which had declared itself on the title page, '*as Performed at the Theatre Wolverhampton*', a provincial town quite near to the scene of the Ashford murder over twenty years later. Eyre's claim of a Wolverhampton performance presents something of a conundrum although it may intriguingly point to some of the tactics of evasion and avoidance which provincial theatres practised. Of course, printed editions of suppressed plays were perfectly legal but Eyre had dated his *errata* slip as late as 16 March 1794, yet John and Anna

Larpent read the play aloud only on the evening of 14 April 1794, nearly one month later and apparently after the Wolverhampton performance signalled on its title-page. Anna had detailed in her diary that *The Maid of Normandy* had come to them in Bedford Square as 'a MSS Tragedy from a Country Theatre', without specifying the location.[1] On the basis of the printed edition, it looks likely that *The Maid of Normandy* had already been staged in Wolverhampton at some time before the middle of March 1794 when Eyre compiled his *errata* slip. In the Midlands region of England there may have been, from time to time, quite different practices of theatrical production operating from those which obtained in London. That same year, Eyre had published a Dublin printed edition of the play but, more importantly, there was also a second edition, similarly printed by Longman of London, whose title-page claimed that *The Maid of Normandy* had by that time been performed at the Theatres Royal, Dublin and Cheltenham, as well as at theatres in Worcester, Wolverhampton, and Shrewsbury.[2] It is probable, that by the time the manuscript reached the Larpents in April 1794, Eyre's *Maid of Normandy* had already been performed at Wolverhampton (where the Examiner's remit did not run) but that their copy of a 'MSS ... from a Country Theatre' emanated belatedly from the Theatre Royal, Bath (since Dublin's Theatre Royal was regulated by the Lord-Lieutenant of Ireland).[3] In other words, despite Eyre's designation of Wolverhampton as its only venue for the purposes of the first edition, and with evidence of the play's interdiction evident in the personal notations of the Larpents,

---

[1] *Diaries of Anna Magaretta Larpent*, vol. i, 14 April 1794, Huntington Library, Calif.

[2] John Edmund Eyre, *The Maid of Normandy; or, The Death of the Queen of France: A Tragedy, in Four Acts, as performed at the Theatres Royal, Dublin and Cheltenham, theatres, Worcester, Wolverhampton, and Shrewsbury, second edition* (1794).

[3] The designation of Cheltenham's playhouse as a Theatre Royal is complicated. There may have been a custom and practice of self-designation (for the purposes of status, considering local rivalry with Bath Theatre Royal) but Tracy C. Davis notes that Cheltenham is not included in theatres officially holding the patent licence at that time. Davis also notes that while Norwich Theatre Royal had been created a Royal theatre in 1768 by Act of Parliament, it never had a patent, *The Economics of the British Stage 1800–1914* (Cambridge: Cambridge University Press, 2000), 384 n. 58.

the surviving details do not relate the whole story of the play's fate. If the manuscript received by Larpent in April 1794 relates to the application for licensing by the Theatre Royal, Bath, there could have been any number of other performance venues besides the ones listed on the title-page of the second edition, although probably not at other provincial Royal theatres. The issue is a complicated piece of contemporary cultural practice. Quite clearly, the Larpents prohibited only the performance they had been asked to license (presumably for Bath) and continued to do so when the Theatre Royal, Norwich, next resubmitted it in 1804, irrespective of the play's possible performances ten years earlier at a number of provincial theatres.

By the time of the Ashford murder, English provincial print culture was much more developed than it had been in the 1790s when Eyre was evading theatrical regulation. The picture as viewed from London alone might have been quite misleading as to the depth of feeling the case had provoked in the regions and, therefore, the energies and opportunities which might have been implemented in portraying the woman's murder in dramatic form. Aspects of the trial were the subject of letters and articles in several national and regional newspapers and journals including the *Taunton Courier, The Examiner, The Independent Whig*, and the *Lichfield Mercury*. Oddly, although James Chandler's *England in 1819* (1998) shows Regency Britain to have been consciously aware of fashioning its own historicity, apart from increasing our sensitivity to the age's 'self-historicism', his otherwise suggestive critical trope of the 'case' offers only general assistance when attempting to understand the political, legal, and social fall-out of Mary Ashford's grim demise in a Warwickshire backwater. As the language of contemporary pamphlets makes clear, Ashford's death and Thornton's trial were exactly considered a 'Case'. While the sexually threatened heroine is a staple of Gothic literature, the persistent public opening and reopening of the Ashford and Thornton cases, both judicially and in print, indicates a cultural fascination with casuistry originating in a decidedly plebeian public sphere notably predating the moment of Shelley's *Cenci* (1819), a drama much examined in Chandler's book. Although Shelley's *Cenci* received no public performance in the author's lifetime, within the plebeian public sphere readers and audiences took increasing advantage of both an expanded print culture and the opportunities afforded by new playhouse spaces to absorb the implications of topical cases connected with crime and the lawcourts. There is much to suggest that this type of plebeian casuistry was at least as complex in its intertextuality as those relevant to elite literary authors such as Hazlitt, Byron, Scott, and Shelley (the chief examples focused on by Chandler). It might even be necessary to posit a quite distinct plebeian, provincial—even explicitly rural—popular casuistry whose expressions culminated in the now obscure dramas this chapter will consider.

Execution speeches and verbatim reports of prominent trials had long been published for popular audiences but cases like the Ashford murder demonstrate the extent to which emerging late-1810s and early-1820s print culture and playhouse infrastructures coincided with a discernible appetite amongst the public to come to deeper understandings of memorable events and their circumstances. A feature common to such occasions was the intersection of competing discourses articulated through a variety of public genres. Although many of the cases were concerned with murder, the variety of discourses they engendered distanced them from crudely sensationalist reportage. Sermons, forensic reconstructions, augmented trial transcripts, prison and execution accounts, as well as morally didactic fictions, all competed for popular attention along with—almost invariably—some type of drama.

Mirroring much of what had happened during the Ashford case in 1817, seven years later there was a flurry of popular interest in the murder of the gambler and tavern-waiter William Weare, in Hertfordshire in October 1823. Weare's convicted murderer, John Thurtell, was similarly a gambler but had also been an amateur pugilist and the keeper of a tavern in Long Acre which had a reputation as a 'free-and-easy' singing venue, no doubt drawing on its Covent

Garden locality and theatrical associations. As well as straightforward printed trial records, Weare's murder elicited similar types of
reconstructive narrative and public discussion to those produced
during the Ashford incident. These included prisoner depositions,
portraits, autographs, ground plans, sermons (both sober and melodramatic), broadsides (including one published by the Seven Dials
pressman Johnny Catnach and another printed as far away as Glasgow) together with semi-fictionalized moral tales.[4] While no single
genre of discourse dominated, the case was also quickly impelled
towards stage dramatization. Thurtell's own propensity towards theatricality (an aspect of the social anthropology of dramatics this
book has discussed throughout) was quickly recognized by his contemporaries. At his Covent Garden tavern he was reported to have
been 'greatly attached to theatricals, and prided himself in no small
degree upon his imitations of Kean, the actor'.[5] Thurtell's theatrical
tastes are circumstantially corroborated by the theatre historian John
Payne Collier who, oddly, 'knew Wear[e], the victim, well, having

---

[4] *The Hertford Genuine Edition of the Trials of John Thurtell and Joseph Hunt, for the*
Murder of Mr. Weare, etc. (1824); George Henry Jones, *Account of the Murder of the late*
Mr. William Weare . . . : including the circumstances which first led to the discovery of the
murder, and the detection of the murderers. The depositions taken before the Magistrates, the
coroners inquest, the trials of the murderers, and the execution of John Thurtell . . . portraits
of the prisoners, John Thurtell, Jos. Hunt, and Wm. Probert. Drawn by Mr. George Lewis;
with their autographs. Illustrated with a ground plan of Gill's-hill cottage and garden and a
map of the surrounding country (1824); J. Louis Chirol, *A Sermon on Gaming; occasioned*
by recent deplorable events, etc. (1824); Solomon Piggott, *The Voice of Blood, and the*
Voice of Conscience! or, the causes of sanguinary atrocity traced . . . A sermon [on Gen. 4:
10–13] *occasioned by the . . . murder of Mr. Weare, etc.* (1824); [J. Catnach, broadside],
The Hertfordshire Tragedy; or, the fatal effects of gambling. Exemplified in the murder of
Mr. Weare, and the execution of J. Thurtell (1824); [broadside], *Account of one of the most*
horrid murders ever read of, committed by three gentlemen, of the names of Hunt, Thurtell
and Probart, on the body of Mr William Weare of London, by murdering him and cutting
his throat, and throwing his body into a pond; they likewise robbed him, with an account of
a house which they had taken for the express purpose of committing murders and robberies
(Glasgow, 1823); Hannah Maria Lowndes, *The gamblers; or, The treacherous friend: a*
moral tale, founded on recent facts . . . Embellished with engravings (1824).

[5] *The Fatal Effects of Gambling Exemplified in the Murder of Wm. Weare, and the Trial*
and Fate of John Thurtell, The Murderer . . . to which is added, The Gambler's Scourge; a
Complete Exposé of the Whole System of Gambling in the Metropolis; With Memoirs and
Anecdotes of Notorious Blacklegs (1824), p. xv n.

played hundreds of games of billiards with him', a recollection which incidentally figures for us Collier's own remarkable predilection for low life and eventual involvement in Shakespeare forgery.[6]

As with the Ashford case of 1817, Weare's murder inspired two dramas, the anonymous two-actor *The Gamblers* (1824) for the Surrey Theatre, and H. M. Milner's *Hertfordshire Tragedy; or, The Victims of Gaming* (1824) for the Royal Coburg. The Surrey's *Gamblers* was 'suppressed by Order of the Court of King's Bench' in November 1823, apparently because of its being too closely based on real-life events (although it was re-licensed in early January 1824).[7] H. M. Milner's *The Hertfordshire Tragedy* (1824), which appears to have attempted to spoil The Surrey's audience by opening at The Royal Coburg the same night *The Gamblers* was re-licensed at the Surrey, ended on a firmly moralistic note with, Freeman (the Thurtell character), declaiming in court before sentencing that 'had I never entered ... a Gaming House, I had not stood here this day'.[8] Nearly ten years later, at the Parliamentary *Select Committee on Dramatic Literature* (1832), the legal foundations for the attempts to suppress the Coburg's *Hertfordshire Tragedy* were still being discussed.[9]

The issues surrounding Ashford's murder, as with that of Weare in 1824, engendered a dramatized casuistry of the incident which defined a populist tendency—debated almost entirely within a plebeian public sphere—which became even more strongly embedded as the years passed. By 1828–9, the murder of Maria Marten at

---

[6] John Payne Collier, *An Old Man's Diary, Forty Years Ago; For The First Six Months Of 1832* (London: Thomas Richards, 1871), ii. 65.

[7] *The Gamblers, A new Melo-Drama, in Two Acts, Of Peculiar Interest, As Performed for the 1st and 2d Times November 17 & 18, 1823, Suppressed by Order of the Court of King's Bench, Re-Performed For the 3d Time, Monday, January 12, 1824, at the New Surrey Theatre* (1824).

[8] H. M. Milner, *The Hertfordshire Tragedy; or, The Victims of Gaming. A Serious Drama. In Two Acts. (Founded upon Recent Melancholy Facts,) as First Performed at The Royal Coburg Theatre, On Monday, Jan. 12, 1824* (1824), 32.

[9] *Report from the Select Committee on Dramatic Literature: With The Minutes of Evidence ... 2 August 1832*, Parliamentary Papers (1831–2), vol. vii, questions 1270 ff., pp. 79 ff.

Polstead, Suffolk, stimulated a parallel set of discourses, the case
once again producing a set of trial transcripts, crime-scene reconstructions, sermons, broadsides, and at least one drama. By 1829,
The Red Barn; or, The Polstead Murder, had been produced at
the Theatre, Stamford, Lincolnshire, a quiet backwater of English
provincial life.[10] Quite at variance with Chandler's focus on elite
literature and a metropolitan emphasis, a noticeable recurrent feature of the distinctive casuistry of popular culture surrounding
these cases was its rural and provincial focus and its tendency for
the process of dissemination to diversify rapidly into a number
of genres. At the risk of being reductive of Chandler's *England
in 1819* (1998)—and certainly to evade assessing the national
psychic mood of the age—the sort of plebeian casuistry presented in this chapter, unlike Chandler's account, falls into a set of
readily articulated phenomena that even retain elements of predict-
ability. For Ashford, as with Weare and Maria Marten's murder,
the sequentiality of public casuistry is striking, with the incident
first creating local accounts in newspapers, then forensic reconstructions, moral debates (sermons, moralizing tales), and finally
semi-fictionalized dramas. In addition, these discourses are notably
sited within the plebeian public sphere (not least evidenced in the
regulatory impetus of recurrent moralizing sermons). The murder
dramas denote a complex set of responses which were clearly ranging
over a national scale.

[10] James Curtis, *An Authentic and Faithful History of the Mysterious Murder of Maria
Marten ... To which is added, the trial of William Corder ... with an account of his
execution ... Many interesting particulars relative to the village of Polstead and its vicinity;
the prison correspondence of Corder, etc.* (1828); Charles Hyatt, *The sinner detected: A
sermon preached in the open air near the red barn at Polstead, and at the meetinghouse,
Boxford, Suffolk, and in the afternoon and evening of ... the 17th of August, 1828, on
occasion of the execution of William Corder for the murder of Maria Marten, including
particulars of his life never before published* (1828); [broadside] *The confession and dying
declaration of Willm. Corder, who was executed at Bury on Monday last, the 11th Aug.
1828, for the cruel and barbarous murder of his own sweetheart, Maria Marten, a long time
back, and the wonderful way in which her body was discovered in the barn by means of a
dream* (Glasgow, 1828); playbills, 3 April 1829, Theatre, Stamford, Lincolnshire. The
play appears to be a spin-off from Robert Huish, *The Red Barn. A Tale, Founded on
Fact* (1828).

Indeed, the problematic hermeneutics of evidence, precedent, and cross-examination at Thornton's trial invited a sharply defined set of cultural contexts owing as much to contemporary attitudes towards sentiment, law, class, and gender as to courtroom procedure. To this can be further added a complex network of provincial mentalities, often reflective of the most rural parts of England, all of them interacting with metropolitan discourses. In particular, the publication chronology of texts related to Ashford's death suggests the pre-existence in the provincial population of the kind of collective grief and frustration exhibited a few months later on a national scale at the death of Princess Charlotte, in November 1817, at the height of the retrial of Ashford's alleged murderer.[11] The expressive public sentiment portrayed at Charlotte's funeral, and of her mother Queen Caroline in 1821, were clearly preceded by similar anxieties and depths of feeling at the perceived injustice of Ashford's fate. *The Mysterious Murder* (1818) and *The Murdered Maid* (1818), although written by elusive provincial authors, with sharply contrasting views of the event, presented the public not only with the basic elements of the case but also with a structure for commenting on the social and cultural implications of her death.

The bare outlines of the case can be briefly stated. On 27 May 1817 Mary Ashford was found dead in a water-filled sandpit the morning after attending a dance at the Tyburn House Inn near Penn's Mills, near Sutton Coldfield, in the English Midlands. The body had signs of bruising but otherwise provided no certain indication as to the cause of death. Drowning following an accidental fall could not be ruled out, although there were strong suspicions that she had been raped. Fresh blood was found on a grassy bank close to the water's edge. Abraham Thornton, who was also at the dance, and who was seen leaving with her, was charged with rape and murder. At his subsequent trial at Warwick Assizes, Thornton was acquitted.

---

[11] Stephen C. Behrendt, *Royal Mourning and Regency Culture: Elegies and Memorials of Princess Charlotte* (Basingstoke: Macmillan, 1997).

In this Regency world before expert autopsies, finger-printing, or DNA, the authorities had the body (which was dead), a pond (in which the body had been found), and traces of blood (which could not conclusively be related to the body) but little else to go on. An unexpected series of legal twists brought the case to the attention of a national audience when, after Thornton's acquittal in August 1817, such was the extent of public and legal disquiet at his release that Thornton was rearrested in October by the Sheriff of Warwick. This came about through the activation of the medieval statute of an 'appeal of murder' which allowed Mary Ashford's brother to reopen proceedings against him. Rearrest for a crime for which the defendant had already been charged and acquitted was rare but the 'appeal of murder' also allowed scope for the distinctly Gothic counter-plea of the 'wager of battle' or 'trial of battle'. The 'wager of battle' (or 'battel') provided a legal statute whereby a defendant could elect to prove his innocence through mortal combat. With full-blown Gothic theatricality, Thornton had a pair of 'medieval-style' gauntlets made and, at his retrial proceedings in November 1817, threw the gloves down on the floor of the court to formally challenge Mary's farm labourer brother to combat. At this point, the judiciary realized they were somewhat out of their depth, the trial was adjourned, and the case was dismissed in April 1818 at the decision of Lord Chief Justice Ellenborough. Shortly afterwards, still the subject of public obloquy, Thornton emigrated to the USA and did not return.

In recounting this narrative, it is important to distinguish between the two stages of the case: that is, between its local and provincial beginnings in Thornton's first trial, and its national and metropolitan manifestations in the higher courts when the 'appeal of murder' and 'wager of battle' became the principal issues. The switch from local/provincial to national/metropolitan agendas does not imply that the first stage was immune from influences derived from the second, but the retrial was beyond doubt the outcome of intense local dissatisfaction at the acquittal. Of course, the most fundamental difference between the two stages of the case was a transition from a focus on the deceased to a focus on Abraham Thornton as 'victim'. The first summary of the trial appeared under a local Warwick imprint in 1817, to which was added a Birmingham printed *Map of the Roads near to the spot where Mary Ashford was murdered*, a sure indication of the public's wish to analyse the available facts and reach their own conclusions.[12] When the proceedings moved from Warwick assizes to the retrial at London's King's Bench, another Warwick pamphlet and a further Birmingham account appeared.[13] At some point after the trial of August 1817, the London veteran scandalmonger, printseller, and radical publisher John Fairburn raised the melodramatic reception of the case by publishing the trial under the title of *Horrible Rape and Murder!! The Affecting case of Mary Ashford, A beautiful young Virgin, Who was diabolically Ravished, Murdered, and thrown into a Pit, as she was returning from a Dance; Including The Trial Of Abraham Thornton For The Wilful Murder Of The Said ... To Which Is Added ... A Correct Plan Of The Spot Where The Rape And Murder Were Committed, &c. &c* (1817).[14] Fairburn's edition appeared long enough after the first trial for him to be aware of the agitation for a retrial because he also reprinted letters arguing for Thornton's rearrest which had appeared in the *Taunton Courier* and in the national-circulation *Examiner*. Fairburn eventually went on to publish an edition of *Thornton's Second Trial* in 1818 but, in any event, his *Horrible Rape and Murder!!* was itself an amplification of a Warwick-printed *Thornton's*

[12] *Thornton's Trial!! The Trial of Abraham Thornton, At the Warwick Summer Assize, On Friday the 8th day of August, 1817, for the murder of Mary Ashford, in the Lordship of Sutton Coldfield* (Warwick, 1817); *Map of the Roads near to the spot where Mary Ashford was murdered* (Birmingham, 1817). There is a 'Vignette' of the 'Fatal Pit'. The printer was James Belcher, a link with Midlands 1790s Jacobinism. Belcher had been prosecuted in the Charles Pigott, *Jockey Club,* libel of 1793, see PRO TS 11/578/1893.

[13] *Murder of Mary Ashford ... Report of the Proceedings against A. Thornton in the Court of King's Bench etc.* (Birmingham, 1817); J. Cooper, *A Report of the Proceedings against A. Thornton ... in the Court of King's Bench* (Warwick, 1818).

[14] On Fairburn, see Iain McCalman, *Radical Underworld: Prophets, Revolutionaries and Pornographers in London, 1795–1840* (Cambridge: Cambridge University Press, 1988) and David Worrall, '*Mab* and Mob: The Radical Press Community in Regency England', in Stephen C. Behrendt (ed.), *Romanticism, Radicalism, and the Press* (Detroit: Wayne State University Press, 1997), 137–56.

Trial!! and both were joined by a luridly titled London edition, *Rape and Murder!!* (1817).

Fairburn's involvement at the metropolitan end of the case was not in itself decisive in transforming either its national public profile or the tendency to situate the event within the discourse of melodrama. At the provincial level, a fascinating play had been written by George Ludlam, the chief prompter at the Birmingham Theatre Royal.[15] Ludlam's *The Mysterious Murder, Or, What's the Clock, a Melo Drama, in Three Acts. Founded on a Tale too True* (1818) had appeared under a Birmingham imprint shortly followed by a second, 'Revised and Corrected Edition'.[16] By this point in late-Georgian Britain, the existence of a rapidly networked metropolitan and provincial press must be understood as a fundamental factor of national infrastructure enabling the swift proliferation of publications responding to the consequences of Ashford's murder and Thornton's trial. The cultural function of Ludlam's *Mysterious Murder* was to allow the issues raised in an otherwise bewildering array of pamphlets and counter-pamphlets to be encapsulated within the detachment conferred by dramatic form. It is also important to understand the complex structure of local rural, economic, theatrical, and print cultures which provide the case's material context.

The Sutton Coldfield area was part of a rapidly industrializing rural landscape. Ashford's whole reason for being at Penn's Mills was that it was an overnight 'stopover' on the journey to her home village of Erdington after selling dairy produce in Birmingham market, some five miles distant. Her fatal journey was determined by these classic rural–urban economics, a situation indicated as much by the name of the location (Penn's Mills) as by the man-made sandpit in which her body was discovered. Even the occasion of the dance, the annual feast of a Friendly Society, is indicative of emergent urban working-class

---

[15] John Hall (ed.), *Trial of Abraham Thornton* (Edinburgh and London: William Hodge & Co., 1926) 42.

[16] The subtitle about the striking of the clock (also followed in the title of S.N.E.'s play discussed below) derives from crucial witness evidence about the timing of Thornton's movements. Some of these witnesses were alleged to have been bribed.

economic co-operative structures.[17] George Ludlam himself was also
the product of a similarly industrializing theatrical culture with
increasingly complex commercial and political manifestations. His
work at the Birmingham Theatre Royal meant that he was employed
by the actor manager Robert William Elliston. Elliston also owned
the Olympic Theatre in Wych Street, London, a circumstance which
forced him into an increasingly contradictory relationship with
the Lord Chamberlain, the Duke of Montrose, since Elliston was,
simultaneously, the owner of a Royal Patent theatre (Birmingham
Theatre Royal) but also of the non-patent Olympic, which was the
subject of repeated closure attempts by the nearby Royal theatres
at Covent Garden and Drury Lane.[18] The manufacturing industry
of Birmingham, which provided the population catchments with
surplus income necessary for theatre attendance and the purchase
of pamphlets, was highly visible to contemporaries. The Theatre
Royal was considered 'very pretty' by Edmund Shaw Simpson,
who visited it a few months later in mid-1818 while scouting for
acting talent to lure away to New York, but he also noted that
'Birmingham is a dirty town— ... the perpetual dirt of Smoke
from the Factories render it very disagreeable. It contains about
90,000 Inhabitants.'[19]

The 'Melo Drama' genre of Ludlam's *Mysterious Murder* was
perfectly suited to this unevenly developing background of politics,
theatre, transformative economics, and widely dispersed print culture. Despite the histrionic implications of the title, Ludlam's play
allowed an essential space for local reflection on the case's implications. Nevertheless, instead of a performance at the Theatre Royal,

[17] *Thornton's Trial!! The Trial of Abraham Thornton, At the Warwick Summer Assize, On Friday the 8th day of August, 1817, for the murder of Mary Ashford, in the Lordship of Sutton Coldfield* (Warwick: 1817), 5.

[18] Robert William Elliston, *Copy Of A Memorial Presented To The Lord Chamberlain, By The Committee Of Management Of The Theatre-Royal Drury-Lane, Against The Olympic And Sans Pareil Theatres; With Copies Of Two Letters, In Reply To The Contents Of Such Memorial, Addressed To The Lord Chamberlain* (1818).

[19] Diary of Edmund Shaw Simpson, 29 May 1818 (Folger Shakespeare Library, Washington, DC).

according to a later commentator, *The Mysterious Murder* was shown only 'at fairs and halls of a popular character'.[20] This circulation of the play in venues frequented by lower classes may explain the appearance of a direct riposte, *The Murdered Maid; or, The Clock Struck Four!!! A Drama, in Three Acts* (Warwick, 1818) written by the anonymous 'S.N.E.'[21] Its author wrote that 'A Pamphlet, called a "Melo Drama", compiled from this "Tale of Woe", has been lately published, and although possessed of no recommendation, save the publicity of its subject, it has met with a most extensive circulation' (p. iii). S.N.E. aimed to refute by displacement Ludlam's narration of 'every disgusting circumstance' (p. iv) of the case, believing that the 'many details . . . narrated and scenes disclosed, [are] as unfit for the public eye, as they are ill-calculated for dramatic representation; and still more improper for the inspection of the fair sex, or of the rising generation' (p. iii). S.N.E. disarmed its local significance by removing the setting to France but there were also other evasions.

Compared to Ludlam's play, *The Murdered Maid* is highly decorous in its language and dramatization, presenting a landscape of conventional literary pastoral, 'A Lawn before a Village Inn,— . . . Musicians, with Pipe and Tabor, Violins, Hurdigurdeys, &c. followed by a group of young Male and Female Peasants, with Garlands' (p. 11). Even Marie's rape scene protestations are constructed of

---

[20] Hall, *Trial of Abraham Thornton*, 42. The lack of a performance at the Theatre Royal does not mean that Ludlam's work was undramatic: the reverse is true. However, not only would the Examiner of Plays, John Larpent, have been likely to refuse it a licence or demand unworkable cuts, the Birmingham Theatre Royal was manifestly not a venue for new writing. The Birmingham journal *The Theatrical Looker-on*, 1822–3, shows that a staple of standard repertory and 'big hits' from London formed the theatre's programmes. Little is known about George Ludlam who signed the *Mysterious Murder* 'G.L.' The only other work attributed to him is *Dalmanutha; or, The Monster of Venice: a Romance. By the author of the Mysterious Murder* (c.1820). See also L. W. Conolly, *The Censorship of English Drama, 1737–1824* (San Marino, Calif.: Huntington Library, 1976).

[21] Curiously, a manuscript of S.N.E.'s play *The Murder'd Maid* was later submitted to John Larpent for the Theatre Royal, Norwich (25 April 1820) but without an application for a licence. The date is Larpent's, not the theatre's. Larpent Plays, 2148, Huntington Library, Calif. The inclusion of a 'gauntlet' scene at the end of *The Murdered Maid* suggests the play was written no earlier than November 1818.

ornate sub-clauses: 'Begone, and learn that the humble and low born Marie abhors the wretch, though a diadem sparkled on his brows, who would shock her ears with such base proposals, and try to lure her from the paths of rectitude and honour' (pp. 12–13). Marie's visitation to Thornville as a ghost, 'supported by Invisible Agency', with 'deep wounds ... on her bosom, from whence issue streams of blood', emphasizes the presence of spiritual values above those of the English justice system (pp. 36–7). Also, because *The Murdered Maid* was probably written before Ellenborough's final judgment, the ending is contrived so that Thornville is simply struck with remorse, goes mad in the witness box, and promptly commits suicide ('[*Draws a concealed Pistol, and shoots himself ...*]' (p. 43)). In other words, as a play about virtue-warned and vice-punished, *The Murdered Maid* is strongly didactic and suitable for its avowed aim of being an immediate warning to young women.

A strong candidate for the identity of its author is Luke Booker, vicar of the nearby town of Dudley and Chaplain-in-Ordinary to the Prince Regent. Dr Booker was the author of a score of sermons, hymns and poems, some of them locally printed but several also published by the London 'Church and King' publishers Rivington and Hatchard.[22] Booker's professional association with the work of the judicial system is evidenced by his loyalist pamphlet *Britain's Happiness; an Assize Sermon: preached at ... Warwick ... April 1792: Exhibiting an Historical Review of Providential Interpositions in Favour of the British Empire* (1792). Booker became involved with the Ashford case when he wrote *A Moral Review of the Conduct and Case of Mary Ashford, In Refutation of the Arguments Adduced in Defence of her Supposed Violator And Murderer* (Dudley, 1818) which was itself a reply to a letter arguing for Thornton's innocence which had appeared in the *Birmingham Commercial Herald*.[23] In

---

[22] Rivington was also the London bookseller for *The Murdered Maid*.

[23] *Birmingham Commercial Herald*, 20 September 1817. The letter's author replied to Booker's pamphlet in 'A Friend to Justice', *A Reply To The Remarks Of The Rev. Luke Booker, L.L.D. In A Pamphlet Entitled 'A Moral Review' Of The Conduct And Case Of Mary Ashford, &C.* (1818).

his *Moral Review*, Booker clearly shows himself alarmed at the potential social and sexual discursive promiscuities invited through the Ashford case having become 'the chief topic of conversation, not only in the Cottage, but in the Drawing Room, among Companies consisting of both Sexes' (Preface). In short, he aimed his pamphlet as 'an admonitory Lesson to young Women; deterring them from repairing to Scenes of amusement, unsanctioned and untended by proper Protection' (p. 3). For Booker, it was not just the facts of the death and trial which concerned him but also their discursive repercussions in their reception via the popular press and everyday conversation. He was no stranger to such lofty patrician perspectives on potential domestic or social unrest, as he had shown in his *Sermon Preached ... at Dudley ... to the Common People, &c on the Subject of Riots* (1793).[24]

So what was it about Ludlam's modest, provincially printed, *Mysterious Murder* that provoked S.N.E.'s three-act riposte? The answer lies in his surprisingly worldly and equivocal portrayal of Maria Ashfield, Ludlam's fictionalization of the victim. Ludlam presents her as a complex character who experienced a cautious, but quite definite, sexual interest in Thorntree while at the same time remaining acutely conscious of the potential personal and moral dangers she might encounter. By contrast, as the choice of title itself suggests, S.N.E.'s *Murdered Maid* idealized the Ashford character into a stereotypical naïve virgin. Of course, this is not too surprising as the author's self-declared motive was to protect women and youth ('the fair sex, or ... the rising generation') from the 'disgusting' events encountered in both the reportage of the case and in Ludlam's *Mysterious Murder*. Paradoxically, in this respect, S.N.E. was following a model similar to Fairburn's straightforwardly melodramatic pamphlet *Horrible Rape and Murder!!*

[24] My account of *The Murdered Maid* differs from Sir John Hall's *The Trial of Abraham Thornton*. Hall believed that Ludlam's *Mysterious Murder* was 'revived' under the title of *The Murdered Maid*. This is clearly not the case although I have agreed with his report that there was a local rumour implicating Booker as having 'had a hand in composing' *The Murdered Maid* (p. 42).

(1817), which closed with an 'Elegy' to Mary Ashford running through the gamut of contemporary virginal female stereotypes. For example, at the dance, Fairburn portrays Ashford as demurely ignorant of her sexual attractiveness:

> Unused to scenes like this, she, slow,
> Thro' the gay crowd in graceful figure moved,
> With downcast eye, beholding not, and, yet,
> By all around, with joy, beheld . . .
> But, on thy sprightly form, amid the dance,
> When all around thee bore the smile of bliss,
> A wretch had fixed his eye's remorseless lust. (pp. 62–3)

In comparison, Ludlam's Maria Ashfield is much more complexly presented. She is never portrayed as simplistically provocative (to take the eternal fable of rape reportage) but neither is she ignorant of the danger into which her sexual desire is leading her, given the circumstances of meeting a male stranger on a dance-floor a long way from home at midnight.

At the end of the dance, Ashford left with Thornton in company with her friend, Hannah Cox, and her boyfriend, Benjamin Carter. The four young people walked together as far as a place called Old Cuckoo where Hannah and Benjamin went off in another direction and Ashford and Thornton were left alone (in Ludlam's version they are on a turnpike road). In *The Mysterious Murder*, Maria Ashfield is aware of the moral and, perhaps, the sexual dangers of her predicament ('I must acknowledge I am acting very imprudent, but my heart is innocent;' 'I'm not accustomed to tell untruths, but perhaps this time it may be pardon'd, should it ever be found out' (pp. 12, 14)). Nevertheless, she is content to go off alone with Thorntree. Representing one of the witnesses who saw them that night, Ludlam's character Country-Man comes in to soliloquize, ostensibly to de-romanticize the dramatic implications of the two lovers' disappearance off-stage but also to widen the context of the event. Country-Man's speech flirts with local dialect, and presents predictable domestic and gender stereotypes, but it also contains fleeting reference to the social and economic conditions which made 1817 a year of national unrest:

> Sweethearts, I suppose? so they were afraid of being seen! Ah, poor souls! when they have been married as long as poor Margery and me, they'll have something else to do, than stop out till this time o' the morning, courting! Od, rabbit it! how anxious some people are, and what deal o' trouble they're at to get married! as for me, I shouldn't care what I did to get unmarried. These curs'd hard times makes women so crabb'd and ill-temper'd, they're like Magpies! chatter, chatter, chatter! their tongues go like the larum of our old clock. (p. 14)

Similarly, Ludlam introduces another rustic witness, Milkman, to comment again on rural hardship, the dependence of rural Sutton Coldfield on the urban markets of Birmingham, and the inequalities of the class system:

> What a wearisome life is this? here am I forced Morning and Night, to come five miles, tugging and toiling!—for what? a mere subsistence. . . . 'Tis well for many of 'em, that they were born with silver spoons in their mouths! or they would not have had ingenuity enough to have got iron ones to eat with, and must have been contented with wooden spoons, like myself. (pp. 18–19)

Ludlam's third stratification of the class system lies in the character of the lawyer, Quibble, who takes Thorntree as his client. He is discovered '[*Reading a Newspaper; over a bottle*]' and commenting on the increased number of adultery cases:

> Were it not for these Crim Con's, Scandal, &c. What would become of half the lawyers of this Country, I know not. . . . 'The Lawyer's Harvest, the increase of Crim Cons'. That's a good toast . . . I think I made pretty well of my last job; when I shall have another such, God knows! I must confess there was no mighty matter of honour in it: honour now-a-days is out of the question. (p. 23)

Of course, Ludlam must have been aware that his own play was deeply implicated amongst the reported cases of 'Criminal Conversation' (adultery) and sexual scandal that Quibble was reading about in his newspaper. John Fairburn, the publisher of *Horrible Rape and Murder!!*, was probably the country's leading exponent of 'Crim. Con' and royal scandal. The Ashford murder pamphlet, with its prurient sexual detail, must have fitted neatly into the pressman's list. Nevertheless, *The Mysterious Murder*'s dramatic point is adroitly made: it is lawyers, not authors such as Ludlam or Fairburn, who are the real beneficiaries of this complicated legal case.

Any or all of these comments on contemporary social disaffection may have been sufficient to prompt S.N.E.'s *Murdered Maid* (and enough to ensure a popular reception for Ludlam's play in the halls and fairgrounds where it was probably performed), but it is the figure of Maria Ashfield who must have caused most discomfort to the patrician class because of Ludlam's portrayal of her wavering morality. At one point she soliloquizes:

> if ever I am found out, I shall never hear the last on't. What a simpleton I was! I cannot think what could possess me, to stop with him? As for his promises, I don't expect he's at all sincere! I'm a fool to think any thing about him! How I must derogate from truth! I don't like it? [*sic*] . . . Yet I've done no harm neither? only the appearance! (p. 17)

The poised, reflective, guilt of Ashfield's speech is remarkable: it is at once regretful and defiant. Her final comment, with its apt punctuation, seems to affirm her continuing virginity but, at the same time, to problematize it. Whatever interpretation one puts on this scene, Ludlam's Ashfield remains remote from Booker's purpose expressed in his *Moral Review* of conveying 'an admonitory Lesson to young Women'.

Nevertheless, although Ludlam attributes to Maria Ashfield conflicts between moral dignity and realism, it is clear that he also intends an educative lesson to young women who might find themselves in similar circumstances. This is done not through pointed moralizing but simply by following the original trial proceedings. During the rape scene at the end of Scene 7, Thorntree 'carries her off the Stage' (p. 18), while the next scene begins by showing '*A Field.—. In which is seen a Pit; and at a distance, a Mill.* MARIA *discovered lying on a Bank senseless; her apparel in a disordered state, &c.*—YOUNG THORNTREE *is taking off her Shoe and Bonnet; after which he takes the Body in his arms*' (p. 19). Added to this accurate forensic detail, Ludlam also introduced into his play the testimony of a surgeon, Mr Bolus. Bolus's statement, with its emphasis on intimate detail, must have been genuinely shocking:

> Being a Surgeon, I was sent for . . . to examine the body of the deceased, who was found in a pit of water: on a strict examination I found there were no wounds inflicted that could occasion her death. She appeared to have been violated; up to this period I do not believe, she had ever had connexion with man. (p. 49)

The Mysterious Murder concludes with a tableau or masque where 'Maria is seen to descend in radiant clouds . . . the fore finger of her left hand pointing towards Heaven' (p. 56). This resolutely sentimental ending, however, is preceded by a 'monument raising' scene, where a tablet is inscribed with her epitaph, '. . . by a monster in human form, [she] fell a victim to Cruelty and Lust. This monument was erected by her Friends, to perpetuate the fatal Effects of Inordinate Passions' (p. 55). There is just about enough equivocation in the final words ('the fatal Effects of Inordinate Passions') to leave it open to question about whose were the 'Inordinate Passions' associated with the night of her death.

After the Warwick trial proceedings in August, that autumn's legal developments of the 'appeal of murder' and 'wager of battle' put the Ashford case (or, at least, its consequences for Thornton) before a national arena of debate. The medieval statutes were dusted off and explained to the public in several publications. The pursuit of Thornton through the courts became a politicized issue. One of the local radical journals supporting the cause was the *Lichfield Mercury*, whose outspoken editor, James Amphlett, was prone to such things as printing hoax anti-flogging handbills, activism for which, in late 1819, he became the subject of a crown prosecution when he libelled the local infantry regiment.[25] One reason for the involvement of the radical press was that there were persistent rumours that three of Thornton's witnesses had been bribed. Ludlam's *Mysterious Murder* had repeated the allegations under the characters of the witnesses Cowherd, Ploughshare, and Clodpole as well as in a sharp exchange between Thorntree and his father when the son declares that 'A little money will soon make up all things' (p. 40). Whether or not the radical press fully anticipated the proceedings reaching the 'wager of battle' stage, the case became sharply politicized at a national level.

The main reason for this was that the linguist and London Corresponding Society 1794 treason trial indictee, John Horne-Tooke, had already 'rediscovered' the archaic statute of the 'appeal of murder' during his 1777 defence in the crown's libel case against him for stating that the King's troops were 'murdering our beloved American fellow-subjects' at Lexington, Massachusetts. Tooke's spirited defence before Attorney-General Thurlow declared that, although Thurlow 'had reviled the right of Appeal in the subject of Murder, as a Gothic custom. Gothic, was the invidious charge brought against it: it was a Gothic custom! Why, gentlemen, so are all the rights, and liberties, and valuable laws which we have; they are all Gothic.'[26] As it turned out, this Anglo-Saxon constitutionalism was not without its repercussions in the popular drama, which reflected the legal implications of (what had now become) the Thornton case. But there were also other far-reaching consequences for the course of English history. Ellenborough's final rejection of the 'appeal of murder' and the 'wager of battle' may certainly have had something to do with settling old scores from Tooke's 1777 Gothic mischief-making, but there were other reasons. At least one commentator, who described the 'wager of battle' as a 'relic of our ancient barbarism,' had also noted

[25] PRO HO 42/198.567 c. Oct 1819; PRO TS 11/73, Rex v. James Amphlett, *c.*1820.

[26] Quoted in Edward Augustus Kendall, *An Argument For Construing Largely The Right Of An Appellee Of Murder, To Insist On His Wager Of Battle, And Also For Abrogating Writs Of Appeal* (London, 1817) 241. Kendall's *Argument* had reached its third edition by late January 1818.

that 'one of the main objects of modern and pseudo-patriots, in the
maintenance of the Appeal of Murder, is the hope of occasionally
entrapping some individual of the King's land or sea service, who, in
the exercise of his duty, shall unfortunately be the cause of the death
of a subject'.[27] Again, in interpreting this contemporary commentator's reflection on the political currency of case history, Chandler's
England in 1819 is not of much assistance, but the historical point
is actually quite electrifying: in April 1818 Lord Ellenborough had
quietly rid the statute books of one possible (Gothic) legal recourse
against the militia soldiers who, fifteen months later in August 1819,
killed the civilian protestors at Peterloo.[28]

Ellenborough's judgment happened to coincide in London with
the opening of the Royal Coburg Theatre (now 'The Old Vic'). The
continuing topicality of the Ashford case is reflected in the theatre's
first-night representation of William Barrymore's *Trial by Battle;
or, Heaven Defend the Right* (1818), 'In which will be portrayed
the ancient mode of decision by Kemp Fight, or Single Combat'.[29]
The decision to run *Trial by Battle* for the theatre's crucial opening
night must, no doubt, have been made on the basis of the management's confidence about widespread topical interest in the case.[30]
The swampy ground on the Lambeth Marsh side of the Thames,
though newly connected to Drury Lane's theatreland by the Waterloo Bridge, was criminally dangerous enough territory for Barrymore
(who doubled as the theatre's manager) to include, in some versions
of the Coburg's debut playbill, the reassurance that 'Extra [police]

---

[27] Ibid. (1817), 275, 260.

[28] A description of the contemporary search for legal precedent is given in *Full Report
of the Trial of Abraham Thornton for the Wilful Murder of Mary Ashford, at Penn's Mills,
Near Sutton Coldfield, in the County of Warwick* (Birmingham, n.d).

[29] *Trial by Battle* played for fifteen nights from 11 May 1818, ten nights in the initial
run and then with further performances in July, August, and September.

[30] The theatre historian Edward Wedlake Brayley recalled that the pantomime
Harlequin and Comus was due to run in tandem with *Trial by Battle*. On 13 May, the
actor playing the clown double-booked himself at Covent Garden, and a dispute ensued
as to whether Barrymore's play or the pantomime should be acted first. After addressing
the audience, the evening began with the pantomime: Brayley *Historical and Descriptive
Accounts of the Theatres of London* (1826), 90.

Patroles are engaged for the bridge and roads leading to the theatre, and particular attention will be paid to the lighting of the same.' The American Edmund Shaw Simpson, who went to the Coburg nine days later, thought it 'a very pretty Theater', liked the lighting ('Candles Chandelier has Globes over the Lights') but considered the playhouse had only a 'poor Company' (although he did get to meet Barrymore himself).[31] Produced four weeks after Ellenborough's verdict, *Trial by Battle* has every appearance of having been written to exploit the most obviously dramatic aspects of the Ashford case but also to have been a vehicle of independent comment. In Barrymore's play, a cottager's daughter, Geralda, is abducted by Baron Falconbridge. During the affray, her father is killed. Falconbridge, in a scene set in a 'Gothic Chamber', is brought before other nobles to answer both charges, whereupon a blood-stained dagger is produced to proclaim his guilt. Glancing, as it does in its abduction scene at the rape of Ashford by Thornton, Barrymore's *Trial by Battle* particularly emphasizes aspects of the case's relationship to class. Ludlam's *Mysterious Murder*, assisted by reportage in the radical press, had rather exaggerated the class differences between the victim and the murderer, making it appear that Abraham Thornton was of a significantly higher social class than Mary Ashford, a gardener's daughter. Trial transcripts make it clear that Thornton was only slightly more well-to-do than Ashford, but it is revealing of these sensitivities to precise class gradations in early nineteenth-century Britain that the murderer in *Trial by Battle* is elevated to a distinctly higher social sphere. Ludlam's play appears to have all but initiated Barrymore's representation of Thornton as the haughty aristocratic Baron Falconbridge in *Trial by Battle*'s accusation scene:

BARON. [*Aside*] Damnation! Am I discovered? [*feigning indifference*] Gentlemen, there is a strange mistake; and I am at a loss to know how my name
could be coupled with so foul a crime. My rank and birth should place
me above suspicion: besides, what proofs exist? (p. 19)

---

[31] Diary of Edmund Shaw Simpson, Wednesday 20 May [1818], Folger T.a. 5, Folger Shakespeare Library, Washington, DC.

At this point, in a remarkably straightforward link to the play's parallels with the 'real-life' case, which Lord Ellenborough had dissolved just a few weeks earlier, the next scene begins with the 'silly peasant', Morrice (a shrewd if clumsy component of the play), who walks on stage to give a pretty explicit, if heavily ironized, summary of how the Ashford case had concluded:

Scene III.—Outside of Albert's Cottage.
MORRICE. [*entering*] So! so! here's another pretty bit of business—another
 specimen of dependence [*sic*] on the law: a guilty man found innocent—acquitted—turned loose upon the world, and no other chance
 left of meeting with his desserts [*sic*], but getting his head cracked in a
 trial by battle. Oh! Wise and upright law to give a chance to might, to
 knock down right. (p. 20)

True to its generic description as being *A Melodramatic Spectacle*, Barrymore's *Trial by Battle* ends with significant 'Grand Combat'. Following exactly the idea of Ashford's brother becoming a possible champion for her cause in single combat, *Trial by Battle* has some quite complicated arrangements of dramatic business for its conclud- ing sword fight. Geralda's brother, Hubert, cannot fight Falconberg because he was wounded trying to save her and his father. Henrie, the smuggler leader's son who is in love with Geralda, becomes Geralda's champion in his place. Meanwhile, Falconbridge has appointed his own champion, Rufus. Echoing—but reversing—the courtroom scene at Thornton's second trial, Henrie '*throws down the gauntlet. Rufus picks it up*' (p. 23). When Rufus is slain, Falconbridge is forced to fight for himself and is, of course, killed outright. With these crude but effective devices, Barrymore's *Trial by Battle* comments on, and redefines, the shortcomings of English law using drama exactly as a means of detached contemplation of civic and judicial processes.

However, this was far from being the end of public interest in the Ashford case, nor of interest in projecting its issues into popular drama. Discussion of the 'wager of battle' reopened questions about the original case and led to many grim details being re-presented. A central problem with the conviction of Thornton (his alleged

bribing of witnesses apart) was that the body gave no absolute clue
as to the cause of death. A key question for finding a motive was
whether Ashford had had consensual or non-consensual sex with
Thornton. Further pamphlets returned to the issue. The *Wager Of
Battle. Thornton And Mary Ashford; Or An Antidote To Prejudice*
(1818) was written anonymously but printed in Holywell Street,
Strand, a thoroughfare in an area of London closely linked to the
radical press but where, in the late 1810s, working-class attitudes
towards women lagged far behind the middle-class followers of Mary
Wollstonecraft.[32] Despite emanating from the heart of London's
radical press 'industry', the *Wager Of Battle* argued against the use
of the medieval statute, finding it 'uncongenial and contrary to all
our ideas of British Justice' (p. 14). Worse still, the author (we can
be sure he was male) argued that there had been no rape:

the virgin female ... seldom, nay, never, yields consent without much
previous solicitation—backwardness, and at least apparent reluctance,
however well disposed she may be towards the individual to whom she
either intends, or ultimately does, surrender her person. (p. 16)

Because this was a pamphlet war about legal, sexual, and social
attitudes which was amplified by a substantial artisan press, the
Holywell Street *Wager Of Battle* received a prompt reply in the
anonymous *An Investigation of the Case of Abraham Thornton ...
Tried ... For The Wilful Murder and Afterwards Arraigned for
the Rape, of Mary Ashford; (Of Which Charges He Was That Day
Acquitted) ... Being An Answer To A Work ... Entitled, Wager Of
Battle* (1818). In keeping with the noticeable contemporary interest
in understanding the exact pathology of the body and the relative
disposition of the victim, witnesses, and accused on the night of the
incident, there continued to be intense discussion of maps, time,
movements, and walking distances. However, public understanding
of the case (perhaps in the light of the publication of Ellenborough's

[32] For the significance of this area of London and the press, see David Worrall,
'Artisan Melodrama and the Plebeian Public Sphere: The Political Culture of Drury
Lane and its Environs, 1797–1830', *Studies in Romanticism*, 39 (2000), 255–302.

judgment) was now also shifting towards focusing on this lack of precise evidence that Ashford had been raped, and whether Thornton had been in the right place, at the right time, to have attacked her.[33]

The descriptive terminology employed began to turn around the *Wager Of Battle*'s subtitle, *An Antidote To Prejudice*. By the end of 1818 it had begun to be argued that the evidence against Thornton was flimsy and 'presumptive'. Edward Holroyd's *Observations Upon The Case of Abraham Thornton ... Shewing The Danger Of Pressing Presumptive Evidence Too Far, Together With The Only True And Authentic Account Yet Published Of The Evidence Given At The Trial, The Examination Of The Prisoner, &c. And A Correct Plan Of The Locus In Quo* (1819) not only completed this reversal of attention away from victim to violator (it is now '*The Case of Abraham Thornton*' rather than of Mary Ashford), but Holroyd also added further lurid arguments that the case was based upon '*Presumptive Evidence*'. His argument hinged on the presence of the blood found near the body. He said that the blood came from Ashford but was the result of her first experience of sexual intercourse and not because of wounding (for which there were few marks) or of the onset of menstruation. Her choice of a thin dancing dress (exhibited at the trial) proved that she was not preparing to menstruate (pp. 18–19). Distasteful though Holroyd's views were, he also reprinted the original trial transcript, showing that he was only repeating the evidence of the official surgeon, George Freer: 'I saw the coagulated blood on the ground; the menses do not produce such blood as that; that coagulated blood proceeded from the lacerations; the lacerations were from the sexual intercourse' (p. 54). In other words, the surgeon's testimony claimed that Ashford had had intercourse but that he could not establish whether or not it was consensual.

That Holroyd's *Observations* were treated seriously, and with renewed attention nearly two years after the incident, is evidenced

---

[33] Thornton admitted having intercourse with her but claimed that it was consensual. His defence evidence argued that Ashford had been attacked later, during which struggle she was stunned and fell unconscious into the water, or else that she accidentally fell.

not only by his pamphlet appearing in at least three editions, but also by his revisiting, in the appended '*Correct Plan of the Locus In Quo*', the original problem of Thornton's exact location on the night of Ashford's death.[34] This continuing pamphlet war, attempting to sway public opinion about the case, coincided with new manifestations of theatricality. One indicator of this is Abraham Thornton's histrionic, but obviously carefully prepared, hurling of the mock-medieval gauntlets during his retrial.[35] Of course, the connection between theatricality and the courtroom was a commonplace of cultural behaviour which does not necessarily suggest the social functioning of literary tropes. Although he does not mention having been at Thornton's retrial, the Shakespeare editor John Payne Collier, who was well connected to the contemporary theatre, recalled being an avid visitor to courtroom galleries, attending the treason trials of Watson and Thistlewood in 1817, all three of William Hone's blasphemy trials of 1818, as well as the Cato Street conspirators' trials in 1820.[36] The popular reception of the minutiae of the Thornton case, after Ellenborough's decision to dissolve the proceedings, settled around whether Thornton had been wrongly accused. The issue is reflected in the subtitle of Holroyd's *Observations*, that is, '*The Danger Of Pressing Presumptive Evidence Too Far*'. Holroyd had quoted the great eighteenth-century legal authority Sir William Blackstone that 'presumptive evidence of felony should be admitted cautiously, for the law holds that it is better that ten guilty persons escape, than one innocent should suffer' (p. 27). 'Presumptive evidence' was exactly the state of the allegations against Thornton. The anticlimax of Ellenborough's verdict was quickly replenished by literary intervention. As with *The Mysterious Murder*, drama was the preferred public mode of reflection for events which remained problematic in the legal and political arena.

---

[34] The engraved plan is dated 18 January 1819.

[35] A photograph of an engraving of the gloves is included in Hall, *Trial of Abraham Thornton*.

[36] Collier, *An Old Man's Diary*, 65.

John Kerr's *Presumptive Guilt, Or The Fiery Ordeal; A Grand Melo Dramatic Spectacle In Three Acts. Performed At The Regency Theatre Of Variety, With Universal Approbation; For The First Time On Monday, Oct. 19, 1818* (1818) was actually quite important to the publishing history of nineteenth-century drama because its reprinting into at least two editions must have helped its publisher, John Duncombe, hasten his family's escape from the increasingly repressive field of radical publishing into the publishing of drama.[37] Just how closely the radical press at this time was kept under surveillance can be judged by the fact that Duncombe had put out Kerr's *Presumptive Guilt* for printing to the Newcastle Street, Strand, printers Hay and Turner (in the same thoroughfare as Elliston's Olympic Theatre) who had themselves been the subject of *agents provocateurs* intrigues also tried out on William Hone in 1817.[38] The Regency Theatre of Variety in Tottenham Street, north of Oxford Street, was a venue which had begun the century in 1802 as the private Cognoscenti Theatre (the Prince of Wales's membership of its exclusive 'Pic-Nic' club helped designate its name) but since then it had fallen on hard times and become a circus, indeed, the Regency's latest owner, Harry Beverly, himself arranged the combat scenes for *Presumptive Guilt*.[39]

On the face of it, Kerr's '*Melo Dramatic Spectacle*' appears to offer little in the way of analysis, but its cultural message is revealed by knowing the contemporary context of the Ashford case. The '*Fiery Ordeal*' of the subtitle refers to the play's elaboration of the story of 'The Ordeal of Queen Emma', a tale repeated in such standard works as Rapin de Thoyras's much reprinted *History of England*. In the legend, Queen Emma had been accused of adultery by her son, King Edward I (the 'Confessor'), but had proved her innocence by successfully walking unharmed over a 'fiery ordeal' of red-hot ploughshares. Contemporary commentators on Thornton's retrial had noted that the 'wager of battle' was reminiscent of

---

[37] On the Duncombes, see Worrall, 'Artisan Melodrama', 218.

[38] PRO HO 40/10. 176; *Hone's Reformists' Register*, 28 June 1817.

[39] For plate and description of the Regency theatre, see Brayley, *Accounts of the Theatres of London*, 83–4.

'the old trial by ordeal', a contextualization which is immediately established by the Gothic setting of *Presumptive Guilt* (Emma's ordeal was said to have taken place in Westminster Abbey but Kerr shifts it to Winchester Castle).[40] In the play, Emma starts off as the stereotypical weak woman but suddenly becomes an assertive, warrior-like queen who kills an attacker with a sword and goes on to save the life of the King from conspirators ('Emma, who has already slain Hastale, rushes forward and preserves his life' (p. 14)). Queen Emma's struggle against a false sexual allegation, in the context of the play's opportunistic allusion to 'Presumptive Evidence', invites a comparison with the situation of Mary Ashford. In other words, Kerr's play forces a reconsideration of the damage done to Ashford's posthumous reputation rather than furthering the question of Thornton's innocence or guilt. The exaggerated actions, sudden changes, and reversals of melodrama are crude but effective in distilling the problem for contemporaries: how can a woman whose virtue has been questioned prove her own innocence? The definitive connection between Kerr's *Presumptive Guilt* and the conduct of the Ashford case is established by the plot's apparently crude dramatic device of the betraying gauntlet. Just as when Thornton had thrown his antique gloves across the courtroom floor, soon afterwards the Regency Theatre audience could see a misplaced gauntlet seal the fate of the conspirator, Leofric of Murcia, in *Presumptive Guilt*. When Emma, sword in hand, had driven off the King's attackers, 'Murcia dropping his gauntlet as he retreats, the King picks it up' (p. 14). Seconds after Queen Emma has successfully undertaken the fiery ordeal of 'nine burning plough-shares' (p. 19) confirming her virtue, the King spots the 'other' glove tucked in Murcia's belt, thereby identifying him as his attacker. Murcia is immediately subjected to the ordeal himself: 'Officers ... lead him up to the plough-shares; reluctantly he advances over

[40] *Full Report of the Trial of Abraham Thornton for the Wilful Murder of Mary Ashford, at Penn's Mills, Near Sutton Coldfield, in the County of Warwick* (Birmingham, c.1818), 13.

them, when just as he reaches the centre of the ordeal, a livid flame burst forth and envelopes him; he falls and expires on the bars' (p. 20).

The Anglo-Saxon Gothic of *Presumptive Guilt* is heavily figured into the contemporary context of law and politics framed by the Ashford case. Far from being simplistic vehicles of exploitative reaction to current events, mere sensation drama, both Kerr's play and Ludlam's *Mysterious Murder* illustrate how dramatic writing and an emerging artisan theatre acted as a focus for discussion of contemporary questions of legality, justice, politics, and, not least, the role of women. The counter-drama *The Murdered Maid* reflects patrician anxieties about the effectiveness of dramatic writing in accelerating moral disaffection. All three plays were linked to the late Regency's rapid and innovative print culture which provided the infrastructure for this distinctive plebeian public sphere. The intensity and unpredictable development of the responses to Ashford's death show that, although there were different varieties of provincial and metropolitan political culture, drama became the primary mechanism for consolidating and reflecting its issues. The case also illustrates the emerging presence of organized public opinion. The quiet and forgotten provincials reading their copies of *Thornton's Trial!!* or perusing a map of Penn's Mills, conversing and arguing in their own homes in mixed groups, or else metropolitan artisans trying to fathom an obscure Warwickshire death armed with Fairburn's *Horrible Rape and Murder!!,* all could be grateful that, by the late 1810s, a distinct artisan drama, founded in the non-patent theatres, was emerging as a fast and efficient contemporary literary form.

10

Theatre of Subversion: Carlile's Rotunda and Captain Swing

In the late autumn of 1830, the veteran radical pressman Richard Carlile took over the running of a rambling building called the Rotunda in Blackfriars Road on the south side of the Thames.[1] It already had a chequered history having been at various times a museum of curiosities, 'a coffee-room, wine and concert-room, billiard-room, and afterwards an amphitheatre for Cooke's equestrian performances, to which succeeded a panorama'. The Rotunda was quite commodious. As well as providing Carlile with a living space, its buildings included two large 'billiard-rooms', an 'extensive bar' and a separate 'coffee-room' together with a 'long room' which had once been the original museum's library. Most attractive of all to Carlile, however, was that the museum space, after adaptation by the equestrian showman company, was now fitted out as 'a small circular theatre' complete with a gallery supported by 'marble' pillars and balustrades from which peered down a statue of 'Contemplation'.

That Richard Carlile was contemplating opening a theatre at all is itself highly revealing of the extent to which rationalist radical politics by then felt obliged to modify the means of delivering their message in order to reach London's working class. That this was a change in the mode of political delivery rather than in the

---

[1] For an important discussion of the background of Carlile, Robert Taylor, and the Rotunda (including the rhetorical context of the *Swing* play) see James Epstein, *Radical Expression: Political Language, Ritual, and Symbol in England, 1790–1850* (Oxford: Oxford University Press, 1994) 136–45.

substance of the message is quite clear: as Carlile proudly put it in the opening editorial of his journal, *The Prompter*, 'This establishment [the Rotunda] affords the most rational and most cheap way of spending an evening that has yet been presented to the public of any country.'[2] Carlile's choice of the journal title, *The Prompter*, with its particularly theatrical nuance must reflect his initial ideas about the new potentially dramatic space he found himself occupying and his intention of capitalizing on its existing infrastructure for supporting semi-staged dramas. Nevertheless, *The Prompter* and the Rotunda of 1830 were a far cry from the earnest asceticism advocated by Carlile's shopmen and women in the *Newgate Monthly* scarcely five years previously.

Although Carlile admitted that the theatre was 'but roughly fitted up', he could see its potential as a meeting place for radical and blasphemous lectures, particularly in view of its proximity to the Royal Circus or Surrey Theatre's and the Royal Coburg, which lay just a short distance towards the west along a track then still semi-rurally marked by a large windmill.[3] Within a few months he would be producing a dramatic tragedy at the Rotunda in competition with these local playhouses. Around the same time, William Cobbett was similarly turning to dramatic mode in his (unperformed) three act anti-Malthus comedy *Surplus Population: And Poor-Law Bill* (*c.*1831) as both men realized the potential of dramatic form. But the most immediate usage to which Carlile put the Rotunda were the infidel 'theologic-astronomical' lectures of his associate, Robert Taylor, which were heavily based on the influence of Volney's *Ruins of Empires* but also drawing on the stock anticlericalism so frequently found in contemporary drama. In part, Carlile's exploitation at the Rotunda of Taylor's astronomical lectures may itself be a part

[2] *The Prompter*, 13 Nov 1830 1. In the first issue, Carlile provided a history of the building from which these details are taken, Richard Carlile, 'The History of the Rotunda', *The Prompter*, 13 November 1830, 7–9.
[3] Edwin Fagg, *The Old 'Old Vic': A Glimpse of the Old Theatre, from its Origin as 'The Royal Coburg', First Managed by William Barrymore, to its Revival under Lilian Baylis* (London: Vic-Wells Association, 1936), 5.

of a hidden history of rationalist polemics infiltrated into such astronomical lectures presented in a theatre. While such exhibitions were a common fall-back for end of season slots at many theatres, it is noticeable that the Royalty in Tower Hamlets were using the 'Eidouranion: Or, Large Transparent Orrery' to explain, in the wake of Volney's *Ruins of Empires*, the workings of the universe within a wholly mechanistic pedagogic technology.[4] With Taylor's lectures in mind, Carlile had the ceiling of the theatre painted with the signs of the zodiac, a sure indication of Taylor's ancestry in Volney's influential work and an indication of the theatrical effects Taylor had begun to import into his lectures which were already present in Taylor's nickname 'Robert the Devil'. In other words, Carlile's shift to a dramatic format which will be explained with his production of Taylor's five-act spoken tragedy *Swing*, was already an aspect of a deeper tradition of religious and political iconoclasm exemplified both by Taylor's deistical or atheistical lectures as well as by a tradition of rationalist science promoted in theatrical London spaces.

As soon as Carlile opened in November 1830 the Rotunda became a hotbed of political and theological controversy. As early as the beginning of that month the Home Office began to receive unsolicited informer reports of how

a gang of Ruffians at night assemble at a Place called the Rotunda in Blackfriars Road for the avowed purpose of political discussions. The exaggerated statements put forth at these meetings, together with the inflammatory nature of their harangues, have gone far, I fear, towards creating that spirit of disaffection now so prevalent among the lower orders.[5]

Within two months Carlile himself had been indicted for a seditious lecture addressed 'To the Insurgent Agricultural Labourers' and by

---

[4] *Royalty Theatre, Well-close-Square. The Theatre is perfectly aired, having had Fires in it for some Time. Eidouranion: Or, Large Transparent Orrery. On this elaborate and splendid Machine, which is 15 Feet Diameter, and has been exhibited Five Seasons in the Theatres-Royal Haymarket and Covent Garden, Mr. Walker, Jun. Will Deliver His Astronomical Lecture . . . Books of the Lecture may be had of the Box-keeper, at the Theatre . . . April 10 1793* (1793).

[5] PRO HO 44/22.97 8 November 1830.

July 1831 Taylor had been arrested for blasphemy.[6] At Taylor's trial, witnesses told of how he had already semi-dramatized his lectures which began with readings from Volney's *Ruins* before Taylor came on stage wearing 'a dress like the Archbishop of Canterbury'. The dramatized lecture (which would soon modify itself into staged drama) is an obvious precursor for how Carlile would use the didactic possibilities offered by the Rotunda's theatrical space. In his lectures Taylor employed minimal but effective props consisting of a table from which he removed a cloth to show 'a cup, a wine-cooler, a tumbler, and wine glass'. In an inversion of the sacrament, Taylor then took the bread and wine before declaring '"Now I drink in my Saviour's health"' and then imitating intoxication. 'The result was, continued roars of laughter' from the three to four hundred people in the Rotunda theatre's audience, proceedings Taylor concluded by saying 'Gammon' (that is, a lie) in place of 'Amen'.[7] As Carlile termed it, the audience came to witness 'the *Raising of the Devil*'.[8]

The theatricality of Taylor's lecturing style was instantly noticeable to contemporaries, as the prosecution counsel in one of his earlier blasphemy trials angrily observed:

Is he a Socrates, assembling and arguing with his disciples? No; he is the mountebank of a little theatre, at a chapel which had been formerly a place of public worship; and where you may see him, for aught I know, trample the Bible under his feet; and that with a theatrical air, which he thinks gives grace and energy to his arguments. This is what the authorities of the city of London thought they ought not to allow.[9]

This combination of Taylor's theatricalized lectures and Carlile's polemical interest in agricultural distress were the two components

---

[6] Richard Carlile, 'To the Insurgent Agricultural Labourers', *The Prompter*, 27 November 1830, 35. The blasphemy charge was Taylor's second indictment for such an offence, see *The Judgment of the Court of King's Bench Upon the Rev. Robert Taylor, A.B. M.R.C.S. on a Conviction of Blasphemy Toward the Christian Religion . . . 7th of February, 1828* (1828).

[7] Richard Carlile, *The Prompter*, 23 July 1831, 643–9.

[8] *The Prompter*, 11 December 1830, 88.

[9] *Judgment of the Court of King's Bench Upon the Rev. Robert Taylor*, 14.

which resulted in Taylor's remarkable play *Swing: or, Who Are The Incendiaries?* performed in the Rotunda's theatre from February 1831.

The issue of the mythical 'Captain Swing', the legendary hayrick incendiarist, was highly topical at the time of Carlile's opening of the Rotunda. Alarmist stories and rumours of his whereabouts, as well as the actual incidence of agricultural fire-raising were frequently discussed at the time and have been well documented by modern historians.[10] As well as Carlile's indicted lecture on agricultural distress, he had himself also contributed a pamphlet, *The Life of Swing, the Kent Rick-Burner. Written by Himself* (1830), in which Swing's child only accidentally sets fire (through an upset oil lamp) to a hayrick. Carlile portrays Swing as an out of work labourer impressed by the parish and 'harnessed like a horse' to drag a gravel cart in return for poor law subsistence, about which treatment he concludes 'in a very short time, Reform or Revolution must release me from it' (pp. 23–4). Carlile's *Life of Swing* provoked enough disquiet to prompt at least two pamphlets which attacked the 'falsehoods or errors contained in a pretended life [of Swing] ... published by Carlile, the Fleet-street infidel'.[11]

The debunking of the myth of Captain Swing, and its explanation through a combination of the outcome of genuine economic distress and the myth-making of the ruling class, were the twin targets of Taylor and Carlile's production of *Swing: or, Who Are The Incendiaries?* The vying for mastery of the authenticity of the myth of Swing as a threat to either agricultural labourers or else their farming landlords was a site of contestation fought out in pamphlet wars for the minds of the urban, as much as the rural, populace. That the authorities intended farm labourers to be cowed by the dangers of

---

[10]   E. J. Hobsbawm and George Rudé, *Captain Swing* (London: Lawrence & Wishart, 1969), Andrew Charlesworth, *Social Protest in a Rural Society: The Spatial Diffusion of the Captain Swing Disturbances of 1830–1831* (Norwich: Geo Abstracts 1978).

[11]   [G. W. S ____ e] *A Short Account of the Life & Death of Swing, the Rick-Burner; Written by One Well Acquainted with Him. Together with the Confession of Thomas Goodman, Now under Sentence of Death, in Horsham Jail, for Rick-Burning* (1830), 3.

following Swing is clear from such things as the printed semi-literate confession of a Horsham incendiarist under sentence of death who claimed to have been inspired by William Cobbett's speaking tours of Kent and Sussex ('i hird of one Mr Cobbit going a bout gaving out lectures'), a commonplace contemporary connection linking radical oratory with incendiarism, as informer reports indicate.[12] The reportage in the loyalist press that incidents such as 'Mr Cobbit going a bout' lecturing, and the danger that they might be 'hird', is a good indicator of how uneasy the authorities felt about the twin terrors of Carlile and Cobbett. Remarkably, the counter-Carlile propaganda in London's local print culture also included specific references to the Rotunda as well as to Robert Taylor, warning against deluded orators who assure 'the people that their only friends were Cobbett, Carlile, and Taylor' and even accurately citing the Rotunda's threepenny admission price.[13] Another one-sheet dialogue printed by the loyalist pressman Hansard purported to be a *Conversation Near The Rotunda, Blackfriars-Road*, subtitled *The Mud-Volcano, Or A Dialogue Between Jack And Will*, which told of a 'mighty clever gentleman . . . talks like a book' but which counselled the timid 'Who gave away all those Coals and Candles last winter? Not the Lecturing Gentlemen I'll be bound.' A nervous government informer, perhaps fearing the very mention of the word 'Rotunda', duly filed a copy back to the Home Office.[14] All of these incidents betray the growth and efficient distribution of a counter-plebeian press culture raised in order to confront and engage the effectiveness of polemicists such as Carlile and Cobbett.

This counter-plebeian press was sorely needed because these were heady times fully exhibiting the manifestations of a mature plebeian public sphere. Millenarianism, never far removed from metropolitan popular culture, had resurfaced again in 1829 in such forms as

---

[12] Ibid. 25–6. PRO HO 44/22. 59. [autumn 1830] Battle, Sussex, 'Lord . . . tells me that his Daughters were riding there & saw one of the fires break out, in the middle of the Day; he also tells me that Cobbett was there about ten day ago giving Lectures.'

[13] *The Genuine Life of Mr. Francis Swing* (1831), 9, 13, 21.

[14] PRO HO 64/17. 89.

fugitive printings addressed to the Duke of Wellington warning of 'the Destruction of London in less than two years by Fire (like Moscow) for all the Abominations of the Church and people' or pamphlets entitled *Is God's Hand Shortened in 1829 Years? Yet Forty Days and* BABY-LONDON *shall be Overthrown by The Modern March of Mind in England and Ireland towards Liberty and Equality.*[15] The millenarianism of Joanna Southcott and 'Shepherd' Smith was the subject of at least one 1831 debate at the Rotunda.[16] In more practically politicized modes, radical newspapers such as the *Poor Man's Guardian* were carrying advertisements for William Benbow's *Grand National Holiday, and Congress of the Productive Classes* (1832) with its plan of a general strike of labour, while another Home Office informer in the same weeks filed back to his controllers a copy of the pamphlet on the *Major And Minor Theatres. A Concise View Of The Question* (1832), which argued against the 'Boroughmongers of the Playhouses . . . that . . . do not wish for a reform' (p. 13).[17] Meanwhile, Carlile was engaged in issuing his own handbills to drum up audiences for the lectures (*Rotunda, Blackfriar's Bridge Englishmen! Fellow Countrymen! Attend*).[18]

It was this immediate context, of polemic and counter-polemic, plus the spate of agricultural disturbances which Carlile had already himself helped polemicize, that Taylor and Carlile began to think of employing, harnessing the Rotunda's theatre space to the full by producing Taylor's 'politico-monological tragedy' *Swing: or, Who Are The Incendiaries?* playbilled under Taylor's 'Robert the Devil' byline. Ironically, although the Coburg had been prosecuted in 1820 for their *King Richard Third* compilation, there appears to be no evidence that the Royal theatres knew of the spoken tragedy of *Swing*

---

[15] H. Burridge, *The Last Days & Works Or The Battle Of Armageddon. Destruction By Deceit, Dogs, Traitors, Liars, Adulterers, Fornicators, Gluttons, Drunkards, Oppressors, Extortioners, Usurers, Blasphemers, Thieves, Murderers, Wolves, Vipers, &C., Containing Death Warrants Against Christendom, Alias Devildom, Or The Gospel's Last Sparks In England And Europe* (1829); PRO HO 64/16. 57, 7 April 1829; PRO HO 64/16. 66.

[16] PRO HO 64/12. 171.

[17] *The Poor Man's Guardian* 28 January 1832; PRO HO 64/17.

[18] PRO HO 44/21. 414.

at the Rotunda although, in any event, with the issue of the patentees' rights becoming ever more politicized, they may have simply judged *Swing* not worth the bother since Carlile was hardly in a position to reinvent himself as a playhouse owner. Carlile may simply have been taking advantage (but also indirectly indicating) the erosion of the patentee privileges.

Whatever the circumstances of its inception, however, Carlile and Taylor did little or nothing by way of publicizing *Swing* for the local audiences, a factor which may suggest that Taylor's increasingly unpredictable drinking problems had marred their planning. Carlile wrote that it was 'the inspiration of two days' but it had already been performed five times before its first notice in *The Prompter* at the end of the first week of February 1831. Whatever had happened, it seems certain Carlile could count upon the proximity of his audience and Taylor's iconoclastic reputation to draw the crowds. Carlile and Taylor obviously had great hopes for *Swing*. *The Prompter* claimed that 'This piece, itself, is sufficient to produce all the desired Reforms' and went on to claim that '"Venice Preserved" shall not outlive it, as it does not excel it.' In particular, Carlile said that 'the plot beats that of any other popular tragedy; for here an injured people finally triumphs; hitherto all dramatic efforts to exhibit a resistance to tyranny have represented that resistance as unsuccessful'.[19] These comments clearly show that Taylor and Carlile thought *Swing* a politically innovative and committed play which would make a decided intervention.

In the British Library's printed copy, gifted to Charles Kemble, Taylor proudly wrote in the fly-leaf that *Swing* was of a 'specimen what the Drama should be—'. In other words, Carlile and Taylor were certainly aware of the political culture of the theatrical context in which their play existed. Taylor's inscription that *Swing* was a 'specimen [of] what the Drama should be' noticeably ironizes the role of Kemble in failing to invigorate 'the national drama' (as the common phrase of the time put it) by producing plays on seriously topical

[19] *The Prompter*, 5 February 1831, 223–4.

subjects. Taylor and Carlile's proud boast that *Swing* was the 'People's Tragedy, In Five Acts' not only comments on the lack of a responsible populism in much of the Theatre Royal repertoire, it blazons itself as in 'Five Acts', sniping at the very terms of their patents.

Although principally a space for political oratory, Carlile was keen to use the Rotunda to the full for its theatrical potential; but there were also several other, more pragmatic, considerations prompting Carlile to experiment in this way. When the Rotunda had first opened, Carlile had the use of Robert Taylor's notoriety but there is evidence to suggest that his efforts to run the premises on an even footing were meeting with only mixed success. For example, he was forced to run Taylor in tandem with the aged orator John Gale Jones, a veteran of mid-1790s 'Jacobinism' who had once starred alongside John Thelwall. As Carlile rather optimistically put it in *The Prompter*, Gale Jones's 'taper, though near its end, still burns brilliantly'.[20] On Christmas day 1830, Carlile admitted that 'the Reverend Robert Taylor's audience did not exceed one hundred persons' and by the middle of January 1831 he was giving the Rotunda's theatre over to fraternal organizations such as 'the British Association, for the promotion of co-operative knowledge', noting rather hopefully that 'the gist of co-operation is anti-aristocratical'.[21] Carlile's decision to present some kind of dramatic performance at the Rotunda must have been based on several factors, not least the proximity of the Royal Coburg and Surrey Theatres.

Despite its specialism as a venue for political meetings, the Rotunda was reasonably competitive with regard to its seating capacity although, of course, it was a lot smaller. In 1820 the Olympic Theatre was judged to hold around 1,320 persons.[22] In early 1831 a Home Office spy reported an audience of 378 people for a Tuesday night performance of *Swing* at the Rotunda, a respectable enough figure for Carlile to work with.[23] There may even have been prior

---

[20] *The Prompter*, 13 November 1830, 8.
[21] *The Prompter*, 1 January 1831, 141; 15 January 1831, 176.
[22] *Particulars and Conditions of Sale of the Olympic Theatre ... 13th June, 1820*.
[23] PRO HO 64/11.206.

usage of the building for performance purposes. If the records of the early historians of music hall are reliable, Charles Sloman, an *improvisatore* who also attended the 'song-and-supper' Coal Hole, Fountain Court, had appeared at the Rotunda as early as 1829, even before Carlile's use of the building.[24] Taylor's five-act structure for *Swing* may even have been designed deliberately to draw the fire of the patent theatres and provoke a confrontation although, being beyond Westminster, the play did not fall under the strict boundaries of the Lord Chamberlain's control (although the Coburg case of 1820 proved that the patentees were prepared to migrate their jurisdiction if they were able). As to its licensing by magistrates, Carlile had already had a stand-off with local magistrates almost as soon as he had opened in November 1830 when he had been forced to barricade 'the stable-yard door of the theatre' against a charge by police officers accompanied by a senior magistrate.[25] It is possible that, as a result of this defiance, the local magistracy decided to leave him alone or, rather, to take out against him the more legally reliable and more sharply focused indictment for sedition for his 'To the Insurgent Agricultural Labourers' lecture. Whatever the case in the early 1830s, the memories of the authorities were long. As Tracy C. Davis notes, when new owners of the Rotunda applied for a theatre licence, they were refused in 1844, 1847, and 1858 on the grounds that the premises had been used 'for propagating infidel principles and socialism'.[26]

Extraordinarily, throughout the run of performances of *Swing*, a Home Office spy was present to keep the Rotunda and all of its events under surveillance. Although his identity is not known, it is evident

---

[24] Charles Stuart and A. J. Parks, *Variety Stage: A History of the Music Halls from the Earliest Period to the Present Time* (1895), 23, 46–7. Charles Sloman, *Fitful Fancies of An Improvisatore* (c.1850). Sloman was a veteran by this time, having sung a 'Three part' comic medley added to *Crockery's Misfortunes; or, Transmogrifications. A Burletta, In One Act. Performed for the First Time, on Monday, July 11th, 1821, At the Royal Cobourg Theatre* (1821).

[25] *The Prompter*, 20 November 1830, 20.

[26] Cited in Tracy C. Davis, *The Economics of the British Stage 1800–1914* (Cambridge: Cambridge University Press, 2000), 52–3.

from one of his reports that the spy had a good working knowledge
of the personnel involved in contemporary metropolitan radicalism,
apparently having a personal knowledge of Arthur Thistlewood,
the Cato Street conspirator, and James Watson, one of the leaders
of the 1816 Spa Fields rising indicted for high treason.[27] As it
happens, amidst the climate of fear associated with the agricultural
incendiarism, the spy failed to report on the opening night of the
production although, by this time, he had concluded that 'I have
not nor cannot as yet arrive at their real intentions, such is their
divided opinions at present that I am certain there is no reason to
expect that anything of a dangerous tendency will occur anywhere.'
It appears that Taylor's lectures, about which the spy delivered very
full reports, were of more concern to the authorities than the play.
However, nevertheless, the number of people at *Swing*'s audiences
were noted and passed on.

Swing was billed as 'The People's Tragedy' and, in keeping with
the sentiments expressed in his inscription for Kemble, Taylor's
Prologue reflected his awareness of the role of theatrical censorship as an aspect of a wider political corruption impacting
on literature:

> The ancient tragedy was first designed,
> From slavish bonds to free th'insulted mind;
> To speak the people's voice with magic art,
> And launch keen satire to the tyrant's heart;
> It was the people's tragedy. The stage,
> The people's House of Commons was, till th'age
> When an usurping censorship arose,
> And sold the people to their deadliest foes . . .
> Dare to be wise yourselves, and SWING shall be,
> If you approve, THE PEOPLE'S TRAGEDY. (p. 9)

As has been indicated earlier with respect to the *Newgate Monthly
Magazine*'s 1824 championing of the reputation of P. B. Shelley
instead of engaging with the issue of theatrical censorship, both

---

[27] PRO HO 64/11. 119.

Carlile's use of the Rotunda in 1831 for drama, and this Prologue by Taylor, reflect something of a change of heart for that brand of rationalist radical polemic and activism which assembled around Carlile.

The plot of *Swing* is otherwise quite simple, involving the machinations of the Archbishop of Canterbury against the Swing family. Old Swing had been a faithful farmer on the Archbishop's lands at Sevenoaks, Kent, ('Old Swing, my good old friend, old Swing') who, until recently, had been a loyal and placid tenant ('Is't the old man himself; that good old man, | That always paid his tithes on quarter-day[?]'). However, his 23-year-old son, John, and cousin, Francis Swing, experience hardship differently. In an incident similar to the ending of Carlile's *The Life of Swing, the Kent Rick-Burner. Written by Himself* (1830), Francis falls foul of the poor law:

> cousin Swing, five children, and his wife—
> Paid but three shillings for his whole week's labour
> And four additional from the parish rates—
> In all, but seven—and himself for this
> Yoked to a cart, and made to draw gravel
> Like a beast of burden. (p. 26)

He and his friend, Richard Jones, are eventually caught poaching pheasants (III.i) for which Swing is hanged after an incriminating stolen watch (planted by the Vicar of Sevenoaks, Elijah Brimstone) has been found under his bed (pp. 32–3). Taylor's whole presentation of *Swing* shows the oppression of the Swing family and how resistance becomes not only ingrained into the family but also how the economic distress and political discontent experienced in extended family relationships under pressure become the source of the elusive identity of the Swing phenomenon.

The whole of *Swing*, however, is also a continuous celebration of Carlile's Rotunda and its place in working-class radical rationalist politics. Of course, the Archibishop 'of Cant ____' (an obvious Taylor pun for the printed edition built upon his blasphemous sermons), is a figure of patrician unease at the growth of unchecked plebeian print culture:

> But is there no way,
> To check the publication of those tracts,
> Pamphlets, and registers, and weekly trash,
> That hold our sacred order up to scorn,
> Expose the secrets of the Government,
> Set forth the amount of salaries and pension,
> And rail at that appointment of the Lord,
> The tithes—on which all true religion is founded? (p. 9)

Taylor's brushstroke characterization of the Archbishop is broad but gives some idea of how he portrayed the dangerously smug ignorance of the church leader. Imagining that unrest in Sevenoaks is the result of religious fanaticism (perhaps millennialist) the local vicar disabuses him:

BRIMS. O no, your Grace! O, no;
　　The danger is from infidelity;
　　The very opposite quarter. The people are
　　Beginning to inquire, to think, to reason,
　　To be curious, to be critical; and e'en
　　Into my well-ordered parish, spread
　　The effect of that infernal institution,
　　Call'd the Rotunda
ARCHB. Why, who preaches there?
BRIMS. Robert the Devil!
ARCHB. The devil he does! [*faints*] (p. 10)

Felling the Archbishop 'of Cant ____' by a swoon is in itself a wonderfully vivid dramatic gesture contrasting with a previous tradition of ardent but ascetic rationalist anticlericalism. To anyone familiar with the unrelenting anticlericalism of Carlile's *Republican*, the replacement of empirical argument by physical demonstration indicates a prodigious shift in Carlile's own positioning of his polemic within a more embracing populist sphere. This odd disjuncture between Carlile's preferred rationalism and the dramatic reach of *Swing* the play is revealingly figured in some of the tragedy's self-reflexive postures when it is said that even old Swing himself has been touched by the Rotunda rationalism ('And has old Swing turned rational at last; | Has he been at that horrible Rotunda, | Where nothing is going on but REASON?' (p. 13)).

Besides the clerics, the only other major figure in *Swing*'s portrayal of members of the patrician class is Judge Jefferies, again a stock lawyer character 'admirably pourtrayed and embellished with some modern instances of Jefferyism', as Carlile put it in a puff for the play in *The Prompter*.[28] Again, the presentation (as with the Archibishop of Canterbury) makes much of Jefferies's foolishness:

BRIM. 'tis whispered,
    He [John Swing] reads Carlile's publications.
ARCHB. Blessed Jesu!
JEFF. Then 'twas he
    That set the ricks on fire! (p. 13)

Despite the number of characters involved, the acting seems only to have been done two-handed with Taylor playing alongside a man called Harrison when they performed *Swing* twice a week, on Tuesday and Friday evenings.[29] Although evidence for performance is sparse, one indication for how it was played, moving in and out of different types of clerical character or between different members of the Swing family, is made clear by the ending of Act I where Taylor came on stage as himself ('Robert the Devil, or The Genius of Reason' as the Dramatis Personae listed him), to comment on the Judge and Archbishop, 'Aye, there they go, the pillars of the state, | Trusted too soon, to be found out too late' (p. 18). The aim

---

[28] *The Prompter*, 5 February 1831, 224.
[29] PRO HO 64/11.189, 199, 206.

must have been to dramatically dispel the myth of a conspiratorial bogey-man 'Captain Swing' by replacing him with the living figure of Taylor, the locally popular (and therefore highly identifiable) Robert the Devil of the Rotunda. By suddenly materializing Robert the Devil (or 'raising the Devil' as the Rotunda's own popular myth-making put it), one brand of subversive politics (a fictitious one though real enough in its incendiarism) is replaced by its actual, living, counterpart.

The presence of the daily Home Office spy, plus Carlile's own account in *The Prompter*, gives an interesting snapshot not only of the material culture of the Blackfriars Road area but also of the persistent low-level harassment to which *Swing* was subjected in a sort of cat-and-mouse between the Rotunda and the authorities. Typical of this was the surveillance of Carlile's attempts to promote the play. To advertise *Swing*, Carlile not only had a playbill printed but he also touted performances by using a placard bearer: both activities were carefully observed by the Government spy.[30] By the time *Swing* was ready for performance, Carlile was already in prison and Taylor was himself aware of how dangerously he courted (as happened in the spring) blasphemy charges. This culture of harassment is reflected in the play: 'JEFFERIES. Though all is not achieved, yet much is done. Richard [Carlile] is put in bonds, Robert in fear' (p. 11).

An unemployed Irishman called Joseph Walker was issued with placards and playbills of *Swing* not only to carry around the streets but also to sell, having been given them by the Rotunda's caretaker. On account of this simple act, Walker was arrested, taken into custody, and fined £5. Carlile's response was to use the pages of *The Prompter* to compare his treatment with the bill-stickers of the Society for Promoting Christian Knowledge, noting how 'not an officer is sent to disturb them. Is this fair play, or equal justice?' In addition, Carlile opened a subscription book for Walker where well-wishers could make donations while he was kept in prison.[31]

---

[30] A copy of the *Swing* playbill is at PRO HO 64/17. 86.

[31] PRO HO 64/11. 207; *The Prompter*, 19 February 1831, 256.

Evidence for wider political support for Carlile and Taylor in the local artisan community comes from the shoemaker Allen Davenport's 'Ode To the Reverend Robert Taylor, A.B.' which appeared in *The Prompter* shortly after Taylor's imprisonment for blasphemy. As Anne Janowitz has shown, Davenport was a significant figure in the history of early nineteenth-century radicalism, journeying from Spenceanism into co-operative movements and finally into Chartism while remaining influenced by a communitarian version of Shelley's poetry: 'Sky-searching sage! thy towering soul, | No daring tyrant shall controul, | Thy spirit shall be free;— ').[32] This ability to polemicize, dramatize, and commit to a local plebeian print culture is a significant indicator of the political impact of Carlile's work at the Rotunda. Given the contemporary historicity of the material structure of Carlile's support for the *Swing* play, the presentation within the text of the centrality of the Rotunda to connections between rural and urban political cultures must be given considerable credence.

Taylor would probably be liable to exaggerate the Rotunda's role in radical agitation but the material background of *Swing* shows every indication that such emphases were not totally misplaced when he has Elijah Brimstone (the vicar of Sevenoaks) and Ebenezer Sanctity (a local religious zealout) discuss how John Swing used to walk to London to visit the Rotunda:

BRIMS. I've heard, too, of his walking frequently to London to hear some sort of lectures that are going on in an unsanctified and unholy place, called the ROTUNDA.

OLD SWING. [*Trembling*] Called the what, sir—what?

BRIMS. The Rotunda!

EBENEZER SANCTITY. There, Mr. Swing! ... He goes to hear the Devil's Chaplain; him what says the Bible's all my eye, and explains it all away by the stars—and says that folks may be quite as good men without religion as with it. (p. 21)

[32] Anne Janowitz, *Lyric and Labour in the Romantic Tradition* (Cambridge: Cambridge University Press, 1998), 115–33; *The Prompter*, 10 September 1831.

That 'the Bible's all my eye' was, of course, one of Carlile's most strenuous assertions but, as with the *Republican* case, it did not go unchallenged by the more orthodox. Again, evidence from the material historical context supports the view that Taylor was right to think religious activists carried out their own interventions at the Rotunda. The Home Office spy, reporting a Friday evening performance of *Swing* with over two hundred people present, noted that the Rotunda was visited by '39 respectably dressed Women' and a 'Mr Asgood', their pastor. As soon as *Swing* began, they 'laid a quantity of Religious Tracts about the Seats of the Boxes and Pit' and left immediately.[33] This climate of intervention by religious activists is paralleled in *Swing* by the fictionalized warnings of Elijah Brimstone to old Swing about owning pamphlets bought at the Rotunda:

BRIMS. Now, take this friendly warning from me, Mr Swing; I warn you
    as a friend, and as a Christian minister, that if I find any of those
    inflammatory, blasphemous, or seditious publications, to have crept into
    my parish, I shall know the channel through which they were introduced;
    and I shall feel it to be my duty as a Christian, as a minister of the gospel,
    and as guardian of the souls committed to my care, to turn you and your
    family out of this house and farm, and send you all adrift as vagabonds,
    and beggars, as you will have deserved to be! (pp. 21–2)[34]

With this degree of proximity between dramatic writing and a radicalized print culture, it is hardly surprising that *Swing* could confidently proclaim a revolutionary ending.

Towards the conclusion of the third act of the tragedy, Robert the Devil is materialized onto the stage in a portentously melodramatic moment:

[*Enter Robert the Devil.*]
I see the gathering tempest big with fate;
    . . . Too late, too late; the cruel wrong of the Swings

---

[33] PRO HO 64/11. 212.
[34] For evidence that books were sold at the Rotunda, see *The Prompter*, 23 July 1831, 644.

Shall fatal be to Bishops and to Kings.
I made the man for't [*sic*], ye have made the strife:
Now Swing, for they revenge, and life for life [*Vanishes*] (p. 38)

The next Act begins with an equally graphically and emblematized display of revolutionary gravitas:

[*John Swing leaning, with his face hid in his hands, upon a pedestal of the figure of Justice. Midnight; thunder and lightning; dreadful storm. Enter Richard Jones, unobserved by Swing, with a tri-coloured flag, which he waves over the head of Swing, and then puts down.*] (p. 39)

Again, the medium of the melodrama is superbly suited to the revolutionary overtones of the speeches. Richard Jones summons up the revolutionary fervour induced by agricultural distress:

Th'agricultural labourers are up in arms
At Sevenoaks.—and thro' Kent, Sussex, and Hampshire,
The name of Swing echoes from hill to hill.
A hundred thousand voices call for Swing . . .
. . . the voice of the people is
The voice of God—that voice is now for Swing;
Speak with it. (p. 41)

Swing finally ends with the Archbishop's palace set ablaze, a total revolution, and John Swing's instatement as King.

Of course, sudden melodramatic reversals of fortune were common in the drama of the period. The sudden reversals of fortune witnessed in the French Revolution and, not least, in the more recent national fortunes of battle at Trafalgar and Waterloo all tended towards affording melodrama its credibility. The ending of *Swing* is no exception. In *Swing*, 'the People's Revolution' is proclaimed by the newly subdued Archbishop of Canterbury but fast followed by the abdication of King Swing:

Then Swing resigns his Kingship,
And will return, a British Cincinnatus,
To the plough, from whence he sprang. (p. 46–7)

Significantly, Taylor portrays a successful people's revolution. In the Rotunda's *Swing*, as Carlile had correctly described in *The Prompter*, 'the denouement of the plot beats that of any other popular tragedy; for here an injured people finally triumphs; hitherto all dramatic efforts to exhibit a resistance to tyranny have represented that resistance as unsuccessful'.[35]

Carlile and Taylor planned to write and produce another play at the Rotunda in order to build on the success of *Swing*. Carlile clearly hoped that the allegorical nature of *Swing* ('it is all an allegory') would place the work beyond prosecution as seditious, but he himself remained acutely aware of the political context of other historical dramas, comparing *Swing* to Southey's *Wat Tyler* (1817) and making a clear connection between Tyler and Swing as 'Kentish Heroes'.[36] The new play, another tragedy, was to have been set 'more remote in time and place, than that of "Swing"' but would attack 'the principles of kingcraft, priestcraft, and donkeyism' by finding their 'living likenesses'.[37] Perhaps partly led on by the Home Office spy who described how Taylor was 'drinking to excess', sending 'opposite for a quantity of Gin' after the meetings and then sitting 'drinking by himself till two three and four in the morning', Taylor never finished the project. The spy reported that 'the truth is that he has not written one word of what he meant to deliver' and the as yet untitled play was never completed.[38]

Swing: or, Who Are The Incendiaries? represents the radicalized end of the theatrical spectrum dealing with agricultural unrest. The earnest polemic of Taylor's 'People's Tragedy' amongst contemporary working-class politics is best contextualized by relating it to the competitive spin-off *Swing! A Farce* (1831) by Charles Zachary Barnett. Not least, the creation of Barnett's *Swing!* is indicative of the controversy and competition provoked by Taylor's namesake

---

[35] *The Prompter*, 5 February 1831, 224.
[36] *The Prompter*, 26 March 1831, 336; 2 April 1831, 351.
[37] *The Prompter*, 26 February 1831, 269.
[38] PRO HO 64/11. 209.

play since the farce was shown at the nearby Surrey Theatre in close proximity to the Rotunda. That it was the Rotunda *Swing* which set the agenda is clear from the chronologies of Taylor's *Swing* and Barnett's *Swing! A Farce*. The Surrey had produced Barnett's *Swing!* with amazing rapidity. The first productions of Taylor's *Swing* had been staged at the Rotunda by the end of the first week of February 1831; Barnett's *Swing!* was shown at the Surrey Theatre on 14 February, scarcely more than one week later.[39] It is not inconceivable that some theatregoers would even have got the playhouses muddled and inadvertently witnessed farce rather than tragedy, and vice versa.

Barnett's *Swing! A Farce* is based upon a plot concerning a rather tiresome but extensively elaborated practical joke (there is even a character called Jokely) about mistaken identity amongst showmen and features an unrestrained series of puns. Daniel Roper (a rope dancer, of course) is tricked into going as a stranger to the Red Lion, a country tavern in rural Reading, dressed entirely in red and doing such things as insisting on eating only carrots and red cabbage. The context, of course, is the arrival of an unaccountable stranger in a country tavern during a period of anxiety about the exploits of Captain Swing (the play opens with the inn displaying a bill 'Two Hundred Pounds Reward, for the Apprehension of Swing, the Rick Burner' (p. 3)). The trick is eventually happily exposed but the more serious point that can be made about Barnett's inconsequential farce, apart from its obvious intention to rival the Rotunda play, is that it is symptomatic of the extent to which Londoners were not intimidated or fearful of Swing's exploits.

Swing! A Farce is an exercise in both containment of and meditation on a still controversial contemporary political topic. Written for the audiences of the south-bank theatres, Barnett's play—for all of its tiresome puns—represents a confrontation of the issue raised in Taylor's subtitle: *Who Are The Incendiaries?* The playgoing public

[39] BL Playbills, Surrey Theatre, 14 February 1831. The eleventh (and apparently final) performance of *Swing!* was on 14 April 1831.

Conclusion

ELIZABETH MACAULEY's remarkable vision in *Theatric Revolution* (1819) of 'one unanimous body' of theatre workers 'aiding and assisting each other; the wise instructing the ignorant, and the strong protecting the weak' was an ideal embodied in much of the history of drama and theatre described in this book. Sociabilities established around spirituality, skill and trade which were located amongst immigrant theatre workers of the 1770s gradually became economically assimilated into the rise of a popularist theatricality whose social anthropology has been described in Chapter 6. The continuing political valency of the dramatic into the second decade of the nineteenth century was demonstrated in the behaviour of Queen Caroline in her manipulation of London's public spaces. Caroline's example is definitive in fixing the political role of theatre within contemporary popular British political culture. Between the loose alliances of theatre workers of the 1770s and Caroline's late Georgian choreography of dramatic politics, lies the vast groundswell of popular theatricality traced in this book. At the other end of the class spectrum, Carlile's early 1830s theatre in the Rotunda, belying his earlier asceticism, is as definitive as Caroline's visit to the nearby Royal Coburg in establishing the social demography traced by London's theatre.

In the period between 1774 and 1832, British drama emerged out of the cultural politics of its own formation. The structures of belief, skill, and occupation centred around de Loutherbourg in the

1770s, together with their attendant sociabilities, were assimilated into the cultural life of the capital. The route between Garrick and de Loutherbourg's masonic spectacle of *A Christmas Tale* and the survival tactics adopted by the Royalty Theatre in the 1780s was paralleled by the eruption of Spitalfields co-operative ideologies into Dibdin's suppressed *The Two Farmers* in 1800. Fraternal structures of confederation and association which had enabled the assimilation of de Loutherbourg and his friends at Drury Lane and Marylebone Gardens migrated across to the defensive and resistive local strategies of the Royalty as they engaged in energetic pamphleteering and debunking stagings of Charles Bannister's adaptation of Hippesley's Drunken Man or their *Apollo turn'd Stroller*.

The suppression of the Royalty, like the opposition to the patentees which gathered pace in the 1820s mirroring attacks on a corrupt and unreformed parliament, were the laboratories not only of social activism but also of regulatory tactics. Suppressing the Royalty implied the Government's willingness to maintain the monopolies of the patentees. Whatever state of embarrassment the Government was in during its defence of the capital interests of the patent holders, continuing acts of censorship was legitimized by their support for the Royal theatres. Their policies of coercion through surveillance and intimidation, the prosecution of any encroachment upon their monopoly, the sponsoring of prosecutions by proxy, all became models for the suppression of the radical presses and later political organizations of the 1790s such as the London Corresponding Society. The example of the dramatist spy James Powell's infiltration of the London Corresponding Society illustrates the vantage point which the Government realized existed between drama and radical politics, enabling the regulation of both. Similarly, the Spencean activists who published *Plots And Placemen* of 1817 were much more prescient than their ideological counterpart, Richard Carlile, in realizing the potential reach of dramatic writing into the urban subcultures which composed the body of their supporters. Of course, the thorough permeation of dramatic taste, of theatricality itself, into contemporary popular culture was the structural precondition for both the projection and the regulation of theatrical forms. The louche private theatres of Soho and Camden, like the 'spouting clubs' of the late eighteenth century or the 'song-and-supper' clubs of the 1830s, promoted an articulate working class increasingly taking its examples and role models from the plebeian public sphere. Personal histories disseminated in the new print culture, such as the extraordinary real-life career of the 'tumbler' James Pack or the *faux* memoirs of *The Lady of Pleasure and Fashion ... Mary Morris, The Chaunting Beggar-Girl, and Strolling Actress*, all testify to models of empowerment enabled through contact with the playhouses.

This plebeian public sphere, in its dramatic configuration at least, is definable not merely by its products, such as the Royalty's *Panto-mimic Preludio, And ... Paris Federation* or the Coburg's *Crockery's Misfortunes*, but also by its regulatory framework. Burletta was defin-itively conferred by the Royal patentees as a working-class dramatic genre as soon as the agitation for a third playhouse evolved in parallel with a reasonably prosperous artisan audience situated to the south and east of Westminster. The inability of the patentees to release spoken drama from their stranglehold ensured that both burletta and pantomime became the twin vehicles through which an emerging class could find their aspirations and condition articulated and reflec-ted. Again, Queen Caroline's south-bank travels conveniently serve to validate the growing political power of the Thames's working-class hinterlands. The examples of new 'local' dramas surrounding the murder of Mary Ashford, both in their provincial Birmingham mani-festations and in the Coburg Theatre's opening night *Trial by Battle; or, Heaven Defend the Right*, are indicative of the overwhelming presence of an underpinning national print infrastructure, in place by the mid-1810s, which empowered popular debate and provided a critique of English natural justice and legal casuistry.

Censors such as John Larpent (unofficially assisted by his wife, Margaretta), with George Colman the Younger following him in 1824, worked to contain this growing tide of populist dramatics. After Larpent's demise, Colman became increasingly aware of the ideological implications of his post as Examiner of Plays. Unlike

Larpent, Colman articulated his views in an ideologically formulated way. In 1829, re-circulating a pamphlet first written in 1825 for private circulation, Colman called for even greater powers for his office, believing that 'It is evident, then, that our Theatres . . . should be under a Controlling Power; and such Power is wisely and naturally vested,—particularly in later times, when Europe has been shaken with revolutionary convulsions,—in The King, The Lord Chamberlain, and (in some instances) the Magistracy'. Colman saw drama as a straightforward agent of destabilizing social change: 'Produce, constantly, before Spectators nothing but fascinating Debauchees, and heroick Conspirators, and the weak part of the multitude, (which is the majority,) would, in time, turn Profligates, and Rebels'. Unsurprisingly, he singled out the south-bank theatres as posing a particular danger:

> It only remains to remark, that, The Lord Chamberlain's control seems rather to require extension than curtailment; in order that the scandalous and illegal encroachments upon grants from the Magistrates may be checked, in respect to certain Scenick Exhibitions, on the Surrey side of the Thames, and in some other places of Theatrical Amusement, out of His [*sic*] present jurisdiction; of which there may be occasion to speak hereafter.[1]

In other words, if the *de facto* powers of the patentees were waning as they failed to engage with an increasingly dispersed and varied theatrical culture, there was no diminishment in the understanding of the political and social changes which might arise in the wake of the 'fascinating Debauchees, and heroick Conspirators' nightly displayed 'on the Surrey side of the Thames'.

The monopolistic rights and privileges of the Royal theatres were continuously protected by Government through threats of prosecution by the patentees paralleled by official censorship administered through the Lord Chamberlain's office, a structure typifying the struggles of an unreformed Parliament to both placate its supporters and regulate potential opposition. Colman's pamphlet, as

---

[1] George Colman, *Observations On The Notice Of A Motion To Rescind Certain Powers Of His Majesty's Lord Chamberlain* (1829) 1–4.

confirmed in a covering letter, was submitted to the 1832 Select Committee on Dramatic Literature but it had also been previously 'circulated among some Members of Parliament, & given to a very few private friends'.[2] Together, the letter and pamphlet confirm the covert workings of exactly the kind of 'Theatrical Oligarchy' against which the counter-pamphleteer Eugene Macarthy had protested.[3] Colman's ideology of theatrical suppression was fully formulated, distributed, and empowered by his continuing presence, until his death in 1836, in the sinecure post of Examiner of Plays.

Outside of these workings of the state in its official sanction-dom over drama, and beyond the elite drawing-room exhibition of Caroline's representation of Shakespeare's Hermione to sway her political followers, there existed the steady rise of the new theatres. Robert Taylor's *Swing* (1831), produced by the unlikely impresario figure of the Zetetic rationalist Richard Carlile, comes nearer than any other contemporary drama to enacting a theatrical revolution. By virtue of its venue in the south-bank Blackfriars Road, and the subversive topicality of its plot enabled by Carlile's proselytizing over a decade to legions of followers prepared to face imprison-ment for their beliefs, *Swing* comes the closest to becoming a full-blown manifestation of a principled ideological revolution in drama presented before a working-class audience. As it happened, the Royal theatres did not need to suppress the Rotunda's *Swing*: there was always a Home Office spy present at every performance and Carlile was already indicted for his lecture on the 'Insurgent Agricultural Labourers'. And in any case, the Rotunda had been raided by police as soon as it opened its doors under Carlile's man-agement. Meanwhile, cosily sited on the other side of the Thames, the West End Covent Garden and Drury Lane theatres continued their monopolistic productions of both the spoken 'National Drama' and of Shakespeare, uninterrupted and undisturbed.

---

[2] Folger Y.d. 23 (104) 10 June 1833, Folger Library, Washington, DC.
[3] Eugene Macarthy, *A Letter To The King, On The Question Now At Issue Between The 'Major', And 'Minor' Theatres* (1832), 10.

Bibliography

Primary Sources

Manuscripts

British Library, London: Additional Manuscripts 2776; 3289; 16922; 27808; 27899; 33, 964; 42865; 42869; 50746.

Corporation of London, Record 27780.

Folger Shakespeare Library, Washington, DC: Folger Manuscript T.a. 78; Folger Manuscript, Y.c. 901 (1); Folger Manuscript Y.d. 23 (104), 483 (10, 11); Folger ART, vol. 619.

Diaries of Anna Margaretta Larpent, Huntington Library, San Marino, California.

John Larpent Collection, Huntington Library, San Marino, California: Plays 851; 963; 976; 1093; 1110; 1301; 1413; 1449; 1533; 2148; 2166; 2322; 2410.

P[ublic] R[ecord] O[ffice] and National Archives, Kew:

PRO Chancery and Supreme Court of Judicature: Patent Rolls 66/3706.

PRO Home Office 40/9; 40/10; 44/22; 42/23; 42/33; 42/162; 42/168; 42/193; 42/198; 44/21; 44/22; 48/12; 64/11; 64/16; 64/17; 119/4.

PRO King's Bench 10/56;10/63 pt. 1.

PRO Lord Chamberlain 5/164; 5/205.

PRO Privy Council 1/18/19; 1/34/90;1/41/138; 1/41/139; 1/3117.

PRO PRO 30/55/87.

PRO Treasury Solicitor 11/73; 11/204/875; 11/578/1893; 11/939/3362; 11/966.

Diary of Edmund Shaw Simpson, Folger Shakespeare Library, Washington DC.

Periodicals and Newspapers

The Adviser (Boston, Lincolnshire)
The Artist
Blackwood's Magazine
The British Stage, and Literary Cabinet

The Cornucopia, or Literary and Dramatic Mirror
The Devil's Pulpit
The Dramatic Censor; or, Weekly Theatrical Report
European Magazine
The General Magazine, and Impartial Review
The Lichfield Mercury
The Monthly Mirror
The Morning Post
The Newgate Monthly Magazine, or Calendar of Men, Things and Opinions
The Poor Man's Guardian
The Prompter
The Rambler's Magazine, or, Man of Fashion's Companion
The Republican
The Theatrical John Bull (Birmingham)
The Thespian Review; an Examination of the Merits and Demerits of the Performers on the Manchester Stage, Pro & Con (Manchester)
The Townsman . . . Addressed to the Inhabitants of Manchester on Theatricals.
The Profits Given to the Patriotic Fund (Manchester)

Books and Pamphlets

Account of one of the most horrid murders ever read of, committed by three gentlemen, of the names of Hunt, Thurtell and Probart, on the body of Mr William Weare of London, by murdering him and cutting his throat, and throwing his body into a pond; they likewise robbed him, with an account of a house which they had taken for the express purpose of committing murders and robberies (Glasgow, 1823).

Account of the Proceedings Before His Majesty's Most Hon. Privy Council Upon the Petition For A Third Theatre in the Metropolis (1810).

An Account of the Rise and Progress of the Dispute Between the Masters and Journeymen Printers (1799).

ADOLPHUS, JOHN, *Memoirs of John Bannister, Comedian* (1839).

Address to the People, On the Distresses of the Nation, Stating the Causes, Effects, and proposed Remedy; also an Examination of the Letters of the Rt. Hon. G. Rose, and the Rt. Hon. G. Canning, in Answer to the 19,000 Memorialists of Bolton (1816).

ANGELO, HENRY, *Reminiscences of Henry Angelo, With Memoirs of his Late Father and Friends* (1828).

Angelo, T., *The Art of Making Fireworks, by Plain and Easy Rules* [c.1816].

Apollo turn'd Stroller; or, Thereby hangs a Tale. A Musical Pasticcio [c.1787].

Arnold, S. J., *Forgotten Facts in the Memoirs of Charles Mathews, Comedian, recalled in a letter to Mrs. Mathews, his biographer* (1839).

Barham, R. H. Dalton, *The Life and Remains of Theodore Edward Hook* (1853).

Barnett, Charles Zachary, *Swing! A farce, in one act, etc.* (1831).

Barrymore, William, *Trial by Battle; or, Heaven Defend the Right: A Melodramatic Spectacle* (1818).

———— and W. Reeves, [*Giovanni in the Country*] *Songs, Choruses &c in the New Comic, Melo-Dramatic, Hippodrame Entitled Giovanni in the Country; or, A Gallop to Gretna Green. as performed at Astley's Royal Amphitheatre* (1820).

Barthélemon, Francois-Hippolyte, *Selections from the Oratorio of Jefte in Masfa, Composed at Florence in the Year 1776* . . . [with] *Memoir of the Late F. H. Barthélémon, Esq.* (1827).

Barthélemon, Maria, *The Weavers Prayer Composed and Sung by Mrs. Barthelemon at the Concert For the Benefit of the Distress'd Weavers London: Printed for the Authoress* . . . (c.1780).

Bellamy, Thomas, *The Life of Mr. William Parsons, Comedian* (1795).

Betson, A., *Miscellaneous Dissertation Historical, Critical, and Moral, On the Origin and Antiquity of Masquerades, Plays, Poetry, &c. With an Enquiry into the Antiquity of Free Masonry, and several other old Heathenish Customs* (1751).

Booker, Luke, *Britain's Happiness; an Assize Sermon: preached at* . . . *Warwick* . . . *April 1792: Exhibiting an Historical Review of Providential Interpositions in Favour of the British Empire* (1792).

———— *A Moral Review of the Conduct and Case of Mary Ashford, In Refutation of the Arguments Adduced in Defence of her Supposed Violator And Murderer* (Dudley, 1818).

Brayley, Edward Wedlake, *Historical and Descriptive Accounts of the Theatres of London* (1826).

B[ritish] L[ibrary], Marylebone Gardens, collection of cuttings (shelfmark: 840.m.29).

BL Playbills, Peckham Theatre.

BL Playbills, Regency Theatre, Queen's Theatre, 1817–32.

BL Playbills 174 vol. 1, 1818–23, Royal Coburg Theatre.

BL Collections Relating to Sadler's Wells, vol 2, 1787–95.

Bryan, William, *A Testimony of the Spirit of Truth, Concerning Richard Brothers* (1795).

BULL, JOHN [JOHN FAIRBURN], *Remarks on the Cause of the Dispute Between the Public and Managers of the Theatre Royal, Covent Garden, With a Circumstantial Account of the Week's Performances and the Uproar ... illustrated with a large Caricature Frontispiece of the House that Jack built* (1809).

BURRELL, SOPHIA, *Theodora* (n.d.)

BURRIDGE, H., *The Last Days & Works Or The Battle Of Armageddon. Destruction By Deceit, Dogs, Traitors, Liars, Adulterers, Fornicators, Gluttons, Drunkards, Oppressors, Extortioners, Usurers, Blasphemers, Thieves, Murderers, Wolves, Vipers, &C., Containing Death Warrants Against Christendom, Alias Devildom, Or The Gospel's Last Sparks In England And Europe* (1829).

CARLILE, RICHARD, *The Life of Swing, the Kent Rick-Burner. Written by Himself* (1830).

Case of Mr. John Palmer, The Renters and Creditors of the Royalty Theatre, Occasioned by a Bill now before the House of Peers, for amending the Acts made in the Tenth and Twenty-fifth Years of the Reign of his late Majesty, relative to Players of Interludes, and Persons keeping Houses of Public Entertainment (1788).

The Catch Club: A Collection of All the Songs, Catches, Glees, Duets, &c. As sung by ... Mr. Leoni ... at the Royalty Theatre, Well-Street, Goodman's-Fields: To which is Added Hippesley's Drunken-Man, As altered and spoken by Mr. Lee Lewes (1787).

CATNACH, JAMES, *The Hertfordshire Tragedy; or, the fatal effects of gambling. Exemplified in the murder of Mr. Weare, and the execution of J. Thurtell* (1824).

CAWDELL, JAMES, *The Miscellaneous Poems of J. Cawdell, Comedian: ... to which is annexed An Answer to a late libellous Compilation called The Stockton Jubilee* (Sunderland, 1785).

CHIROL, J. LOUIS, *A Sermon on Gaming; occasioned by recent deplorable events, etc.* (1824).

Choice Cabinet Pictures; With a Few Portraits Done to the Life (1817).

Coade's Gallery, or, Exhibition in Artificial Stone (Lambeth, 1799).

COBBETT, WILLIAM, *Surplus Population: and Poor-law Bill. A comedy, in three acts* (1834).

Coggeshall, An Inhabitant of, *C____ll Volunteer Corps. A Farce. In Two Acts* (Colchester, 1804).

COLLIER, JOHN PAYNE, *An Old Man's Diary, Forty Years Ago; For The First Six Months Of 1832* (London: Thomas Richards, 1871).

COLMAN, GEORGE, THE YOUNGER, *Observations On The Notice Of A Motion To Rescind Certain Powers Of His Majesty's Lord Chamberlain* (1829).

The confession and dying declaration of Willm. Corder, who was executed at Bury on Monday last, the 11th Aug. 1828, for the cruel and barbarous murder of his own sweetheart, Maria Marten, a long time back, and the wonderful way in which her body was discovered in the barn by means of a dream (Glasgow, 1828).

Conversation Near The Rotunda, Blackfriars-Road. The Mud-Volcano, Or A Dialogue Between Jack And Will (1831).

COOPER, J., *A Report of the Proceedings against A. Thornton . . . in the Court of King's Bench* (Warwick, 1818).

Covent Garden Journal (1810).

COWELL, JOE, *Thirty Years Passed Among The Players In England And America: Interspersed With Anecdotes And Reminiscences Of A Variety Of Persons, Directly Or Indirectly Connected With The Drama During the Theatrical Life Of Joe Cowell, Comedian. Written By Himself* (New York, 1845).

COXE, PETER, *A Catalogue of the all the Valuable drawings &c. of James Philip de Loutherbourg Esq R.A., 18 June 1812 . . . And Extensive Library of Scarce Books* (1812).

Crockery's Misfortunes or, Transmogrifications (1821).

Crosby's Pocket Companion To The Playhouses (1796).

CROSS, JOHN CARTWRIGHT, *Songs, Recitatives, Chorusses, &c. in the New, Grand, Local, and Temporary Divertisement, Called, Our Native Land, and Gallant Protectors: Performed at the Royal Circus, For the First Time, On Thursday, June 23d, 1803* (1803).

CURTIS, JAMES, *An Authentic and Faithful History of the Mysterious Murder of Maria Marten . . . To which is added, the trial of William Corder . . . with an account of his execution . . . Many interesting particulars relative to the village of Polstead and its vicinity; the prison correspondence of Corder, etc.* (1828).

Declarations, Resolutions, and Constitution of the Societies of United English-men (1798).

[*Deserter of Naples*] *Songs, &c. in the Deserter of Naples; or, Royal Clemency: To Which is Added, An Ode to Friendship, A Tale from Baker's Chronicle, Address for the Marine Society, Mr. Lee Lewes's Farewell Address, and other favourite Pieces Performed at the Royalty Theatre* (1787).

DIBDIN, CHARLES, *Vineyard Revels; or, Harlequin Bacchanal* [c.1775].

_____ *Royal Circus Epitomized* (1784).

_____ *Observations on a Tour Through Almost the whole of England, and a considerable part of Scotland* (1801).

_____ *The Professional Life of Mr. Dibdin, written by himself. Together with the words of six hundred songs selected from his works*, 4 vols. (1803).

_____ *Songs &c. In Britons Strike Home A New Entertainment of Sans Souci* (1803).

DIBDIN, CHARLES ISAAC MUNGO, *The Water Spectre: or, Kitty o' the Clyde: A Romance* (1805).

_____ *History and Illustrations of the London Theatres* (1826).

_____ *Professional and Literary Memoirs of Charles Dibdin the Younger, Dramatist and Upward of Thirty Years Manager of Minor Theatres*, ed. George Speaight (London: Society for Theatre Research, 1956).

DIBDIN, THOMAS JOHN, *The Mouth of the Nile: or, The Glorious first of August, a musical entertainment, etc.* (1798).

_____ *The Naval Pillar: a musical entertainment, etc.* (1799).

_____ *Songs, Chorusses, &c. In The New Pantomime of Harlequin's Tour; or, The Dominion of Fancy* (1800).

_____ *Airs, Chorusses, &c. and A List of the Scenery, in the New Comic Pantomime, called Harlequin in his Element, or Fire, Water, Earth, & Air. As Performed At the Theatre Royal, Covent-Garden Theatre* (1806).

_____ *Scales's Edition. A Description of Harlequin in his Element, or Fire, Water, Earth, & Air. A New Popular Pantomime Performing with Universal Applause, At Covent-Garden Theatre* (1806).

_____ *Harlequin in his Element: or, Fire, Water, Earth, & Air* (Appleyards, 1807).

_____ *Harlequin in his Element; or, Fire, Water, Earth, & Air; A Favourite Pantomime. As Performed at The Theatre Royal, Covent Garden* (London: Appleyards, 1807–8 [*sic*]). This edition is in Beinecke Library, Yale University.

DIBDIN, THOMAS JOHN, *The Reminiscences of Thomas Dibdin*, 2 vols. (1837).

Dreadful Catastrophe [Sadler's Wells, Thursday, 15 October 1807], BL Shelfmark Crach I. Tab. 4.5. 4/3/1.

The Duke's Coat; or, The Night After Waterloo: A Dramatick Anecdote; Prepared For Representation on The 6th September, At The Theatre-Royal, Lyceum, And Interdicted By The Licenser Of Plays (1815).

E., S. N., *The Murdered Maid; or, The Clock Struck Four!!! A Drama, in Three Acts* (Warwick, 1818).

EATON, DANIEL ISAAC, *Politics for the People* (1793).

EGAN, PIERCE, *The Life of an Actor* (1825).

⸻ *Show Folks!* (1831).

ELLISTON, ROBERT WILLIAM, *The Venetian Outlaw, A Drama in Three Acts, As Performed at the Theatre Royal, Drury Lane* (1805).

⸻ *Copy Of A Memorial Presented To The Lord Chamberlain, By The Committee Of Management Of The Theatre-Royal Drury-Lane, Against The Olympic And Sans Pareil Theatres; With Copies Of Two Letters, In Reply To The Contents Of Such Memorial, Addressed To The Lord Chamberlain* (1818).

EVANS, THOMAS, *Christian Policy the Salvation of the Empire* (1816).

EVERARD, EDWARD CAPE, *Memoirs Of An Unfortunate Son Of Thespis; Being A Sketch Of The Life Of Edward Cape Everard, Comedian* (1818).

EYRE, EDMUND JOHN, *The Fatal Sisters; or, The Castle of the Forest: A Dramatic Romance, of Five Acts. With a Variety of Poetic Essays* (1788).

⸻ *The Maid of Normandy; or, The Death of the Queen of France, A Tragedy in Four Acts; as Performed at the Theatre Wolverhampton* (1794).

FAIRBURN, JOHN, *The Life of Wm. Henry West Betty, The Celebrated and Wonderful Young Roscius: Containing the Particulars of his Theatrical Career, His Education, Character, & Abilities; Together with an Impartial Account of his Astonishing Performances on* [sic] *the London Theatres* (1804).

⸻ *Fairburn's Laughable Songster, and Fashionable Quizzer, For 1809* (1809).

⸻ *Remarks on the Cause of the Dispute Between the Public and Managers of the Theatre Royal, Covent Garden, With a Circumstantial Account of the Week's Performances and the Uproar . . . illustrated with a large Caricature Frontispiece of the House that Jack built* (1809).

[FARINGTON, J.], *The Diary of Joseph Farington* ed. Kenneth Garlick and Angus Macintyre (New Haven and London: Yale University Press for the Paul Mellon Centre for Studies in British Art, 1978).

The Fatal Effects of Gambling Exemplified in the Murder of Wm. Weare, and the Trial and Fate of John Thurtell, The Murderer ... to which is added, The Gambler's Scourge; a Complete Exposé of the Whole System of Gambling in the Metropolis; With Memoirs and Anecdotes of Notorious Blacklegs (1824).

FENNELL, JAMES, *An Apology for the Life of James Fennell. Written by Himself* (Philadelphia, 1814).

FOOTE, HORACE, *A Companion to the Theatres; and Manual of The British Drama* (1829).

Fraternal and Philanthropic Policy, or Articles of the British Fraternal and Philanthropic Community, United against Monopoly and Extortion (1797).

Friend to 'Fair Play and a Free Stage', A, *Letter To The Right Hon. Robert Peel, Respecting The Proposed Introduction Of A Bill, To Repeal So Much Of The Act Of 10th Geo.Ii.Cap.28, As Requires Notice To Be Sent To The Lord Chamberlain ... And Showing That The Consequence Of Such An Act Would Be, To Confirm The Monopoly Claimed By The Proprietors Of Drury Lane And Covent Garden, And To Enable Them To Annihilate The Minor Theatres* (1829).

Friend to Justice, A, *A Reply To The Remarks Of The Rev. Luke Booker, L.L.D. In A Pamphlet Entitled 'A Moral Review' Of The Conduct And Case Of Mary Ashford, &C.* (1818).

FROST, THOMAS, *The Old Showmen, And the Old London Fairs* (London: Tinsley Brothers, 1874).

Full Report of the Trial of Abraham Thornton for the Wilful Murder of Mary Ashford, at Penn's Mills, Near Sutton Coldfield, in the County of Warwick (Birmingham, n.d.).

The Gamblers, A new Melo-Drama, in Two Acts, Of Peculiar Interest, As Performed for the 1st and 2d Times November 17 & 18, 1823, Suppressed by Order of the Court of King's Bench, Re-Performed For the 3d Time, Monday, January 12, 1824, at the New Surrey Theatre (1824).

GARRICK, DAVID, [*A Christmas Tale*] *A New Dramatic Entertainment, Called A Christmas Tale. In Five Parts. As it is Performed at the Theatre-Royal in Drury Lane. Embellished with an Etching, by Mr. Loutherbourg, 2nd ed.* (1774).

The Genuine Life of Mr. Francis Swing (1831).

GILLILAND, THOMAS, *A Dramatic Synopsis, Containing an Essay on the Political and Moral Use of a Theatre; Involving Remarks on the Dramatic Writers of the Present Day, and Strictures on the Performers of the Two Theatres* (1804).

―――― *Elbow Room, A Pamphlet: containing remarks on the shameful increase of the private boxes of Covent Garden, with a variety of original observations relating to the management of that theatre. Also a comparative view of the two houses, shewing the puerility of a great man's prophecy, who was to have turned Drury Lane Theatre into a 'splendid desert', &c. &c.* (1804).

GLOVER, RICHARD, *London: or, The Progress of Commerce* (1739).

GRANT, JAMES, *Sketches in London* (1838).

GRAVES, RICHARD, *Senilities; or Solitary Amusements: in Prose and Verse: With a Cursory Disquisition on the Future Condition of the Sexes* (1801).

GRAY, THOMAS, *An Elegy, Written in a Country Church-yard. A New Edition: As Deliver'd By Mr. Palmer At the Royalty Theatre, Goodman's Fields* (1787).

Great Sea Snake, and Gaffer Grey (c.1800).

GREVILLE, HENRY FRANCIS, *Mr. Greville's Statement Of Mr. Naldi's Case* (1811).

HARRAL, T., *A Monody On the Death of Mr. John Palmer, The Comedian. To Which is Prefixed a Review of his Theatrical Powers* (1798).

HARRIS, MICHAEL (ed.), *The Proceedings of the Old Bailey*, microform (Brighton: Harvester Microform, 1984); www.oldbaileyonline.org

HAWES, ROBERT, *Constitutional Toasts, Good Wishes, &c. An humble Offering To the Friends of Liberty* (c.1789).

The Hertford Genuine Edition of the Trials of John Thurtell and Joseph Hunt, for the Murder of Mr. Weare, etc. (1824).

HITCHIN, EDWARD, *A sermon Preached at the New Meeting, in White-Row Spital-Fields, On Thursday 29 November 1759* (1759).

HOLROYD, EDWARD, *Observations Upon The Case of Abraham Thornton . . . Shewing The Danger Of Pressing Presumptive Evidence Too Far, Together With The Only True And Authentic Account Yet Published Of The Evidence Given At The Trial, The Examination Of The Prisoner, &C. And A Correct Plan Of The Locus In Quo* (1819).

HOOK, THEODORE EDWARD, *Facts Illustrative of the Treatment of Napoleon Buonaparte in Saint Helena* (1819).

____ *Radical Harmonist; or, A Collection of Songs and Toasts given at the late Crown and Anchor Dinner* (1820).

____ *The Choice Humorous Works, Ludicrous Adventures, Bon Mots, Puns and Hoaxes of Theodore Edward Hook With a New Life of the Author* (1873).

Horrible Rape and Murder!! The Affecting case of Mary Ashford, A beautiful young Virgin, Who was diabolically Ravished, Murdered, and thrown into a Pit, as she was returning from a Dance; Including The Trial Of Abraham Thornton For The Wilful Murder Of The Said . . . To Which Is Added . . . A Correct Plan Of The Spot Where The Rape And Murder Were Committed, &c. &c (1817).

HUISH, ROBERT, *The Red Barn. A Tale, Founded on Fact* (1828).

The Humble Petition of the Proprietors of the Theatres Royal Drury Lane and Covent Garden (1832).

HUMPHREYS, R., *The Memoirs Of J. Decastro, Comedian . . . Accompanied By An Analysis Of The Life Of The Late Philip Astley, Esq. . . . Also An Accompanying History Of The Royal Circus, Now The Surrey Theatre* (1824).

HUNT, JAMES HENRY LEIGH, *Leigh Hunt's Dramatic Criticism, 1808–1831*, ed. Lawrence Huston Houtchens and Carolyn Washburn Houtchens (New York: Columbia University Press, 1949).

HUTCHINSON, WILLIAM, *Spirit of Masonry in Moral and Elucidatory Lectures* (1775).

HYATT, CHARLES, *The sinner detected : A sermon preached in the open air near the red barn at Polstead, and at the meetinghouse, Boxford, Suffolk, and in the afternoon and evening of . . . the 17th of August, 1828, on occasion of the execution of William Corder for the murder of Maria Marten, including particulars of his life never before published* (1828).

An Investigation of the Case of Abraham Thornton . . . Tried . . . For The Wilful Murder and Afterwards Arraigned for the Rape, of Mary Ashford; (Of Which Charges He Was That Day Acquitted) . . . Being An Answer To A Work . . . Entitled, Wager Of Battle (1818).

IRELAND, WILLIAM HENRY, *Vortigern. A Tragedy in five Acts* (1796).

____ *Chalcographimania; or, The Portrait-Collector and Printseller's Chronicle, with Infatuations of every Description. A humorous poem in four books. With copious notes explanatory. By Satiricus Sculptor* (1814).

____ *Something Concerning Nobody, Embellished with Fourteen Characteristic Etchings* (1814).

IRELAND, WILLIAM HENRY, *Memoirs of a Young Greek Lady* (1823).

Is God's Hand Shortened in 1829 Years? Yet Forty Days and BABY-LONDON shall be Overthrown by The Modern March of Mind in England and Ireland towards Liberty and Equality (1829).

JACKMAN, ISAAC, *Royal and Royalty Theatres. Letter to Phillips Glover, Esq of Wispington, In Lincolnshire; in a Dedication to the Burletta of Hero and Leander, now performing, with the most distinguished applause, at the Royalty Theatre, in Goodman's Fields* (1787).

JOHNSON, CAPTAIN C., *Lives of the Most Remarkable Female Robbers* (1801).

JONES, GEORGE HENRY, *Account of the Murder of the late Mr. William Weare. . ..: including the circumstances which first led to the discovery of the murder, and the detection of the murderers. The depositions taken before the Magistrates, the coroners inquest, the trials of the murderers, and the execution of John Thurtell ... portraits of the prisoners, John Thurtell, Jos. Hunt, and Wm. Probert. Drawn by Mr. George Lewis; with their autographs. Illustrated with a ground plan of Gill's-hill cottage and garden and a map of the surrounding country* (1824).

JONES, ROBERT, *Artificial Fire-Works, Improved to the Modern Practice*, 2nd edn. (1766).

The Judgment of the Court of King's Bench Upon the Rev. Robert Taylor, A.B. M.R.C.S. on a Conviction of Blasphemy Toward the Christian Religion ... 7th of February, 1828 (1828).

KEMBLE, JOHN PHILIP, *The Dramatic Scorpion. A Satire, in Three Cantos, With Explanatory Notes* (1818).

KENDALL, EDWARD AUGUSTUS, *An Argument For Construing Largely The Right Of An Appellee Of Murder, To Insist On His Wager Of Battle, And Also For Abrogating Writs Of Appeal* (1817).

KERR, JOHN, *Presumptive Guilt, or, The Fiery Ordeal; A Grand Melo Dramatic Spectacle In Three Acts. Performed At The Regency Theatre Of Variety, With Universal Approbation; For The First Time On Monday, Oct. 19, 1818* (1818).

KILHAM, ALEXANDER, *The Hypocrite Detected And Exposed; And The True Christian Vindicated And Supported: In a Sermon Preached From A Passage In A Play-Bill, December 15, 1793, In The Methodist Chapel In This City. With A Reply, In an Appendix, To A Paper Signed Civis, Concerning Dancing. And A Postscript, With Remarks, On The Mr. Lee Lewes's Answer* (Aberdeen, 1793).

The Lady of Pleasure and Fashion. Being the Remarkable Adventures of the Celebrated Mary Morris, The Chaunting Beggar-Girl, and Strolling Actress. Displaying Vicissitudes of Low and High Life, As Led by a Beautiful Girl; Through the Metricious Arts of Seduction, Intrigue, and Cyprian Amours [*c*.1821].

LANCE, EDWARD JARMAN, *The Golden Farmer, Being an Attempt to Unite the Facts Pointed Out by Nature, in the Sciences of Geology, Chemistry, and Botany* (1831).

LARCHER, ANDREW, *A Remedy For Establishing Universal Peace And Happiness, Against Universal Oppression, And Dangerous Tumults, Or, The Friendly Dictates Of Common Sense, To All Working People, Especially To The Silk Weavers Of London* ... ONE FIRMLY UNITED FRIENDLY AND PHILANTHROPIC SOCIETY OF FREE TRADESMEN (1796).

——— *A True Description of the Real Causes and Principles of the British Fraternal and Philanthropic Community, United against Monopoly and Extortion* (1796).

Laugh When You Can; or, The Monstrous Droll Jester ... To Which is added, The Benevolent Jew, as Recited at The Royalty Theatre [*c*.1795–8].

LEE, RICHARD, *By General Desire ... On the Grand Theatre at St. James's, An Entire new Pantomime, called the Royal Vagabonds* [*c*.1791].

LEWES, CHARLES LEE, *Comic Sketches; Or, The Comedian His Own Manager ... The Whole Forming Matter Sufficient for Two Evenings' Entertainment; Originally Intended for the East Indies* (1804).

The Life of Joseph Balsamo, Commonly Called Count Cagliostro (1791).

LOWNDES, HANNAH MARIA, *The gamblers; or, The treacherous friend: a moral tale, founded on recent facts ... Embellished with engravings* (1824).

LUCIA, *The Life of the Count Cagliostro* (1787).

LUDLAM, GEORGE, *The Mysterious Murder, or, What's the Clock, a Melo Drama, in Three Acts. Founded on a Tale too True* (1818).

MACARTHY, EUGENE, *A Letter To The King, On The Question Now At Issue Between The 'Major', And 'Minor' Theatres* (1832).

MACAULEY, ELIZABETH, *Theatric Revolution; or, Plain Truth Addressed To Common Sense* (1819).

——— *Facts Against Falsehood! Being A Brief Statement Of Miss Macauley's Engagements At The Winter Theatres; The Subterfuges By Which She Has Been Driven From The Regular Exercise Of Her Profession, And Withheld*

From At Least Two Thirds Of The Public Of This Metropolis. Also Her Letters Of Appeal To The Present Managers (1824).

Major And Minor Theatres. A Concise View Of The Question, As Regards, The Public, The Patentees, And The Profession With Remarks On The Decline Of The Drama, And The Means Of Its Restoration To Which Is Added The Petition Now Lying For Signature (1832).

MALCOLM, JAMES PELLER, *Anecdotes Of The Manners And Customs Of London During The Eighteenth-Century Including The Charities, Depravities, Dresses, And Amusements, Of The Citizens Of London During That Period; With A Review Of The State Of Society In 1807*, 2 vols. (1810).

——— *Essay on the Principles of Population* (1798).

——— *An Investigation of the Cause of the Present High Price of Provisions* (1800).

Map of the Roads near to the spot where Mary Ashford was murdered (Birmingham, 1817).

MATHEWS, ANNE, *Memoirs of Charles Mathews, Comedian*, 2 vols. (1838).

MATHEWS, CHARLES, *Second Edition/Duncombe's Edition. The Theatrical Album; or, Comedian at Home . . . Sketches from Mr. Mathews's Entertainment of Earth, Air, And Water* (1821).

——— *Entirely New Entertainment. Mathews in America; or, The Theatrical Wanderer: A Cargo of New Characters, Original Songs And concluding Piece of the Wild Goose Chase, Or the Inn At Baltimore* (1823).

MAYHEW, EDWARD, *Stage Effect: or, The Principles which Command Dramatic Success in the Theatre* (1840).

MEISTER, HENRY, *Letters Written During a Residence in England* (1799).

MILNER, H. M., *The Hertfordshire Tragedy; or, The Victims of Gaming. A Serious Drama. In Two Acts. (Founded upon Recent Melancholy Facts,) as First Performed at The Royal Coburg Theatre, On Monday, Jan. 12, 1824* (1824).

Mr. Lutherburg [sic] A true Copy of the Writing put up in his Room, where Patients wait, on Thursday, the second of July, 1789 (BL *Lysons Collectana.* C.191. c.16 vol. 1 (2). fol. 161).

The Modern Stage. A Letter To The Hon. George Lamb, M.P. On The Decay And Degradation Of English Dramatic Literature: With A Proposal For The Encouragement Of Composition For The Stage, By The Legislative Protection Of New Pieces; So That They Might Be Produced In The

Provincial Theatres, Or Otherwise Published, With An Adequate Reward, Independent Of The Caprice Of Arbitrary Judges (1819).

MONCRIEFF, WILLIAM THOMAS, [*Giovanni in the Country*] *Songs, Duets, Choruses &c. &c. &c. Sung in the New Comic Operatic Melo-Dramatic Pantomimic Moral Satirical Gallymaufrical Parodiacal Salmagundical Olla Podriadacal Extravaganza Bizarro Entertainment* ... *Yclept Giovanni in the Country; or, the Rake Husband: as performed at the Royal Coburg Theatre* (1820).

——— *Modern Collegians; or, Over The Bridge. A Half Hours Comic Sketch Before Dinner* ... *As Performed At The Royal Coburg Theatre, October 9th 1820* (1820).

——— *Prison Thoughts* (1821).

——— [*Actors Al Fresco*] *Songs, Duets, Trios, Choruses, &c. &c. in Actors Al Fresco; or, the Play in the Pleasure Grounds; (an Occasional Vaudeville) First Produced at the Royal Gardens, Vauxhall, 4ᵗʰ June, 1827* ... *To be had only in the Gardens* (1827).

——— *Selection from the Dramatic Works of William T. Moncrieff* (1851).

MORTON, THOMAS, *The Slave; A Musical Drama, in Three Acts; As Performed at the Theatre-Royal, Covent-Garden* (1816).

Murder of Mary Ashford ... *Report of the Proceedings against A. Thornton in the Court of King's Bench etc.* (Birmingham, 1817).

MURPHY, ARTHUR, *Songs, &c. in the Deserter of Naples; or, Royal Clemency: To Which is Added, An Ode to Friendship, A Tale from Baker's Chronicle, Address for the Marine Society, Mr. Lee Lewes's Farewell Address, and other favourite Pieces Performed at the Royalty Theatre* (1787).

MURRAY, LINDLEY, *Sentiments of Pious and Eminent Persons on the Pernicious Tendency of Dramatic Entertainments, and other Vain Amusements*, 4th edn. (1823).

The New British Theatre; a Selection of original drama, not yet acted; some of which have been offered for representation but not accepted (1814).

New Lights on Jacobinism, Abstracted from Professor Robison's History of Free Masonry. With an Appendix, Containing An Account of Voltaire's behaviour on his Death-bed, and a Letter from J. H. Stone, (Who was tried for Sedition,) To his Friend Dr. Priestley, Disclosing the Principles of Jacobinism (1798).

NICHOLSON, RENTON, *Autobiography of a Fast Man* (1863).

The number of little Theatres already opened ... having greatly injured the Theatres Royal ... [c.1810].

OULTON, WALLEY CHAMBERLAIN, and BENJAMIN VICTOR, *The History of the Theatres of London ... Being a Continuation of Victor's and Oulton's Histories, From the Year 1795 to 1817 Inclusive* (1818).

PACK, JAMES, *Some Account Of The Life And Experience Of James Pack, Late A Celebrated Actor, In The Pantomime Department, At ... Drury Lane ... But Now, By The Grace Of God, A Disciple And Follower Of The Lord Jesus Christ* (1819).

[*Pantomimic Preludio, And The Paris Federation*] *A Sketch Of The Entertainment, Now Performing At The Royalty Theatre, In Two Parts: Consisting Of A Pantomimic Preludio, And The Paris Federation. To which is added, The Popular French Music* (1790).

Particulars and Conditions of Sale of the Olympic Theatre ... 13th June, 1820 (1820).

PATERSON, PETER, *Behind the Scenes: Being the Confessions of a Strolling Player* (Edinburgh: D. Mathers, 1859).

PERKINS, ERASMUS [CANNON, GEORGE] *The Trial of the Rev. Robt. Wedderburn, (A Dissenting Minister of the Unitarian persuasion,) For Blasphemy, Before Sir Charles Abbott, Knight, Lord Chief-Justice, and a Special Jury, in the Court of King's Bench, Westminster, The Sittings after Hilary Term, 1820; Containing a Verbatim Report of the Defence* (1820).

PIGGOTT, SAMUEL, *The Voice of Blood, and the Voice of Conscience! or, the causes of sanguinary atrocity traced ... A sermon* [on Gen. 4: 10–13] *occasioned by the ... murder of Mr. Weare, etc.* (1824).

PINDAR, PETER Jr., [George Daniel], *The Plotting Managers, A Poetical Satyrical Interlude: To Which is Prefixed A Letter to Lord S—dn—y, On his recommending the Suppression of the Royalty-Theatre* (1787).

—— *Bubbles Of Treason; Or, State Trials At Large. Being A Poetical Epistle From An Irishman In London To His Brother In Paris; And Containing A Humorous Epitome Of The Charge, Evidence And Defence* (1817).

[PLACE, F.], *The Autobiography of Francis Place, 1771–1854* ed. Mary Thale (Cambridge: Cambridge University Press, 1972).

PLAGIARY, PETER [pseud.], *The Song Smith and Story Stitcher; Or, the Humours of a Strolling Player: A Dramatic Olio ... With a Portion of Original Matter* (1818).

A Poetical Epistle; Being the Farewell Address of the Royalty Theatre, to its late beloved Master, John Astley, Esq. (1807).

POWELL, JAMES, *The Narcotic and Private Theatricals. Two Dramatic Pieces by James Powell of the Custom House* (1793).

____ *The Venetian Outlaw, His Country's Friend. A Drama, in Three Acts, Now Performing at the Theatre Royal, Drury-Lane, with unbounded Applause . . . Altered from the French of A. Pixiricourt* (1805).

____ *Furibond; Or, Harlequin Negro. The Songs Choruses &C. With A Descriptions Of The Pantomime. As Performed At The Theatre Royal, Drury-Lane. Monday, December, 28th* (1807).

PRATT, MARY, *A List of a Few Cures performed by Mr and Mrs de Loutherbourg . . . without Medicine* (1789).

PRATT, S. J., *Sympathy, and Other Poems* (1807).

PRIESTLEY, JOSEPH, *Dr. Priestley's Letter to the Inhabitants of Birmingham* (1791).

Proposals for the Royal Coburg Theatre [c.1817].

The Recruiting Serjeant, A Musical Entertainment, As it is Performed at the Royalty Theatre, Wellclose-Square (1787).

REID, WILLIAM HAMILTON, *The Rise and Dissolution of the Infidel Societies in this Metropolis: including the origin of modern deism and atheism . . . from the publication of Paine's Age of Reason till the present period* (1800).

Remarks on the Cause of the Dispute Between the Public and Managers of the Theatre Royal, Covent Garden, With a Circumstantial Account of the Week's Performances and the Uproar . . . illustrated with a large Caricature Frontispiece of the House that Jack built (1809).

The Report Of The Lord Chancellor And The Other Judges To His Majesty On The Investigation Of The Subject Of The Different Theatrical Petitions Was As Follows [19 February 1831].

Report of the Trial of Mrs. Susannah Wright, for publishing, in his shop, the Writings and Correspondences of R. Carlile; Before Chief Justice Abbott . . . Monday, July 8, 1822. Indictment at the Instance of the Society for the Suppression of Vice (1822).

Report from the Select Committee on Dramatic Literature: With The Minutes of Evidence . . . 2 August 1832, Parliamentary Papers (1831–2), vol. vii.

A Review of the Present Contest Between the Managers of the Winter Theatres, the Little Theatre in the Hay-market, and the Royalty Theatre in Well-close Square. To Which are Added, Several Authentic Papers (1787).

RITCHIE, J. EWIN, *The Night Side of London* (1857).

Robbery. Whereas the Office belonging to the Theatre, was last Night between the Hours of Eleven and Twelve, burglariously entered by some Villain or Villains, who broke open the Desk and stole the following Property: . . . Reward of Twenty Pounds . . . Theatre Royal, Margate, Saturday, August 2, 1794.

ROGERS, CHARLES, *The Book of Wallace* (1889).

Royal Coburg Theatre. In order to form a just opinion . . . (1817).

Royalty Theatre, Well-close-Square. The Theatre is perfectly aired, having had Fires in it for some Time. Eidouranion: Or, Large Transparent Orrery. On this elaborate and splendid Machine, which is 15 Feet Diameter, and has been exhibited Five Seasons in the Theatres-Royal Haymarket and Covent Garden, Mr. Walker, Jun. Will Deliver His Astronomical Lecture . . . Books of the Lecture may be had of the Box-keeper, at the Theatre . . . April 10 1793 (1793).

RYLEY, SAMUEL WILLIAM, *The Itinerant, or Memoirs of an Actor* (1817).

S____ E, G. W., *A Short Account of the Life & Death of Swing, the Rick-Burner; Written by One Well Acquainted with Him. Together with the Confession of Thomas Goodman, Now under Sentence of Death, in Horsham Jail, for Rick-Burning* (1830).

S., J. W., *The Innocent Usurper, A Musical Drama, founded upon the Demofoonte of Metastasio. As offered to the Managers of Covent Garden Theatre, June, 1819* (1821).

SHEE, MARTIN ARCHER, *Alasco: A Tragedy, in Five Acts . . . Excluded from the Stage by the Authority of the Lord Chamberlain* (1824).

SHELLEY, P. B., *A Philosophical View of Reform* (1819).

SIBLY, MANOAH, *A Collection of Thirty Remarkable Nativities* (1789).

____ *Supplement to Placidus De Titus; Containing The Nativity of that Wonderful Phaenomenon, Oliver Cromwell* (1790).

SLOMAN, CHARLES, *Fitful Fancies of An Improvisatore* (c.1850).

SMITH, JOHN THOMAS, *A Book for a Rainy Day: or, Recollections of the events of the Last Sixty-Six Years* (1845).

Stamford, Lincolnshire, playbills.

STEDMAN, JOHN GABRIEL, *Curious Adventures of Captain Stedman, During an Expedition to Surinam, In 1773; Including The Struggles of the Negroes, And the Barbarities of the Planters, Dreadful Executions, The Manner of Selling Slaves, Mutiny of Sailors, Soldiers, &c. And various Other Interesting Articles* (1805).

STEVENS, GEORGE ALEXANDER, *The Celebrated Lecture on Heads; which has been exhibited upwards of Two Hundred and Fifty successive Nights* (1766).

—— *The Trip to Portsmouth; A Comic Sketch of One Act, With Songs* (1773).

STRUTT, JOSEPH, *The Sports and Pastimes of the People of England* (1801).

The Surprising Life and Adventures of Robin Hood . . . To which is added, The Wonderful Life of William Davis, Commonly called the Golden Farmer (1805).

TAYLOR, ROBERT, *Swing: or, Who Are The Incendiaries? A Tragedy, Founded On Late Circumstances And As Performed At The Rotunda.* (1831).

The Temple of Virtue, A Masonic Ode; As performed at the Theatre in Southampton, on Monday the 15th of September, 1777 (Southampton, 1777).

THACKERAY, THOMAS JAMES, *On Theatrical Emancipation, And the Rights of Dramatic Authors* (1832).

Theatre, Haymarket, Feb.17, 1794 [handbill].

Theatrical Monopoly; Being an Address to the Public on the Present Alarming Coalition of the Managers of the Winter Theatres (1779).

THIRLWALL, THOMAS, *Royalty Theatre. A Solemn Protest Against The Revival Of Scenic Exhibitions And Interludes, At The Royalty Theatre; Containing Remarks On Pizarro, The Stranger, And John Bull; With A Postscript* (1803).

Thornton's Trial!! The Trial of Abraham Thornton, At the Warwick Summer Assize, On Friday the 8th day of August, 1817, for the murder of Mary Ashford, in the Lordship of Sutton Coldfield (Warwick, 1817).

TOMLINS, F. G., *A Brief View of the English Drama . . . with Suggestions for Elevating the present condition of the art, and of its professors* (1840).

The Trial of James Hadfield, At the Court of King's Bench, Before Lord Kenyon, on the 26th of June, 1800, for High Treason in Attempting the Life of the King on the Fifteenth of May, Last (Newcastle upon Tyne, 1800).

True Blue: or, The Press-Gang. And the Story of John Gilpin . . . As Performing at the Royalty-Theatre, Wellclose-Square (1787).

A Very Plain State of the Case, or The Royalty Theatre Versus the Theatres Royal (1787).

A View Of London, Or, The Stranger's Guide Through The British Metropolis (1803–4).

WALCOT, JOHN, *The Works of Peter Pindar* (1816).

WALDRON, FRANCIS GODOLPHIN, *The Man With Two Wives; or, Wigs For Ever! A Dramatick Fable; By F. G. Waldron. Set To Musick By Mr. Sanderson. And First Performed At The Royalty Theatre, Saturday, March 24th. 1798* (1798).

WALLACE, EGLANTINE, *The Ton; or, Follies of Fashion. A Comedy* (1788).

—— *The Conduct of the King of Prussia and General Dumourier, Investigated* (1793).

——*A Sermon Addressed to the People, Pointing out the only sure method to obtain a speedy peace and reform* (1794).

—— *The Whim, A Comedy In Three Acts . . . With an Address to the Public, Upon the Arbitrary and Unjust Aspersion of the Licenser Against its Political Sentiments. Offered to be Acted for the Benefit of the hospital and Poor of the Isle of Thanet, But Refused the Royal Licence* (Margate, 1795).

WEBSTER, BENJAMIN NOTTINGHAM, *The Golden Farmer; or, The Last Crime: A Domestic Drama* (1833).

WIGHTWICK, GEORGE, *Theatricals 45 Years Ago* (Portishead, Somerset, 1862).

WILSON, F. A., *Epistolary Remonstrance to Thomas Morton Esq, Dramatic Writer And Professed Critic and Reader to Captain Polhill and His Majesty's Servants of Drury Lane Theatre* (1832).

WINSTON, JAMES, *The Theatric Tourist; Being A Genuine Collection Of Correct Views, With Brief And Authentic Historical Accounts Of All The Principal Provincial Theatres In The United Kingdom. Replete With Useful And Necessary Information To Theatrical Professors, Whereby They May Learn How To Chuse And Regulate Their Country Engagements; And With Numerous Anecdotes To Amuse The Reader* (1805).

The Words of the Most Favorite [sic] Songs, Duets, &c. Sung at the Royal Amphitheatre, Westminster-Bridge, and the Royalty Theatre, Well-Close Square (Lambeth, 1802).

The Woman of the Town; or, Authentic Memoirs of Phebe Phillips . . . Well Known in the vicinity of Covent Garden. Written by Herself (1801).

WRIGHT, SUSANNAH, *Report of the Trial of Mrs. Susannah Wright, for publishing, in his shop, the Writings and Correspondences of R. Carlile; Before Chief Justice Abbott . . . Monday, July 8, 1822. Indictment at the Instance of the Society for the Suppression of Vice* (1822).

Wager Of Battle. Thornton And Mary Ashford; Or An Antidote To Prejudice (1818).

ZEALOUSHEAD, ZACHARY [pseud.], *Plots And Placemen, Or Green Bag Glory, An Historical Melo Drama, In Two Acts . . . As performed at the Boroughmongers' Private Theatre. In the Course of the Piece are Introduced Original Parodies On Part of the Works of Shakespeare. Milton. Pope. Rowe. Walter Scott. Lord Byron. Southey, &c. And also An Original Parody on Rule Britannia* (1817).

Secondary Sources

ALLEN, RALPH G., '*A Christmas Tale*, or, Harlequin Scene Painter', *Texas Studies in Literature*, 19 (1974), 149–61.

ALLERTON, JAMES F., and JOHN W. ROBINSON, *English Theatrical Literature 1559–1900* (London: Society for Theatre Research, 1970).

ALTICK, RICHARD, *The Shows of London* (Cambridge, Mass.: Belknap Press of Harvard University Press, 1978).

ARUNDEL, DENNIS *The Story of Sadler's Wells, 1683–1977* (Newton Abbot: David & Charles, 1978).

BAER, MARC, *Theatre and Disorder in Late Georgian London* (Oxford: Clarendon Press, 1992).

BARRELL, JOHN (ed.), *Painting and the Politics of Culture: New Essays on British Art 1700–1850* (Oxford: Oxford University Press, 1992).

——— *Imagining the King's Death: Figurative Treason, Fantasies of Regicide 1793–1796* (Oxford: Oxford University Press, 2000).

——— '*Exhibition Extraordinary!!': Radical Broadsides of the Mid-1790s* (Nottingham: Trent Editions, 2001).

BATE, JONATHAN, *Shakespearian Constitutions: Politics, Theatre, Criticism 1730–1830* (Oxford: Clarendon Press, 1989).

BAUGH, CHRISTOPHER, *Garrick and Loutherbourg* (Cambridge and Alexandria, Va.: Chadwyck-Healey, 1990).

BEAUDRY, HENRY R., *The English Theatre and John Keats*, Salzburg Studies in English Literature (Salzburg: University of Salzburg, 1973).

BEEDELL, A. V., 'John Reeves's Prosecution for Seditious Libel, 1795–1796: A Study in Political Cynicism', *Historical Journal*, 36: 4 (1993) 810–11

BEHRENDT, STEPHEN C., *Royal Mourning and Regency Culture: Elegies and Memorials of Princess Charlotte* (Basingstoke: Macmillan, 1997).

BERG, MAXINE, 'New Commodities, Luxuries and their Consumers in Eighteenth-Century England', in Maxine Berg and Helen Clifford (eds.), *Consumers and Luxury: Consumer Culture in Europe 1650–1850* (Manchester: Manchester University Press, 1999), 63–85.

BINDMAN, DAVID (ed.), *The Shadow of the Guillotine: Britain and the French Revolution* (London: British Museum, 1989).

BOLTON, BETSY, *Women, Nationalism, and the Romantic Stage: Theatre and Politics in Britain, 1780–1800* (Cambridge: Cambridge University Press, 2001).

BREWER, JOHN, '"The Most Polite Age and the Most Vicious": Attitudes towards Culture as a Commodity, 1660–1800', in Ann Bermingham and John Brewer (eds.), *The Consumption of Culture 1600–1800: Image, Object, Text* (London: Routledge, 1995), 341–61.

—— 'Reconstructing the Reader: Prescriptions, Texts and Strategies in Anna Larpent's Reading', in James Raven, Helen Small, and Naomi Tadmore (eds.), *The Practice and Representation of Reading in England* (Cambridge: Cambridge University Press, 1996).

—— *The Pleasures of the Imagination: English Culture in the Eighteenth Century* (London: HarperCollins, 1997).

BROADBENT, R. J., *A History of Pantomime* (London: Simpkins, Marshall, Hamilton, Kent & Co., 1901).

BROCK, ALAN St. H., *A History of Fireworks* (London: Harrap, 1949).

BURROUGHS, CATHERINE B., *Closet Stages: Joanna Baillie and the Theater Theory of British Romantic Writers* (Philadelphia: University of Pennsylvania Press, 1997).

—— *Women in British Romantic Theatre: Drama, Performance, and Society, 1790–1840* (Cambridge: Cambridge University Press, 2000).

BYRNE, PAULA, *Jane Austen and the Theatre* (London: Hambledon, 2002).

CHANDLER, JAMES, *England in 1819: The Politics of Literary Culture and the Case of Romantic Historicism* (Chicago: University of Chicago Press, 1998).

CHASE, MALCOLM, *'The People's Farm': English Radical Agrarianism 1775–1840* (Oxford: Clarendon Press, 1988).

CHARLESWORTH, ANDREW, *Social Protest in a Rural Society: The Spatial Diffusion of the Captain Swing Disturbances of 1830–1831* (Norwich: Geo Abstracts, 1978).

CLARK, ANNA, 'Queen Caroline and the Sexual Politics of Culture in London, 1820', *Representations*, 31 (1990), 47–68.

_____ *Scandal: The Sexual Politics of the British Constitution* (Princeton: Princeton University Press, 2003).

CLAYTON, TIMOTHY, *The English Print, 1688–1802* (London and New Haven: Yale University Press, 1997).

COLOMBO, CLAIRE MILLER, '"This pen of mine will say too much": Public Performance in the Journals of Anna Larpent', *Texas Studies in Literature and Language: A Journal of the Humanities*, 38:3/4 (1996), 285–301.

CONOLLY, L. W., *The Censorship of English Drama, 1737–1824* (San Marino, Calif.: Huntington Library, 1976).

COX, JEFFREY N., and MICHAEL GAMER (eds.), *The Broadview Anthology of Romantic Drama* (Peterborough, Ont.: Broadview Press, 2003).

CUNNINGHAM, JOHN E., *Theatre Royal: The History of the Theatre Royal Birmingham* (Oxford: George Ronald, 1950).

DANIELS, STEPHEN, 'Loutherbourg's Chemical Theatre: Coalbrookdale by Night', in John Barrell (ed.), *Painting and the Politics of Culture: New Essays on British Art 1700–1850* (Oxford: Oxford University Press, 1992), 195–230.

DAVIS, TRACY C., *The Economics of the British Stage 1800–1914* (Cambridge: Cambridge University Press, 2000).

DIRCKS, PHYLLIS T., 'David Garrick, George III, and the Politics of Revision', *Philological Quarterly*, 76:3 (1997), 289–312.

_____ *The Eighteenth-Century English Burletta* (Victoria, BC: English Literary Studies, 1999).

DOBSON, HENRY AUSTIN, *At Prior Park and Other Papers* (London: Chatto & Windus, 1912).

EASTWOOD, DAVID, 'John Reeves and the Contested Idea of the Constitution', *British Journal for Eighteenth Century Studies*, 16 (1993) 197–212.

EPSTEIN, JAMES, *Radical Expression: Political Language, Ritual, and Symbol in England, 1790–1850* (Oxford: Oxford University Press, 1994).

ERICKSON, LEE, *The Economy of Literary Form: English Literature and the Industrialization of Publishing, 1800–1850* (Baltimore: Johns Hopkins University Press, 1996).

FAGG, EDWIN, *The 'Old Vic': A Glimpse of the Old Theatre, from its Origin as 'The Royal Coburg', First Managed by William Barrymore, to its Revival under Lilian Baylis* (London: Vic-Wells Association, 1936).

FAHRNER, ROBERT, 'The Turbulent First Year of the Royal Circus (1782–1783)', *Theatre Survey*, 19 (1978), 155–70.

FLAHERTY, GLORIA, *Shamanism and the Eighteenth Century* (Princeton: Princeton University Press, 1992).

FLECK, LUDWIK, *Genesis and Development of a Scientific Fact*, (ed.) Thaddeus J. Trenn and Robert K. Merton, trans. Fred Bradley and Thaddeus J. Trenn (Basel: Benno Schwebe, 1935; Chicago: University of Chicago Press, 1979).

GAGE, JOHN, *Colour in Turner: Poetry and Truth* (London: Studio Vista, 1969).

GARSTANG, DONALD (ed.), *Colnaghi, Established 1760, Art, Commerce, Scholarship: A Window onto the Art World—Colnaghi 1760 to 1984* (London: P. & D. Colnaghi, 1984).

GAY, PENNY, *Jane Austen and the Theatre* (Cambridge: Cambridge University Press, 2002).

GILMARTIN, KEVIN, *Print Politics: The Press and Radical Opposition in Early Nineteenth-Century England* (Cambridge: Cambridge University Press, 1995).

GRIFFITHS, ANTONY, with the collaboration of Robert A. Gerard, *The Print in Stuart Britain, 1603–1689* (London: Trustees of the British Museum, 1998).

HADDON, ARCHIBALD, *The Story of the Music Hall from Cave of Harmony to Cabaret* (London: Cecil Palmer, 1924).

HALL, JOHN (ed.), *Trial of Abraham Thornton* (Edinburgh and London: William Hodge & Co., 1926).

HANDFIELD-JONES, R. M., *The History of the Royal Masonic Institution for Girls 1788–1974* (1974).

HAY, DOUGLAS, 'The State and the Market in 1800: Lord Kenyon and Mr Waddington', *Past and Present*, 162 (1999), 163–94.

HOBSBAWM, E. J., and GEORGE RUDÉ, *Captain Swing* (London: Lawrence & Wishart, 1969).

HÖHER, DAGMAR, 'The Composition of Music Hall Audiences, 1850–1900', in Peter Bailey (ed.), *Music Hall: The Business of Pleasure* (Milton Keynes: Open University Press, 1986).

HOGAN, CHARLES BEECHER, *The London Stage 1660–1800* (Carbondale, Ill.: Southern Illinois University Press, 1968).

HONE, J. ANNE, *For the Cause of Truth: Radicalism in London, 1796–1821* (Oxford: Clarendon Press, 1982).

HUME, ROBERT D., *Henry Fielding and the London Theatre, 1728–1737* (Oxford: Clarendon Press, 1988).

JANOWITZ, ANNE, *Lyric and Labour in the Romantic Tradition* (Cambridge: Cambridge University Press, 1998).

JERROLD, CLARE, *The Story of Dorothy Jordan* (London: Eveleigh Nash, 1914).

JEWETT, WILLIAM, *Fatal Autonomy: Romantic Drama and the Rhetoric of Agency* (Ithaca, NY: Cornell University Press, 1997).

JOHNSTON, KENNETH, *The Hidden Wordsworth* (London: Norton, 1998).

JOPPIEN, RÜDIGER, *Philippe Jacques de Loutherbourg, RA, 1740–1812, Kenwood, 2 June–13 August* (Exhibition catalogue; London, 1973).

KINSERVIK, MATTHEW J., 'The Censorship of Samuel Foote's *The Minor* (1760): Stage Controversy in the Mid-Eighteenth Century', *Studies in the Literary Imagination*, 32: 2 (1999), 89–104.

——— *Disciplining Satire: The Censorship of Satiric Comedy on the Eighteenth-Century London Stage* (Lewisburg, Pa.: Bucknell University Press, 2002).

KUHN, THOMAS S., *The Structure of Scientific Revolutions* (Chicago: University of Chicago Press, 1962).

KWINT, MARIUS, 'The Legitimization of the Circus in Late Georgian England', *Past and Present*, 174 (2002), 72–115.

LACQUEUR, THOMAS W., 'The Queen Caroline Affair: Politics as Art in the Reign of George IV', *Journal of Modern History* (Sept. 1982), 417–66.

LINEBAUGH, PETER, and MARCUS REDIKER, *The Many-Headed Hydra: Sailors, Slaves, Commoners, and the Hidden History of the Revolutionary Atlantic* (London: Verso, 2000).

LLOYD, STEPHEN (ed.), *Richard and Maria Cosway: Regency Artists of Taste and Fashion* (Edinburgh: Scottish National Portrait Gallery, 1995).

McCALMAN, IAIN, *Radical Underworld: Prophets, Revolutionaries and Pornographers in London, 1795–1840* (Cambridge: Cambridge University Press, 1988).

McDOWELL, PAULA, *The Women of Grub Street: Press, Politics, and Gender in the London Literary Marketplace 1678–1730* (Oxford: Clarendon Press, 1998).

MCKENDRICK, NEIL, 'Commercialization and the Economy', in Neil McKendrick, John Brewer, and J. H. Plumb (eds.), *The Birth of a Consumer Society: The Commercialization of Eighteenth-Century England* (London: Europa Publications, 1982), 9–196.

MCVEIGH, SIMON, 'Freemasonry and Musical Life in London in the Late Eighteenth Century', in David Wyn Jones (ed.), *Music in Eighteenth-Century Britain* (Aldershot and Burlington, Vt.: Ashgate, 2000).

MAXTED, IAN, *The London Book Trades, 1775–1800: A Preliminary Checklist of Members* (Folkestone: Dawson, 1977).

MAYER, DAVID, *Harlequin in his Element: The English Pantomime, 1806–1836* (Cambridge, Mass.: Harvard University Press, 1969).

MOODY, JANE, *Illegitimate Theatre in London, 1770–1840* (Cambridge: Cambridge University Press, 2000).

MURRAY, CHRISTOPHER, 'Elliston's Coronation Spectacle, 1821', *Theatre Notebook*, 25 (1970/1), 57–64.

NELSON, RONALD ROY, *The Home Office, 1782–1801* (Durham, NC: Duke University Press, 1969).

NICHOLSON, WATSON, *The Struggle for a Free Stage in London* (London: Archibald Constable, 1906).

NICOLL, ALLARDYCE, *A History of English Drama, 1660–1900* (1930) (Cambridge: Cambridge University Press, 1960), vol. iv.

NORTHCOTT, RICHARD, *Charles Dibdin's Masonic Pantomime 'Harlequin Freemason'* (Printed privately, 1915).

OLIVER, J. W., *The Life of William Beckford* (London: Oxford University Press, 1932).

PALEY, MORTON D., *The Apocalyptic Sublime* (New Haven: Yale University Press, 1986).

PASCOE, JUDITH, *Romantic Theatricality: Gender, Poetry, and Spectatorship* (Ithaca, NY: Cornell University Press, 1997).

PEDICORD, HARRY WILLIAM, 'White Gloves at Five: Fraternal Patronage of London Theatres in the Eighteenth Century', *Philological Quarterly*, 45 (1966), 277–8.

—— 'Masonic Theatre Pieces in London 1730–1780', *Theatre Survey*, 25 (1984), 154–7.

—— and FREDERICK LOUIS BERGMANN (eds.), *The Plays of David Garrick* (Carbondale and Edwardsville: Southern Illinois University Press, 1980), vol. ii.

PLOMER, H. R., G. H. BUSHNELL, and E. R. McC. DIX [*sic*], *A Dictionary of the Printers and Booksellers who were at Work in England, Scotland and Ireland from 1726 to 1775* (Oxford: Bibliographical Society, 1932).

PLUMB, J. H., 'Commercialization and Society', in Neil McKendrick, John Brewer, J. H. Plumb (eds.), *The Birth of a Consumer Society: The Commercialization of Eighteenth-Century England* (London: Europa Publications, 1982), 265–334.

POULTER, G. C. B., '*Golden Farmer*': *The Inn and the Highwayman* (Camberley, Surrey: 1934).

RICHARDSON, ALAN, *A Mental Theatre: Poetic Drama and Consciousness in the Romantic Age* (University Park and London: Pennsylvania State University Press, 1988).

ROE, NICHOLAS, *Wordsworth and Coleridge: The Radical Years* (Oxford: Clarendon Press, 1988).

'Romantic Drama: Origins, Permutations, and Legacies', Special Issue, *European Romantic Review*, 14 (2003).

ROSENFELD, SYBIL, 'The Eidophusikon Illustrated', *Theatre Notebook* 18:2 (1963), 52–4.

_____ *Temples of Thespis: Some Private Theatres and Theatricals in England and Wales, 1700–1820* (London: Society for Theatre Research, 1978).

_____ *Georgian Scene Painters and Scene Painting* (Cambridge: Cambridge University Press, 1981).

RUSSELL, GILLIAN, 'Playing at Revolution: The Politics of the O.P. Riots of 1809', *Theatre Notebook*, 44:1 (1990), 16–25.

_____ *The Theatres of War: Performance, Politics, and Society 1793–1815* (Oxford: Clarendon Press, 1995).

_____ '"Keeping place" servants, theater and sociability in mid-eighteenth-century Britain', *Eighteenth Century: Theory and Interpretation* (Texas Tech. Univ., Lubbock), 42:1 (2001), 21–42.

_____ and CLARA TUITE (eds.), *Romantic Sociability: Social Networks and Literary Culture in Britain, 1770–1840* (Cambridge: Cambridge University Press, 2002).

SALATINO, KEVIN, *Incendiary Art: The Representation of Fireworks in Early Modern Europe* (Los Angeles: Getty Institution for the History of Art and the Humanities, 1997).

SANDS, MOLLIE, *The Eighteenth-Century Pleasure Gardens of Marylebone* (London: Society for Theatre Research, 1987).

SCHAMA, SIMON, *Citizens: A Chronicle of the French Revolution* (London: Viking, 1989).

SIMPSON, MICHAEL, 'Re-Opening after the Old Price Riots: War and Peace at Drury Lane', *Texas Studies in Literature and Language*, 41 (1999), 378–402.

SOLKIN, DAVID H., '"This Great Mart of Genius": The Royal Academy Exhibitions at Somerset House, 1780–1836', in David H. Solkin (ed.), *Art on the Line: The Royal Academy Exhibitions at Somerset House, 1780–1836* (New Haven and London: Paul Mellon Center for Studies in British Art and the Courtauld Institute Gallery, 2001).

SPEAIGHT, GEORGE, *Bawdy Songs of the Early Music Hall* (Newton Abbot: David & Charles, 1975).

——*A History of the Circus* (London: Tantivy Press, 1980).

STEPHENS, JOHN RUSSELL, *The Censorship of English Drama 1824–1901* (Cambridge: Cambridge University Press, 1980).

STONE, GEORGE WINCHESTER JR., and GEORGE M. KAHRL, *David Garrick: A Critical Biography* (Carbondale and Edwardsville: Southern Illinois University Press, 1979).

STUART, CHARLES, and A. J. PARKS, *Variety Stage: A History of the Music Halls from the Earliest Period to the Present Time* (London: Fisher, Unwin, 1895).

SWINDELLS, JULIA, *Glorious Causes: The Grand Theatre of Political Change, 1789 to 1833* (Oxford: Oxford University Press, 2001).

TAYLOR, GEORGE, *The French Revolution and the London Stage, 1789–1805* (Cambridge: Cambridge University Press, 2000).

THIEME, JOHN A., 'Spouting, Spouting-Clubs and Spouting Companions', *Theatre Notebook*, 29 (1975), 9–18.

THOMPSON, E. P., *The Making of the English Working Class* (1963; Harmondsworth: Penguin 1980).

——*Customs in Common* (Harmondsworth: Penguin 1993).

WALVIN, JAMES, *Slaves and Slavery: The British Colonial Experience* (Manchester: Manchester University Press, 1992).

——*Fruits of Empire: Exotic Produce and British Taste, 1660–1800* (Basingstoke: Macmillan, 1997).

WEATHERILL, LORNA, *Consumer Behaviour and Material Culture in Britain, 1660–1760* (London: Routledge, 1988).

WELLS, ROGER, *Wretched Faces: Famine in Wartime England 1763–1803* (Gloucester: Alan Sutton, 1988).

WILLIAMSON, GEORGE C., *Richard Cosway, R.A. and his Wife and Pupils* (London: George Bell & Sons, 1887).

WORRALL, DAVID, *Radical Culture: Discourse, Resistance and Surveillance, 1790–1820* (Hemel Hempstead: Harvester, 1992).

_____ 'The Mob and "Mrs Q": William Blake, William Benbow, and the Context of Regency Radicalism', in J. DiSalvo, G. A. Rosso, and Christopher Z. Hobson (eds.), *Blake, Politics, and History* (New York and London, Garland Publishing and Taylor & Francis, 1998), 169–86.

_____ 'Artisan Melodrama and the Plebeian Public Sphere: The Political Culture of Drury Lane and its Environs, 1797–1830', *Studies in Romanticism*, 39 (2000), 255–302.

_____ 'Robert Hawes and the Millenium Press: A Political Microculture of Late-Eighteenth-Century Spitalfields', in Tim Fulford (ed.), *Romanticism and Millenarianism* (Basingstoke: Palgrave, 2002), 167–82.

_____ 'Kinship, Generation and Community: The Transmission of Political Ideology in Radical Plebeian Print Culture', *Studies in Romanticism*, 43 (2004), 283–95.

Index